An Introduction to the Bible

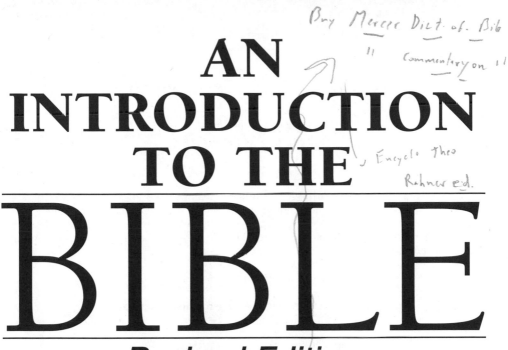

AN INTRODUCTION TO THE BIBLE

Revised Edition

Buy Mercer Dict. of. Bib
" Commentary on "

Encyclo Theo
Rahner ed.

Clyde E. Fant
Donald W. Musser
Mitchell G. Reddish

Abingdon Press
Nashville

AN INTRODUCTION TO THE BIBLE, REVISED EDITION

Library of Congress Cataloging-in-Publication Data

Fant, Clyde E.
  An introduction to the Bible / Clyde E. Fant, Donald W. Musser, Mitchell G. Reddish.—Rev. ed.
    p. cm.
  Includes bibliographical references (p.) and index.
  ISBN 0-687-08456-3
    1. Bible—Introductions. I. Musser, Donald W., 1942-   II. Reddish, Mitchell Glenn, 1953-
III. Title.

BS475.3 .F36 2001
220.6'1—dc21

                                                                          2001045139

02 03 04 05 06 07 08 09 10—10 9 8 7 6 5 4 3 2

MANUFACTURED IN THE UNITED STATES OF AMERICA

In memory of

Dr. O. LaFayette Walker
Professor of Religion
at
Stetson University
from 1945 to 1981

and

Dr. E. Earl Joiner
Professor of Religion
at
Stetson University
from 1955 to 1992

Figure A. This photograph of the Sinai Peninsula was taken by the crew of *Discovery* while on orbit during Space Shuttle Mission STS-26. Note the Dead Sea and the Sea of Galilee to the north. *(Photograph by NASA)*

CONTENTS

LIST OF ILLUSTRATIONS. 11

PREFACE 15

ABBREVIATIONS OF THE BOOKS OF THE BIBLE
WITH THE APOCRYPHA 17

PART I: INTRODUCTION TO THE STUDY OF THE BIBLE

1. The Bible and Western Culture 21

    The Roots of Western Civilization 21
    The Cultural Influence of the Bible 23
    What Is the Bible? 28
    Approaches to the Bible 31

2. Methods and Tools for Studying the Bible 35

    Types of Biblical Criticism. 35
    Related Disciplines 51
    Tools and Reference Works 52
    Consolidating the Results 53

3. The Origins and Development of the Bible 55

    Formation of the Hebrew Bible 55
    Formation of the Christian Bible 62
    The Process of Translation. 68

4. The Cultural and Geographic Context of the Bible 75

    The Shape of the Ancient Near East. 75
    The Land Called Palestine. 80
    Vital Evidence: Archaeological Discoveries 89

PART II: ORIGINS AND EARLY DEVELOPMENT OF THE JEWISH TRADITION

5. Hebrew Origins and Early History. 97

    Israel's Ancestral Narratives. 98
    Characteristics of the Ancestral Narratives 101

The Ancestral World. 103
Ancestral Religion. 106
The Exodus and Wilderness Traditions 109
Characteristics of the Exodus-Wilderness Narratives. 112

6.   The Era of the Judges 121

The Settlement in Canaan. 121
Tribal Life and Leadership. 126
The Divine-Human Encounter in the Era of the Judges 129

7.   The United Kingdom and the Yahwistic History 135

The Desire for a King. 135
The First Kings: Saul and David 139
The Reign of Solomon 146
Theological Developments During the Monarchy. 150
The Yahwistic History. 150

8.   The Divided Kingdom: Israel and Judah 155

The Nature of the Sources. 155
The Division of the Kingdom 159
The Northern Kingdom (922–722 B.C.E.). 160
The Southern Kingdom (922–587 B.C.E.). 167

9.   The Institution of Prophecy. 175

Background of Hebrew Prophecy. 175
The Nature of Hebrew Prophecy 176
Functions of the Hebrew Prophets. 177
Representatives of Preliterary Prophecy 180
The Divine-Human Encounter in the Preliterary Prophets. 184

10. The Preexilic Prophets 185

Amos. 185
Hosea. 189
Isaiah. 192
Micah 197
Jeremiah. 198
Zephaniah 202
Nahum 203
Habakkuk 203
The Preexilic Prophets and the Divine-Human Encounter. 204

11. The Exile, Exilic Prophets, and Exilic Histories 205

The Historical Situation 205
The Exilic Prophets. 208
The Exilic Histories 216

12. The Restoration of Judah 221

The Restoration (538–424 B.C.E.). 221
The Literature of the Restoration 225
The Divine-Human Encounter in the Restoration 230

13. The Psalms and Wisdom Literature 233

Psalms 233
Wisdom Literature 240

14. Judaism in the Hellenistic and Roman Eras 251

Political Developments in Palestine 251
Religious Developments in Judaism 259
Literary Developments in Judaism 266

15. Daniel and the Books of the Apocrypha 271

The Book of Daniel. 271
The Books of the Apocrypha 277
The Influence of the Apocrypha 285
The Divine-Human Encounter in the Hellenistic and Roman Eras. . . . 288

PART III: ORIGINS AND EARLY DEVELOPMENT OF THE CHRISTIAN TRADITION

16. The Life and Teachings of Jesus 295

Sources of Information 297
Obstacles to Achieving a Biography of Jesus. 303
Core Elements of a Life Sketch of Jesus 305

17. The Development of the Gospels: From Oral Traditions to Mark . . . 319

From Oral Traditions to Written Gospels 319
The Gospel of Mark 326

18. The Further Development of the Gospels: Matthew, Luke, and John . . 337

The Gospel of Matthew. 337
The Gospel of Luke 343
The Gospel of John. 350
Beyond the Four Gospels 357

19. The Development of the Early Church: The Acts of the Apostles . . . 359

"Beginning in Jerusalem" (Acts 1–6) 361
"In Samaria and Judea" (Acts 7–8). 366
"To the Ends of the Earth" (Acts 9–28) 370
The Kerygma of the Emerging Church and the Divine-Human Encounter . 375

20. Paul and His Cultural Environment. 379

The Greco-Roman World 379
Sources for the Life and Teaching of Paul. 386
The Life of Paul 387

21. Paul and His Writings 395

Paul as a Letter Writer. 395
The Contents of Paul's Letters 398
The Divine-Human Encounter in Paul. 412

22. The Developing Institutional Church. 417

From Charisma to Institution 417
Sources for Study 418
The Church Distinguishes Right Belief from False Teachings (James; 1, 2,
    3 John; Jude; 2 Peter; Colossians; 2 Thessalonians) 420
The Church Establishes Its Structure (1 and 2 Timothy, Titus, Ephesians) . 426
The Church Encourages Fidelity in Difficult Times (Hebrews, 1 Peter) . 431
The Divine-Human Encounter: Keeping the Faith in Later Generations. . 435

23. The Church in Conflict 437

Conflict with Judaism. 437
Conflict with Rome. 441
A Response to Persecution: The Book of Revelation 446

SELECTED BIBLIOGRAPHY 457

INDEX 465

LIST OF ILLUSTRATIONS

Figure	Description
A	Sinai Peninsula
1.1	Socrates
1.2	The Dome of the Rock Mosque
1.3	*The Crucifixion* by Salvador Dali
1.4	Chart: The Books of the Bible
1.5	The Western Wall
2.1	St. Catherine's Monastery
2.2	The Rosetta Stone
2.3	Tutankhamen
2.4	Anatolian Mother Goddess
3.1	*Thanksgiving Scroll*
3.2	Chart: Dates for Writings in the Hebrew Bible
3.3	Codex Sinaiticus
3.4	Chart: Dates for Writings in the New Testament
3.5	Jerome
3.6	Title page from King James Version of the Bible
4.1	Map: The ancient Near East
4.2	Prince Rahotep and his wife Nofret
4.3	Map: Palestine
4.4	Sea of Galilee
4.5	Olive press
4.6	Amarna letter
4.7	Caves at Qumran
5.1	Bedouin camp
5.2	Chart: Major Periods in Israel's History
5.3	Mudbrick gate at Dan
5.4	Jabbok River
5.5	The Great Temple at Hattusa
5.6	Sharruma, one of the ancient Hittite gods
5.7	Ramesses II
5.8	Map: Route of the Exodus
5.9	Jebel Musa (Mount Moses)
6.1	Stone watchtower at Jericho
6.2	Hazor
6.3	Canaanite altar at Megiddo
6.4	Anthropoid clay coffin
6.5	The Gezer calendar
7.1	Beth-shan

7.2	Stepped structure in Jerusalem
7.3	Drawing: Solomon's Temple
7.4	The step pyramid at Sakkara
8.1	Water tunnel at Megiddo
8.2	Grain silo at Megiddo
8.3	Chart: The Hebrew Kings
8.4	Assyrian man praying
8.5	Assyrian royal chariot
8.6	A cultic stand
9.1	Chart: The Hebrew Prophets
9.2	Elijah
9.3	Megiddo
9.4	The Black Obelisk of Shalmaneser
10.1	The Old City of Jerusalem
10.2	Lachish
10.3	The Jezreel Valley
11.1	The Babylonian Chronicle
11.2	Ivory carving: "The woman at the window"
11.3	The Babylonian god Marduk
11.4	*Adam* by Auguste Rodin
12.1	The Cyrus Cylinder
12.2	*Ruth and Boaz with the Reapers*
12.3	Jonah
13.1	A Palestinian woman caring for her sheep
13.2	An Egyptian scribe
13.3	A coney or badger
14.1	Alexander the Great
14.2	Chart: Major Historical Events in Palestine 332 B.C.E.–135 C.E.
14.3	Burnt house in Jerusalem
14.4	Drawing: The Jerusalem Temple
14.5	The Western Wall
14.6	The Qumran settlement
14.7	The Arch of Titus
15.1	Antiochus IV
15.2	Daniel in the lion's den
15.3	*Judith and Her Maidservant with the Head of Holofernes*
15.4	Palestinian tombstone ornament
15.5	Masada
16.1	"The Treasury" at Petra
16.2	*The Return of the Prodigal Son*
16.3	Mosaic of Jesus
16.4	Map: Palestine during the time of the New Testament
16.5	Machaerus

16.6	The Jordan River
16.7	Model of Herod's Temple
16.8	Jesus in the Garden of Gethsemane
17.1	Fishermen on the Sea of Galilee
17.2	Drawing: The Two-Source Theory
17.3	Drawing: The Synoptics and John
17.4	The synagogue at Capernaum
17.5	The Garden of Gethsemane
17.6	The Via Dolorosa
17.7	The crucifixion of Jesus
18.1	The Church of the Beatitudes
18.2	The evangelist Matthew
18.3	The Garden of Gethsemane
18.4	The Pool of Bethzatha
18.5	Jesus raising Lazarus from the dead
19.1	Fair Havens, Crete
19.2	Areopagus (Mars' Hill) in Athens
19.3	The goddess Artemis
19.4	Paul preaching in Beroea
19.5	The Roman theater at Caesarea
19.6	The Fortress of Antonia
20.1	*The Apostle Paul* by Rembrandt
20.2	The Dionysian cult
20.3	Epicurus
20.4	The Khazneh, or Treasury, at Petra
20.5	Map: The journeys of Paul according to Acts
20.6	Chart: A Chronology of Paul's Life
20.7	The Parthenon in Athens
21.1	Zeus, chief of the Greek gods
21.2	Chart: Writings Attributed to Paul
21.3	The Roman Forum in Thessalonica, Greece
21.4	The Fountain of Peirene in Corinth
21.5	The Library of Celsus in Ephesus
21.6	The Via Egnatia in Philippi
21.7	The Roman aqueduct at Caesarea
22.1	Theater in Jerash
22.2	Colossae
22.3	Titus, a coworker with Paul
22.4	Theater in Ephesus
22.5	Dionysus, the Greek god of wine
22.6	Cappadocia
23.1	Vespasian and Titus
23.2	Chart: Roman Emperors During New Testament Times
23.3	Domitian

23.4   Trajan
23.5   The island of Patmos
23.6   Map: Locations of the island of Patmos and the
            seven churches addressed in Revelation
23.7   Bath-gymnasium complex at Sardis
23.8   Megiddo

PREFACE

This revised edition of *An Introduction to the Bible* has been developed after a decade of its use in teaching nearly five hundred students a year in a first course in biblical study. The authors have attempted to incorporate both their experiences and those of other professors in varied settings who have offered valuable suggestions for this revision. As in the first edition, this volume is intended as the basic text for a survey course in the life, literature, and faith of the early Jewish and Christian traditions. It is arranged to be used either for a single course surveying both the Hebrew Scriptures and the New Testament or for two separate courses dealing individually with each body of literature. The advantages of this text for those teaching two introductory courses are the coherence of using the same volume from one course to another and the economy of a single text for the students.

As in the first edition, our approach has been guided by four basic convictions. First is the belief that students should be encouraged to read extensively from the Bible as their primary text. Accordingly, at the beginning of each chapter this edition lists suggested biblical texts to be read by the students prior to the lectures by the instructor. Our experience has shown that students who have read this biblical material in advance are much better prepared to understand lectures and engage in class discussion. We recommend The New Oxford Annotated Bible with the Apocrypha for this purpose.

Second, our experience in using various approaches in past years of teaching has convinced us that the historical/chronological framework is the best arrangement for a text intended for an introductory-level course in biblical studies for undergraduate students.

Third, we believe that an introduction to the Bible should acquaint students with the history and culture of the biblical world and also give them a sense of the profound religious conviction that was responsible for the biblical story. The faiths of early Judaism and early Christianity were based on the belief that God had entered into a direct relationship with humanity. The recurring theme of this text is the development of this idea and its particular expression in the Jewish and Christian traditions.

Fourth, an introductory text should reflect the consensus of scholarship in the field of biblical studies. Consequently, we have adhered to the most widely accepted results of critical scholarship. This revised edition has sought to incorporate recent advances in the critical understanding of the Bible.

In addition to updated information throughout the book based on recent scholarly discussions, this edition of the text contains additional historical charts, maps, and photographs. An index has been added for the convenience of students. Finally, we have attempted to further improve the organization and clarity of this work.

We are grateful to many colleagues who read portions of the manuscript and contributed helpful observations to our work: Walter Brueggemann, Moody Smith, Adela Yarbro Collins, James Charlesworth, James Sanders, Clarice Martin, Kandy Queen-Sutherland, Dixon Sutherland, Justo and Catherine Gonzales, David Gregory Sapp, Alice Hudiburg, Russell Gregory, Reginald H. Fuller, Rabbi Barry Altman, Roger Woods, Teresa Hornsby, G. Todd Wilson, and Marilyn Metcalf-Whittaker. Others who contributed invaluable assistance in the production of this volume include Lisa Guenther, Kati Bentley, and Elizabeth Clark. Further appreciation must be expressed to our editors who encouraged us in the development of this revised edition. We also acknowledge our indebtedness and gratitude to Stetson University for its support; to James Ridgway, Jr. and Educational Opportunities for their help in our travels to Israel, Jordan, Egypt, Greece, and Turkey; to Ünver Gazez of Azim Tours, Turkey, for his gracious assistance; and to Necdet (Net) Özeren, our good friend and expert guide in Turkey.

CEF
DWM
MGR

ABBREVIATIONS OF THE BOOKS OF THE BIBLE WITH THE APOCRYPHA

Hebrew Bible

Gen.	Genesis	Eccl.	Ecclesiastes
Ex.	Exodus	Song	Song of Solomon
Lev.	Leviticus	Isa.	Isaiah
Num.	Numbers	Jer.	Jeremiah
Deut.	Deuteronomy	Lam.	Lamentations
Josh.	Joshua	Ezek.	Ezekiel
Judg.	Judges	Dan.	Daniel
Ruth	Ruth	Hos.	Hosea
1 Sam.	1 Samuel	Joel	Joel
2 Sam.	2 Samuel	Amos	Amos
1 Kings	1 Kings	Ob.	Obadiah
2 Kings	2 Kings	Jon.	Jonah
1 Chr.	1 Chronicles	Mic.	Micah
2 Chr.	2 Chronicles	Nah.	Nahum
Ezra	Ezra	Hab.	Habakkuk
Neh.	Nehemiah	Zeph.	Zephaniah
Esth.	Esther	Hag.	Haggai
Job	Job	Zech.	Zechariah
Ps.	Psalms	Mal.	Malachi
Prov.	Proverbs		

Apocrypha

Tob.	Tobit	Pr. Azar.	Prayer of Azariah and
Jdt.	Judith		the Song of the
Add. Esth.	Additions to Esther		Three Jews
Wis.	Wisdom	Sus.	Susanna
Sir.	Sirach (Ecclesiasticus)	Bel.	Bel and the Dragon
Bar.	Baruch	1 Macc.	1 Maccabees
1 Esd.	1 Esdras	2 Macc.	2 Maccabees
2 Esd.	2 Esdras	3 Macc.	3 Maccabees
Let. Jer.	Letter of Jeremiah	4 Macc.	4 Maccabees
		Pr. Man.	Prayer of Manasseh

Matt.	Matthew	1 Tim.	1 Timothy
Mark	Mark	2 Tim.	2 Timothy
Luke	Luke	Titus	Titus
John	John	Philem.	Philemon
Acts	Acts of the Apostles	Heb.	Hebrews
Rom.	Romans	Jas.	James
1 Cor.	1 Corinthians	1 Pet.	1 Peter
2 Cor.	2 Corinthians	2 Pet.	2 Peter
Gal.	Galatians	1 John	1 John
Eph.	Ephesians	2 John	2 John
Phil.	Philippians	3 John	3 John
Col.	Colossians	Jude	Jude
1 Thess.	1 Thessalonians	Rev.	Revelation
2 Thess.	2 Thessalonians		

Part I
Introduction to the
Study of the Bible

Chapter 1

THE BIBLE AND
WESTERN CULTURE

Family stories provide an understanding and appreciation of our family traditions. Children often are fascinated by stories of significant people, places, and events that matter to their relatives. These stories create in children a sense of self-identity and community identity that links them to the past. We are all figuratively "children" of a cultural heritage that includes stories of people, places, events, and traditions of art, music, literature, science, values, and ideas. In Western culture the Bible is a central part of the literary heritage. Thus, to understand and appreciate Western culture one must acquire knowledge of biblical literature.

THE ROOTS OF WESTERN CIVILIZATION

Every culture is shaped by its traditions and forges its future in the light of those traditions. Western culture is no exception. The three primary sources that have provided the foundations of this culture are Greco-Roman traditions, Jewish and Christian traditions, and the modern sciences.

A "culture" includes the products of human activity that bind people together into a society. Among the products of a culture are language, science, art, philosophy, government, law, beliefs, customs, habits, and technologies. These creations provide a social heritage that one generation passes on to another. Cultures are inherently conservative in that they conserve past human achievements. For instance, Americans celebrate the Constitution of the United States as a valued achievement of the past. But at the same time, lasting cultures are also dynamic, revising and reinterpreting their historical traditions in the light of new challenges. Americans, for example, have amended their Constitution and continue to debate its application in changing circumstances.

For centuries Western culture was influenced primarily by Greco-Roman and Judeo-Christian traditions. With the conquests of Alexander the Great in the fourth century B.C.E. (Before the Common Era), Palestine, the Jewish homeland, came under Greek domination. Moreover, Jews had dispersed throughout the Greek-dominated Mediterranean world. Although most Jews resisted Greek ways, some Jews nevertheless adopted Greek ideas during this period. Later, when the Romans conquered the lands along the Mediterranean, their culture became dominant. Few major cultural shifts took place, however, because Roman culture had itself adopted much of Greek culture. Scholars often refer to the cultural traditions of the Greeks and Romans as "Greco-Roman."

Christianity emerged from Judaism in the first century C.E. (Common Era) as an independent religious tradition and quickly spread throughout the Greco-Roman world. In the fourth century the emperor Constantine embraced Christianity. Since then, most Western views of the nature of God, the nature of human beings, and morals and values were shaped in dialogue with Greco-Roman traditions and Christian traditions.

Leading Western thinkers have disagreed over how the traditions of the Bible and the traditions of Greece and Rome should be related. Some, such as the Jewish philosopher Philo of Alexandria, saw them as stating essentially similar ideas. He believed that the claims of Jewish faith and Greek philosophy could be harmonized. Others, such as Tertullian, the Christian lawyer-theologian, thought that the traditions of Christian faith had little in common with Greco-Roman culture. He believed they dealt with separate realms. Still others, such as Augustine of Hippo and Thomas Aquinas, sought a synthesis of the two traditions within a larger historical or philosophical framework. An analysis of this clash of cultural traditions leads to the conclusion that most of Western culture's basic ideas and values derive from the faith traditions of *both* the Bible *and* Greece and Rome. In law, for example, one finds traces of both biblical precepts *and* Roman law in statutes pertaining to the property rights of citizens. With regard to values, one finds views that derive from the moral codes of *both* the Jewish Bible *and* the Greeks. Dante, for example, defined seven virtues in his *Divine Comedy*. Four were from classical Greece (prudence, justice, fortitude, and temperance) and three were biblical (faith, hope, and love). Basic conceptions of the divine also reflect *both* biblical *and* Greco-Roman traditions. The Western notion that God is holy, merciful, and righteous finds roots in the Bible, while the idea that God is infinite, all-knowing, and all-powerful finds its sources in Greco-Roman thought and belief. Finally, Western views of life after death include *both* the biblical view of the resurrection of the body *and* the Greek view of the immortality of the soul.

With the rise of modern physics and mathematics in the seventeenth century, followed by the emergence of the disciplines of chemistry, biology, psychology, sociology, and history in the eighteenth and nineteenth centuries, the modern natural and social sciences became a third main ingredient in Western culture. The natural and social sciences provided new traditions out of which contemporary people now think and act. The modern sciences have not replaced the older traditions, but they have provided new, alternative views about nature, humanity, and divinity that have challenged and often modified older views. The sciences have offered new ways of discovering truth, fresh views of the natural world, and extensive empirical information about human beings. These sciences and their offspring, technology (the application of science), have stimulated renewed considerations of traditional Western viewpoints.

Figure 1.1. Socrates exemplifies Greco-Roman philosophy, which together with the Jewish and Christian traditions and modern science has greatly influenced Western civilization. *(Photograph by Mitchell G. Reddish)*

Western culture has emerged, then, from Greco-Roman traditions, from Judeo-Christian traditions, and, more recently, from the modern sciences. The remainder of this chapter and the balance of this book will focus specifically on the religious traditions that undergird Western culture. The next section of the chapter will illustrate a multitude of ways that the biblical traditions have influenced the culture and suggest that an informed understanding of Western culture requires an acquaintance with the biblical traditions.

THE CULTURAL INFLUENCE OF THE BIBLE

The Bible has had a pervasive influence on Western religion, politics, law, art, literature, ethics, language, and history. Its most obvious influence is in *religion*. The Bible, or portions of it, provides the basis for codes of moral conduct,

Figure 1.2. The Dome of the Rock, a Muslim mosque in Jerusalem, stands on the approximate location of the former temples of Solomon, Zerubbabel, and Herod. *(Photograph by Clyde E. Fant)*

theological beliefs, and worship rituals for Judaism and Christianity, the major faith traditions of the West. Jewish faith is rooted in the Hebrew Bible (which is called the Old Testament by Christians). Christian traditions derive from the Hebrew Bible and the New Testament. Islam, the third of the Western monotheistic religions, also considers the Hebrew Bible authoritative, although it has its own sacred Scripture, the Qur'an. Many recent new religious movements—and even nonreligious movements like atheism and humanism—often find themselves dependent on, in dialogue with, or in opposition to the biblical literature.

Politics and Law

Other illustrations of the Bible's impact beyond its clear religious influence abound. Many Western communities, for example, have attempted to construct systems of politics and law upon principles found in the Bible. Such attempts began in earnest once Christianity became an acceptable and popular religion in the Roman Empire in the fourth century C.E. Powerful Christian popes, leaders who were modeled after the biblical kings David and Solomon, emerged in the church, often exercising both religious and civil authority that rivaled and at times superseded secular authority during the Middle Ages. During the Protestant Reformation of the sixteenth century, John Calvin established an ill-fated experiment in Christian political and legal authority in Geneva, Switzerland. In the seventeenth century the founders of New England sought to establish a society conformed to the Bible, believing that God had established a "new world." In later American history various religious groups, such as the Shakers, the Amish, and the commune at Koinonia Farms near Americus, Georgia, have sought to shape communities by employing ideas found in biblical texts. Numerous other social and political movements have based their premises on ideas in the Bible.

A considerable number of Westerners believe that their nation prospers to the extent that its citizens follow the teachings of the Bible. Christian churches in America often display both an American flag and a Christian flag in their worship centers; such displays are intended to indicate the close alignment of the nation with Christian faith. Although the American Bill of Rights prohibits the legal establishment of any particular religion, the predominance of Christians in American culture often has given them an unofficial privileged status. Americans generally consider themselves "godly" people, and a great majority of them believe the Bible is divinely inspired. They include in the pledge to the national flag the phrase "one nation under God" and have placed the words "In God We Trust" on their currency. Historian Sidney Mead's remark that America is a nation with the soul of a church contains considerable truth.

Art

Western nonliterary art (music, painting, and sculpture) widely depicts Christian themes. Much classical music is religious music, often written for church worship. Bach, Beethoven, Brahms, Buxtehude, and Handel are just a few of the composers who created music for worship. The text of Handel's *Messiah*, which has become a staple in the American celebration of Christmas, consists almost exclusively of biblical quotations. Western painting has been, until the last few centuries, a gallery of religious painting in which themes were explicitly Jewish and Christian. Even today, one finds explicit religious themes in the works of Picasso, Dali, Chagall, and Rothko. Sculptors such as Michelangelo depicted biblical figures—see, for example, his *Pieta* and *David*.

Figure 1.3. *The Crucifixion* by Salvador Dali is a dramatic, modern interpretation of the death of Jesus. (*The Metropolitan Museum of Art*, Gift of Chester Dale Collection, 1955. [55.5])

Literature

Biblical themes and symbols appear regularly in Western literature. Both classic and contemporary writers and poets have extensively mined the Bible for resources. Its influence in Western literature is pervasive. Some writers and poets have written with a distinctly Jewish or Christian outlook. Included among this number are Dante, John Milton, John Bunyan, Chaim Herzog, C. S. Lewis, T. S. Eliot, W. H. Auden, Graham Greene, Elie Wiesel, Flannery O'Connor, Robert Penn Warren, and Walker Percy. Other writers, such as Shakespeare, John Steinbeck,

John Updike, Mark Twain, and Nikos Kazantzakis, also utilized motifs from the Bible. Some writers of fiction have modeled characters after such biblical figures as Moses, David, Jesus, Jezebel, and Satan. Other writers have employed biblical themes or motifs such as the Exodus of the Hebrews from Egypt, the suffering of Job, or the temptations of Jesus.

Ethics

The Bible has also influenced Western ethics. The Ten Commandments, the Sermon on the Mount, and the ethical teachings of Paul and the Hebrew prophets have traditionally set the tone for what many Westerners consider right and wrong. Theories of pacifism and just war both are argued from the biblical texts. Ideas about sexual practice, marriage, property rights, personal rights, justice, love, and family owe a great debt to the Bible. Liberation and equal rights movements have called upon biblical texts for inspiration. Even opposing moral positions are argued from biblical standpoints. Examples might include arguments about the justice or injustice of capital punishment, the legality of prayer and Bible reading in public schools, and the morality or immorality of abortion.

Language

The language of the West is well seasoned with idioms, aphorisms, words, and allusions from the Bible. One sees this in phrases such as "a house divided against itself cannot stand" and "Am I my brother's keeper?" Words and epithets such as "sodomy," "shibboleth," "manna," "jezebel," and "Judas" derive from biblical texts. The names of children, such as Simon, Isaiah, Christa, Caleb, Elizabeth, Timothy, and Michael, are drawn from biblical figures. Towns, cities, and regions are named for locations in the Bible (for example, Mt. Zion, New Bethlehem, Bethany, Nazareth, East Salem, and Emmaus (all in Pennsylvania). Hospitals that were founded by Jews and Christians retain religious names such as Good Samaritan, Mt. Sinai, St. Jude, and St. Joseph. Elementary and grammar schools, colleges, and universities carry biblical names like Resurrection, Ascension, and St. John's. During the civil rights movement in America in the 1960s, Martin Luther King, Jr. was seen as a Moses figure who would lead African Americans out of bondage to economic and political freedom. One who suffers an unjust death is often referred to as being "crucified." Symbols and phrases such as the Ark of the Covenant, the tablets of the Ten Commandments, the "chosen people," "manna in the wilderness," and the cross are amply utilized in contemporary culture. Even in modern sports one hears of a "Hail Mary" pass in football, a spectacular catch as an "immaculate reception," and the "resurrection" of a team hopelessly buried in last place.

History

Finally, knowledge of the history of ancient Palestine, the origins and development of Judaism, and the origins of early Christianity depends upon the biblical texts. They are the primary literary sources for these traditions.

This section has suggested that the biblical tradition has had broad influence in the many sectors of Western culture. If people gain an understanding of the Bible, they can better appreciate Western culture.

WHAT IS THE BIBLE?

Writings that are regarded as authoritative for a religious community are known collectively as that group's "canon" (from the Greek word *kanon*, meaning "reed"). In the ancient world a reed was often used as a measuring rod, and therefore "canon" came to refer to a norm or standard by which to judge or measure. Jews and Christians often call their canon, or collection of accepted texts, the Bible. The term "bible" is derived from the Greek word *biblia*, meaning "books." What makes the term "bible" confusing is that it can refer to a variety of collections. The Jewish Bible, known as the Tanak or Hebrew Bible, consists of twenty-four books arranged in three divisions. The first division is called the Torah (Law), the second is the Nevi'im (Prophets), and the third is the Ketuvim (Writings). The term "Tanak" derives from the first letters of the three divisions, T, N, and K. A Christian Bible contains two major sections, the Old Testament and the New Testament ("Testament" in this usage refers to a "covenant" or "agreement" with God). For Protestant Christians, the Old Testament contains the exact same material as that found in the Jewish Bible. In a Protestant Old Testament, however, this material is divided into thirty-nine books rather than twenty-four. Christians who are Roman Catholic include in their Old Testament several additional books termed deuterocanonical (second canon) that were added later than the other books. Most Protestant Christians refer to the deuterocanonical books as the Apocrypha and do not accept them as Scripture. Most Eastern Orthodox Christians accept the deuterocanonical writings as Scripture. Greek Orthodox Christians also accept 1 Esdras, the Prayer of Manasseh, Psalm 151, and 3 Maccabees. (Although not regarded as canonical, 4 Maccabees is included as an appendix in their Bible.) Some Russian Orthodox Bibles include, in addition to the deuterocanonical works, 1 and 2 Esdras, Psalm 151, 3 Maccabees, and the Prayer of Manasseh. The second section of a Christian Bible, the New Testament, contains twenty-seven writings and is the same for Protestants, Roman Catholics, and the Eastern Orthodox.

In the present volume the word "Bible" will refer to the Old Testament, New Testament, and Apocrypha since all of the materials provide knowledge of the development of the Jewish and primitive Christian traditions. (The Protestant Old Testament will be referred to as the Hebrew Bible.)

Figure 1.4. The Books of the Bible

The Hebrew Bible	The Septuagint (Greek version of the Hebrew Bible)	Roman Catholic and Eastern Orthodox Bibles	Protestant Bible
TORAH		OLD TESTAMENT	OLD TESTAMENT
Genesis	Genesis	Genesis	Genesis
Exodus	Exodus	Exodus	Exodus
Leviticus	Leviticus	Leviticus	Leviticus
Numbers	Numbers	Numbers	Numbers
Deuteronomy	Deuteronomy	Deuteronomy	Deuteronomy
	Joshua	Joshua	Joshua
	Judges	Judges	Judges
NEVI'IM	Ruth	Ruth	Ruth
	1-4 Kingdoms	1 Samuel	1 Samuel
Former Prophets	(1-2 Samuel,	2 Samuel	2 Samuel
Joshua	1-2 Kings)	1 Kings	1 Kings
Judges	1-2 Paralipomena	2 Kings	2 Kings
Samuel	(1-2 Chronicles)	1 Chronicles	1 Chronicles
Kings	1 Esdras+	2 Chronicles	2 Chronicles
	2 Esdras (Ezra-	Ezra	Ezra
Latter Prophets	Nehemiah)	Nehemiah	Nehemiah
Isaiah	Esther	Tobit	
Jeremiah	Judith+	Judith	
Ezekiel	Tobit+	Esther (with	Esther
	1-4 Maccabees+	Additions)	
The Twelve	Psalms	Job	Job
Hosea	Odes (includes	Psalms	Psalms
Joel	Prayer of	Proverbs	Proverbs
Amos	Manasseh)+	Ecclesiastes	Ecclesiastes
Obadiah	Proverbs	Song of Solomon	Song of
Jonah	Ecclesiastes	(Song of Songs)	Solomon
Micah	Song of Songs	Wisdom of	
Nahum	Job	Solomon	
Habakkuk	Wisdom (of	Sirach	

Zephaniah	Solomon)+	(Ecclesiasticus)	
Haggai	Sirach+	Isaiah	Isaiah
Zechariah	(Ecclesias-	Jeremiah	Jeremiah
Malachi	ticus)+	Lamentations	Lamentations
	Psalms of	Baruch (including	
	Solomon+	the Letter of	
	Hosea	Jeremiah)	
KETUVIM	Amos	Ezekiel	Ezekiel
	Micah	Daniel (including	Daniel
Psalms	Joel	Susanna,	
Job	Obadiah	Prayer of	
Proverbs	Jonah	Azariah and	
Ruth	Nahum	Song of the	
Song of Songs	Habakkuk	Three Jews	
Ecclesiastes	Zephaniah	and Bel	
Lamentations	Haggai	and the Dragon)	
Esther	Zechariah	Hosea	Hosea
Daniel	Malachi	Joel	Joel
Ezra-Nehemiah	Isaiah	Amos	Amos
Chronicles	Jeremiah	Obadiah	Obadiah
	Baruch+	Jonah	Jonah
	Lamentations	Micah	Micah
	Letter of	Nahum	Nahum
	Jeremiah+	Habakkuk	Habakkuk
	Ezekiel	Zephaniah	Zephaniah
	Susanna+	Haggai	Haggai
	Daniel	Zechariah	Zechariah
	(including	Malachi	Malachi
	Prayer of	1 Maccabees	
	Azariah+ and	2 Maccabees	
	Song of the	3 Maccabees*	
	Three Jews+)	4 Maccabees*	
		1 Esdras*	
	Bel and the	2 Esdras*	
	Dragon+	Prayer of	
		Manasseh*	
		Psalm 151*	

NEW TESTAMENT	NEW TESTAMENT
Matthew	Matthew
Mark	Mark
Luke	Luke
John	John
Acts	Acts
Romans	Romans
1 Corinthians	1 Corinthians
2 Corinthians	2 Corinthians
Galatians	Galatians
Ephesians	Ephesians
Philippians	Philippians
Colossians	Colossians
1 Thessalonians	1 Thessalonians
2 Thessalonians	2 Thessalonians
1 Timothy	1 Timothy
2 Timothy	2 Timothy
Titus	Titus
Philemon	Philemon
Hebrews	Hebrews
James	James
1 Peter	1 Peter
2 Peter	2 Peter
1 John	1 John
2 John	2 John
3 John	3 John
Jude	Jude
Revelation	Revelation

+These works are not included in the Hebrew Bible.
*These works are not included in Roman Catholic Bibles but are contained in some Eastern Orthodox Bibles.

APPROACHES TO THE BIBLE

Some students enter a college course on the Bible with a prior knowledge of its content, perhaps having studied it to enrich their personal faith. This approach may be called the devotional or spiritual approach to Bible study. Several features typically characterize this approach. First, it assumes that the

Figure 1.5. Among the places most holy to Jews, the Western Wall (also known as the "Wailing Wall"), the only remaining portion of the wall around the Herodian Temple, has become the site of continual prayers by devout Jews. *(Photograph by Mitchell G. Reddish)*

Bible does or may have relevance to one's personal spiritual life. For such students the Bible may be referred to as "the Word of God" or as a "living" book. In this approach the key question one brings to the Bible is "How do these texts bear upon my faith?" This question assumes the Bible's relevance, and students attempt to discern how the Bible "speaks" to them. Second, such students read the Bible from a stance of commitment to the Bible's authority as a reliable guide in matters of faith. The Bible functions as their source of religious truth. Third, the devotional or spiritual approach may tend to ignore the context or historical setting of the biblical texts in the ancient world. The text and the reader are all that is necessary to discern the Bible's present relevance for faith. Fourth, people who use this approach often come to their study with an attitude of deep reverence and prayer, asking that God's Spirit lead them in their study. This approach to Bible study is simple, uncluttered, and uncomplicated. It requires neither formal training nor academic study. Millions of devoted Jews and Christians over the centuries have found inspiration through such study.

Although many devout believers study the Bible in this fashion, this approach has limitations. First, the books of the Bible were not written as chapters in one unified narrative, as anyone who attempts to "read the whole Bible straight through" quickly discovers. The Bible emerged from the history of the Jewish and early Christian communities and does contain the originating "stories" of these faiths. But books of poetry, law, proverbs, and letters are intermingled with historical narrative. Furthermore, the books of the Bible are not arranged in chronological order, and in some cases events are told several times and in different ways. Without an understanding of the special nature of this "book," the Jewish and Christian stories often become a series of isolated and confusing incidents that are tied together loosely at best.

A second limitation of the devotional approach is that persons who read the Bible apart from its historical contexts run the risk of misunderstanding its texts. For example, some biblical texts justify the killing of noncombatant women and children in battle, prohibit women from having leadership roles in the synagogue or church, and advise that one should remain single rather than marry. A careful reading of the passages in their originating contexts may lead a contemporary reader to understand them quite differently today.

Third, without analytical study one is less likely to understand the idioms, colloquialisms, and cryptic references that often occur in the Bible. The symbolism of Daniel 7–12 or Revelation is difficult to understand without scholarly guidance. A devotional reader strains to discover what is meant in these books by "the little horn," "the whore of Babylon," "the dragon from the sea," or the number 666.

Fourth, a subtle danger of using the devotional or spiritual approach alone is that a student may come to the texts with preconceived notions that will distort the interpretation. For example, an uninformed reader who assumes that the Hebrew prophets were primarily foretellers of the future will misunderstand the role and contributions of these important figures.

Since the eighteenth century, an alternative approach to the study of the Bible, called the critical approach, has developed. ("Critical" in this usage does not mean "negative" but refers to an analytical and objective approach, which will be further explained in the following chapter.) Because chapter 2 will formally introduce this approach, this chapter will introduce only two of its general features in regard to how it differs from the devotional method. First, the critical approach emphasizes the understanding of the texts in their original settings. It asks such questions as: "How was the text understood in its original context?" "How did it function for its early hearers?" "How do its literary form and literary setting affect our understanding of the text?" Second, the critical approach makes no assertion about the inspiration or spiritual authority of the Bible, although it by no means obviates or weakens such claims.

The critical approach has at least three advantages. First, it does not imply or require a faith stance. Any inquirer, whether a believer or not, may study the texts and become conversant with Jewish and Christian origins. Second, the critical approach imposes none of the claims of either Judaism or Christianity upon students outside of those faiths. Third, at the same time it may assist persons of faith who seek to enrich their understanding of the Bible. Acquaintance with the original settings of the texts can provide a fruitful basis for the interpretation and application of biblical teachings. This approach need not be a threat to faith. If one's faith is to be based upon the Jewish and Christian Scriptures, it is essential to understand what those writings actually teach.

The critical approach to biblical study, the one taken in this volume, can benefit all students who seek an understanding and appreciation of the origins and development of early Judaism and Christianity. The following chapter will explain this approach to biblical study in more detail and summarize its methods and conclusions.

Chapter 2

METHODS AND TOOLS FOR STUDYING THE BIBLE

Communication, both written and oral, is a complex process in which the receiver constantly tries to analyze and understand the meaning of the message from the sender. Interpretation is a necessary task because the meaning of words and phrases, either oral or written, is not always self-evident. The reader or listener, using certain clues and prior information, formulates an opinion on the meaning of a particular message, then continually refines or corrects that understanding as new information is gained. This process of explanation or interpretation, particularly when applied to the study of written documents, is called exegesis. The term "exegesis" comes from a Greek word that means "to lead or bring out"; thus, to exegete is to bring out the meaning of a text.

The scholarly study of the Bible is an attempt to systematize the process of asking questions of the text. It is a way of helping the reader gain a better understanding of the biblical writings. Biblical exegesis is necessary because misunderstanding can occur in reading biblical texts just as it does in other forms of communication. The possibility of misunderstanding is even greater with biblical texts, however, for three reasons. First, a great cultural divide separates the Western reader from the world of the ancient Near East. Second, a time gap as great as three thousand years or more separates the modern reader from the writing of some of the biblical texts. Third, the special status accorded the biblical writings by many individuals makes the interpretation of those texts more difficult. Many individuals regard the Bible as a sacred text, as Scripture. This status means that people often ask questions of the Bible that are not asked of other writings (What meaning does this have today? What authority does this text have?). It also means that many people approach the Bible with presuppositions or assumptions different from the ones with which they approach other literature. The individual who considers the Bible a source of religious authority is apt to interpret the text differently from the individual who does not view the Bible as religiously authoritative. All of these problems point to the need for a reliable, informed approach to the study of biblical literature that is appropriate for all inquirers.

TYPES OF BIBLICAL CRITICISM

Biblical scholars use certain tools and methods to assist them in understanding biblical literature. Their approach to the study of the Bible is known as critical study of the Bible, and the various methods are known as criticisms, such as textual criticism, source criticism, redaction criticism, or narrative criticism. Results from the scholarly use of these methods have increased our knowledge of the Bible and have provided the source materials for the writing of this textbook.

The words "critical" and "criticism" are often misunderstood. To study something critically does not mean that one takes a negative approach to the subject. Rather, to study a subject critically is to examine it carefully, analytically, and as objectively as possible in order to make well-founded and intelligent judgments about it. Art critics or literary critics are not individuals who disparage works of art or literature; they are people who appreciate the value of these works, try to assess their meaning, and attempt to share informed judgments with others. Likewise, biblical critics are persons who study biblical literature, using critical methods to understand the texts, and then share insights and information from their studies with others. Biblical critics are not attempting to destroy or alter the message of the biblical texts; on the contrary, they are seeking to understand these ancient writings.

The following discussion intends to provide a basic understanding of the most common approaches used by biblical scholars in their study of biblical literature. This discussion does not cover all approaches; other approaches are also used. The following methods, however, are the major ones used by biblical scholars. Each method of study will be defined and discussed, and each will be followed by one or two examples demonstrating how the method is actually used.

Textual Criticism

The formation of the Bible was a long and complex process. The Bible developed over several hundred years and was written by many different people in various locations. The Bible is a compilation of many writings; it was not written as one single book. Furthermore, no original manuscript of any portion of the Bible exists today. What remain are copies of manuscripts that were made from earlier copies, which were themselves copied from earlier copies. Scholars have discovered thousands of biblical manuscripts, some containing the entire Bible, some containing only a fragment of a verse. As one would expect, these thousands of manuscripts do not always agree on the contents of a particular text. Variations occur in spelling, in word choice, in names, and in meaning.

Textual criticism is the study of these various manuscripts in order to determine as accurately as possible the original wording of a passage. Since no original copies of any biblical manuscripts exist, and the multitude of manuscripts that we do have do not always agree, decisions have to be made about the best wording of a text. Any version of the Bible in use today owes its existence to the work of textual critics who have decided what likely was written in the original texts.

The method used by textual critics deals with two main areas of study: external evidence and internal evidence. External evidence is concerned with the dates of the manuscripts in question, the quantity of manuscripts, the types of manuscripts, the relationships among manuscripts, and the general reliability of the manuscripts being examined. How do textual critics use this external evidence to determine the best wording of a text? Generally, the text represented in early manuscripts, in numerous manuscripts, in manuscripts that are found over a wide geographical distribution, and in manuscripts that have already shown themselves to be reliable is usually preferred.

Internal evidence deals with the variations in wording among different manuscripts. Ancient manuscripts were reproduced by being painstakingly copied by hand, either by scribes with another copy of the manuscript in front of them or by scribes who copied the texts as they were read aloud. Changes occurred in numerous ways. Scribes involved in the transmission of the manuscripts could have accidentally changed a text. Anyone who has ever typed a paper from a manuscript or rewritten a term paper is familiar with the kind of accidental changes that can occur. Letters, words, or even entire lines may be inadvertently omitted or duplicated. Letters may be transposed. Sometimes scribes made the mistake of inserting into a new manuscript notes and comments that were written in the margins of the text from which they were copying. A scribe could have misunderstood the text as it was being read aloud and thus could have produced an erroneous version of the text.

Figure 2.1. St. Catherine's Monastery at the foot of traditional Mount Sinai is an Orthodox monastical center dating from the sixth century C.E. In 1844 Constantine von Tischendorf discovered in its library one of the most important manuscripts of the Bible, Codex Sinaiticus. (*Photograph by Clyde E. Fant*)

Other scribal changes could have been intentional. A scribe may have changed a passage to make it agree with a similar passage elsewhere in the Bible or to "improve" the grammar, the spelling, or even the theology of the passage. All these types of changes actually have occurred in biblical texts. The task of the textual critic is to examine all the evidence and then decide what the original author most likely wrote.

Psalm 49 provides an example of a textual problem from the Hebrew Bible. In some manuscripts verse 11 of this psalm reads, "Their inward [thoughts] are their homes forever." In the context of this psalm, this line does not seem to make sense. When one examines other ancient manuscripts of this psalm, the verse reads, "Their graves are their homes forever." The latter certainly makes better sense. Which wording is probably original? The answer to this question lies in noticing that the Hebrew word for "inward" is spelled *qrbm*, whereas the word for "graves" is *qbrm*. One can easily understand how a scribe might have accidentally transposed the letters in this verse and changed *qbrm* (graves) to *qrbm* (inward). This explanation of the change, along with the better contextual support for "graves," has led most scholars to conclude that Psalm 49:11 originally stated, "Their graves are their homes forever."

With the thousands of variations that exist in biblical texts, how reliable are the Bibles that are used today? They are very reliable, for several reasons. First, the Bible was such an important writing that a large number of copies of biblical writings were produced and preserved. There are more copies of ancient biblical manuscripts than of any other ancient document. Because of this fact, scholars are more certain of the accurate wording of biblical texts than they are of some passages from other ancient writings. Second, many of the variations are obvious changes, and scholars can, with virtual certainty, reconstruct the original wording. Third, very few of the questionable passages that remain in biblical texts are of major importance. Many of the questionable passages involve only minor issues such as spelling or grammar. Fourth, scholars have made significant gains in understanding the production and transmission of ancient documents and have developed specialized methods for helping them reconstruct ancient documents. The modern reader of the Bible needs to be aware that uncertainty does exist over the exact wording of some biblical passages, but the reader should proceed with confidence, assured that the texts from which modern translations are made are highly reliable.

Historical Criticism

Historical criticism involves two areas of study. First, historical criticism is the study of a text in order to determine the historical accuracy of information contained within the text. A careful study of the Bible sometimes suggests that events did not occur exactly as described. Questions about the historical accuracy of biblical information may arise for several reasons: discrepancies between parallel accounts in the Bible, discrepancies between biblical sources and nonbiblical evidence, information that seems inherently improbable or unbelievable, or material that seems to reflect later ideas or events.

An example of a historical question in the Bible is found in Luke 2:1-7, which states that Jesus was born during the time when Quirinius was governor of Syria. (Quirinius was legate or governor of Syria from 6 to 9 C.E.) According to Matthew 2:1 (and seemingly supported by Luke 1:5), however, Jesus was born during the time of Herod the Great, who died in 4 B.C.E., more than a decade before Quirinius became governor. Was Jesus born during the time of Quirinius or during the time of Herod? A reasonable suggestion, accepted by most scholars, is that Luke, writing toward the end of the first century, was confused about the time of Quirinius's rule. The Herodian tradition, therefore, is probably more accurate.

A second focus of historical criticism is a study of the historical factors that shaped a particular text. Biblical writings, like all other literature, did not arise in a vacuum. Although religious in focus, they were also the product of social, cultural, geographical, and political forces. The more one understands about the background of a particular writing (its date and place of composition, its author, and its intended audience), the better equipped one will be to understand the contents of that document.

One of these historical factors is the date of composition of a text. Sometimes specific indications of dates are given in the writing itself. For example, the book of 2 Kings ends with a reference to Jehoiachin, former king of Judah, living in exile in Babylon. Since Jehoiachin was taken into exile around 597 B.C.E., the final form of 2 Kings obviously could not have been written until after that date. With most writings, however, dating is not that easy. Scholars must look for internal clues in the writing, use information gained from archaeology, compare the writing to other ancient writings whose dating has been ascertained, and look for references to the writing in other documents.

Closely related to the date of a writing is the place where the writing was produced. By knowing the date and place of composition, scholars can study the political, social, and economic situations present when the writing was produced and explore how these factors might have shaped the message of the writing and the form in which it was presented. All of the biblical writings were produced in the area around the Mediterranean Sea. Scholars, however, try to pinpoint the location of the various writings more precisely. In some cases, scholars have reliable evidence of the city in which a document was produced. In 1 Corinthians 16:8, for example, Paul indicates that he is in the city of Ephesus when he writes the letter known today as 1 Corinthians.

Historical critics are also interested in determining the actual authors of biblical texts. Determining authorship is not always possible, however. Many of the biblical writings make no claim concerning authorship. Names in the titles of books in English Bibles today were often added decades after the books were written and represent only what later tradition believed about authorship. For example, some English versions of the Bible entitle the book of Hebrews in the New Testament "The Epistle of Paul the Apostle to the Hebrews." That title was not originally a part of the work but was added later. A careful comparison of the book with Paul's known writings in the New Testament shows that Hebrews was not written by Paul because the differences in style, vocabulary, and theology are too great.

Even when the book itself names a particular person as author, that claim is not necessarily a reliable indication of authorship. Pseudonymity, or writing under the name of someone else, was a fairly common—and, unlike today, apparently acceptable—practice in the ancient world. As a result, biblical scholars must look for internal as well as external clues to help them determine authorship. The problem is compounded by the fact that many biblical writings did not have one single author. As will be discussed in chapter 3, some of the biblical writings are the products of various traditions involving different individuals who shaped and edited the material along the way. In many cases it is more appropriate to talk in terms of the author or editor of a particular section of the material or a certain edition of the document.

Another concern of historical critics is to determine the identity of the intended audience of a particular writing. To whom was the author writing? What was the relationship between author and audience? Once again, the answers to these questions are sometimes relatively easy. The book of Philippians, as indicated in the writing itself, is a letter from Paul the apostle to the church in Philippi. Paul writes as their spiritual leader, giving them encouragement and advice. On the other hand, some writings, such as the Gospel of Matthew, make no explicit statements concerning the identity of their intended readers, leaving scholars to make educated judgments about the intended recipients of the writings.

The question of the authorship of the book of Isaiah illustrates one aspect of the work of historical critics. The book as it now stands contains sixty-six chapters. The casual reader usually assumes that the book is the work of one person, the eighth-century prophet Isaiah. As scholars have studied the book closely, however, that understanding of authorship has changed. For the most part, chapters 1–39 do seem to originate from Isaiah the prophet. These chapters portray Isaiah interacting with the political and military events of the latter part of the eighth century B.C.E. Beginning with chapter 40, though, Isaiah is never mentioned again. Furthermore, the historical situation has changed. The political events described in

Figure 2.2. The Rosetta Stone, with its inscription written in Egyptian hieroglyphics, demotic script (also Egyptian), and Greek, provided the key for deciphering hieroglyphic writings. The granite block was discovered in Egypt in 1799 by Napoleon's soldiers. *(Photograph by Clyde E. Fant)*

the text are those of the sixth century B.C.E. following the fall of Jerusalem to the Babylonians. In addition, chapters 56–66 seem to reflect an even later period of Israel's history. This information, along with other evidence, has led most scholars to conclude that the biblical book of Isaiah was not composed by one individual but was the work of at least two and probably three different writers, each reacting to different historical, social, and religious situations.

The value of studying a writing's historical setting is illustrated by the book of Revelation in the New Testament. The bizarre imagery and strange symbolism of this book have left readers wondering how to understand it. Drawing upon information in the writing itself, such as references to persecution and emperor worship in chapter 13, as well as upon information from early Christian writers and Roman historians, most scholars today locate the place and time of the composition of Revelation as Asia Minor during a time when some

Christians had been persecuted by the government. The most likely date of composition would be during the end of the reign of the Roman emperor Domitian, sometime around 95 C.E. Read in this light, much of the strange symbolism in the book becomes understandable. The bizarre creatures (such as the seven-headed beast from the sea in chapter 13) are often the author's way of describing the Roman officials. The author portrays them as frightening beasts because he is convinced that the emperors with their claims to divine status represent a threat to Christians who refuse to participate in the cult of emperor worship. By depicting the emperor as a beast, the author is saying to his readers that the emperor is not divine but evil. Understanding the historical context of Revelation helps one see that the book is not a prediction of events in the distant future, but a document addressed to a first-century audience that offers its readers words of comfort and consolation about their current predicament.

Source Criticism

Source criticism is a study of the sources that underlie a particular text. Biblical writers, like the authors of many other writings, often borrowed materials from other sources, editing and shaping the material to fit their own purposes. Source critics attempt to determine what—if any—sources authors used in composing their works. Sometimes the use of sources is obvious, such as in Numbers 21:14-15 or Luke 1:1-4, in which the writer explicitly states that a source is being used. In most cases, however, the use of sources is not that easy to determine. Since biblical writers did not use quotation marks or footnotes, how do we detect the presence of sources? Scholars have identified several clues that indicate the likelihood of dependence upon another source. Some of these clues are changes in vocabulary and phrasing, changes in literary style, interruptions in the flow of a passage, inconsistencies within a text, and duplication of a story or event.

One of the most well-known results of source criticism in the Hebrew Bible occurred in the study of the Pentateuch, the first five books. In studying these texts, scholars noticed several interesting facts. First, differing accounts of the same story are found. Genesis 1:1–2:4*a* contains one account of creation while Genesis 2:4*b*-25 presents another version. Second, different names for God seem to prevail in particular passages throughout the Pentateuch. In some places the name Yahweh is prevalent; in other places Elohim is the preferred name. For example, in Genesis 1:1–2:4*a*, Elohim (NRSV: God) is the name used for God. Beginning at Genesis 2:4*b*, however, the name for God that is used consistently is Yahweh Elohim (NRSV: Lord God). Third, the style of writing differs in several places. Chapter 1 of Genesis is a tightly organized and formal account of creation. The second creation account, however, flows more easily and reads like a well-crafted story. Fourth, even the portrayals of God differ. The God of the first creation account is distant and austere: God commands, and the created world comes into existence. The God of the second creation account is more intimate: God creates by shaping and crafting, like a skilled potter. God is personal, breathing the breath of life into the first man and being concerned about the man's need for companionship.

These and other differences throughout the first five books of the Hebrew Bible led scholars to conclude that the Pentateuch is composed of at least four different sources or strands of tradition. This theory, known as the Documentary Hypothesis, labels the four sources as J, E, D, and P. The J (or Yahwist) strand is so named because it prefers the name Yahweh for God. (In German "Yahweh" begins with a J; thus, the source is called J.) According to the classic version of the Documentary Hypothesis, the traditions contained in this material were likely written down around 1000–900 B.C.E. and were dominant in Judah, the southern part of Israel. The E (or Elohist) material derives its name from its preference for the term *Elohim* for God. It seems to reflect the ideas of the northern part of Israel. Although difficult to date, the Elohist material was probably preserved in written form approximately one hundred years after the Yahwist material. Sometime later, the J and E strands seem to have been combined into one account, the JE material. D stands for Deuteronomic because the majority of D material in the Pentateuch is in the book of Deuteronomy. This material probably arose in the Northern Kingdom and was later shaped and augmented sometime during the seventh century in the Southern Kingdom. The Priestly material, designated P, is so named because of the intense interest of the writer in cultic matters—priests, worship, sacrifices, the Temple. The Priestly writer composed the work during or just after the time of the Exile of the Jewish people in Babylon (ca. 587–538 B.C.E.). Shortly thereafter, the JE material was combined with the P tradition. Then, during the fifth century B.C.E., the JEP material was combined with the D material, and the Pentateuch, roughly as we know it today, took shape. In recent decades, the Documentary Hypothesis has been challenged and modified in different ways by various scholars. Many scholars dispute the dating and even the existence of some of these sources. Other disagreements concern the allocation of various texts to the different sources. In spite of these arguments over the details of the sources underlying the Pentateuch, almost all scholars concur that multiple authors and sources contributed to the development of these writings. In studying the Pentateuch, therefore, one should be aware that several sources were brought together at varying stages to produce the work as it exists in the Bible today.

Form Criticism

Communication occurs in typical patterns or forms: a joke is told in a particular way, a newscast is delivered in a set form, a telephone conversation has a typical pattern. People use these various forms of communication subconsciously. The forms, however, are an important clue to understanding the message. Form critics study biblical passages to identify the various forms of communication that are contained within them. Form critics are particularly interested in trying to go behind the written text and discover the oral stages of the tradition. They seek to ascertain the form in which the material circulated orally. By categorizing the material into different forms, scholars are able to learn more about how the material was used in its earlier stages. For example, the form may indicate that the material was originally used in worship, or that it was part of a wedding ceremony, or that it was part of a legal document. Form critics also attempt to trace the development and changes of the tradition as it went through various oral and written stages. (This latter concern is sometimes known as tradition criticism.)

Form criticism can be applied not only to the oral stage of the tradition but also to the written stage. The Bible contains a wide variety of literary forms or genres: letters, histories, hymns, gospels, miracle stories, parables, legends, apocalypses, and so on. Reading a text without paying attention to its proper literary form can lead to misunderstanding. Messages, simply by their form, communicate. The form of the message produces certain expectations in the mind of the reader. For example, two distinct literary forms in a newspaper are the editorial and the front-page story. When one reads the editorial, one expects to find the editor's opinion on a certain issue. The purpose of the editorial is to persuade or convince. The front-page story, on the other hand, should be factual, objective writing. The purpose of the material is to present information, not to persuade or convince. If one ignored these forms and read an editorial as objective information, one could be misled. The same is true when dealing with biblical texts. The reader must take notice of the literary form or genre in which the material is presented. To do otherwise may cause one to misunderstand the text. For example, one should not read the book of Revelation, which is an apocalypse, in the same way that one would read the writings of Paul, which are letters.

A literary form in the New Testament that has generated considerable interest is the hymn. The early church, like religious communities today, expressed its faith through the singing of hymns. Some of those hymns are embedded in the New Testament. One such hymn is found in Philippians 2:6-11. Scholars do not agree on the exact division of the text into strophes or verses, but most accept the designation of this passage as a hymn based on the presence of several hymnic characteristics: rhythm, parallelism, poetic style, extensive use of participial constructions, arrangement in strophes or verses, and exalted language. As an ancient hymn, this text was probably sung by the early Christians in worship. Paul, the author of Philippians, borrowed this hymn and adapted it to convey his message to the church members at Philippi.

Redaction Criticism

Whereas form criticism concentrates on small units of tradition, studying their setting and function independent of the larger work of which they are a part, redaction criticism arose in an effort to look at the larger picture. Biblical writers were not just collectors and compilers of isolated traditions but were creative writers and theologians. A redactor is an editor, one who corrects, rearranges, deletes, complements, or otherwise modifies material. Redaction critics are interested in how writers shaped, structured, and edited their material in order to present their message. Recognizing that biblical writers were often dependent on sources, redaction critics attempt to determine how an author has used those sources. Redaction criticism is an attempt to understand the theological viewpoint, the literary interests, and the life setting of the author, as well as how those factors might have shaped the author's presentation of the material.

Figure 2.3. Archaeology sometimes uncovers rare treasures such as this gold mask of Tutankhamen, made of twenty pounds of solid gold and inlaid with turquoise and lapis lazuli. More often, common pottery or other remains of ancient daily life are uncovered. *(Photograph by Clyde E. Fant)*

A good example of the value of redaction criticism is found in the study of 1 Chronicles. Scholars generally agree that the author of 1 Chronicles used 1 and 2 Samuel as sources. A comparison of the same events described in 1 Chronicles and 1 and 2 Samuel reveals that the author of 1 Chronicles made several changes in the source material. The story of David in 1 Chronicles 20:1-3 illustrates these changes. The Chronicler is obviously adapting material from 2 Samuel 11–12. The Chronicler, however, omitted some material in the retelling of the story. The author of 1 Chronicles begins by rephrasing 2 Samuel 11:1-2, then skips to 2 Samuel 12:26 and picks up the story again, omitting the material in the intervening verses. The omitted material contains the account of David's adulterous affair with Bathsheba, the murder of her husband, and David's rebuke by the prophet Nathan. The Chronicler likely omitted this material because it was not consistent with the overall purpose of portraying David as the exemplary leader of Israel. This conclusion is reinforced when one notices that such redaction of material in favor of David is not an isolated incident but occurs regularly in 1 Chronicles. The author of 1 Chronicles did not simply report information that was available but instead creatively shaped that material to express certain religious convictions.

Canonical Criticism

Rather than dealing with earlier stages of a text or isolated segments of texts, canonical criticism is concerned with the final form of a text, the way it appears in the canon. Canonical criticism arose out of a concern to interpret biblical passages not just as isolated texts but as parts of a larger work, the entire Bible. Canonical critics ask questions about the theological significance of biblical texts, both their significance for the communities of faith that preserved them and their significance for the communities of faith that still use these texts today.

The acceptance of particular texts as sacred and normative by believing communities—and their inclusion in the canon of those communities—affects the interpretation of those texts in several ways. For instance, biblical texts are approached differently from other texts. The reader brings presuppositions and assumptions to the Bible different from those he or she brings to the reading of other texts. Likewise, biblical texts, although originally written as individual documents, are now parts of a larger work. For example, the Gospel of Mark does not stand by itself but circulates along with the Gospels of Matthew, Luke, and John, as well as with the other biblical writings. The church has placed them together and in so doing has said either implicitly or explicitly that they must be interpreted together. A canonical reading of Mark is sensitive to the portrayals of Jesus in the other Gospels.

Furthermore, as part of a larger work now in use by believing communities, biblical texts may acquire meanings in addition to those that they had in their original settings. As a part of faith communities, biblical texts continue to speak to those communities. Canonical criticism, therefore, asks what meaning biblical texts have for contemporary readers of the Bible. Moreover, canonical criticism recognizes that no one idea or teaching can be considered normative on its own. The teachings of other biblical passages on the same subject must also be considered. The teaching of the whole canon must be heard.

Isaiah 53 is a text in the Hebrew Bible that has sparked much discussion. Who is the Suffering Servant figure about whom the author speaks? Scholars, approaching the text from a historical-critical standpoint, have usually argued that there are several possibilities. The Servant may be the nation of Israel, a recent Judean king, a prophet, the author himself, or some individual whom the author expects to appear within a short time. As this text was read and interpreted within the Christian community centuries later, a new identification was given to the Suffering Servant. The early church—and Christians ever since—saw in this figure a foreshadowing of Jesus of Nazareth. New Testament writers described Jesus in terms borrowed from Isaiah 53. A canonical reading of Isaiah 53 by a Christian allows for this added meaning of the text, a meaning not intended by the author. To read the text in this manner is not to claim that the original author of Isaiah 53 was predicting the coming of Jesus several hundred years later. Rather, a canonical reading allows new meanings to arise from texts as they function in different settings and different times.

A canonical reading of Romans 13 illustrates how the message of a text may be affected by other biblical passages. In Romans 13, Paul advises his readers to obey the governmental authorities—to resist the government is to resist God. Taken alone, this passage could, and has, led to the conviction that Christians must always be obedient to the government no matter what it demands. This strict view is altered, however, when Romans 13 is placed alongside other New Testament texts such as Acts 4 and Revelation 13, which affirm that civil disobedience is acceptable and even necessary on certain occasions. These passages teach that when the will of God and the will of government are at odds, the Christian must resist the claims of the government and follow the will of God. Romans 13, on the other hand, relativizes Acts 4 and Revelation 13 by showing that civil authorities are not always to be resisted. They render a valuable service and, given certain conditions, should receive the support of Christians. Canonical criticism reminds us that biblical texts stand alongside one another and must be interpreted in dialogue with one another.

Social-Scientific Criticism

Social-scientific criticism attempts to understand the biblical texts by situating them within the social world out of which they came. A great social distance separates the modern world from the biblical world. Our customs, languages, values, social systems, economic systems, political systems, and worldviews are different from those of the Bible. Uninformed modern readers are apt to assume that their world closely resembles the world of the Bible and thus will impose their values and belief systems on the texts. Through methods and insights gained from the social sciences, particularly sociology, anthropology, economics, and political science, social-scientific criticism reconstructs and illuminates the social world of antiquity so that the biblical texts from that world can be better understood. In order to enhance information gained from historical studies, social-scientific criticism often makes use of crosscultural models and comparative studies.

An example of a social-scientific approach to the New Testament might be a study of the status and social relationships of slaves in the first-century Roman world. Modern American readers, when they encounter references to slavery in the New Testament, are likely to conceptualize it in terms of the experience of African slaves in the United States from the seventeenth to the nineteenth centuries. Yet, as social historians have demonstrated, slavery in the Mediterranean world of the first century was greatly different from the institution of slavery in America. Slavery in the Roman world was not racially based or necessarily a lifelong experience. Slaves could earn their freedom through various means. Moreover, Roman slaves were often granted Roman citizenship upon receiving their freedom. In Roman society, slaves did not constitute a separate social or economic class; rather, their social and economic standing was determined in large part by the status of their owners. These examples of differences between ancient slavery and slavery in America should not be understood to imply that ancient slavery was a benign or neutral practice. On the contrary, slavery in the ancient world was an unfortunate and often cruel experience. Families were sometimes torn apart when parents were forced to sell their children into slavery in order to pay their debts. Slaves could be tortured, beaten, or sexually exploited by their masters. Because of the differences between slavery in the Roman world and in America, however, modern readers must take care not to interpret slavery in the Bible in terms of their knowledge of slavery in the American experience, but rather should seek to understand how slavery functioned in the world of the Bible.

Narrative Criticism

Narrative criticism is one of several methods of biblical study that can be grouped together as literary criticisms. These literary approaches study the text as an independent work, apart from its historical and cultural setting, on the basis that the text creates its own world and must be understood within that world.

Literary critics, therefore, are only secondarily interested in such issues as authorship, social and political contexts, and place and date of writing. The concern of literary critics focuses on matters internal to the text.

Narrative criticism studies biblical texts in the same way that other literature is studied. It focuses on such issues as plot, characters, setting, themes, narrator, point of view, style, figures of speech, symbolism, narrative patterns, conflict, order, implied author, and implied reader. The implied author is not the real author of the text (who may be anonymous) but the hypothetical author created by the way the narrative is told. Likewise, the implied reader is not the actual reader (neither the original reader nor the modern reader) but an idealized reader presupposed by the narrative itself. Narrative critics are interested in how the implied author guides and gives clues to the implied reader throughout the narrative. Narrative critics try to enter the world of the text and hear the story in the same way that the implied reader is supposed to hear it. Thus, narrative critics are not interested in determining whether an event actually happened historically, but rather in how the event functions within the narrative itself. How is the implied reader expected to understand the event?

One example of a narrative-critical approach to a text might be the study of the use of intercalation, or "sandwiching," in the Gospel of Mark. On several occasions the author begins to tell one incident, interrupts it with another incident, and then completes the first incident, thus "sandwiching" one story between the two parts of another. One of the classic examples of this literary technique occurs in Mark 11:12-25, which brackets the story of Jesus "cleansing" the Jerusalem Temple by placing on either side of it the beginning and ending of the story of Jesus cursing a fig tree. On a strictly historical level, the fig tree story creates several problems. Why, for example, would Jesus become angry at a fig tree for not having figs when it was not the season for figs? If one looks at the fig tree incident, however, as primarily a literary device that the author uses to help the reader interpret the incident in the Temple, then the meaning of the story becomes clearer. By surrounding the story of the Temple with the story of the cursing of an unproductive fig tree, the author indicates to the reader that Jesus' activity in the Temple was not simply the "cleansing" of an institution with minor problems but the condemnation of a system that had failed to produce the "fruit" it was intended to bear.

Reader-Response Criticism

Another literary methodology sometimes used in biblical study is reader-response criticism. As its name suggests, reader-response criticism focuses less on the role of the text and more on the role of the reader of the text. According to reader-response critics, meaning is not found within texts; rather, meaning is created by readers in their interaction with a text. Reader-response critics are not interested in the intention of the author (claiming it cannot be known anyway) because meaning is created by the reader of the text, not by the author. All texts have "literary gaps," places in the text in which certain information is not supplied. The reader must make connections across these gaps that occur in a text. Different readers understand texts in different ways partly because they "fill the gaps" differently. Reader-response critics emphasize that no reader is ever objective or neutral. Every reader brings her or his experiences, biases, and expectations to a text that are different from those brought by another reader. Reader-response critics are interested in how a reader engages the text and interacts with it as she or he reads the text. How does reading the text affect the reader? Does the text change the reader's point of view? Does the reader identify with certain characters in the text? Reader-response critics stress that reading is a temporal rather than a static activity; that is, as one reads from one sentence or paragraph to the next, one's understanding of the text changes and new meanings occur. The reader starts with a meaning, develops other meanings as he or she continues to read, then alters or confirms those meanings. The very act of reading through the text, then, creates meaning for the reader. The reader-response critic is interested in how the different elements in the text (for example, structure, repetitions, and anticipatory statements) affect the reader's engagement with and response to the text.

Genesis 18, for example, tells the story of the visit to Abraham of three strangers. In studying this text, a reader-response critic might note the different identifications and descriptions that are given of these visitors and ask how this information affects the reading of the text. In 18:1 the text says, "The LORD appeared to Abraham by the oaks of Mamre, as he sat at the entrance of his tent in the heat of the day." Verse 2 states, "He looked up and saw three men standing near him." A literary gap occurs between the two verses. What is the connection between "the LORD" (Yahweh) and "the three men"? Are they the same or different beings? As the reader moves through the text, the question continues to surface because the text alternates between presenting the major characters (other than Abraham and Sarah) as either the LORD or the three men. Additional insight (or confusion?) occurs when the reader continues into chapter 19 and encounters "the two angels" (19:1). What is their connection to the characters in chapter 18? What effect does this interplay in character identification have on the reader's understanding of Yahweh and how Yahweh interacts with humanity? Furthermore, how do the reader's own experiences and biases influence him or her in making judgments about the identities of the characters?

RELATED DISCIPLINES

In addition to the nine critical methodologies described above, biblical scholars benefit from information gained from other sources and other disciplines. Two areas that have been especially helpful in the study of the Bible are archaeology and literary parallels.

Archaeology

Archaeology is the study of the material remains of a culture for the purpose of helping to provide a better understanding of how ancient peoples lived and worked. Although some ancient remains lie exposed, most archaeological work requires painstaking excavation of ancient cities and tombs. By examining ancient documents, pottery, household utensils, tools, weapons, jewelry, buildings, sculptures, and bones, archaeologists learn much about the political,

Figure 2.4. Archaeological discoveries, such as this clay figurine of the Anatolian Mother Goddess from south central Turkey, provide insights into ancient customs and beliefs. This statuette, about four inches tall, dates from approximately 5750 B.C.E. (*Photograph by Mitchell G. Reddish*)

economic, social, and cultural history of a people. Archaeological studies have been valuable to biblical studies because they have yielded a better understanding of the customs, beliefs, and lifestyles of the ancient Israelites and early Christians.

Literary Parallels

Valuable information can also be gained by studying documents that in some way parallel biblical texts. Literary parallels drawn from Egyptian, Canaanite, Greek, Roman, and other sources (including noncanonical Jewish and Christian sources) can shed light on vocabulary, literary styles, literary forms or genres, ancient customs or beliefs, or historical events encountered in the Bible. The serious student of the Bible will study these nonbiblical documents and apply the information gained to his or her understanding of the Bible.

TOOLS AND REFERENCE WORKS

The methods described above are the major ones used by biblical scholars today. Others could be mentioned: structuralism, rhetorical criticism, deconstructionism, ideological criticism, and linguistics. No one scholar is adept at the use of all of these techniques. Even the best scholars must depend upon the expertise of others who are better qualified in certain areas than they are. The average reader of the Bible is likely not skilled in any of these methods of study, but that does not mean that she or he cannot benefit from them. Several tools and reference works are available that make accessible the results of the various scholarly studies of the Bible. The person who is seriously interested in learning more about biblical texts would be wise to consult these works.

Dictionaries and Encyclopedias

Several good, reliable biblical dictionaries and encyclopedias are available. Some are one-volume works; others are multivolume sets. These works provide an enormous amount of helpful information derived from critical studies about terms, ideas, customs, and people related to the Bible.

Concordances

A concordance is like a large index. It gives the scriptural location of each occurrence of major words in the Bible. A concordance can be of great use in locating a particular passage or in trying to find all the biblical references to a particular topic.

Commentaries

Perhaps the most helpful tool in understanding a text, commentaries usually follow either a verse-by-verse or a section-by-section approach to Bible study. Commentaries explain the meaning of texts by discussing the historical and literary background of the passage, the literary form and style, the themes and motifs that are present, the sources that were used, and any textual problems that might exist. Most commentaries deal with only one biblical book, or in the case of small books, two or three. Less helpful, but still valuable, are commentaries that cover the entire Bible in one volume.

Atlases

An atlas is a collection of maps. Maps of the ancient Near East and the Mediterranean world help put biblical places and locations in perspective. Many Bibles include a small collection of maps. Separately bound atlases, however, contain more maps along with supplementary information about various locations, peoples, and cultures.

Introductions

As the name implies, introductions to the Bible are written to help individuals become acquainted with the biblical texts. Some cover only the Hebrew Bible or only the New Testament, whereas others discuss the entire Bible. Reading an introduction is one of the best ways to begin one's study of the Bible because introductions present a brief overview of the texts in their religious, historical, literary, and cultural contexts.

A bibliography of basic tools and reference works for the study of the Bible may be found at the end of this book.

CONSOLIDATING THE RESULTS

No one methodology is sufficient to understand the Bible. Scholars must utilize insights gained from all of these methods and disciplines in doing exegesis. Furthermore, the goal of exegesis is not to discover *the* meaning of a passage but to reach *an* understanding of the passage. Texts are multidimensional. An interpreter never fully comprehends or exhausts the meaning of a text. The particular method or approach one uses will shape the understanding of the text one achieves. For example, the person who studies a text using a literary-critical approach may gain insights different from those acquired by the person who studies it from a historical perspective. Each approach is valid; each yields its own insights.

Furthermore, the perspective from which one studies the text will influence one's understanding of the text. Feminist scholars have provided a valuable service to biblical scholarship by pointing out that the study of the Bible has too often been a male-dominated, or at least a male-oriented, discipline. When studied from a feminist perspective and with feminist concerns, the text gives rise to new understandings. In the same way, new insights into the Bible have arisen as it has been studied from an African American, Latin American, or Asian viewpoint. The study of the Bible demands all the resources available. A good student of the Bible will not be content to examine one aspect of a text but will ask what can be learned from other approaches to the passage.

The beginning student of the Bible is likely to feel overwhelmed by the variety of methods and tools discussed here: textual criticism, historical criticism, source criticism, form criticism, redaction criticism, canonical criticism, social-scientific criticism, narrative criticism, reader-response criticism, archaeology, literary parallels, dictionaries and encyclopedias, concordances, commentaries, atlases, and introductions. A logical question to ask is, "Is the Bible that difficult to understand?" The answer is both yes and no. On the one hand, there are some parts of the Bible that are extremely difficult to understand; even scholars still debate their meanings. In other cases, scholars have been able to bring new understandings to obscure and confusing passages by applying the various methodologies discussed above. Modern readers of the Bible are greatly indebted to individuals who have devoted their time and energies to unlocking some of the long-held mysteries of biblical texts.

On the other hand, the Bible is also a book with a message about God and humanity, a message that has spoken to and inspired people for centuries (including long before the advent of biblical criticism). The Bible survived not because it was a book of secrets only for the learned but because it was a book that spoke to the deepest needs and longings of humanity. Throughout the centuries, people have read the Bible and seen within its pages a reflection of their own predicament and found in its teachings answers to some of their most important questions. The goal of the biblical scholar is not to take the Bible out of the hands of the average reader but rather to help the reader better understand the Bible and its message.

Chapter 3

THE ORIGINS AND DEVELOPMENT OF THE BIBLE

The Bible is a diverse collection of writings composed over a long period of time by many people, reflecting various social and historical situations. How were these writings produced? Why and how were they collected into one volume? Why were these works selected and not others? Judaism and Christianity have traditionally claimed divine guidance or inspiration for the writing, selection, and preservation of the books of the Bible. These assertions are faith claims, however, and not objective, verifiable data that help the scholar to understand the complex historical processes behind the production of the Bible. The question of the origins of the biblical materials is not easy to answer. Although some of the biblical works first appeared as written works produced by one person (some of the letters of Paul, for example), many of the writings give evidence of several stages of composition. Early traditions passed through oral and written stages in which the content was reviewed, enlarged, and adapted to new situations.

FORMATION OF THE HEBREW BIBLE

The Hebrew Bible was a community product; that is, it developed out of the Israelite and Jewish communities. It contains the stories and traditions that the Hebrew people considered important to their understanding of God. These traditions, some of which circulated orally for generations before being cast into written form, were formulated, shaped, and later given authoritative status by these communities of faith. On the other hand, these writings also helped shape and nurture the communities as people looked to them for guidance in faith and daily living.

Oral Stage

Like most ancient cultures, ancient Israel was an oral culture. Through stories it remembered its past, reflected on the meaning of life, and speculated on the origin of the world. The Israelites told sagas and sang songs about the exploits of ancestral heroes and tribal leaders and about military victories. They crafted prayers and confessions to express their feelings toward God. They used proverbs and legal sayings to transmit the social and religious values and norms of the

Figure 3.1. The partially rolled *Thanksgiving Scroll,* one of the many biblical and nonbiblical scrolls found at Qumran near the Dead Sea, contains forty psalmlike hymns of thanksgiving. Many biblical manuscripts have been discovered on similar scrolls. *(Courtesy of Israel Museum, Jerusalem)*

community. Over the centuries that these oral traditions were passed down through Hebrew culture, they were revised and refined by storytellers in succeeding generations. By the time the first written documents of the Bible appeared, the Israelites had formed an immense body of oral traditions from which they drew.

Although not all of the material in the Hebrew Bible originated in oral traditions, much of it did. The bulk of the ancestral sagas in Genesis 12–50, for example, were almost certainly composed orally and then told and retold for generations before they were ever written down. Similarly, the sayings in the book of Proverbs, the material in the book of Psalms, the story of Job, and the Song of Deborah in Judges 5 are examples of the extensive oral prehistory of the biblical material. As these traditions were recounted in varied settings and for different purposes, they helped shape Israel's understanding of itself and its God, and the traditions themselves were in turn shaped and modified in the retelling.

The Writing Stage

Few books in the Hebrew Bible are the product of a single author. Most are composite works that grew from a diverse assortment of oral and written sources. The earliest written materials now contained in the Hebrew Bible were not complete books but literary traditions embedded in the current writings. For example, the Song of Deborah in Judges 5 likely began as oral tradition, then circulated as an independent written work, and later was incorporated into the book of Judges. Although scholars disagree over the dating of the Song of Deborah, some authorities say that it was possibly written down as early as the twelfth century B.C.E. Likewise, the Song of Miriam in Exodus 15:21, considered one of the earliest examples of Hebrew poetry, originating perhaps in the twelfth century B.C.E., also probably had an independent written history prior to its inclusion in the Torah. The earliest lengthy preservation of traditions in writing among the Israelites, according to most scholars, took place during the time of David and Solomon (tenth century B.C.E.). During this period one or more persons produced an early version of Israel's history, the Yahwistic History or J material that later became a part of the Torah. Even after the production of literary documents became more common, however, oral traditions did not cease. Instead, oral and written traditions were preserved parallel to each other for much of Israel's history.

Most of the Torah (Law) comprised the first major literary collection within the Hebrew Bible. There are, however, some materials in the other two major collections, the Nevi'im (Prophets) and the Ketuvim (Writings), that predate certain portions of the Torah. The growth of these writings from their smallest literary units to the books of the Hebrew Scriptures was a complicated process. An initial orientation to this history of composition can be accomplished by examining the process of writing, collecting, and editing that resulted in the finished form of each of the three major sections of the Hebrew Bible.

Torah (Law). The first five books of the Bible (Genesis, Exodus, Leviticus, Numbers, and Deuteronomy) constitute the Torah (or Pentateuch). Analysis of the contents of these books reveals that the community that composed them used numerous oral traditions and written sources. Evidence for these multiple sources includes special names for God that are peculiar to some sections of the Torah, multiple descriptions of the same event, differences in vocabulary, abrupt changes in style, and breaks in the continuity of certain narratives. As discussed in the previous chapter, biblical scholars have proposed the Documentary Hypothesis to explain how four different strands of tradition (J, E, D, and P) were used in the composition of the Torah. The earliest of these traditions (J) was probably written down around 1000–900 B.C.E. The last tradition (P) was likely composed during the sixth or fifth century B.C.E. All of these materials were combined into their final form as the Torah sometime during the fifth century B.C.E.

Nevi'im (Prophets). At the same time that much of the literature of the Torah was being written, several of the works that constitute the second section of the Hebrew Bible, the Nevi'im, were also taking shape. The Nevi'im contains two parts, the Former Prophets and the Latter Prophets. The first part (Joshua, Judges, 1 and 2 Samuel, and 1 and 2 Kings) tells of certain prophets (such as Elijah and Elisha) who did not produce literary works. It also provides the historical and political contexts for the "latter prophets," who do have books about them in the Hebrew Bible. The works that comprise the Former Prophets were written in an early form during the seventh century B.C.E. and then later revised in the sixth century as the major portion of what scholars call the Deuteronomistic History (see chapter 11 for an extended discussion of the Deuteronomistic History).

Many of the writings known as the Latter Prophets show evidence of a complex history of composition involving several authors or editors and various alterations, expansions, and revisions. For example, the writing of most of the book of Amos dates from the mideighth century B.C.E., the time of the prophet Amos. The final five verses of the book, however, are often considered a later addition by a person or persons who tempered Amos's predominantly pessimistic message with a word of hope. Any attempt to date the writing of these works, then, is only approximate. The Latter Prophets can be divided roughly into three historical periods based on the date of the writing of the major portion of each work. The writings of Amos, Hosea, Isaiah 1–39, Micah, Zephaniah, Nahum, and Habakkuk appeared between 750 and 587 B.C.E., prior to the Babylonian Exile. The books of Jeremiah and Ezekiel and some of the additions to Isaiah (chapters 40–55) were produced during the Exile (between 587 and 538 B.C.E.). After the Exile, portions of Isaiah (chapters 56–66) and the books of Haggai, Zechariah, Joel, Obadiah, Jonah, and Malachi were written (between 538 and 400 B.C.E.).

Ketuvim (Writings). Other books that came to be part of the Hebrew Bible were 1 and 2 Chronicles, Ezra, Nehemiah, Ruth, Esther, Job, Psalms,

Figure 3.2. Approximate Dates for Writings in the Hebrew Bible (all dates are B.C.E.)

12–10th centuries	10th cent.	9th cent.	8th cent.	7th cent.	6th cent.	5th cent.	4th cent.	3rd cent.	2nd cent.
Various poetic passages (e.g., Judg. 5 Ex. 15:21) circulate orally and are possibly written down	Yahwistic History	Elohistic History	Amos Hosea Isaiah 1–39 Micah	Deuteronomy (early form) Zephaniah Nahum Habakkuk Early form of DH*	Jeremiah Ezekiel Lamentations Final form of DH* Priestly History Isaiah 40–55 Haggai Zechariah Obadiah Job	Isaiah 56–66 Malachi Joel Jonah Ruth Torah (Gen., Ex. Lev., Num., Deut.) reaches its final form	Esther Song of Solomon Ezra Nehemiah 1 and 2 Chronicles	Ecclesiastes	Daniel

------Various portions of Proverb written------Final form of Proverbs

------Various portions of the book of Psalms written------Final version of Psalms

*DH = Deuteronomistic History (Deuteronomy, Joshua, Judges, 1 and 2 Samuel, and 1 and 2 Kings)

Note: The dates for some of these writings (e.g., Job, Song of Solomon, Ecclesiastes, Ruth) are uncertain and strongly disputed. Some writings (e.g., Ruth, Job, Daniel) contain material that is much earlier than the final form of the work.

Proverbs, Ecclesiastes, Song of Solomon, Lamentations, and Daniel. Some of the stories or traditions upon which these texts were based likely circulated in oral form long before they were written, including many of the psalms, the story of Job (which was likely borrowed from a common folk tale and adapted to special theological problems of the postexilic period), wisdom sayings in Proverbs and Ecclesiastes, Song of Solomon, portions of Lamentations, and portions of Daniel. Although some of the material in these books may have been written before the Exile, the books themselves did not reach their present form until the Exile or, in most cases, after the Exile. The last book of the Hebrew Bible to be written was probably the book of Daniel, composed around 165 B.C.E.

Canonization of the Hebrew Bible

Within Judaism, the development of the canon was a lengthy process rather than a singular event. As various writings were used repeatedly in Jewish communities, these works were gradually recognized as having authority for Jewish belief and practice. The first section of the Hebrew Bible to be granted authoritative status was the Torah. Portions of the Law may have been accepted as authoritative by the time of Josiah's reform in 621 B.C.E., which occurred as a result of the discovery of some early form of the book of Deuteronomy. Not until after the Exile, however, during a reform effort by Ezra and Nehemiah, did a significant move toward developing or recognizing a body of sacred Scriptures take place. By 400 B.C.E. the Law was generally recognized in all Jewish communities as authoritative.

The next group of writings given authoritative status was the Prophets. By the time the Law was recognized, the four books that came to be known as the Former Prophets (Joshua, Judges, 1 and 2 Samuel, 1 and 2 Kings) and much of the literature that came to be known as the Latter Prophets (Isaiah, Jeremiah, Ezekiel, Hosea, Joel, Amos, Obadiah, Jonah, Micah, Nahum, Habakkuk, Zephaniah, Haggai, and Malachi) were enjoying increasing recognition, although they were not yet universally regarded as authoritative Scripture. The growing interest in these books was probably heightened by some common concerns they shared with the Torah, such as obedience to the covenant. By approximately 200 B.C.E. the Jewish community had accepted these prophetic writings as normative.

The third section of the Hebrew canon remained undefined for several centuries after the Law and the Prophets had gained authoritative status. Most of the works that presently constitute the third section of the Hebrew canon (the writings) were, as evidenced by their usage and popularity, accepted with little or no controversy very early. The authority of other works, such as Ecclesiastes, Ezekiel, Esther, and the Song of Solomon, although eventually accepted, was initially disputed by some Jews. Furthermore, other writings that were later not accorded authoritative status were being accepted and used as sacred Scripture by some Jewish groups. Included in this latter category are some of the works contained in the Apocrypha and the Pseudepigrapha. (The latter term refers to a loose collection of mainly Jewish writings produced between about 300 B.C.E. and 200 C.E. that is not a part of the Hebrew Bible or the Apocrypha.) A date for the closing of the third section of the Hebrew Bible is difficult to assign since Jewish leaders made no official pronouncements regarding the limits of the Jewish canon. Toward the end of the first century C.E., Judaism seems to have been moving toward consensus in regard to the general parameters of the Jewish canon, although contrary opinions continued to be voiced for several more centuries.

Around 90 B.C.E. at the town of Jamnia, a group of Jewish leaders met to discuss how the faith of Judaism could survive without the Temple (which had recently been destroyed) and the sacrificial system associated with it. Among the items discussed at Jamnia was the authority of certain Jewish religious writings. Frequently scholars have claimed that the meeting at Jamnia (often referred to as the "Council" of Jamnia) fixed the Jewish canon for all time. This claim is an overstatement, however, for at least two reasons. First, this meeting was not a "council" in the sense of a body of official delegates who wielded authority over all of Judaism. Rather, it was an assembly of Jewish scholars from Palestine who sought ways to restructure and preserve Judaism. The assembly had no official authority in Jewish life, especially outside Palestine. Second, the list of books considered to be improper expressions of the Jewish faith continued to vary until the end of the fourth century C.E. A more careful reading of the evidence about Jamnia suggests that the religious leaders at Jamnia made no binding decisions regarding the Jewish Scriptures. What the meeting at Jamnia indicates is that the question of "canon" or authoritative writings was being discussed at the end of the first century and possibly that the books that were still in dispute were few in number.

Additional evidence that the Jewish community was beginning to reach a consensus on the limits of its canon by the end of the first century C.E. is provided in two sources: Josephus and 2 Esdras (also called 4 Ezra). Josephus, a first-century Jewish historian who wrote toward the end of the century, indicated that the Jews had twenty-two books of special status. Josephus was possibly describing the same twenty-four works that make up the Hebrew Bible today, since Jeremiah and Lamentations were sometimes considered one work, as were Judges and Ruth. The author of 2 Esdras, a Jewish work written around 100 C.E., mentions two groups of writings: twenty-four works that were to be read by everyone (the books of the Hebrew Bible), and seventy works (other Jewish writings) that were to be reserved for the "wise" among the people (2 Esd. 14).

Scholars are not certain about what criteria were used to exclude certain writings and to include others. Comments found in ancient writings suggest four possible criteria: conformity, inspiration, Hebrew language, and widespread use. Works that were accepted as authoritative had to conform to the teachings of the Torah and other writings that were already normative for Jewish belief and practice. Furthermore, works that were accepted had to have been written by divinely inspired prophets. Among some Jewish groups, the assumption was that divine inspiration of the prophets had ceased after the time of Ezra (fifth century B.C.E.). Works believed to have been written after that time were possibly excluded on that basis. (In actuality, some of the accepted works were written well after the fifth century.) In addition, works that were not originally written in Hebrew were excluded. The Jews believed that works produced in Greek were likely to be corrupted by Hellenistic influences; furthermore, since Hebrew was the language of the prophets, they were sure Greek writings could not be inspired writings. The most important criterion, however, was widespread use of the writings. The works that were eventually recognized as authoritative within Judaism were those that had already found general acceptance among the people on the basis of their contents. These were the works that conveyed most clearly the Jewish understanding of God's dealings with the Jewish people.

The precise reasons for the limiting or closing of the Jewish canon are unclear. One factor was likely the growth of the early Christian church, which brought about a review of the Jews' understanding of themselves as the people of God, especially after the destruction of the Temple in 70 C.E. Since the Jews, like the Christians, defended their beliefs on the basis of Scripture, it was important to define which writings belonged to the Scriptures and which did not. Another possible factor was the decline in the popularity of messianic and apocalyptic literature within Judaism (see chapter 15) after the ill-fated Jewish rebellion against the Romans in 132–135 C.E. A result of this decline was the rejection of most apocalyptic literature, although the apocalyptic works of Daniel and Isaiah 24–26 survived this movement.

FORMATION OF THE CHRISTIAN BIBLE

Because Christianity arose from within Judaism, the early Christians naturally accepted the Hebrew Scriptures as authoritative. At the time Christianity separated from Judaism, however, the Jewish canon had not been closed. The Christians, therefore, inherited a larger canon than the twenty-four books that comprise the Jewish Bible today. Evidence of this is seen in the more than one hundred and fifty references and allusions to apocryphal or pseudepigraphal works by New Testament writers. The version of the Hebrew Scriptures used by most of the New Testament writers, as well as by most others in the early church, was the Greek translation known as the Septuagint (discussed later in this chapter). The Septuagint contained not only the books currently in the Hebrew

Figure 3.3. Codex Sinaiticus, written in the fourth century C.E., is one of the most important copies of the entire New Testament. Originally the manuscript also contained the entire Hebrew Bible and the Apocrypha, but some of these books are now missing from the scroll. (*By permission of the British Library [43725]*)

Bible but also the books of the Apocrypha. Even though there was some dispute in the early church about the status of these additional works, the prevailing view held that the books of the Apocrypha were also Scripture.

The acceptance of the Apocrypha was normal practice in the Christian church until the Protestant Reformation in the sixteenth century, at which time the Reformers chose to exclude these works and to use only the books in the

Hebrew Bible as their Old Testament. The Roman Catholic Church, in response to the Protestant Reformers, declared that the works of the Apocrypha (or deuterocanonical writings) were equally authoritative with the other writings in the Old Testament. Today, Roman Catholics and Eastern Orthodox Christians continue to accept these additional works as canonical, whereas Protestants exclude them.

Concurrent with their use of the Hebrew Scriptures, the early Christians produced religious writings of their own. Through a process similar to that which resulted in the Hebrew Bible, the early Christian community gradually recognized many of these writings as sacred Scripture. These authoritative Christian works came to be known collectively as the New Testament.

Oral Stage

Some of the material that formed the contents of the New Testament, especially material incorporated into the Gospels, circulated orally for several decades. The teachings of Jesus and the stories about him were valued in the early church and were used in preaching and in teaching, in settling disputes or problems that arose, in determining correct beliefs or practices, and in defending the Christian faith. In the excitement of expectation that a new age was dawning, the early Christians did not immediately set about writing the story of Jesus and his teachings but preserved the traditions about him in oral form. The writing process was further deterred by the confidence of the early Christians in the oral transmission of traditions. In fact, after the written Gospels began to circulate in the church, some church leaders still valued the oral traditions as more reliable than the written Gospels.

Writing Stage

Several circumstances created the need to record some of the early Christian traditions. First, the church became aware of the need to preserve a record of the eyewitnesses to Jesus' life. When some of Jesus' first disciples began to die, the community was prompted to preserve the memory of his life and teaching in written form. Second, the end time did not appear as some early Christians expected, and some instruction was needed to interpret both the present and the future. Third, as the movement spread, problems arose in the churches that demanded the attention of knowledgeable church leaders, who then wrote to solve the problems. Fourth, as the number of converts increased, documents were written to instruct the new believers in the basics of the Christian faith.

The first written materials of the New Testament were the letters of Paul, beginning around 50 C.E. The authentic letters of Paul in the New Testament

Figure 3.4. Approximate Dates for Writings in the New Testament (all dates are C.E.)

50–51	1 Thessalonians
52–56	Galatians 1 Corinthians Philippians Philemon 2 Corinthians Romans
68–70	Gospel of Mark
70–90	2 Thessalonians Colossians
80–90	Gospel of Matthew Gospel of Luke and the book of Acts
80–95	James Hebrews Ephesians 1 Peter
90–100	Gospel of John
95	Revelation
95–110	1 John 2 John 3 John
100–125	1 Timothy 2 Timothy Titus Jude
125–150	2 Peter

include at least the following: 1 Thessalonians, Romans, 1 and 2 Corinthians, Philippians, Philemon, and Galatians. Authorship of the other books attributed to Paul is debated.

The first Gospel, Mark, was written around 70 C.E. Next came Matthew (80–90 C.E.) and Luke (80–90 C.E.). The Gospel of John (90–100 C.E.) was the last of the canonical Gospels to be written, and though it contains some of the same information as the other three Gospels, it was written independently of them.

Several works were produced in the late first century and early second century that are designated by scholars as deutero-Pauline. The direct authorship of these books by Paul is doubted. They are attributed to Paul and share some of his ideas. Differences in setting, vocabulary, style, and theological emphasis between these documents and the undisputed Pauline letters indicate that in their present form Paul probably did not write them. Among the deutero-Pauline letters are 2 Thessalonians, Colossians, 1 and 2 Timothy, Titus, and Ephesians.

Other writings in the New Testament are Hebrews, Revelation, and the Catholic, or "universal," Epistles. Hebrews was attributed by later church tradition to Paul but was likely written by an anonymous Christian of the first century. The book of Revelation, written by a church leader in Asia Minor named John, dates from the last decade of the first century. The Catholic Epistles are so named because, as the word "catholic" suggests, they were addressed to the church at large and were intended to be widely circulated. They include 1, 2, and 3 John, Jude, and 1 and 2 Peter. The Letter of 2 Peter may be the last of the New Testament writings to have been written, perhaps as late as 125–150 C.E.

In addition to the canonical books of the New Testament, a number of other books came into being between the closing decades of the first century and the end of the second century. They include *1* and *2 Clement*, the *Epistle of Barnabas*, the *Didache*, the *Shepherd of Hermas*, the *Gospel of Peter*, the *Apocalypse of Peter*, the *Gospel of Thomas*, and the *Acts of Paul*. While some of these were given the status of sacred Scripture in some circles, and a few were included in some of the earliest lists of canonical books, none survived in the canon that finally developed.

Canonization of the New Testament

As was true with the Hebrew Bible, the development of the New Testament canon was a lengthy process rather than a single event. The writings deemed authoritative for the Christian church were those works that had proved their value through widespread use in churches throughout Christianity.

As noted above, the oral traditions concerning Jesus, along with the Hebrew Bible, functioned as the earliest canon for the Christian community. By the end of the first century C.E., the letters of Paul were probably collected, circulated, and regarded as authoritative in some churches (2 Peter 3:15-16 may reflect this fact). Sometime near the middle of the second century, the Gospel of Luke was separated from Acts and the four Gospels were collected. The earliest evidence that passages from the Gospels were being regarded as Scripture comes from *2 Clement*, about 150 C.E.

By the end of the second century, then, the letters of Paul and the four Gospels were widely recognized as authoritative for the Christian faith. The status of the other books now in the New Testament, however, varied. The book of Acts gained ready acceptance because the church recognized that the same person who wrote the Gospel of Luke also wrote Acts. The letters known as 1 John and 1 Peter were accepted without much difficulty, likely because they were believed to have been written by the apostles John and Peter. Some works, however, had a more difficult time before they were regarded as canonical. The book of Revelation, for example, was used and accepted widely in churches in the western part of the Roman Empire but was rejected by churches in the East. The book of Hebrews, on the other hand, had the opposite experience—it was accepted in the East and rejected in the West. Furthermore, some of the Christian writings that were later denied canonical status were read and accepted as Scripture in the first few centuries by some Christian groups. The *Shepherd of Hermas*, *1 Clement*, and the *Epistle of Barnabas* are only three examples of such works that had strong early support for inclusion in the New Testament. During the first two or three centuries of the Christian church, then, the number and identity of Christian writings recognized as authoritative differed to some degree in churches throughout the Christian world.

The first person known to have attempted the formation of a canon was *Marcion*, a second-century Christian whose views on the canon were eventually rejected. He believed the twelve apostles had corrupted the pure doctrine of Christ by connecting it with the Hebrew Bible, which he rejected. Marcion accepted only portions of Luke's Gospel and ten of Paul's letters. His enemies accused him of mutilating both Paul and Luke. His complete rejection of the Hebrew Bible placed him in opposition to the prevailing views of the church. In response to Marcion's canon, the church began making careful judgments as to which documents the church should regard as canonical.

Although the earliest consensus on the twenty-seven books that make up the New Testament cannot be dated with certainty, the earliest list of these books was given by *Athanasius*, bishop of Alexandria, in 367 C.E. Later at the Council of Hippo in 393 C.E. and at the Council of Carthage in 397 C.E., the same list received the approval of the church in North Africa. These councils did not represent the formal authority of the whole church, however. Like the Jewish canon, the Christian canon was determined not by the formal action of a governing body but through gradual use and recognition by the religious community. Eventually, Christianity concurred in the limiting of the New Testament canon to these same twenty-seven writings.

Several criteria influenced the early church in its acceptance or rejection of individual writings as authoritative. The first was apostolicity, which means that those writings were considered authoritative that preserved the tradition of the apostles of Jesus. Of special importance were those works that were considered to have been written by one of the early apostles. The second criterion was that of orthodoxy, or "true doctrine." Writings were considered authoritative if their teaching was in line with the faith of the apostolic church. The third criterion was antiquity, meaning that it was written in the apostolic age—that is, while the authors could have had contact with the apostles. (Some writings, however, that were rejected were written prior to some that were accepted. Thus this criterion could not function independently of the others.) A fourth criterion was inspiration, or divine influence. All of the individuals in the early church who suggested a canon believed their list of writings was inspired. But while several of the early lists included many of the same books, these lists varied. Moreover, those books that were ultimately included in the canon were not the only ones believed to be inspired of God. The belief, then, that a work was inspired, while a necessary condition for canonical acceptance, was not a sufficient reason alone for a work to be considered authoritative. The fifth, and most important, criterion was widespread use by the early church. Those texts that were used widely and met the needs of the Christian communities were the ones that eventually won acceptance as Scripture. In these writings, the church said, the divine-human encounter is most clearly and compellingly expressed.

THE PROCESS OF TRANSLATION

The Jewish Scriptures were originally written mainly in Hebrew, with a few sections in Aramaic, a related language. Because the main language of the Mediterranean world in the first century was Greek, the New Testament writings were written in Greek. Eventually, however, translations of the Hebrew Bible and the New Testament into other languages were needed.

While the Hebrew canon was still developing, many of the Jews who lived outside Palestine had forgotten (or never knew) Hebrew and had adopted the language of the land in which they lived. Following the spread of Greek culture by Alexander the Great, most Jews outside Palestine, as well as some in Palestine, spoke only Greek. This situation created the need for a translation of Hebrew writings into Greek. During the third century B.C.E., possibly in Alexandria, Egypt, a translation of the Torah into Greek was made. By the first part of the first century B.C.E. the Prophets and the Writings were also translated from Hebrew into Greek. The name given to this translation was the Septuagint (the Latin word

Figure 3.5. In the fourth century Jerome, depicted in this statue in Bethlehem, produced the Vulgate, the most influential Latin translation of the Bible. *(Photograph by Clyde E. Fant)*

for seventy, the number of translators who supposedly worked on the project). Soon the Septuagint was being used in Alexandria and in other Jewish communities. (It was also widely used in the early Christian communities.)

Latin translations of the Christian Bible began to appear as early as the end of the second century. In an effort to bring some uniformity to the diverse Latin translations that had been produced by the fourth century, Pope Damasus in 382 C.E. asked the biblical scholar Jerome to prepare a revision of the Christian Scriptures into Latin. In revising the Old Latin versions, Jerome consulted Greek manuscripts of the New Testament (although at times he simply retained translations found in the Old Latin versions) and used both the Septuagint and Hebrew manuscripts in his work. His version became widely accepted throughout the Western church. It therefore earned the title of Vulgate, which means "common" version, for it was the main translation used in the Western church for several hundred years.

Although the Bible was translated into many other languages (including Syriac, Armenian, Coptic, Ethiopic, and Georgian) at a very early date, the following discussion will focus only on the production of English-language Bibles.

The translation of some sections of the Bible into English began as early as the seventh century C.E., but it was not until 1382 that the first complete Bible in English appeared. The person who is given credit for this major milestone is John Wycliffe, although scholars are uncertain about how much of the translation was actually done by Wycliffe himself. The Wycliffe Bible was basically a word-for-word translation of the Latin Vulgate. The translation of the Bible into English was staunchly resisted by the church leadership for several reasons, including their belief that English was too vulgar a language for the Scriptures, their fear that the Bible in the hands of the common people would lead to false interpretations and erroneous doctrines, and their desire to maintain authority over the people. Wycliffe's Bible was officially condemned, and over forty years after his death, his body was exhumed and burned in retaliation for his work as a translator. In spite of the official reaction to the work, the Wycliffe Bible survived and continued as the only complete Bible in English for nearly 150 years.

Wycliffe's work had been based on the Latin text, but in the early sixteenth century a number of English Bibles based on the Hebrew and Greek manuscripts appeared, which was a major advance in the production of English Bibles. The first of these was produced by William Tyndale, who published his English translation of the New Testament in 1525 from Germany, where he had fled to escape opposition from the church in England. He began work on translating the Hebrew Bible from Hebrew manuscripts but completed only the Pentateuch and the book of Jonah. In 1536 the Church of England (which only two years earlier had declared itself independent of Rome) had Tyndale arrested and burned at the stake. Tyndale's translation, however, exerted a major influence on subsequent English translations.

Another milestone in the production of English Bibles occurred in 1535 with the appearance of a translation by Miles Coverdale, who produced the first complete printed edition of the Bible in English. (Tyndale's translation was also printed, but it did not contain the entire Bible.) Coverdale's translation drew heavily from the work of Tyndale and certain Latin and German translations

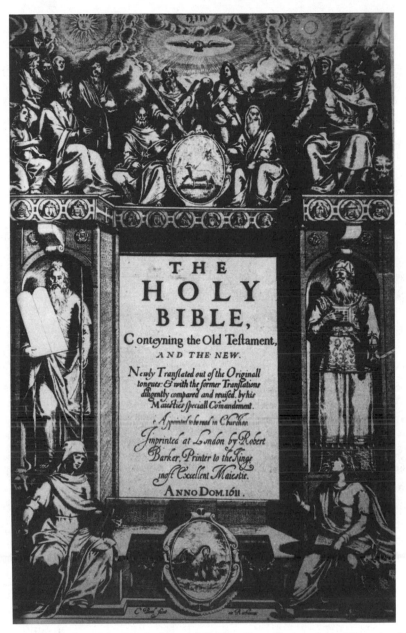

Figure 3.6. Title page from the original edition of the King James Version of the Bible, printed in 1611. *(Photograph is owned and copyrighted by the American Bible Society.)*

instead of being a fresh translation from the Hebrew and Greek. Coverdale's Bible circulated without opposition from the king or the Church of England. Other English Bibles that appeared in the next few years included the Thomas Matthew

Bible in 1537, the Great Bible in 1539, and the Geneva Bible in 1560. (The Geneva Bible was the translation used by Shakespeare and the version brought to America by the Pilgrims. Because this translation referred to the clothing of Adam and Eve in Genesis 3:7 as "breeches," the Geneva Bible was popularly known as the "Breeches Bible.")

After being unsuccessful in preventing the translation of the Bible into English by others, the Roman Catholic Church in the seventeenth century decided to correct the errors they believed were made by the Protestant translations, which were regarded as corrupt. The official Catholic version was begun at the English College in Douay, France, and then moved to Rheims, where the translation was completed in 1609–10. Translated from the Vulgate, the Rheims-Douay version remained the standard Roman Catholic Bible into the twentieth century.

In 1604 James I ascended to the British throne and ordered a new translation from the original Hebrew and Greek. Fifty-four scholars were appointed for the task. Completed in 1611, this version, known as the King James Version or the Authorized Version, soon became the most widely used English translation of the Bible among Protestants, a position it maintained until late in the nineteenth century. From 1881–85 the Revised Version, a revision of the King James Version, was produced by British and American scholars. In 1901 the American scholars who worked on the Revised Version published the American Standard Version, in which many English words of the Revised Version were adapted to American usage.

In the twentieth century new manuscript discoveries, archaeological findings, and linguistic changes brought about the need for new translations. One of the most notable translations was the Revised Standard Version, completed in 1952; a new edition of the entire work (the New Revised Standard Version) was published in 1989. The Revised Standard Version gained widespread popularity because it incorporated the fruits of modern biblical scholarship while retaining much of the basic literary structure of the King James Version. Several other modern translations have appeared in the last few decades. Among them are the New American Standard Bible (a revision of the American Standard Version), the Jerusalem Bible, the New American Bible, the New English Bible (and its revision, the Revised English Bible), the Good News Bible, the New International Version, the New King James Version, the Contemporary English Version, and the New Jewish Version. The New Jewish Version, published in its entirety in 1985, was produced by the Jewish Publication Society. It was a major milestone in Jewish translations of the Bible into English because it was the first truly new English translation of the Hebrew Bible. Previous English versions of the Jewish Scriptures were basically editions of the King James Version or the Revised Version that had been slightly modified for Jewish usage.

The average reader is likely to be surprised and even confused at the multiplicity of translations of the Bible. As confusing as this situation may seem, the abundance of biblical translations is solid evidence of the continuing importance of this collection of writings and the commitment of scholars to produce the best possible translation of these texts. No single version of the Bible presents the best translation for every passage in the Bible. Scholars often disagree over the best way to render a passage from the ancient Hebrew or Greek language into modern English. For this reason, serious students of the Bible should consult several English translations when studying biblical literature.

Chapter 4

THE CULTURAL AND GEOGRAPHIC
CONTEXT OF THE BIBLE

Geography played a particularly important role in the biblical story. Both the location of Palestine and the physical features of the land itself were instrumental in shaping the history of the people of Israel. Palestine was bordered for centuries by major players in the shaping of the modern world, while within its boundaries significant variations in climate and topography influenced the development of a surprisingly diverse culture.

These external and internal geographic influences produced two results. On the one hand, Palestine was a land united by the common experience of a people exposed to the same international influences and pressures; on the other, it was a land divided by localizing geographic features that often separated its inhabitants into highly individual cultural regions. The result of these diverse influences was a land more often divided than united, more often ruled by others than by itself, and more often confessing its beliefs in diverse accents.

To understand the biblical account of the history and beliefs of the people of Palestine, therefore, we must gain some knowledge of both its physical and historical geography. Physical geography studies the topography, natural resources, and climate of a land. Historical geography refers to the entire effect of the location, physical features, and use of the land upon the history of its inhabitants.

Furthermore, extensive archaeological efforts have yielded significant evidence of the ancient history and customs of the people of Palestine as well as of other nations with whom they were related. Recently, important finds in Lebanon, Jordan, and Syria have emphasized the influence of the larger Near Eastern region on the biblical story. Acquaintance with these discoveries sheds further light upon the history of Israel and its religious tradition.

This chapter will describe in turn each of these significant elements in the biblical story: the larger context of Palestine within the ancient Near East, the key physical features of Palestine itself, and archaeological discoveries of importance to an understanding of the biblical accounts.

THE SHAPE OF THE ANCIENT NEAR EAST

The Fertile Crescent

The ancient Near East was largely an arid, barren region due to the scant rainfall it received. Such rain as occurred was seasonal, frequently falling torren-

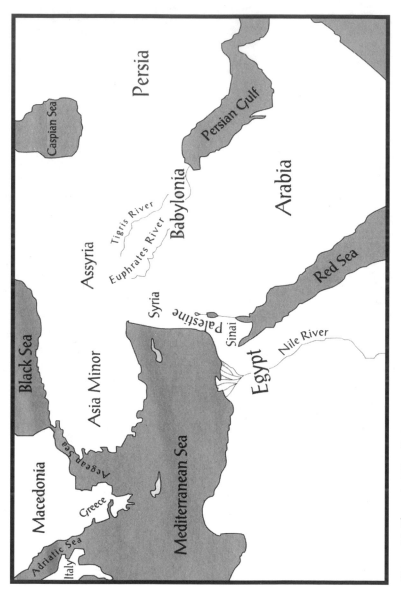

Figure 4.1. The ancient Near East

tially in a matter of days. The subsequent rapid runoff and erosion, coupled with the searing heat of the dry season, resulted in barren terrain across much of the area. Parts of the region received only traces of rain each year. These places formed the vast desert regions that surrounded the biblical world: the Arabian Desert to the east; the Sahara Desert to the west, extending to the Nile River; and the desert of the Sinai peninsula to the south. To the north, rugged mountain ranges discouraged extensive settlement and cultivation.

Only a few areas provided locales hospitable to human life: a narrow belt of land along the eastern Mediterranean coast, the fertile lands bordering the Tigris and Euphrates rivers of Mesopotamia ("between the rivers") in the north, and the Nile River of Egypt and its delta to the south. In these regions arable land permitted civilizations to flourish between the rugged mountain ranges and barren desert expanses. The periodic overflow of these rivers provided rich alluvial soil along their banks, although the erratic flooding of the Tigris and Euphrates created more problems for their region than the regular, annual floods of the Nile. Nevertheless, at least as early as 3000 B.C.E. irrigation methods had been sufficiently developed along both river systems to permit extensive farming and increased population densities.

A line connecting these two fertile areas, arcing from Mesopotamia across the coastal plains of the eastern Mediterranean to Egypt, would form a crescent with Palestine in its center. The name "Fertile Crescent," now commonly used for this area, was first applied to the region by an Egyptologist, James H. Breasted. Israel traced the journey of its historic ancestor Abraham along this Fertile Crescent from Mesopotamia to the region of Palestine. Later, due to famine, the family of Joseph would continue that route into Egypt. In the following centuries Moses would reverse that path, leading "the children of Israel" back from Egypt to Palestine, and subsequent wars would see the Israelites return to Mesopotamia as captives.

The history of the Hebrew people, then, was bound up with the influences of the Fertile Crescent. With the Mediterranean Sea on the west and the Arabian Desert barring travel in the east, Palestine became a land bridge over which for centuries passed the countless caravans of traders and the marching armies of invaders. The biblical story is one of constant movement across this small region, a story of the upheavals of nations and the overthrow of rulers as the land of Palestine was occupied by a succession of world powers. Egypt, Assyria, Babylonia, Persia, Greece, and the Roman Empire each became the dominant power over the land and its people. Much of the fascination of the biblical narratives is due to the encounter of these mighty nations with the sturdy faith of the Hebrew people in their "Promised Land."

Figure 4.2. Prince Rahotep, son of Pharaoh Cheops and high priest of Heliopolis in Egypt, and his wife, Nofret, lived during the fourth dynasty (around 2613–2498 B.C.E.). Egypt was one of the important lands of the Fertile Crescent. *(Photograph by Clyde E. Fant)*

The Semitic Quadrangle

To some extent, however, "the Fertile Crescent" is not a completely satisfactory description of the arena of the biblical story. Another term has been coined to incorporate the Fertile Crescent into a larger area: the "Semitic Quadrangle" (sometimes also referred to as the "Semitic Quadrilateral").

Beyond the arc of the Fertile Crescent lie mountains and deserts. The Semitic Quadrangle includes these areas. Its boundaries form an uneven rectangle bounded by the Red Sea on the south, the Indian Ocean on the southeast, the Persian Gulf and Mesopotamia on the east, the Iranian plateau on the north, and the Taurus mountains and the Mediterranean on the northwest. This rectangle encompasses the Arabian Peninsula, Mesopotamia, Syria, and Palestine. But it would be even more inclusive of the lands of the biblical story if the southwestern border of the rectangle were pushed farther west, to the Nile River, to include Egypt.

The name "Semitic Quadrangle," however, was intended to describe the region of the Semitic peoples in the biblical story—that is, those who spoke one of the many Semitic languages, such as Hebrew, Syriac, and others. Since the language of the Egyptians was not Semitic, they were not included in the quadrangle. Nevertheless, Egypt should be kept in mind in any geographic image of the region of the biblical story.

The Westward Crescent

Beginning with the conquest of Palestine in 333 B.C.E. by Alexander the Great of Macedonian Greece, the orientation of the biblical world turned westward. With the collapse of the Persian Empire under the onslaught of Alexander, Palestine was infused with Greek culture. Following the death of Alexander, his former generals and rival successors, the Ptolemies of Egypt and the Seleucids of Syria, alternately ruled Palestine. After a brief period of independence, Palestine was ruled by the Roman Empire following the capture of Jerusalem in 63 B.C.E. At the close of the biblical story in the New Testament, the Romans were still in control.

To understand this period (about 333 B.C.E.–100 C.E.), which includes the "Common Era" of Jews and Christians, a new geographical orientation is required. A new crescent developed, a "Westward Crescent" facing in the opposite direction. Egypt was still at its southern base, but in this later era it formed the southeastern tip of the crescent rather than its southwestern point. Palestine remained in the central section, as did Syria. But then the crescent bent westward, including Asia Minor, Greece, and Italy. Even Spain, "the end of the earth" for these peoples, received mention in the New Testament. The Mediterranean Sea no longer touched the western boundary of the biblical arena; now it touched its eastern boundary and formed the southern base of its activity.

This Westward Crescent, with its brilliant cultures and dominating armies, exerted a powerful pull on both the Jewish and Christian faiths. Both faiths were modified by their contacts with these Western cultures, and to a significant degree the future movement of these religions would be westward, not eastward. The traffic across the land bridge of Palestine had changed from east to west.

THE LAND CALLED PALESTINE

One Land, Many Names

Anyone encountering the biblical story for the first time likely will be puzzled by the variety of names that refer to the land of the Bible: Canaan, the Promised Land, the Holy Land, Israel, Judah (or Judea), Palestine. Each of these names, though sometimes used interchangeably, has its own distinctive reference.

Canaan. The early inhabitants of the land were called Canaanites, and their land, Canaan. The name appears as early as 3000 B.C.E. in texts from Ebla (Syria). Its meaning is obscure, and none of the attempts to define it (as, for example, "Westland" or "The Land of the Sunset") have proved convincing.

The Promised Land. The early ancestors of the Jewish people cherished the belief that Yahweh had promised this land to them as their "land of promise." Much of the biblical story is involved with seeking, finding, occupying, and defending this "Promised Land."

The Holy Land. Because three of the world's great religions—Judaism, Christianity, and Islam—trace their history to this land, it is referred to as the Holy Land.

Israel. The earliest recorded mention of "Israel" occurs on a victory stele (stone marker) erected by the Egyptian pharaoh Merneptah ca. 1207 B.C.E. It boasted that "Israel is laid waste, his seed is no more." The determinative, or prefix, on the hieroglyphic symbol for "Israel" indicates that the name refers to a people rather than a nation. Originally, then, "Israel" likely referred to an ethnic minority group within the multiethnic society of Canaan. The Hebrew Scriptures identify these Israelites as the children of Jacob. Later, for a brief time before the death of King Solomon, the whole country was referred to as "Israel." After the death of Solomon the kingdom split into two nations. Then "Israel" referred strictly to the Northern Kingdom—the region north of Jerusalem—while "Judah" referred to the Southern Kingdom. As commonly used, however, "the children of Israel" refers to all those who followed and worshiped Yahweh in any period of biblical history. "Israelites" as used today generally refers to the Jewish people in all their history prior to their return from exile in Babylon, after which they are referred to as "Jews." "Israeli" refers to a citizen of the modern state of Israel.

Judah. During the Divided Kingdom period, "Judah" designated the Southern Kingdom, which occupied the region from Jerusalem southward. Later the name "Judea," the Greco-Latin form of "Judah," was applied to the whole

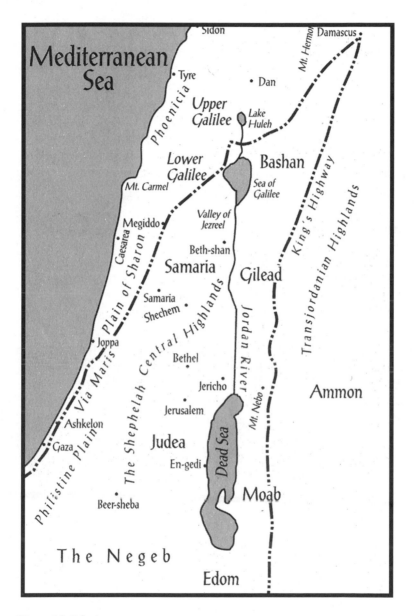

Figure 4.3. Palestine

province. The name was later abolished during the reign of the Roman emperor Hadrian in reprisal for the second unsuccessful revolt of the Jews (132–135 C.E.), and the name "Provincia Syria Palaestina" was adopted.

Palestine. The most widely accepted name for the land, Palestine, was derived from "Philistia," the name for the land of the Philistines. The Philistines, one of the tribes of the "Sea Peoples" from the Aegean area, occupied the southernmost coastal region of Canaan. They settled there after the Egyptians under Ramses III repulsed their attempted invasion of Egypt (ca. 1190 B.C.E.). Later the name was modified by Greek writers (Herodotus and others) to "Palaestina." Under the Roman emperor Hadrian, as mentioned above, "Provincia Syria Palaestina" was established as the official name of the country. Later it was known simply as Palestine.

The Land in Perspective

Because Palestine is situated at the juncture of three continents—Africa, Asia, and Europe—and surrounded by powerful nations, its historical importance was proportionately much greater than its size. Probably no other country of comparable size has exerted such a powerful, long-lasting, and worldwide influence.

The boundaries of Palestine were traditionally defined as "from Dan to Beer-Sheba," which, from north to south, comprises about one hundred and fifty miles. From east to west, between desert and sea, the land averaged sixty to seventy miles in width. These boundaries varied greatly, however, from period to period. For example, the greatest expanse of the empire under David and Solomon was slightly less than four hundred miles, from Kadesh on the north to Ezion-Geber on the south, and no more than one hundred miles at its widest point, east to west. Compare these dimensions with those of the world powers around them:

- The Egyptian Empire once extended at least 1,000 miles, from Upper Egypt (the southern portion of the Nile valley) to the northern reaches of Palestine and Syria.
- The Assyrian Empire at its peak covered a great arc of more than 2,000 miles, from Egypt to Babylonia.
- The Persian Empire also reached 2,000 miles, from the edges of Greece and Libya in the west to India in the east.
- The Greek Empire under Alexander the Great included Greece and all of the Persian Empire, some 3,300 miles or more.
- The Roman Empire extended from England in the west to the

Euphrates River in the east. It included Spain, all of Asia Minor, Palestine, Egypt, and the entire North African coast of the Mediterranean Sea—an incredible empire stretching 3,000 miles east to west and 1,200 miles north to south, with some seventy to ninety million inhabitants.

Obviously, even at its greatest period of expansion, Palestine was a small land in comparison to these world powers, each of which swallowed it in turn. The importance of this small land, no larger than the state of Vermont, was due mainly to one factor: its location. Palestine had no significant natural resources, wealth, or harbors, so only its strategic location made it a key piece of the imperial puzzle of each of the great empires that occupied it.

Key Geographical Features

The primary features of the topography of Palestine are not difficult to describe. The land naturally divides itself into four north-south regions parallel with one another and with the Mediterranean Sea. On a map of Palestine, these divisions would appear as long, narrow, "vertical" (longitudinal) strips of land. Only one prominent geographical feature cuts across these strips "horizontally," or latitudinally: the Jezreel Valley. From west to east, these four regions are the Coastal Plain, the Central Highlands, the Jordan Rift, and the Transjordanian Highlands.

The Coastal Plain. The western boundary of Palestine is a long shoreline on the Mediterranean Sea. Along this shore, with some notable exceptions, the land is relatively flat. A famous international highway, the Via Maris ("the Way of the Sea"), ran the length of the coastline. But historically this section of Palestine proved as much a problem as an asset for Israel. In biblical times the Coastal Plain was divided into northern, central, and southern sections. The central section, called the Plain of Sharon, was the only portion held consistently by Israel. There were no natural harbors along this section of coastline to encourage the Israelites in maritime activity. (In Roman times Herod the Great did build the port city of Caesarea there.) Nor was much of the land useful for settlement due to extensive areas of marshy lowlands. Other parts of the Plain of Sharon were partially covered by dense oak forests growing out of infertile red sand unsuitable for cultivation.

Even the one area of rich, fertile soil in this plain was a mixed blessing. The Valley of Jezreel was a fertile valley that extended east and west across the northern edge of the Plain of Sharon and continued to the Jordan River. It was the only valley that completely crossed the country and connected the Mediterranean with the Jordan Valley. But even though the Valley of Jezreel provided good farming and ease of travel, as a major ancient highway it also increased Israel's vulnerability to attack.

The other two sections of the Coastal Plain to the north and south were never under Israel's absolute control. The northernmost section of the coast was under the control of the Phoenicians. Their major ports of Tyre and Sidon made them the foremost maritime power in the region. The southern section of the Coastal Plain was controlled by the Philistines and was known as the Philistine Plain. There the Coastal Plain widens in places to over twenty miles and contains much fertile land. The Philistines had five major cities in this region: Gaza, Ashkelon, and Ashdod along the coast and Gath and Ekron farther inland. Ashkelon served as the principal port of the Philistines.

In summary, even though Palestine bordered on the Mediterranean, for all practical purposes Israel remained landlocked and the northern and southern coasts, with their better harbors, were controlled by their enemies. But the Coastal Plain did provide Israel with one vital link to the outside world. The Via Maris, as it made its way along the coast, turned inland at Mount Carmel and passed through the Valley of Jezreel on its way to Damascus. This road was a great river of commerce, up and down which streamed caravans of merchants, enterprising traders, and invading armies. As such, "the Way of the Sea" introduced Israel, landlocked as it was, to the cultures of distant nations.

Figure 4.4. The Sea of Galilee is an important geographical feature of northern Palestine. Approximately 12.5 miles long and 7 miles wide (at its widest point), this freshwater lake has supported a thriving fishing industry. *(Photograph by Mitchell G. Reddish)*

The Central Highlands. The central portion of Palestine, west to east, consists of low foothills that rise out of the Coastal Plain and end in the central mountain range of Palestine. These mountains slope away to the east as they descend into the third region of Palestine, the Jordan Rift, or Jordan Valley. This mountain range runs the entire length of Palestine, transected only by the Jezreel Valley. Just as the Coastal Plain is divided into northern, central, and southern regions, so the Central Highlands is composed of three regions from north to south: Galilee, Samaria, and Judah.

Galilee, the northernmost district of Palestine, is divided into two distinct geographic zones, northern and southern Galilee. Northern Galilee, also called Upper Galilee, contains the most mountainous region of Palestine, in places reaching over three thousand feet in elevation. Southern or Lower Galilee consists of rolling foothills and becomes increasingly more fertile as it descends into the Valley of Jezreel. Overall, Galilee was a rugged, sparsely settled region of fiercely independent people who were only marginally incorporated into the mainstream of Israel's political and religious life. Josephus, a Jewish historian of the first century C.E. who was once governor of Galilee, said of the Galileans, "They were ever more anxious for honor than for gain" and "They were ever fond of innovations, by nature disposed to changes, and delighted in seditions." Nazareth, the hometown of Jesus, was in the foothills of Lower Galilee, overlooking the Valley of Jezreel.

Samaria, the central portion of the Central Highlands, is separated from Galilee by the Valley of Jezreel. This region was fertile, populous, and noted for cities of historic importance such as Shechem, Dothan, and Samaria, the city from which it took its name. (Earlier the region had been called Ephraim.) Mount Ebal and Mount Gerizim were mountains of significance in Samaria; between them lay the Shechem Pass, where east-west and north-south trade routes converged. Farther to the south these highlands drop several hundred feet to form the "Saddle of Benjamin." This major crossroads area between the coast and the Jordan Valley separated Samaria from Judah and was strategic to the defense of Jerusalem, the capital city of Judah. People in these rival regions often contended for control of the area.

Judah is the southernmost section of the Central Highlands. In the Greco-Roman period it was called Judea, the Greek form of Judah. In biblical times it contained some areas of fertile soil to the west, on its seaward slopes; likewise, south of Jerusalem the land was particularly fertile in the area around Bethlehem, whose very name means "the house of bread." Overall, however, Judah was the least fertile—and therefore least desirable—terrain of the region. (The rabbis said it was easier to raise "a legion of olives in Galilee than one child in Judea.") To the east and west the land drops away rapidly in steep, rocky slopes. Particularly in the east, where the terrain drops abruptly to the Dead Sea, the land is barren and dry. The Bible refers to this eastern sector of Judah as "desert" or "wilderness," a desolate region suitable only for foraging with herds of sheep or goats. Only the oasis at En-Gedi provided shelter for settlement in this barren terrain along the Dead Sea. At the northwest corner of the Dead Sea, however, lived the community that produced the famous Dead Sea Scrolls. Known as the Qumran community, they occupied this area from approximately 140 B.C.E. to 68 C.E.

The western foothills of Judah, known as the Shephelah ("lowlands"), separated the Judean mountains from the coastal Philistine Plain and were the object of much contention between Judah and the Philistines. Heavily fortified cities, either Philistine or Judean, were located in these often-disputed foothills. South of this area, below the ancient capital city of Hebron, lies the Negeb ("Southland"), a parched region with less than eight inches of rainfall annually. Two important places in this region are prominent in the Bible. Beer-sheba, the traditional southern limit of Palestine, was an important frontier city on the upper or northern edge of the Negeb. Kadesh-barnea was an oasis settlement in the lower or southern Negeb. The Israelites spent much time wandering in this region prior to entering their "Promised Land" across the Jordan. Throughout the history of Israel, however, several important north-south roads, including the Via Maris, passed through portions of the Negeb.

The Jordan Rift. The third of the geographic divisions of Palestine, the Jordan Rift, is a major geological fault in the earth's surface that extends from the foot of Mount Hermon in northern Syria through the valley of the Jordan River to the Dead Sea. It then crosses the Arabah ("desert") Plain to the Gulf of Aqabah and continues across the Red Sea into Africa, where it is known as the Great African Rift.

In Palestine this fissure was once an inland arm of the sea; now it is the channel for the Jordan River. This river drops from the foothills of Mount Hermon (about 1800 feet above sea level) to 695 feet below sea level at the Sea of Galilee (first known as the Sea of Chinnereth and later, under the Romans, as the Sea of Tiberias). From the Sea of Galilee the Jordan then meanders two hundred miles to the Dead Sea, although the direct distance between the two bodies of water is only seventy miles. This twisting river cuts through steep gorges and is impassable along most of its route. In the biblical era its banks were covered with such thick vegetation that the valley was called "the jungle of the Jordan," and animal life, including lions, was abundant there.

The Dead Sea, or Salt Sea, is so named because its waters contain six times the concentration of salt found in ocean water (more than 25 percent sodium chloride and other mineral salts). Until recently the Dead Sea was considered completely "dead," but certain microscopic organisms have been discovered there. The surface of the Dead Sea is 1,300 feet below sea level, making it the lowest point on earth; the bottom of the lake at its northern end is an incredible 1,300 feet deeper yet. With no outlet whatsoever, the Dead Sea forms a natural evaporation basin, and its salt was an important commodity in biblical times.

The Transjordanian Highlands. This plateau east of the Jordan consists mostly of tableland interrupted occasionally by wadis (stream beds that may or may not contain water, most flowing only seasonally); the region does contain a few mountains over 3,000 feet. Four perennial rivers flow westward from the Transjordan into the Jordan River. From north to south, they are the Yarmuk, the Jabbok, the Arnon, and the Zered. These streams served as divisions between five geopolitical areas: Bashan (north of the Yarmuk), Gilead (between the Yarmuk and the Jabbok), Ammon (between the Jabbok and the Arnon), Moab (between the Arnon and the Zered), and Edom (south of the Zered).

Bashan, the northernmost district of the Transjordan, is directly east of the Sea of Galilee and was noted for its prosperous grain and grazing lands. Gilead was an area of mixed farming and numerous villages, and in biblical days it was heavily forested. Ammon's boundaries were always somewhat vague. It seems to have been an area on the edge of the desert given mostly to sheep herding. Moab, due east of the Dead Sea, was divided between growing grain and raising sheep. It was also noted for frequent conflict with the Israelites, as was Edom to the south. Edom's territory reached southward to the Gulf of Aqabah, and the Edomites controlled the vital southern access to the King's Highway, an important caravan route from Egypt to Damascus. Tariffs from this trade brought great wealth to Edom and to the other plateau kingdoms of the Transjordan, when they were strong enough to exact them. The Edomites were particularly hated by the Judeans for their occupation of Judah after its conquest by the Babylonians in 587 B.C.E. In New Testament times these Edomites of Judah became known as Idumaeans. Herod the Great, king of Israel at the time of the birth of Jesus, was an Idumaean and therefore never was regarded as truly Jewish by the Jews.

Climate and Agriculture

As the varied topography would suggest, Palestine is a land of climatic extremes. Rainfall, for example, varies from virtually none in eastern Judah ("the wilderness of Judah") to forty inches annually in Upper Galilee. Even a matter of a few miles may spell the difference between relatively fertile land and barren terrain. The coastal regions, the western slopes facing the sea, and the higher elevations of Palestine receive the greatest rainfall. Toward the south rainfall gradually diminishes until desert conditions prevail.

In a normal year rainfall will occur in Palestine between late October and April, with 70 percent of the annual rain falling between November and February.

This rainy season was known in biblical times as "the early rains" (October to November) and "the latter rains" (February to March). If rainfall was deficient in either of these periods—and it frequently was—crops suffered; they could not be planted without the early rains, and the harvest would be limited without the later rains. The volume of rain at any one time was also highly unpredictable. Sometimes torrential downpours did more harm to crops than good, and sudden storms from the sea were common. During such times care had to be taken to store water while also minimizing erosion.

Variations in temperature throughout the region are no less severe. Although the entire area is subtropical, the proximity of ocean and desert and the great extremes in elevation produce widely differing temperatures. The highest mountain elevations receive some snowfall and freezing temperatures; the lower Jordan Valley and the desert regions farther south suffer extreme heat. Upland plateaus enjoy more moderate conditions, as do the Coastal Plains. Nevertheless, hot winds from the desert (known as the Sirocco or Khamsin, the "east wind" of the Bible) frequently blow for days, bringing dust and oppressive heat to the people and scorching crops.

As already noted, soil conditions also vary greatly from region to region. In the biblical period, arable land amounted to less than half of the total land, and even that portion was far from uniformly fertile. The most dependable farming areas were

Figure 4.5. Olive presses, like this one at Capernaum, were used to extract oil from olives, a plentiful crop throughout Palestine. (*Photograph by Mitchell G. Reddish*)

in four locations: along the coast (with the exception of the marshy sections of the Plain of Sharon); the western slopes of the Central Highlands from Galilee to a point south of Hebron (halfway down the length of the Dead Sea); the Jezreel-Esdraelon valleys and a portion of the upper Jordan Valley; and a narrow strip of land, averaging ten miles in width, down the length of the Transjordan. Except for Gilead, where crops of barley, wheat, grapes, and olives produced bread, wine, and oil, the eastern region of Palestine could not produce the variety of crops grown in the west. In many otherwise unproductive areas of the country, sheep, goats, and (to a lesser extent) cattle were raised. In the wilderness regions of the south, there were also some especially fertile oases, such as at En-Gedi and Jericho, but these were exceptions. The Plain of Jericho, in fact, was so lush that the city was known as "the city of palms." In biblical times many wild animals also inhabited areas of dense tropical growth, such as along the Jordan River. The variety of these animals is surprising and included the ostrich, the fallow deer, some antelope species, and even lions and bears, all of which are now extinct in that region.

VITAL EVIDENCE: ARCHAEOLOGICAL DISCOVERIES

Information regarding the biblical world comes from both literary and nonliterary sources. The greater source of information by far, however, is the literature of the biblical era. Sometimes in the past, greater claims have been made for the nonliterary, or archaeological, data than can be established by more recent findings. Nevertheless, archaeology provides valuable sources of knowledge about the cultures of the biblical era. Without the many significant discoveries of artifacts and ruins of ancient civilizations, we could not adequately comprehend the environments that surrounded the writing of the books of the Bible.

Archaeological findings range from the fabulous treasures of Pharaoh Tutankhamen to the pottery shards, or broken pottery, of simple peasants. Sometimes writings are also discovered, either on pottery, clay tablets, parchment scrolls, or papyrus. (Papyrus, from which the word "paper" is derived, is an aquatic plant from which strips were cut, pounded, and woven into a smooth surface for writing.) These remains might be found in pyramids and caves or buried in loose desert sands. Most often, however, they are found in tells, or mounds, which are carefully excavated and sifted, layer by layer, progressively revealing the successive cultures that existed in that place.

An amazing amount of information regarding the culture of Israel and its neighbors has been provided by this painstaking work of archaeologists from many nations. For more than a century, scientific excavations have been conducted in Palestine by various institutions; more recently, intense efforts have been devoted to the wider world of Near Eastern culture. This broader focus is sometimes referred to as Syro-Palestinian archaeology.

Yet in spite of such concerted activity, roughly 90 percent of the more than five thousand sites of interest in Palestine alone remain as yet untouched, and major archaeological excavations have been conducted on less than 5 percent of these sites. Obviously much work remains to be done. In light of the extensive knowledge gained already, future excavations can be expected to provide much greater insight into the world of the Bible.

In many ways our current knowledge of that world is incomplete. For example, we know much more about the wealthy and upper classes because of the extensive remains they left than we know of the peasant classes. Likewise, we know more about the urban areas and less about the rural areas. In Palestine more information has been gained about the period of the Israelite kingdom than about the tribal period. We have more evidence from the Coastal Plain, Samaria, and Judah than from Galilee, the Jordan Valley, and the Transjordan.

The conclusions to be drawn from archaeological remains have their limits, however, no matter how extensive the evidence. Thus far, archaeology's findings seem unable to provide answers to questions of chronology (on which we remain much more dependent on literary texts) or political history, or in determining the meaning of texts. But archaeology has provided invaluable information about the broader context of biblical events, about the customs and practices of Israel's neighbors, and about details of daily life in biblical times. Together with a study of the texts, this evidence yields a much more comprehensive picture of the biblical story than the texts alone provide. Even a partial listing of the major finds of archaeology will give ample evidence of that fact.

The Behistun Stone

In the sixth century B.C.E. the Persian ruler Darius I carved an account of his military victories on the stone face of a mountain in Persia (modern Iran). This inscription was written in three languages, Babylonian, Elamite, and Persian. Its meaning was first decoded in the nineteenth century, providing for the first time an understanding of Babylonian and other cuneiform writings (words formed from wedge-shaped marks). This knowledge in turn made possible the translation of many ancient cuneiform texts of relevance to events in the Hebrew Bible.

The Rosetta Stone

One of the most important archaeological discoveries of all time was made in 1799 by Napoleon's soldiers during his invasion of Egypt. This black granite slab, the key to unlocking the mysteries of Egyptian hieroglyphics, was inscribed with a text in three languages: two forms of Egyptian writing, hieroglyphics and demotics, and a Greek version written below the Egyptian scripts. By comparing the account in Greek, a language already known, with the hieroglyphic version, this unknown language could be translated. Subsequently, thousands of previously untranslatable Egyptian documents and inscriptions yielded their information about Egyptian life. The Rosetta stone is now in the British Museum.

Ugaritic Texts

In 1928 a Syrian farmer discovered a thirteenth-century B.C.E. tomb near Ras-Shamra, the modern name for the ancient city of Ugarit. This led to extensive discoveries of cuneiform texts by French archaeologists at the extensive tell, or mound, of Ras-Shamra, which is nearly a thousand yards long and five hundred yards wide. However, a second variety of text, previously unknown, was deciphered and is now known as Ugaritic. The most important of these texts in Ugaritic come from the fourteenth century B.C.E., but they represent a much older oral tradition. These texts are important because of their description of the gods worshiped in Israel's vicinity, such as Baal, Asherah, and El. But they also mention a legendary figure named Daniel (Dnil), regarded by some scholars as a prototype of the biblical hero Daniel. This information about the culture and religion of the ancient city of Ugarit has proved to be extraordinarily valuable for an understanding of the Hebrew Bible, particularly regarding our knowledge of the Canaanite religions and the poetic texts of the Hebrew Bible.

The Ebla Tablets

In 1964 a group of Italian archaeologists began the systematic excavation of a large tell of approximately 140 acres in Syria, south of Aleppo. Their finds identified the place as the location of the ancient commercial city of Ebla. The most important objects discovered there were more than seventeen thousand clay tablets comprising about four thousand complete texts and inscribed in cuneiform script. These tablets date from approximately the mid–third millennium B.C.E. Although the importance of these tablets seems to have been exaggerated at first (for example, there were reports that biblical persons and places were supposedly named in the texts), they are nonetheless important for an understanding of Near Eastern ideas and customs in the final centuries preceding the biblical ancestral era.

The Mari Tablets

More than thirty archaeological expeditions have explored the ancient city of Mari on the Euphrates River since it was first examined by French archaeologists in 1933–34. As in Ebla, thousands of clay tablets—more than twenty thousand in all—have been discovered. Since Mari was destroyed by Hammurabi, king of

Babylon, around 1765 B.C.E., these tablets provide data from the mid–third millennium to the early eighteenth century B.C.E. The primary value of the Mari tablets, as in the case of the Ebla tablets, thus far seems to be in providing background information for the Hebrew ancestral period (ca. 2000–1750 B.C.E.).

The Nuzi Tablets

Several thousand tablets have also been discovered in the ruins of ancient Nuzi on the upper Tigris River, now in northeastern Iraq. These tablets are a primary source of knowledge regarding the customs and practices of the Hurrians, a people who occupied the middle Euphrates Valley during the time of the biblical ancestors. They are particularly valuable for their description of family law among the Hurrians.

The Black Obelisk of Shalmaneser

Shalmaneser III, King of Assyria (858–824 B.C.E.), had two contacts with kings of Israel that he recorded on an obelisk (a commemorative stone that tapers to a pyramid at the top or, in this case, to a stair-stepped, flat top). In 853 Shalmaneser's march into Syria was stopped at the Orontes River by a coalition of Phoenician and Syrian states, including "Ahab of Israel," said to have provided "two housand chariots and ten thousand foot soldiers" (some scholars believe these numbers to be exaggerated). Later, King Jehu of Israel rendered tribute to Shalmaneser (841 B.C.E.). His submission is depicted on the Black Obelisk. Interestingly, neither of these events is mentioned in the Bible.

The Amarna Letters

These cuneiform tablets were found at Amarna, Egypt, and contain correspondence between Egyptian pharaohs and Canaanite and Phoenician rulers. More than 350 letters have been discovered, many of them describing difficulties encountered by the rulers in attempting to administer Palestinian cities. Particularly interesting are references to the Khapiru, a disruptive, apparently nomadic or semi-nomadic Semitic group. The same term may be connected with the later Hebrews.

The Cyrus Cylinder

The capture of Babylon in 539 B.C.E. by Cyrus the Great of Persia was commemorated on a ten-inch-long clay cylinder now known as the Cyrus

Figure 4.6. The Amarna letters, one of which is shown here, were written in cuneiform on small clay tablets during the fourteenth century B.C.E. *(Photograph by Mitchell G. Reddish)*

Cylinder. The name of Cyrus occurs twenty-two times in the Bible, and his authorization of the rebuilding of the Jerusalem Temple, mentioned in 2 Chronicles and Ezra, is in accord with his policy of tolerance toward the captured nations of his empire. (Isaiah 45:1-3 even describes Cyrus as the "anointed of the Lord".) The release of Israel is not mentioned on the cylinder, but its description of Cyrus's policy of restoring the temples and cities of certain captive populations parallels the biblical account. The Cyrus Cylinder is now in the British Museum.

The Siloam Inscription

In 1880 two boys wading in a tunnel, or aqueduct, discovered the Siloam Inscription. It commemorates the excavation of a water tunnel by King Hezekiah shortly before Sennacherib, the king of Assyria, laid siege to Jerusalem (701 B.C.E.). The text describes the moment when two crews, digging in opposite directions through 1,749 feet of bedrock, finally met. The digging of this aqueduct is described in 2 Chronicles and 2 Kings. The Siloam Inscription is now in the Archaeological Museum of Istanbul, Turkey.

The Dead Sea Scrolls

Undoubtedly the most significant modern archaeological find pertaining to the Bible was the discovery of the Dead Sea Scrolls, which were found between 1947 and 1960 at eleven sites near Qumran on the northwestern shore of the Dead Sea. These scrolls seem to have been preserved by a Jewish separatist community that had withdrawn from conventional Jewish society to practice their understanding of a purified Judaism. The biblical texts of the Dead Sea Scrolls are more than a thousand years older than any other Hebrew manuscripts of the Jewish Bible. First discovered in a cave by young shepherd boys, these scrolls astonished the modern world because it was widely believed that no manuscripts could survive so long in that region. In addition to providing a fragment of almost every book of the Hebrew Bible, they also provide much knowledge of the life and rituals of this group of Jewish separatists.

Although many peoples occupied the geographical region described in this chapter, the biblical record centers upon the story of the Hebrew people. The next chapter will examine evidence of other peoples who lived in the same region and whose cultures, in varying degrees, exercised influence upon the life and times of the people of the Bible.

Figure 4.7. Inside these caves at Qumran were discovered some of the Dead Sea Scrolls, one of the most important archaeological discoveries of the twentieth century. (*Photograph by Mitchell G. Reddish*)

Part II
Origins and Early Development of the Jewish Tradition

Chapter 5

HEBREW ORIGINS AND
EARLY HISTORY

Suggested Biblical Readings: Genesis 12–13; 22:1-19; 32; Exodus 1:1–4:20;
12:1-39; 14; 19; 20; Deuteronomy 32:44-52; 34:1-12

    Ancestral stories are a part of the universal human heritage. They are told and retold with embellishments or deletions by storytellers in each generation. The content of such narratives is drawn from a variety of sources, including individual experiences and family, tribal, and national histories. Biblical ancestral stories display the artistic skill of the ancient Hebrew narrators. Preserved in the text of Genesis, the first book of the Pentateuch, these Hebrew ancestral traditions tell a story in two parts. The first part of the story, in Genesis 1–11, depicts Hebrew understandings of the primeval history of the world. This story does not have as its aim what we regard as historical or scientific accuracy. Rather, it consists of religious affirmations about the beginnings of the world, about the

Figure 5.1. Bedouin camps, like this one in Jordan today, have changed little since biblical times. The early ancestors of the Israelites followed a similar nomadic lifestyle. *(Photograph by Clyde E. Fant)*

human predicament, and about divine interaction in human affairs. By repeating this story, successive generations of Hebrews could better understand themselves and relate themselves to the world around them, to their beginnings, and to God. (This primeval history will be examined more closely in chapter 7, which describes the Solomonic period when it likely was written.)

Figure 5.2. Major Periods in Israel's History

19th century–17th century B.C.E. – Period of the Israelite ancestors

1300–1250 B.C.E. – Hebrew Exodus from Egypt and wilderness wanderings

1250–1020 B.C.E. – Conquest of Canaan and period of the judges

1020–922 B.C.E. – United Monarchy of Israel (Saul, David, and Solomon)

922–722 B.C.E. – Northern Kingdom of Israel (Destroyed by Assyrians)

922–587 B.C.E. – Southern Kingdom of Judah (Destroyed by Babylonians)

587–538 B.C.E. – Babylonian Exile

539–332 B.C.E. – Persian rule

332–142 B.C.E. – Hellenistic rule

164–63 B.C.E. – Maccabean and Hasmonean rulers
(Religious freedom was gained in 164 B.C.E. Political independence from Hellenistic rulers was not gained until 142 B.C.E. and was lost temporarily from 134–129 B.C.E.)

63 B.C.E.–324 C.E - Roman period

ISRAEL'S ANCESTRAL NARRATIVES

The second part of the story, Genesis 12–50, focuses on Israel's memories of the ancestors. This story is composed of three collections of material: the Abraham-Sarah narrative, the Jacob-Esau narrative, and the Joseph narrative. The initial group of stories (Gen. 12–25) focuses on the promise given to Abraham, his response to the divine call, and the tests of his fidelity to the God of promise. In the call, Yahweh says to Abraham: "Go from your country and your kindred and your father's house to the land that I will show you. I will make of you a great nation, and I will bless you, and make your name great, so that you will be a blessing. I will bless those who bless you, and the one who curses you I will curse; and in you all the families of the earth shall be blessed" (Gen. 12:1-3).

In response to the divine call and its promise, Abraham and Sarah leave their homeland in Haran (today in eastern Turkey) in search of the "Promised Land" of Canaan. They soon discover that the Promised Land is suffering a famine and they migrate to Egypt. There the pharaoh's desire to take Sarah as a wife threatens the fulfillment of the divine promise. Sarah's deliverance and the ancestral couple's return to Canaan only temporarily relieve the threat to the promise. A series of further challenges follows in stories of family strife (Abraham and Lot), struggles against the Canaanites, and the inability of Sarah to bear children. In two covenant-making ceremonies in chapters 15 and 17, God renews the promise, and through the performance of ritual acts Abraham commits himself to faithfulness.

The Abraham-Sarah cycle of stories reaches its climax with the birth of

Figure 5.3. This sun-dried mudbrick gate at Dan in northern Israel was built around the middle of the eighteenth century B.C.E. during the period of Israel's early ancestors. (*Photograph by Mitchell G. Reddish*)

their son, Isaac. The promise that God would bless the nations of the earth through Abraham and Sarah now seems possible. Before God seals the promise, however, Abraham must submit to the supreme test of faith: "Take your son, your only son Isaac, whom you love, and go to the land of Moriah, and offer him there as a burnt offering on one of the mountains that I shall show you" (Gen. 22:2). The provision of the ram caught in the thicket (as a replacement for Isaac as a sacrifice) brings the narrative to its theological zenith and asserts that the God of the promise always provides for those who remain faithful. Abraham and Sarah thus serve as prototypes of faithful Israel.

The second group of narratives in Genesis presents the story of Jacob and Esau, the sons of Isaac and Rebekah. The Jacob-Esau narrative (Gen. 26–36) centers upon the rivalry between the two brothers that begins in the womb of Rebekah and explodes into conflict when Jacob tricks his brother into surrendering his rights as the firstborn and his paternal blessing. Forced to flee from Esau's revenge, Jacob travels out of Israel to live in the home of his uncle Laban. As a result of an encounter with God at Bethel, the promise made to his father, Isaac, and to his grandfather, Abraham, is renewed to Jacob. Jacob offers only qualified acceptance of the promise and begins a long-term struggle with God. After many years Jacob returns to Canaan, and the scene is set for a renewal of the conflict with Esau. On the eve of the reunion of the two brothers, Jacob has

Figure 5.4. The Jabbok River in the Transjordanian region is the place where, according to Genesis 32, Jacob wrestled with a divine being. *(Photograph by Mitchell G. Reddish)*

a dramatic struggle by night at Peniel with a mysterious stranger he later recognizes as God. Jacob is transformed as a result of this meeting, and the narrative reaches its theological climax. The man whose life epitomizes conflict with God and with his kinfolk finally submits to the divine call. Given a new name, Israel (meaning "may God rule"), Jacob is now portrayed as the father of the twelve tribes who carry on the ancestral traditions.

The third and final group of narratives in Genesis tells the story of Joseph and his brothers (Gen. 37–50). Joseph, the favorite of Jacob's sons, is sold by his jealous brothers into slavery in Egypt. Joseph subsequently rises to power in the pharaoh's court, marries an Egyptian, and takes an Egyptian name. Because of famine in Canaan, his brothers migrate to Egypt, where food is plentiful. They receive an audience before Joseph and are placed at his mercy. Joseph tests the family loyalty of the brothers and finds that they love their father and one another. Joseph's forgiveness of his brothers provides the resolution of the conflict in the narrative, and Jacob and his family are received by Joseph and settle in the land of Goshen in Egypt.

The Joseph narrative represents a more polished literary document than either of the other two cycles of stories in Genesis 12–50. The narrative also differs from the sagas about earlier ancestors in focusing much more on Joseph than on God. God is seldom mentioned, and never does the divine appear directly to Joseph and make him a recipient of the covenant promise. Nevertheless, the narrative had theological significance for the Hebrew storytellers. Near the conclusion of the story, in a speech to his brothers, Joseph says: "Even though you intended to do harm to me, God intended it for good, in order to preserve a numerous people, as he is doing today" (Gen. 50:20). The narrative was used by Israel to teach that God's mysterious and unseen guidance moves the course of events toward purposeful ends in spite of—and even through—unfaithful persons and powerful empires.

CHARACTERISTICS OF THE ANCESTRAL NARRATIVES

The Hebrew ancestral narratives share a similar interest and exhibit several characteristics in common.

First, the stories grew out of an oral tradition. Instead of an earlier oral tradition and a later written tradition, it seems more likely that there was overlapping development of oral and written traditions. Probably most of the ancestral stories originally circulated orally within family, clan, and tribal settings. Tribal storytellers told stories about Abraham and Sarah, Isaac and Rebekah, and other ancestral heroes to their children and in clan gatherings. Such stories were often grouped together into cycles or collections relating to particular persons or topics, such as the Abrahamic cycle of narratives. Eventually, skilled authors and editors combined these clusters of stories into the narrative preserved in Genesis 12–50. The oral foundation of the narratives does not reflect negatively upon their trustworthiness. Like many other ancient peoples, the Hebrews gave great credence to the spoken word, and the constant repetition of stories probably resulted in a remarkably accurate preservation of traditions.

A second characteristic of the ancestral narratives reflects the interweaving of several older traditions. Although there is no agreement regarding such traditions, scholars traditionally have identified three sources that underlie the narratives in Genesis 12–50: the Yahwist (J), the Elohist (E), and the Priestly (P) sources. According to this theory, the J writer contributed the largest amount of the ancestral narratives—perhaps as much as E and P combined. One of the most fascinating features of the ancestral narratives is that these separate traditions were woven together to form a complex but unified story. For example, the Abraham stories probably circulated among the southern Hebrew tribes as independent collections, while the Jacob and Joseph stories are believed to have circulated among the northern tribes in a similar way. In this theory, these clusters of stories were collected by P or an independent editor, who put them into their final form in the period of 550–450 B.C.E.

Third, the ancestral stories describe the actions of both individual clan leaders and persons who symbolize clan life as a whole. Such symbolic persons are eponyms, persons whose names are associated with a group of stories and traditions or who symbolize the activities of an entire group. In the case of the Abrahamic sagas, the narrative seems to describe the life and activities of a particular person, Abraham. In other parts of the Genesis narratives, such as in the Jacob cycle of stories, the eponymous character of the traditions is more evident. That is, the name of the ancestor describes both an individual and a group. For example, the narrator identifies Jacob's brother, Esau, with the Edomites (Gen. 25:30), and Jacob's sons' names are identical with those of the later twelve tribes of Israel (Gen. 35:22-26). It is by no means clear which usage of the names appeared first. Did the name Israel first refer to a "Jacob clan" and later to an eponymous ancestor believed to be the founder of that clan? Or did the term identify the clan founder whose descendants came to bear his name? Since some of the stories carry individual and tribal meanings simultaneously, the genealogical connection of four generations in the stories of Abraham, Isaac, Jacob, and Joseph may represent a unification of separate tribal traditions. This suggests that the ancestral Hebrews may have been far less unified as a people than the stories of family lineage seem to imply.

Fourth, the Genesis narratives always deal with the Hebrew past from the perspective of God's actions. Specifically, they relate the ancestral sagas against the background of God's deliverance of the Hebrews from Egyptian bondage. The narrators present ancestral "history" as preparation for the decisive encounter with the divine in the Exodus experience. These narratives, therefore, do not present ancestral history from a value-free viewpoint but reflect the faith of later authors and redactors. Likewise, because there are no extrabiblical references to the people and events in Genesis, both the scope and the certainty of the ancestral history is limited.

Fifth, the ancestral narratives of Israel served to define the Hebrews in relation to the other peoples of the ancient Near East. Dating from the period after the establishment of the monarchy in Israel, the written form of these narratives provided background for the new status of statehood achieved by the Hebrews. This narrative prepared the way for the story of Israel as the people of Yahweh, as told in the book of Exodus, and the story of Israel as the nation of Yahweh, as told by the Deuteronomistic history (the books of Joshua through 2 Kings). The story of Israel as an ethnic entity was therefore pushed back into ancestral times, with the effect of describing the ancestral Hebrews as one of the unified peoples of the ancient Fertile Crescent.

Sixth, and perhaps most important, the biblical narrators told ancestral stories primarily to confess the Hebrew understanding of the divine-human encounter. The overall purpose of these stories is to claim that God acts in the history of Israel, that humans are capable of responding, and that the events of history provide the setting for that response. The ancestral narratives introduce the theme of encounter in the story of God's call of Abraham and Sarah. Their response begins a story of pilgrimage in which the Hebrews are continually invited to respond in faith to the divine call.

THE ANCESTRAL WORLD

According to Genesis, the Hebrews' ancestral history began with the movement of Terah, the father of Abram (later Abraham), from Ur of the Chaldeans in the southeastern Fertile Crescent to Haran in northwest Mesopotamia. The task of locating these early Hebrews in the context of political and social events in the ancient Fertile Crescent is not easy because of the lack of extrabiblical information on the Hebrew ancestors. Nevertheless, we can describe society in the Fertile Crescent in general terms.

The first major civilization in the upper Fertile Crescent was that of Sumer. The Sumerians swept into the Tigris-Euphrates Valley about 3200 B.C.E. and overran the local population. Among the Sumerian city-states established in the river plain was Ur, the birthplace of Abraham (Gen. 11:27-28). Sumer struggled for several centuries with successive waves of conquerors who came into Mesopotamia. During the period from 2360–2180 B.C.E., the Sumerian cities were brought under the domination of Akkad, a Semitic kingdom to the northwest. The Akkadians took over many aspects of Sumerian culture, including its religion and its cuneiform style of writing, and established a far-ranging empire. The Akkadians later were subjected by the strong city-state of Ebla, located in northern Syria, and eventually overrun by an onslaught of barbaric peoples from near the headwaters of the Tigris River. Following this destruction of Akkad, there was a resurgence of Sumerian culture under King Ur-nammu of the Third Dynasty of Ur (2050–1950 B.C.E.). This revival of Sumer, which included the construction of the famed ziggurat of Ur and the establishment of the earliest law code known in history, was soon to dissipate in the face of a dramatic invasion of the Fertile Crescent.

Near the end of the third millennium B.C.E., a horde of Semitic peoples flooded into the Fertile Crescent from the Arabian Desert. By 1800 B.C.E. these Amurru (Akkadian: "Westerners") or Amorites ruled most of the larger city-states in Mesopotamia. One of the early centers of Amorite strength was the city-state of Mari, on the middle Euphrates.

Mari fell to another Amorite power, the city-state of Babylon, under its brilliant king, Hammurabi (ca. 1728–1686 B.C.E.). Hammurabi built Babylon into a power recognized for its political, cultural, and religious influence in Mesopotamia. Particularly significant was his enactment of the famous Code of Hammurabi, a remarkable work of literary and legal scholarship. The code reflects the interest of the king in effective and just governance of his people, and it became a model for the subsequent development of law codes in the Fertile Crescent.

In the decades after Hammurabi, increasing numbers of Hurrians, an Indo-European people from the region between the Black Sea and the Caspian Sea, began to infiltrate the northwest Fertile Crescent. These people established a strong kingdom known as Mitanni in upper Mesopotamia (1500–1370 B.C.E.) and eventually extended their influence into Syria and Palestine. At Nuzi, a Hurrian city on the upper Tigris River, archaeologists uncovered a significant collection of tablets and other artifacts that sheds much light on the social customs and family life of these people. Although they are useful as an example of the cultural practices of the middle second millennium B.C.E., these materials can provide only a general comparison with Hebrew ancestral traditions.

The Hittites were another people who contributed to the cultural milieu of the Fertile Crescent during the second millennium. Early in the second millennium these Indo-Europeans had established a strong kingdom in Asia Minor (modern-day Turkey). In the fourteenth century they subjugated Mitanni and other upper Mesopotamian powers and founded an empire that lasted until approximately 1200 B.C.E., when it fell to invaders whose identity is still uncertain. After the destruction of their empire, some of the Hittites migrated south and settled in kingdoms in northern Syria. The references to Hittites in the ancestral narratives probably refer to any number of people in northern Palestine and in Syria who had intermingled with the Semitic cultures of that region.

Figure 5.5. Remains of the Great Temple at Hattusa, capital of the Hittite kingdom, in modern Turkey. (*Photograph by Mitchell G. Reddish*)

The collapse of the Hittite Empire near the end of the second millennium was contemporaneous with the movement of the Arameans into upper Mesopotamia. These Semitic people slowly changed from a nomadic to a settled way of life and established numerous small states, first in Mesopotamia and eventually in Syria and Palestine. Several references in Genesis 12–50 identify the Arameans as Abraham's relatives who lived near Haran. The Arameans did not settle in the region of Haran until at least the twelfth century B.C.E. Unwilling to assign such a late date to the ancestral figures, some scholars claim that the references in Genesis to Arameans are an anachronism (which represents something as occurring or existing outside of its proper time). That is, the biblical narrators writing in and after the tenth century used contemporary terminology (i.e., "Arameans") in constructing their stories of the Hebrew ancestral period. The ancestral narratives, therefore, portray a feeling of kinship with the Arameans, but the precise historical foundations of this sense of identity are obscure.

The final group of people that has been significant in discussions of Hebrew origins is the Habiru (or 'Apiru). These "wanderers" or "foreigners" are mentioned often in documents from all around the Fertile Crescent in the second millennium. The term *Khapiru* refers not to an ethnic or national group, but to a social classification of migrant peoples regarded as rootless and foreign by any of the settled societies in which they appeared. The precise relationship of the biblical word "Hebrew" to Habiru is not clear, but it is generally agreed that the two terms are not identical. On the other hand, it is likely that the Hebrew ancestors belonged to a larger social class of Near Eastern society known as Habiru.

This brief survey of several peoples occupying the Fertile Crescent in the second millennium B.C.E. serves to illustrate the complex population shifts that characterized the ancient Near East. The question of Hebrew origins must be addressed against the background of this cultural intermingling. A scholarly consensus emerged by the middle of the twentieth century that placed Hebrew origins among the Amorite peoples of the upper Fertile Crescent in the Middle Bronze Age (2200–1550 B.C.E.). Many subscribers to this early theory of ancestral origins preferred a specific phase, MB II, which would have placed Abraham in the period of 1900–1750 B.C.E. Recent reevaluations of the archaeological evidence and further studies in historical criticism, source criticism, and literary criticism have called this date into question. There are now several competing theories regarding the historical context out of which the Hebrews came, with proposals ranging from the first phase of the Middle Bronze Age (about 2200–1900 B.C.E.) to the Early Iron Age (about 1200–950 B.C.E.).

With the question of Hebrew origins so unsettled, perhaps the soundest position for the present is to see the ancestral figures as part of the generally unsettled sociopolitical context of the second millennium B.C.E. Any attempt to relate them to a particular ethnic strain or to place them in a specific chronological period of the Bronze Age may be unwarranted by the evidence available at this time. Our inability to make precise correlations between the Hebrew ancestors and the data on Mesopotamian culture means that any effort to describe the "life and times" of the ancestors must be somewhat tentative.

In any case, the story told in Genesis 12–50 was intended to profess Israel's faith that God was working in Hebrew history to accomplish redemption, not record a definitive history of the ancestors. In studying these stories we gain insight into the general pattern of life that characterized the ancestral period and a better understanding of the ways in which later Israel interpreted the traditions of its past.

ANCESTRAL RELIGION

The narrative cycles of ancestral tradition pose particular problems for the student of early Hebrew religious beliefs and practices. The chief difficulty is that the narrators blended the later, more unified religious traditions of their own time period into the religion of the ancestors, somewhat obscuring the distinctiveness of the earlier religious community. However, these stories give us some insight into the ancestral view of the divine-human encounter and display four general features of ancestral religion.

First, ancestral religion seems to have included the worship of separate clan deities. The Genesis narrators use epithets (descriptive names or titles) that

Figure 5.6. This relief, part of a natural rock shrine at Yazilikaya, Turkey, depicts Sharruma, one of the ancient Hittite gods. The carvings at Yazilikaya date from the thirteenth century B.C.E. *(Photograph by Mitchell G. Reddish)*

link the deity with particular ancestral figures. For example, in the renewal of the covenant promise with Isaac, the deity is identified as "the God of your father Abraham" (Gen. 26:24); when Jacob is involved in a similar renewal, the divine identity is "the God of Abraham your father and the God of Isaac" (Gen. 28:13). At other places the narrators use such titles as "Fear of Isaac" (Gen. 31:42) and "Mighty One of Jacob" (Gen. 49:24). This identification of the deity with individual ancestral fathers suggests the existence of a cult of the "God of the fathers." In such a system, the head of the clan would choose a deity to be the patron god of the families in that clan, and the chief ancestor would then establish a contract with that god, thereby creating clan-deity solidarity. This close identification of the deity with the clan/family extended to the thought of the "God of the fathers" as the head of the clan. This clan deity was actively involved in the life of the ancestral family, accompanied the group in all its movements, and was accessible to all members of the clan.

A second characteristic of ancestral religion is the adaptation by the Hebrews of certain elements of Canaanite religion. An example of this influence of Canaanite polytheism is seen in the Hebrew choice of divine names. The most frequently used name for deity in Genesis is Yahweh (usually translated "LORD" in English Bibles). The writings regarded as those of the J writer consistently use this title. However, as we shall see in a later section of this chapter, this usage is probably anachronistic since the name Yahweh likely appeared at the time of Moses. In the documents attributed to E and P there are a variety of divine names and epithets, including Elohim (God or gods), El Elyon (God Most High), El Bethel (the House of God), El Roi (God of Seeing), El Olam (Everlasting God), and El Shaddai (God Almighty). The term "El" was widely used among Semitic peoples in the Fertile Crescent as a generic name for deity. In Canaanite religion El was the chief deity and father of the gods. At times the Hebrew ancestors participated in the cultic activities of this Canaanite religion. They apparently combined the name El with certain descriptive words to arrive at the divine titles mentioned above, which represent the divine as provider for and protector of the ancestral families.

The establishment of covenant relationships with their god was a third feature of ancestral clan religion. Perhaps the best example of a covenant ceremony is in Genesis 15, in which divine initiative is taken to institute a covenant with Abraham. The story, attributed to the J writer, suggests that sacrifice may have been an important part of covenant-making ceremonies. Abraham cuts animals in half and lays them in opposing rows, through which the parties in the contract then pass. If either party fails to keep the agreement, that party will suffer the same fate as the animals. In another covenant ceremony, in Genesis 17, circumcision is instituted as the sign and seal of the contract between Abraham and God. These ceremonies affirm the ancestral notion that the deity makes promises and seals those promises in a covenant with the clan father.

Fourth, in the ancestral narratives God is known primarily through God's participation in concrete events of history, the tasks and conflicts of human life. These stories therefore place great emphasis upon the encounter of the divine with humans. Indeed, once the promise has been given to Abraham, practically every scene in Genesis turns upon some divine intervention. By the end of the Genesis saga, the stage is set for the story of the greatest of Israel's encounters with the divine: the Exodus.

THE EXODUS AND WILDERNESS TRADITIONS

The ancestral stories begun in Genesis continue in the narrative sections of the remaining books of the Pentateuch. The Exodus/wilderness narrative is more firmly set in history than are the ancestral narratives, but like them it has the characteristics of a skillfully and dramatically told story. Because the story was about their deliverance and freedom, it was a favorite of the early Israelites. It recounts the establishment of a religious community, the definition of its place in the purposes of God, and the structuring of its way of life.

The story begins by detailing background material on the oppression of Jacob's descendants, who suffer under the harsh rule of an Egyptian pharaoh "who did not know Joseph" (Ex. 1:8) and who finally decrees that all newborn male

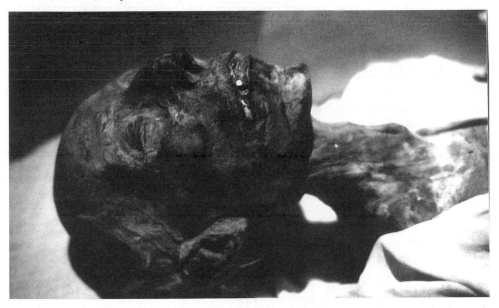

Figure 5.7. Head of the mummified remains of Ramesses II, who reigned over Egypt during the thirteenth century B.C.E. He was possibly the pharaoh at the time of the Hebrew exodus from Egypt. (*Photograph by Clyde E. Fant*)

Israelites be killed. Against the backdrop of this oppression, the story then focuses on one Hebrew, Moses, who as an infant is rescued from death by the Egyptian princess and is reared in the pharaoh's palace by the princess and by his Hebrew mother. Moses, whose childhood and youth are not mentioned in the narrative, becomes the mediator through whom God delivers the Hebrews from bondage in Egypt and calls them into covenant relationship.

Although he was reared as an Egyptian, Moses apparently maintains his sense of being a Hebrew. It is his empathy for the oppressed Hebrews that leads to his killing an Egyptian taskmaster who was abusing a Hebrew slave. Forced to flee Egypt, Moses seeks exile in Midian, where he lives among a community of Kenites led by a priest named Jethro, whose daughter, Zipporah, Moses marries. While tending sheep in Midian, Moses receives his call to lead the Hebrews out of Egypt (Ex. 3:1–4:17). This provocative account of his call includes the theophany (manifestation of God) of the burning bush, out of which Moses hears the voice of God. A significant part of this theophany at the "mountain of God" is the disclosure of God's name, when God is first identified as the God of Abraham, Isaac, and Jacob. But Moses wants to know a name by which he should call God when he speaks to the Israelite captives of his experience on the mountain. So God responds to Moses' request with a name that has been variously translated as "I am who I am" or "I will be who I will be" (Ex. 3:14-15). The focal point of the call narrative, however, is Yahweh's commission to Moses: "So come, I will send you to Pharaoh to bring my people, the Israelites, out of Egypt" (Ex. 3:10).

In confronting the pharaoh with Yahweh's demands, Moses' first audience with the Egyptian ruler results in harsher treatment of the Hebrew slaves. The extended narrative that follows (Ex. 7:8–11:10) recounts the conflict between the pharaoh, who is the incarnation of the sun god, and Yahweh, who is the Lord of the slaves. Ten plagues inflicted by Yahweh upon Egypt are the focal point of this drama. The final scourge, the death of the Egyptian firstborn, breaks Pharaoh's stubborn will. This tenth plague also provided the historical grounding of Israel's most prominent and probably oldest religious festival, the Passover, when the angel of death passed over the Hebrews without harming them.

Following the tenth plague, Yahweh leads the Israelites to escape. Yahweh goes before the Hebrews by day in a pillar of cloud and by night in a pillar of fire. At the Sea of Reeds, the waters are divided and the Israelites march through the sea on dry ground. Then the waters return upon Moses' command and drown the army of the pharaoh. The sister of Moses, Miriam, who had assisted in the rescue of the baby Moses, then led the women in a victory song (Ex. 15:20-21). In this account she also is referred to as a prophet. Many modern scholars have noted the prominence of her role in later events and believe that Miriam likely played an even more significant part in the leadership in the wilderness than emphasized by the patriarchal scribes.

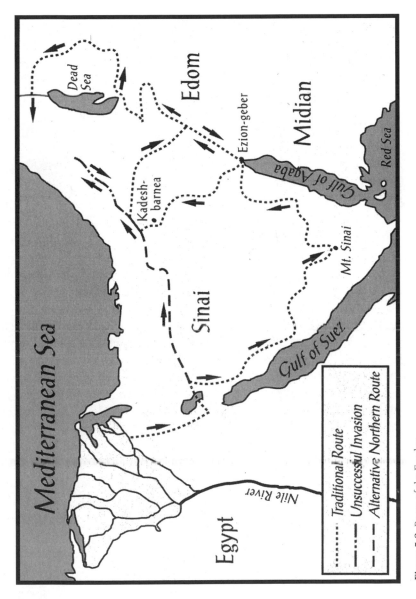

Figure 5.8. Route of the Exodus.

The deliverance at the Sea of Reeds is followed by other crises as Yahweh's newly elected people move beyond the sea toward the holy mountain where Moses had received his initial commission. In the face of thirst, hunger, and war with desert tribes, Yahweh provides fresh water, manna (a mysterious food that appeared on the bushes each morning), quail, and victory over the Amalekites, who were fierce desert warriors. The Israelites are also troubled with internal strife; the people "murmur" against Yahweh and Moses because they begin to realize they had been more comfortable in Egypt than they are now in the wilderness. The Hebrew storytellers emphasize that the uncertainty of life in the wilderness made the life of faith in Yahweh very difficult. The Israelite interpreters of this period believed that even Moses came under Yahweh's judgment for disbelief, with the result that he was not permitted to enter the Promised Land (Num. 20:12).

The escape narrative, recorded in two versions in Exodus 19 and 24, reaches its climax in the story of the covenant made between Yahweh and the people at Mount Sinai. This agreement includes laws whose observance will ensure the continuation of the right relationship between God and the Israelites. The lengthy Sinai narrative (Ex. 19:1–Num. 10:11) points to the importance the Israelites assigned to their new status as the elect people of God.

After almost a year at Mount Sinai, the Israelites set out for the Wilderness of Paran and finally arrive at Kadesh-barnea, where the remainder of the traditional forty years in the wilderness is spent (Num. 10:11–20:21). Among the episodes that have their setting there are those that repeat the themes of Exodus 15–18: further murmuring and rebellion, Moses' persistent intercession for the people, and Yahweh's faithful provision of water, manna, and quail.

After an abortive effort to enter Canaan from the south, the Hebrews take a circuitous route around the two kingdoms of Edom and Moab and arrive in the central Transjordan region north of Moab. Here they conquer a territory extending several miles north of the Dead Sea and encamp to prepare an assault upon Canaan, the land across the Jordan to the west. Deuteronomy tells the story of Moses' last days, his farewell speeches, his commissioning of Joshua as his successor, his final blessing of the Israelite tribes, and his death on Mount Nebo.

CHARACTERISTICS OF THE EXODUS-WILDERNESS NARRATIVES

The narratives of Israel's Exodus-wilderness experiences pose many historical-critical questions. How did these stories come to their present form? When did the Exodus take place and what was the route that the Hebrews followed? Where was the "mountain of God"? How are we to understand such phenomena as the plagues, the crossing of the sea, the manna, the pillars of cloud and fire, and the other unusual means by which Yahweh made nature serve the divine purpose? How did the Hebrews of Moses' time understand the divine-human encounter, and how did the covenant, the Law, and cultic practice reflect this understanding? These questions will be the focus of the remainder of this chapter.

The Development of the Narrative

As noted above, the great majority of the ancestral traditions in Genesis were preserved in the form of sagas. By contrast, the Exodus/wilderness traditions are largely devoted to laws and lists (tribal censuses, land allotments and boundaries, and itineraries). The bulk of this material is found in Exodus 25–31, 35–40, all of Leviticus, Numbers 1–9, and the book of Deuteronomy. Exodus 1–24, 32–34, and Numbers 10–36 form the heart of the narrative portion of the tradition. It is likely that most of the narrative in Exodus was edited by the Priestly redactor during the late–exilic period and that this editor added material that had been preserved in the circle of priests. The story in its present form is therefore the end result of a long and complex development that reaches back to its oral stage of transmission in Israelite culture. The story probably was associated originally with the celebration of Passover, when the Hebrews told the story as the explanation of their existence as a nation and of their special sense of being the people of God. Over the course of many centuries, the story was told and retold until the Priestly writer put it into its final form.

The Historical Context

The historical framework of the Exodus-wilderness narrative poses numerous problems that lead to inconclusive results. Neither Moses nor the flight of the Hebrew slaves is mentioned in any Egyptian text yet discovered, and the biblical accounts themselves are often obscure with regard to historical detail. This historical vagueness results from the narrator's emphasis upon the theological significance of the Exodus. Yahweh's deliverance of the Hebrews from Egyptian bondage is a fundamental premise of Israel's covenant faith and the formative event from which the Hebrews traced their origins as a nation. As one of the primary themes of the Hebrew Bible, the Exodus lies at the heart of Israel's historical experience.

Although the Hebrew narratives speak clearly of the significance of the Exodus, they say almost nothing about when it happened. Several factors complicate efforts to date the Exodus: no specific dates are given in the biblical texts; the Egyptian pharaohs who play a large part in the story go unnamed; Asiatics and even Khapiru captives are referred to over several centuries in Egypt;

Egyptian names are given to people living in Canaan; and even the store cities of Raamses and Pithom are mentioned as late as the fifth century B.C.E. In the face of these difficulties we cannot make absolute claims about the date of the Exodus. However, modern historical-critical assessment of the Exodus traditions against the backdrop of ancient Egypt has led most scholars to accept a thirteenth-century setting for the Exodus, placing the escape early in the reign of Pharaoh Ramesses II, about 1290 B.C.E.

When the Hebrews fled Egypt, they did not take the most direct route to Canaan. The storyteller indicates that the route of the escape was providential: "When Pharaoh let the people go, God did not lead them by way of the land of the Philistines, although that was nearer. . . . So God led the people by the roundabout way of the wilderness toward the Red Sea" (Ex. 13:17-18). The "nearer" way refers to the heavily traveled commercial and military highway that went most directly from the Egyptian delta to Canaan (although at that time it would not have been known as the "way of the Philistines" because the Philistines did not occupy that area until after 1200 B.C.E.). Avoiding this heavily guarded highway, they moved in the direction of *yam suph*, which sometimes has been translated as "Red Sea." Today historians believe that in passages dealing with the Exodus, *yam suph* should be translated as "reed sea." (The word "suph" twice is translated "reeds" in Exodus 2:3-5, the story of Moses being placed in a basket

Figure 5.9. Jebel Musa (Mount Moses), located in the southern part of the Sinai Peninsula, is traditionally identified as Mount Sinai. *(Photograph by Mitchell G. Reddish)*

made of reeds and hidden in the reeds along the Nile.) This "Sea of Reeds" may have designated a marshy area now crossed by the Suez Canal. The text then speaks of God providing a miraculous crossing of this body of water, in which some of the pursuing Egyptians were drowned, through the steadfast faith of Moses. The Hebrews thus made good their escape from Egypt and moved on toward Sinai.

Since the sixth century C.E., tradition has located Mount Sinai on the southern tip of the Sinai peninsula. With this location in mind, it has been surmised that the Israelites traveled down the west coast of the peninsula, stopping at the oases and sites along this route. This traditional view has been called into question, however, and many contemporary scholars argue for a location of Sinai near Kadesh-barnea in the Mount Seir range of the Negeb, far north of the traditional Sinai. Archaeology has been of little help in settling this question, and to date the precise route of the Exodus and the location of Mount Sinai cannot be determined with certainty.

Whatever the route and wherever the mountain, the narrative describes a very large population of Hebrews leaving Egypt. Exodus 12:37 numbers the Hebrews at "about six hundred thousand men on foot, besides [women and] children." This would have placed the total number of Hebrews at about two and a half million. Other references in Exodus suggest that this number probably was exaggerated by a later biblical narrator. One such reference states that two midwives were enough to serve the entire colony (Ex. 1:15-20). Another reference says that when they approached Canaan, the Hebrews were too few to engage the inhabitants in battle (Ex. 23:29-30).

As in the case of the historical questions concerning the ancestral narratives, many of the historical-critical reconstructions of the events described in the Exodus-wilderness narratives must remain incomplete. In the biblical traditions we can only observe how Israelites at various times conceived the course of events and in what locales they placed them. Because these biblical narratives are so indirect and often fragmentary with regard to their historical setting, and because extrabiblical evidence is so slight, a fuller picture of the historical context of the Exodus-wilderness experience cannot be developed.

Mosaic Religion

The effort to elucidate the religious features of Hebrew culture during the lifetime of Moses faces difficulties similar to that of the critical assessment of the historical context. The chief problem is isolating Israel's Exodus-wilderness faith and practice from that of the much later redactors of this story. In spite of this difficulty, there is a core of religious belief and practice that—if not directly traceable to Moses—reflects authentic Mosaic traditions that were remembered and conveyed in the generations after Moses. These religious features deal with aspects of the Hebrew understanding of the divine-human encounter during this era and may be discussed under four headings: the concept of God, the understanding of the covenant, the institution of the Law, and the elements of the Mosaic cult ("cult" refers to everything associated with the worship of a group).

The Concept of God. Moses' question to God in the theophany of the burning bush in Exodus 3:13 ("If I come to the Israelites and say to them, 'The God of your ancestors has sent me to you,' and they ask me, 'What is his name?' what shall I say to them?"—seems to assume a polytheistic environment. In other words, in the midst of many deities, who is this divine being who has spoken? Moses is not only asking the practical question of the god's name; he also wants to know something of the nature of this god. But the answer given to his question is "I AM." "I AM WHO I AM" is related to the Israelite name for God, YHWH, probably pronounced Yah'weh.

The exact derivation and meaning of the name that Moses was given, however, is obscure and has prompted many interpretations. At a minimum, the name suggests that God acts redemptively in Hebrew history. If the phrase was intended to emphasize the dynamic character of God, it may mean "I WILL BE WHAT I WILL BE," or "I CAUSE TO BE WHAT IS." In this sense it suggests that the secret of God's being is shrouded in mystery; it is to be discovered not in the knowledge of God's name but rather in what God was about to do. God becomes known to the Hebrews primarily through historical events, through what God does for them and through them in the arena of human affairs. Specifically, Yahweh is the God whose liberating power is known to the Hebrews in the historical event of the Exodus. For this reason the Exodus became the pivotal event in Hebrew history. Israel came to know its God as the one who delivered them from bondage in Egypt.

From the account in Exodus 3 it appears that the divine name, Yahweh, was first revealed to Moses at Sinai. Likewise, in chapter 6 God says, "I am the LORD. I appeared to Abraham, Isaac, and Jacob as God Almighty, but by my name 'The LORD' I did not make myself known to them" (Ex. 6:2-3). On the other hand, other references trace the name to a much earlier period and reflect the tradition that Yahweh was the name used by at least some of the ancestral clans. Although the origin of the name remains uncertain, it seems probable that the early use of the name in Genesis is theologically anachronistic—that is, the writer imposed the name upon the earlier traditions in order to show that the God who led the Hebrews in the Exodus was the same God known by Abraham, Isaac, and Jacob. The other narrative traditions seem to be more accurate in claiming that the name came into common use only at the time of Moses. Some scholars have argued that Moses learned of Yahweh from the Kenites or Midianites, among whom Moses was living when he received the theophany of the burning bush. This Kenite hypothesis rests on the idea that Yahweh was the mountain God of the Midianites and that Moses was initiated into this tradition by his father-in-law, Jethro.

The Understanding of the Covenant. Recent study of the Mari texts (Syria) and treaties from the Hittite archives has enlarged our understanding of covenants among Near Eastern peoples. There were two distinctive Near Eastern covenant forms: parity covenants and suzerainty covenants. The parity covenant is one in which covenant partners equally share responsibility to cooperate and support one another. The suzerainty covenant, however, is unilateral; one party is more powerful than the other and grants the covenant largely as an act of benevolence. The Sinai covenant is a suzerainty covenant. Yahweh acts as a powerful God of history who grants the covenant as a gift to the people. This alliance requires that Israel accept its role as a covenant people and respond in faithfulness to the commandments of God.

The covenant ceremony at Mount Sinai is described in chapters 19 and 24 of Exodus. (Chapter 19 describes the preparations for the event and chapter 24 describes the ceremony itself.) In chapter 19 the terms of the covenant are stated by God to Moses: If the Hebrews will acknowledge Yahweh as their deliverer and will obey the law that is about to be given to them, then they will be God's people and will enjoy God's blessing. Moses and the people respond that they will do "everything that the Lord has spoken" (Ex. 19:8).

The covenant narrative in chapter 24 reflects the interweaving of two accounts. In the Yahwistic version (24:1-2, 9-11), the ceremony is conducted on top of the mountain. There Moses, his brother Aaron, Aaron's sons, and seventy elders meet with Yahweh and, as representatives of the people, bind the covenant by eating a sacred meal in God's presence. In the Elohistic account (24:3-8, 12-14), the whole assembly of the people meets God at the foot of the mountain and makes a vow to keep the Law. Moses erects an altar there, along with twelve pillars to represent the twelve tribes, and animal sacrifices are offered.

The Institution of the Law. Set within the context of the Mosaic covenant are the codes of Israelite law, representing a variety of legal traditions and developed over a broad span of Hebrew history. Grounded in the divine-human relationship affirmed by Moses' encounter with Yahweh and by the covenant faith, the Law provides the guidelines for the ordering of a human community under God's direction. Consequently, there are no distinctions between civil/criminal law on the one hand and religious/cultic law on the other. The Law is given for the ordering of all aspects of Hebrew life.

Within the Law, the Decalogue (or Ten Commandments) expresses what is most fundamental in the maintenance of the divine-human relationship. The first four stipulations concern especially the worship of God; the last six govern the life of the Israelite community.

The first commandment, "You shall have no other gods before me," requires specific comment because it is often understood as a statement of absolute monotheism. This is not, however, a formal monotheistic claim; instead, it declares that there may be other gods for other peoples, but not for Israel. Some have termed this aspect of Mosaic faith *henotheism* (the worship of only one God, though others may exist). The full implications of this first commandment were long in coming to expression, and an explicit monotheism is not evidenced in Hebrew literature until the exilic period (sixth century B.C.E.).

Immediately following the Decalogue in Exodus is a collection of laws designated the Covenant Code (Ex. 20:22–23:33). These laws cover a wide variety of personal and property rights as well as cultic requirements, many of which presuppose a settled agricultural society. Although some of these laws may survive from the Exodus-wilderness era, most of this material is dated to the period after the settlement in Canaan.

The book of Deuteronomy is a law book and belongs as such among the other legal collections of the Pentateuch. It differs from the typical legal code, however, in consisting not of an itemized list of rules but of exhortation to covenant faithfulness. Most scholars believe that the basic form of the book originated in the late–seventh century B.C.E. during the reign of King Josiah of Judah, for whose reformation of Yahwism the book served as a guide. The core collection was enlarged by later Hebrew historians, and the book eventually served as an introduction to the Deuteronomistic history, which includes the books from Deuteronomy through 2 Kings (to be discussed in chapter 11).

The Priestly Code, found primarily in Exodus 25–31 and in the book of Leviticus, is the last body of law in the Pentateuch and did not attain its final form until the time of the Priestly writers in the sixth century B.C.E. This material focuses on the worship life of Israel, a brief discussion of which will conclude this chapter.

The Elements of the Mosaic Cult. The descriptions of Israel's worship life in the Pentateuch reflect cultic traditions that developed over several centuries, and it is difficult to ascertain which features of that cult were present in the Exodus-wilderness era. It is generally accepted, however, that a minimal description of Mosaic worship should include the following elements.

First, the Israelites worshiped Yahweh through sacrifice. How elaborate this sacrificial system was in the Mosaic cult is not clear. It does appear that through their sacrifices the Hebrews sought to acknowledge God's ownership of all life by giving to God a portion of their flocks and crops, to establish communion with God, and to maintain the covenant relationship.

A second feature of Mosaic worship was the use of the Ark of the Covenant, a wooden chest about the size of an attic trunk. The Ark symbolized Yahweh's presence among the Hebrews. It was a portable throne upon which Yahweh was believed to be invisibly enthroned and also served as a container for the tablets bearing the Decalogue. When carried in battle, it was believed to be an object with the power to protect those who possessed it. The Ark went wherever Israel went, and wherever Israel was, there God would be also.

The Ark was related to a third element of the Mosaic cult, the "tent of meeting." The tent was a movable dwelling that served as a desert shrine where Moses consulted Yahweh and where God's words were proclaimed to the assembled people. This tent is distinguished from the "tabernacle," which is frequently mentioned in the Priestly source. The tabernacle is described as a much more elaborate structure, which seems to be inconsistent with the desert conditions and semi-nomadic life of the Mosaic era. Most scholars have concluded that the tabernacle was not yet in existence during this period but is a retrojection of the Temple (built by Solomon) into the Exodus-wilderness period by the Priestly writer, who assumed that all Hebrew cultic institutions and practices originated at that time.

Finally, all of the activities and objects of cultic activity in the Mosaic era were entrusted to a formal priesthood. From the time of the Sinai covenant, the priesthood was formally an inherited office associated with Moses' brother, Aaron. The priests were keepers of the tent and the Ark, they offered sacrifices, they delivered messages from God, and they preserved, interpreted, and taught the sacred tradition.

Israel's faith and worship in the Exodus/wilderness period is not founded upon a conception of a God who is aloof from the human struggle. Rather, it rests upon a response to the God who is active within the social struggle, guiding and shaping the course of human affairs according to divine purpose. The Hebrew tradition has always affirmed that what God did in Egypt and in the wilderness under Moses' leadership was the foundation for the settlement in the land of Canaan. This land, which had been promised through the ancestral figure Abraham, was not to be a possession about which Israel might boast; rather, it was a gift to be received with gratitude. The next chapter will examine the manner in which the Hebrews claimed this gift.

Chapter 6

THE ERA OF THE JUDGES

Suggested Biblical Readings: Deuteronomy 20:1-18; Joshua 1–2; 23–24;
Judges 2; 4; 5; 13–14; 16

During the two hundred years after the wilderness wanderings, the Hebrews entered the area that would become their "holy land" and began developing the rudimentary political and religious institutions that would eventually result in the creation of an Israelite nation. The books of Joshua and Judges tell of Israel's settlement in Canaan. With Deuteronomy, which serves as an introduction to the material, this collection is known as the Deuteronomistic history because it takes a view of Israel's past that is consistent with the theological principle of Deuteronomy. This history reached its final form around 550 B.C.E. Despite the unique characteristics of the separate books, the narrative has an essential theological unity. The Deuteronomistic historian portrays Israel's fortunes as rising and falling in accordance with the nation's faithfulness to the covenant established with Yahweh at Mount Sinai. The first portion of this history (after the introduction in Deuteronomy) covers approximately two hundred years following the death of Moses. This period is called the era of the judges, after the title given to the military heroes who led the Hebrew tribes during the period of settlement. The narratives describing this period are found in the books of Joshua and Judges. The story begins with the movement of the tribes into Canaan.

THE SETTLEMENT IN CANAAN

The book of Deuteronomy concludes with the death of Moses on Mt. Nebo, his burial in a valley in the land of Moab, and the transfer of leadership from Moses to Joshua. The Deuteronomistic author writes, "Joshua son of Nun was full of the spirit of wisdom, because Moses had laid his hands on him; and the Israelites obeyed him, doing as the LORD had commanded Moses" (Deut. 34:9). With these words the scene is set for the movement of Israel into the land of Canaan. Because the Deuteronomistic historian saw this settlement as a fulfillment of the promise Yahweh gave to Abraham, the importance of this period is clearly discernible in the narrative. However, the record of details in the taking of the Promised Land is overlapping, ambiguous, and even conflicting. This confusion results from the interweaving of multiple traditions regarding the way in which Canaan was claimed as the homeland of the Hebrews. Although the Deuteronomistic editor has skillfully intertwined the stories, the multiplicity of traditions and the preferred theological interpretation of the editor can still be recognized.

The canonical narrative presents two views of the manner in which the Hebrews settled Canaan. On the one hand, the book of Joshua presents a story of rapid and complete conquest of the land by the Hebrews (Josh. 1–12). On the other hand, the book of Judges records a gradual infiltration of Canaan that lasted over several centuries (Judg. 1:1–2:5).

The invasion as described in the book of Joshua proceeded by three swift and decisive campaigns to bring the whole land under the Israelites' control. The first campaign established their hold in the region of Jericho and the Central Highlands. After receiving a favorable report from spies sent to Jericho (chapter 2), the Israelites broke camp in the Plain of Moab and marched toward the Jordan River. Reminiscent of the Sea of Reeds experience, the Jordan's waters stopped their flow and allowed the Israelites passage (chapter 3).

After a brief encampment at Gilgal, the assault on Jericho began. The Israelites ritually marched around the city, led by priests bearing the Ark of the Covenant and blowing trumpets. After seven daily trips around the city, "they raised a great shout, and the wall fell down flat" (6:20). The point of the famous story is clear: Israel's victory was due not to its military prowess but to Yahweh's mighty presence. The city was accordingly placed under the ban or *herem* (a practice of holy warfare whereby a conquered people and their possessions were destroyed as a sacrifice to the conquerors' deity). Joshua also records the execution of the ban against the city of Ai, another Central Highlands town to fall to the invading Israelites (chapter 7). Following the conquest of Jericho and Ai, Joshua built an altar at Shechem, in the center of Canaan, and offered a sacrifice of thanksgiving to Yahweh (chapter 8).

The second phase of the Hebrew invasion, according to the book of Joshua, took the Israelites into the southern hill country of Judah to war against several Canaanite city-states. Bypassing the well-fortified town of Jerusalem, they moved against Makkedah, Libnah, Lachish, Eglon, Hebron, and Debir, a campaign that takes only twelve verses to describe (10:28-39). Each city was placed under the ban.

The third campaign was fought against a coalition of kings north of the Sea of Galilee. Among the northern cities, only Hazor, "the head of all those kingdoms," was subjected to the *herem* and was burned with fire. The Israelite conquest of the area was complete (11:1-15). The Deuteronomistic writer sums up the three campaigns with these words: "So Joshua took all that land: the hill country and all the Negeb and all the land of Goshen and the lowland and the Arabah and the hill country of Israel and its lowland.... Joshua made war a long time with all those kings" (11:16, 18).

The other settlement tradition can be found in scattered passages in the

Figure 6.1. Stone watchtower unearthed at ancient Jericho. This tower dates to approximately 8000–7000 B.C.E. and was part of the walled fortifications of the city. It is one of the oldest human structures still standing. *(Photograph by Mitchell G. Reddish)*

latter half of Joshua and especially in Judges 1:1–2:5. Here a quite different view of the settlement emerges, although the same period and the same events are described. In the Judges account there is no single leader of the conquest, and the struggle against the Canaanites is undertaken by individual tribes or related tribes that are trying to gain a foothold in the hill country of Canaan. There is no unified campaign by "all Israel" as described in the text of Joshua. Moreover, in contrast to the *herem*, which is important to the Joshua narrative, the inhabitants of the land are not completely eradicated; in fact, Judges lists twenty cities that were not conquered by the Hebrews. The Judges narrative preserves a tradition that Canaan was gradually occupied by the Israelites as individual tribes or small groups of

Figure 6.2. Hazor in northern Israel was one of the cities conquered and destroyed by the invading Israelites during the settlement period. This storage building at Hazor dates from the ninth century B.C.E. (*Photograph by Mitchell G. Reddish*)

tribes undertook separate operations of conquest or slowly merged with the Canaanite population.

Both of these biblical perspectives of the Hebrew settlement of Canaan were given their present form in the narrative long after the events actually took place. The redactor of the Deuteronomistic materials selected passages from available ancient sources and told the story of Israel's beginnings from a theological perspective. This Deuteronomistic view of the swift and complete conquest became the normative view transmitted by generations of Israelites, and, as history became obscured by layers of later tradition, the picture in the book of Judges of a slow infiltration was regarded as secondary to this more widely accepted position.

In general, three major models have been proposed for reconstructing the history of Israel's occupation of Canaan. Each of these theories tries to take seriously the tensions within the biblical accounts, and each depends heavily upon archaeology to authenticate its argument.

Conquest Model. The conquest model defends the basic integrity of the normative biblical view in its depiction of military successes under Joshua's leadership. Those battles are dated in the latter half of the thirteenth century B.C.E., at which time archaeology reveals widespread cultural changes in Palestine and the destruction or abandonment of a number of cities. Objections to the conquest theory center particularly on its interpretation of archaeological data. For example, no data definitively connects the cultural changes in thirteenth-century Palestine specifically with the Israelites. Furthermore, archaeological discoveries at some sites present more of a problem than a support for the conquest model. In the case of Jericho, for example, there is no evidence of a walled city dating to the period from about 1400 to 1200 B.C.E., when most scholars would date the Israelite entry into Canaan.

Immigration Model. The immigration model conceives of a long and primarily peaceful infiltration of Palestine by diverse groups—among whom were Israelites—rather than the "all Israel" assault described in the book of Joshua. This theory relies on such details in the biblical narrative as the alliance with the Gibeonites, the absence of fighting in the Shechem area, and the notations that some parts of the land were slow in coming under Israel's domination. This view further envisions the migration of seminomadic peoples into the unoccupied areas of Palestine and the eventual merger of these groups into the nation of Israel. Only much later, toward the end of the period of the judges, did sporadic fighting erupt between these immigrants and the Canaanite city-states.

Revolt Model. The third major alternative, the revolt model, portrays the settlement of Canaan as neither a peaceful immigration nor a military conquest. Rather, the emergence of Israel is connected with a sociopolitical upheaval instigated by the peasantry within Palestine, who sought relief from the oppressive feudal system imposed by the Canaanite city-states. The catalyst for this broad peasant revolt was the arrival in the thirteenth century of the Israelites, led by Joshua. This model is built largely upon speculations concerning the social setting, with virtually no biblical confirmation possible.

As with a number of other issues regarding early Hebrew history, the question of the Hebrew occupation of Canaan is likely to remain an unsettled issue for some time to come. Some general points of agreement in these three models, however, may summarize the scholarly consensus on the issue.

First, Israel emerged from a melting pot of peoples who occupied Palestine in the thirteenth century B.C.E. Some of the people who considered themselves a part of Israel were remnants of the traditional twelve tribes who had not migrated to Egypt, while others were likely members of Canaanite society or wandering Khapiru who aligned themselves with the emerging Israelites.

Second, the Joshua or Exodus group played a crucial role in the emergence of Israel. They brought with them the traditions of the Exodus and the Sinai covenant, and their Yahwism served as a unifying element for the emerging tribal league.

Third, Israel initially occupied the Central Highlands, leaving for later conquest the fortified cities of the plains and valleys. They did not at any time during the two-hundred-year period of settlement completely dominate the land they occupied.

TRIBAL LIFE AND LEADERSHIP

The development of a unified group of tribes called "Israel" spanned most of the period of the judges. The relationships of tribes and groups of tribes were slowly worked out against the background of the tradition that traced each tribe back to one of the twelve sons of Jacob, whose name was changed to Israel. When and how the tribes arose in ancient Israel is not clear. The number of Israel's tribes probably varied from time to time during the period. But the number twelve became fixed in the memory of Israel, even when the existence of twelve Israelite tribes was no longer a historical reality.

Reconstruction of the precise political relationship among the Hebrew tribes during the period of the judges is difficult. The older and once widely accepted interpretation held that Israel was organized into a religious confederacy called an amphictyony (comparable to the amphictyonies that existed among the Greeks). Recent scholarship has challenged this view, charging that it fails to deal with the ambiguity of the biblical evidence about tribal interrelations or the inherent differences between the Hebrew and Greek societies. This does not mean that there was no cooperative alliance through which the Israelite tribes expressed their common allegiance to Yahweh or united in defensive actions. Rather, the Hebrew tribes were bound together in a loose confederacy that allowed the fullest possible autonomy to the separate tribes, but one that also nurtured a common Israelite identity.

Hebrew society in this loosely organized confederacy consisted of three basic social units: the family, the clan, and the tribe. The extended family, which in the Hebrew Bible is called a "father's house," was the basic residential and productive unit within the social structure. Typically the family consisted of several generations (the patriarch, his wife or wives, their married sons and wives, their married grandsons and wives, unmarried children, and grandchildren) and various related figures (uncles, aunts, cousins) as well as slaves and long-term visitors. This extended family generally would have dwelt close together, with some larger families having their own settlement or village. The family was also the basic unit in economic matters such as the ownership of property, cultivation of land, and care of domestic animals.

Groups of extended families made up a clan, which occupied a village or several villages within a larger settlement and which provided support and protection to the member families. Government and the administration of justice in the clans were normally in the hands of elders, themselves the heads of families. Their prominence and position depended not on election but on social status, wealth, and prestige.

Tribes were corporate expressions of extended families and clans and were the basis for membership in the larger entity, Israel. A person could not claim identification with Israel unless he or she held membership in an individual tribe. Tribal divisions tended to be more vague and fluid. The tribes were changing entities; sometimes a union of formerly separate tribes occurred, and at other times tribes divided. This accounts for the variations in the tribal listings in the Scriptures, which variously list six, ten, eleven, and twelve tribes as composing Israel.

During the period of settlement the tribes slowly aligned themselves into two groups that were distinguished primarily by their geographical location. The northern group of tribes came to be designated as the "house of Israel," and the southern group of tribes became known as the "house of Judah." These alignments are reflected in the titles given later to northern and southern regions within Canaan and eventually to the two Hebrew kingdoms after the division of the United Monarchy.

A major feature of Hebrew tribal life in the twelfth and eleventh centuries was the important role given to certain tribal heroes called judges, from which title is derived the historical designation of this period of Israelite history. These leaders of the Hebrew tribes are the subject of much of the book of Judges (2:6–16:31). Six of these figures receive a more detailed treatment and are commonly referred to as the major judges: Othniel (3:7-11), Ehud (3:12-30), Deborah (4:1–5:31), Gideon (6:1–8:35), Jephthah (10:6–12:7), and Samson (13:1–16:31). The so-called minor judges receive little attention and are only briefly mentioned: Shamgar (3:31), Tola and Jair (10:1-5), and Ibzan, Elon, and Abdon (12:8-15).

Israel's judges were primarily military leaders or tribal heroes who arose in times of crisis to deliver their people from the hands of enemy oppressors. They derived their authority from their charismatic personalities and leadership skills rather than from hereditary succession or election. The English word "judge" fails to bring out the meaning encompassed in the Hebrew term *shophet* (from the verb *shaphat*, meaning to "judge," "justify," or "deliver"). A *shophet*, as the title is used in the Hebrew Bible, is not primarily an objective legal arbitrator, though he or she might serve in that capacity. Rather, a *shophet* is one who defends a just or right cause, whether as someone who hears cases and renders judgments or as a military leader who delivers an oppressed people. In either case the result is the same: the judge protects the just parties, punishes offenders, and restores the right order of things.

Accounts of the judges provide some of the best examples of storytelling in the Hebrew Bible. The basic format of the stories is simple: Israel sins against Yahweh and suffers oppression from a non-Israelite foe; a charismatic person is endowed with the blessing of Yahweh; this favored judge rallies one or more tribes into Yahweh's battle; Yahweh delivers the Israelites from their enemies. The stories of Jephthah's battle against the Ammonites (Judg. 10:6–12:7) and Gideon's victory over the Midianites (Judg. 6–8) follow this familiar pattern.

Of the several stories about these heroes of Israel's past, the story of Deborah, the only woman judge mentioned in the biblical narrative, is one of the most unusual. The Deborah story is told in two versions, the Song of Deborah (Judg. 5), one of the oldest examples of poetry in the Hebrew Bible, and a prose account (Judg. 4) that was written considerably later than the poem. Although there are several differences between the two accounts, in both texts a crisis occurs because "the Israelites again did what was evil in the sight of the LORD" (4.1). God then delivered them into the hands of their enemies, who "oppressed the Israelites cruelly twenty years" (4:3). The focus of the story is upon Deborah and the Israelite general Barak, who battle the Canaanite forces and deliver Israel from the enemy.

The Song of Deborah is a masterpiece of ancient poetry. To read it, even in English translation, is to experience the power of its verse to convey the heat of battle and the divine support of the Hebrew cause:

> The kings came, they fought;
> > then fought the kings of Canaan,
> at Ta'anach, by the waters of Megiddo;
> > they got no spoils of silver.
> The stars fought from heaven,
> > from their courses they fought against Sisera.
> The torrent Kishon swept them away,
> > the onrushing torrent, the torrent Kishon.
> March on, my soul, with might! (Judg. 5:19-21)

The waters of the Kishon River, which flowed through the Esdraelon Valley, were apparently swollen from heavy rains. With his chariots bogged down in the mud, Sisera lost a prime military advantage over the Hebrew army and Deborah and Barak were victorious. The Israelites' decisive ally, however, is shown to be Yahweh, who figuratively fights from heaven through the stars. Like all the stories about the judges, this story expresses the familiar pattern: the Hebrews turn away from Yahweh and fall into the hands of their enemies, and Yahweh raises up a judge (Deborah) to deliver them.

One of the best-known stories of a Hebrew judge is that of Samson, whose enemy was the Philistines. In the Samson story a collection of tales presents the heroic deeds of a man of deep passions and wild appetites. The hero is a mighty warrior who kills Philistines with the jawbone of a donkey (Judg. 15:10-17) and burns their fields by using foxes with torches tied to their tails (Judg. 15:4-5). Samson's fatal weakness, however, is Philistine women, especially Delilah, who betrays him and brings him to a tragic end (Judg. 16).

The Samson narrative is not the typical story of a judge who rallies tribes to fight an enemy, but the story of one man's largely personal vendettas against the Philistines. Nonetheless, in the biblical narrative it is always "the Spirit of the LORD" who empowers Samson.

THE DIVINE-HUMAN ENCOUNTER IN THE ERA OF THE JUDGES

Through their loyalty to the judges and their covenant ceremonies, the Hebrews affirmed their tribal unity and their commitment to the Exodus faith. Yet the ideal was not always realized, either in political unity or in religious fidelity. In their continuing effort to understand the divine-human encounter, the Israelites faced two particularly threatening problems, which together set the context in which Hebrew religion developed during the period of the judges.

Figure 6.3. The circular stone structure at the ruins of Megiddo is a Canaanite altar dating back to approximately 2600 B.C.E. Other sacred buildings stood nearby. *(Photograph by Clyde E. Fant)*

The first challenge facing the Hebrews was the necessity of establishing an agricultural lifestyle. The Hebrew tribes came out of a desert background in which a pastoral economy was required. Their ancestry was essentially that of wanderers who had moved about the Sinai peninsula seeking seasonal pasturage for their flocks and herds. If they were to claim the land they believed Yahweh had granted to their ancestors, they had to adapt to the life of farming.

This changing economic basis of Hebrew life precipitated a second challenge—that of preserving their Yahwistic faith from the threat of syncretism with the fertility religion of Canaan. Much has been learned about Canaanite religion from the Ras Shamra texts that were found on clay tablets dating from the fourteenth century B.C.E. at the site of the old Canaanite city of Ugarit on the north Syrian coast.

Canaanite religion centered on the cycles of nature and the sexual pairing of the major gods and goddesses. The pantheon of deities was headed by *El*, the father of the gods and ruler of the sky. El's female counterpart was Asherah, the mother of the gods. Baal, one of the many offspring of El and Asherah, was the god of storm and fertility. He was portrayed as a bull and represented by a standing stone. His female consort was Anath, the warrior goddess who was given to violent sexual passion.

Baal was the most significant figure in this Canaanite pantheon and is mentioned often in the Hebrew Bible. The mythological basis of the religion was the story of the death and resurrection of Baal. Baal is killed by Mot, the god of summer drought, and carried to the underworld, after which all life on earth languishes. Then Anath finds Mot and kills him, and Baal is restored to life. Baal's resurrection is accompanied by a corresponding renewal of nature. The fertility of fields, flocks, and families was thought to depend upon sexual relations between Baal and Anath. Their mating caused the new life of spring to come forth out of the barrenness of winter. This mythology was enacted by devotees of the Baal cult in rites that included ritual prostitution, both male and female. By means of imitative magic, in which the worshipers imitated the actions they desired the gods to perform, they attempted to induce fertility.

The Baal cult was a practical religion for farmers. The people of Canaan believed that the creative cycles of reproduction in the world would cease if proper worship was not offered to Baal. Baal was the lord of the land, the giver of rain, and the sustainer of all life. Since the Israelites were attempting to cope with their new agricultural lifestyle, it is not surprising that they were attracted to this religion of the land. A number of Canaanite religious elements were assimilated into Hebrew faith and culture. For example, some Hebrew parents named their children after Baal (e.g., 1 Chr. 8:34), several Israelite religious celebrations were influenced by Canaanite agricultural festivals (e.g., the Feast of Unleavened Bread, the Feast of Weeks, and the Feast of Booths), and fertility altars and figurines were utilized in some Hebrew households. Some Hebrews, perhaps without consciously abandoning Yahweh, became active participants in the fertility cult. In recent times archaeology has uncovered statuettes of Baal, perhaps kept as good-luck charms, in otherwise orthodox homes of well-to-do Jews in the upper city of Jerusalem, revealing that attachment to the ancient Canaanite god persisted even into first-century Roman times.

The evolution of Yahwism during the period of the judges occurred within this context of pressure to assimilate into an agricultural economy and, simultaneously, the temptation to adopt the gods of the Canaanites. The Deuteronomistic writer presents a view of Yahwism that is contrasted sharply with

Figure 6.4. Anthropoid clay coffin, probably Philistine, from the twelfth century B.C.E., found at Beth-shan in Israel. *(Photograph by Clyde E. Fant)*

the religious beliefs and practices of the Canaanites. In the view of the biblical narrator, Baal worship and Yahwism were incompatible views of the divine-human relationship, despite popular attempts to create a syncretism of the two religions.

The biblical narrator argues that Yahweh, not Baal, is the Lord of history and of the sown land. Baal worshipers encountered the divine through fertility rites in which the gods were controlled in the interest of human well-being. The purpose of the religion was to ensure the fertility of the earth upon which the people were dependent for their existence. The events of nature and human life moved through historical cycles that were dependent upon the performance of fertility rites. On the other hand, the Hebrews believed that history moved in a linear fashion under the direction of Yahweh. They emphasized nonrecurring historical events as the medium of the divine-human encounter. (The Exodus was the most significant of these events in Israel's past.) But this centrality of history for the Hebrews did not mean that Yahweh had no control over the forces of nature. Yahweh was properly conceived of as Lord of both nature and history. The same God who delivered Israel through the Exodus and the Sinai wilderness was the very source of the natural energies upon which human life depended.

Furthermore, according to the Deuteronomistic historian, Yahweh's holiness precluded God's identification with male fertility power. Thus, Yahweh's direction of nature could not be attributed to sexual union with a female consort. As the God who transcends the human world, Yahweh, for the Hebrews, was

Figure 6.5. The Gezer calendar, dating from the tenth century B.C.E., is an agricultural calendar describing the ancient months by their harvests. (*Photograph by Mitchell G. Reddish*)

beyond sexuality. Nevertheless, archaeological discoveries of figures of consorts to Yahweh in Arad and elsewhere indicate that deviation from this orthodox view occurred in some areas.

Finally, Yahwism in the period of the judges is always presented against the background of the Exodus experience and the giving of the covenant. For the biblical writer, the ethical demands of the Sinai covenant prohibited sacred prostitution. There was no proper place in the worship of Yahweh for sexual rites designed to coerce fertility.

Although some of these features of Yahwism may have been characteristic of Hebrew religion during the period of the judges, much of this view has been superimposed on the Judges narratives by the Deuteronomistic writer. The challenge facing the student of Hebrew history is to discern the actual features of the religious tradition as it existed in the period of the settlement. Given the idealistic views of the compilers of the Deuteronomistic history, we can say four things about the nature of Hebrew religion during the period of the settlement.

First, it is evident that there was considerable continuity between the religion of the Israelite tribes and the Canaanite population. Some of the individual narratives in Judges reflect a general religious and cultic situation that is different from the overall interpretation presented by the Deuteronomistic history. An example is the story of Gideon, Jerubbaal, and Abimelech found in Judges 6–9. In this complex narrative there are numerous instances in which features of Baal worship were combined with Yahwism, indicating that the popular syncretism was extensive.

Second, although Yahwistic religion played a significant role among the people, the spread of Yahwism among the tribal groups was probably a gradual phenomenon that would have resulted in local forms of Yahwism varying from place to place. There appears to have been nothing like a uniform religious faith that demanded the allegiance of all the tribes to the exclusion of other forms of faith and worship.

Third, perhaps the most noticeable characteristic of Yahwism during the period of the judges was its militant nature. Most of the Judges narratives point to a strong connection between Yahweh and warfare. The stories suggest that it was during warfare that the tribes joined together in a common cause that transcended local interest. It may have been primarily in connection with Israel's wars that Yahweh gained status as the national god rather than the god of part of Israel. During times of peace some portions of the tribes may have depended heavily upon Baal worship to ensure fertility, but when they came together to wage war against their common enemies they turned to Yahweh, the divine warrior who could provide victory. The Song of Deborah in Judges 5 is typical of the Hebrews' praise of Yahweh as a divine warrior who could be counted on to intervene on behalf of his followers.

Fourth, there were numerous shrines and altars scattered among the Israelite tribes. Some of these cultic centers, such as those at Shechem, Shiloh, Hebron, and Beer-sheba, were obviously more important than others. At these central shrines, tribal groups would gather regularly to observe cultic rites that at times were syncretistic with the surrounding religions and at other times were distinctively Yahwistic. The Yahwistic rites centered upon the observation of the ancient festivals of Passover, Weeks, and Tabernacles. The most important aspect of these festivals was a ceremony of covenant renewal. The key features of this ceremony were a recitation of Yahweh's great acts on behalf of the Hebrews and a reaffirmation of allegiance to the God of the Exodus. Sacred history was reenacted, relived, and made equally binding upon each generation to which it was presented. This is made clear in the Deuteronomistic introduction to the Decalogue: "The LORD our God made a covenant with us at Horeb. Not with our ancestors did the LORD make this covenant, but with us, who are all of us here alive this day" (Deut. 5:2-3).

For the Deuteronomistic editor, the covenant ceremony at Shechem described in Joshua 24 is the clearest cultic expression of this covenant faith: "Joshua gathered all the tribes of Israel to Shechem . . . and they presented themselves before God" (24:1). Joshua then reminded the gathered tribes of all that Yahweh had done for them in the past, beginning with the promise given to Abraham. The speech concludes with an appeal to "therefore revere the LORD, and serve him in sincerity and in faithfulness" (24:14). The Shechem ceremony, although presented in the text as a singular event, most likely reflects a recurring ritual whereby the Israelite tribes reaffirmed and renewed the covenant, perhaps on a regular basis. Furthermore, the ceremony was more than just a renewal rite for the Joshua tribes. It was also a call for those who had not shared in the Exodus experience to make that tradition their own through personal choice. Joshua challenged them to give up the Canaanite gods and take their stand with the God who had provided the deliverance from bondage in Egypt. This call to forsake false gods and to renew the covenant with Yahweh was repeated over and over during the period of the judges and constitutes significant evidence of the gradual adoption of Yahwism by the Hebrew tribes.

During the period of the settlement the Hebrew understanding of the divine-human encounter established in the Mosaic covenant was placed in great jeopardy. Was prosperity in the Promised Land best assured by the fertility rites of nature worship or in relation to the Lord of history? This crucial question was not answered easily or quickly. The true strength of Yahwism was tested over many generations during the settlement of the Promised Land. Nevertheless, under the pressure to adapt to a new style of life in Canaan, and in the presence of a seemingly successful fertility religion, Yahwism not only survived but increasingly became the most powerful force of unification for the Hebrew tribes.

Chapter 7

THE UNITED KINGDOM AND THE YAHWISTIC HISTORY

Suggested Biblical Readings: 1 Samuel 8–10; 18:1-16; 31; 2 Samuel 7; 11:1–12:25; Genesis 1–3; 6:5–9:17; 11:1-9

The term "United Kingdom" is commonly used to describe the beginning of Israel's monarchy, but in many ways the term is not an apt description of the reigns of Saul, David, and Solomon (ca. 1020–922 B.C.E.). The unity of the nation was surely loose under Saul, and David faced divisions and insurrections within his young empire. Even the reign of Solomon was really a rule over two small states, Judah in the south and Israel in the north. In spite of the kingdom's complex administrative districts and its relative stability, which was enforced through Solomon's ruthless purges of enemies, these two states were never really united. The pressures that eventually would split this "United Kingdom" were never absent from these Israelite monarchies.

An important account of the earliest experiences of Israel, traditionally known as the Yahwistic history, has been dated to this period. For that reason, we will examine its composition and message in this chapter also.

THE DESIRE FOR A KING

The transformation of the tribes of Israel into an international power represents an epochal movement in the life of the nation. Some of Israel's historians viewed it as a "Golden Age"; others saw it as a rejection of Yahweh's intended theocracy (government by God). In any case, the days of sporadic leadership by charismatic leaders such as Deborah or Gideon came to an end, replaced by all the strengths and weaknesses of monarchy. What was responsible for this remarkable change?

The Philistine Threat

In the biblical accounts, only the increasing threat of Philistine domination is presented as the reason for the Israelites' demand for a king. It is likely, however, that there was another agenda behind this demand. The desire of the emerging upper classes for a strong central government to guard their holdings was the real drive toward monarchy. In any case, the military prowess of the Philistines provided a convincing argument for a king. The Philistines had established a confederation of five cities on the southern Coastal Plain: Gaza, Ashkelon, Gath, Ekron, and Ashdod. But their territorial goals plainly did not stop there. In one smashing defeat of the Hebrews after another, the Philistines manifested their superiority in war and threatened to overrun the Central Highlands.

Never was this danger more evident than in the battle at Aphek. Using their superior war implements of bronze and iron, the Philistines routed the Israelites and "killed about four thousand men on the field of battle" (1 Sam. 4:2). In desperation the Israelites carried the Ark, symbol of the presence of Yahweh, into battle. At first the Philistines cried out in fear and the Israelite soldiers shouted for joy. But the Philistines rallied, and the Israelites again were defeated; worse yet, the Ark was captured, an unimaginable catastrophe. (Its loss would be attributed to the corruption of the priesthood at Shiloh, where the Ark had been kept [1 Sam. 2:12-17]. The Philistines kept the Ark for seven months but finally returned it after a series of calamities fell upon their cities.) When Eli, priest at Shiloh and mentor of Samuel, learned of the loss of the Ark and the death of his two sons in battle, he collapsed, breaking his neck, and died (1 Sam. 4). His daughter-in-law, who gave birth to a son during this time, named the boy Ichabod ("the glory has departed").

Then the Philistines pushed farther inland, seizing more of the Central Highlands. They also prohibited the Israelites from making weapons (1 Sam. 13:19-22). The use of iron was just beginning in Palestine; bronze was the chief metal in use until approximately 1200 B.C.E. (The Philistines apparently learned the art of smelting and forging iron from the Hittites of Asia Minor, who had developed this technology around 1400 B.C.E.) Their superior weaponry, as well as their more unified organization, allowed the Philistines to threaten all of the territory inhabited by the Israelites. The power figures in Israel seized this situation as an opportune moment to press their desire for a king.

A Favorable International Situation

The international situation, though not prominent in the biblical record, played a vital role in the establishment of the monarchy in Israel. Obviously no such development would have been possible if the Israelites had been under the domination of their usually powerful neighbors. But at this time in the history of the ancient Near East, no nations were strong enough to prevent the rise of a kingdom in Israel.

Egypt, Israel's old foe to the south, held nominal control of Canaan. Around 1175 B.C.E., Ramesses III defeated an attempted invasion of Egypt by the "Sea Peoples," who were invaders from the Aegean Sea and its islands. (The

Philistines were one of the tribes of the Sea Peoples.) The Philistines then settled along a narrow strip of the southern coast of Canaan. But the Egyptians were not as strong as they seemed nor were the Philistines weak. Both historical records and archaeological finds reveal that the Philistines were anything but crushed. Furthermore, in the Twentieth Dynasty of Egypt (ca. 1150 B.C.E.), twenty-five years after Ramesses's victory, Egypt was torn by internal dissent and sank into impotence for some four centuries. One of the later pharaohs even gave one of his daughters in marriage to Solomon, an act that earlier would have been unthinkable for such a powerful state.

To the north, as well, no nation was positioned to control the Israelite expansion. In the thirteenth century B.C.E. when the Sea Peoples left their homelands and attacked civilizations farther east, they defeated the Syrian kings and ended their threat to Palestine. The Assyrians, who earlier had overrun the Hurrians, were no longer strong enough to pose a threat. After the reign of Tiglath-pileser I (1114–1076 B.C.E.), it was not until the ninth century that the Assyrians were again a dominant force in the Fertile Crescent.

These favorable international events allowed Israel to devote its attention to internal problems. The threat of the Philistines was used as an excuse to overcome ancient objections to a monarchy; it was argued that the older, loosely knit organization of tribes could not cope with so formidable a foe. With no overlord nation to forbid them, Israel sought a king.

Choosing a King: The Role of Samuel

The biblical accounts of the selection of Saul as Israel's first king display the tensions created by this decision. The book of 1 Samuel contains three versions of Samuel's choosing of Saul.

In the first account, Saul appears as a tall, handsome youth searching for his father's lost donkeys. He asks advice of Samuel, a priest and seer, and, as instructed by Yahweh, is privately anointed by him as a "ruler" (perhaps better translated as "military commander"; 1 Sam. 9:1–10:16). In the second tradition, however, both Yahweh and Samuel oppose the demands of the people for a king. Yet Saul, who had hidden himself among the baggage of the camp, is chosen by casting lots and anointed by a reluctant Samuel (1 Sam. 10:17-27). The third account portrays Saul plowing a field, when he is told of a threat to the Transjordanian town of Jabesh-Gilead. The Ammonites had laid siege to the town and cruelly refused to make peace with the men of Jabesh-Gilead unless they suffered the disgrace of having their right eyes gouged out. In desperation Jabesh-Gilead sent out messengers throughout Israel looking for aid. When they reached Gibeah, Saul hacked a yoke of oxen into twelve pieces and sent them by messengers to the tribes, threatening to do the same to their oxen unless they came to the aid of Jabesh-Gilead. Subsequently, Saul won a victory over the Ammonites, rescued the city, and with the agreement of Samuel was proclaimed king at Gilgal (1 Sam. 11–12).

How are these accounts to be understood? It should be remembered that Israel retained an early bias against kingship; Yahweh alone was regarded as ruler of the nation. (This idea later becomes emphatic with the prophets. See Hos. 8:4; 9:15; and Jer. 10:7-10.) Gideon had refused to become king for that reason, saying, "the LORD will rule over you" (Judg. 8:23). This antimonarchical attitude regarded kingship as rejection of God's rule over Israel (1 Sam. 8:7-8). Anti-Saul tendencies are also evident in these accounts. Likewise, the role of Samuel is portrayed from two perspectives. One view, favorable to Samuel (and skeptical of Saul), sees Samuel as a leader of Israel and the last and greatest of the judges (1 Sam. 7:3–8:22). He has the authority to speak for God, particularly to warn of the evils of monarchy (1 Sam. 8:10-18) and even to declare the king unfit if Yahweh so orders (1 Sam. 13:7-14; 15:10-29). The other view, favorable to Saul, presents Samuel as a local seer and priest at a shrine as well as a prophet who endorses Saul as God's choice for king (1 Sam. 9:1–10:16).

It is interesting that Israel never felt a need to harmonize these divergent views, which are particularly obvious in that they occur so close to one another in the text. Apparently in this situation, as in others in the Hebrew Scriptures, Israel was content to let each account stand with its own witness to the meaning of these events as the various traditions interpreted them.

Although there are conflicting interpretations of these sources, several conclusions appear warranted from the narratives:

1. The early Israelites regarded themselves as "the people of God," not one of the "nations." ("Nations" likely refers to city-states in Palestine during the period of conquest [1 Sam. 8:19-20].) As such, they considered God alone to be sovereign.
2. The Philistine threat was used as an excuse to overcome Israel's ancient objections to monarchy.
3. Some Israelites regarded the movement toward monarchy as a rejection of Yahweh and a mere desire to "be like other nations."
4. Nonetheless, Saul was chosen: first, likely, as a military commander (a warlord, in effect) and later as a king.
5. Samuel anointed Saul. Those who favored Saul and his tradition saw Samuel as God's agent in this process. Those who opposed Saul and/or kingship, and those who later favored David, his successor, emphasized the reluctance of Samuel.
6. Samuel emerged as a king-maker and king-breaker. His triumph in these narratives is the result of the triumph of the conservative forces of the Shiloh priesthood.

7. Under the heavy hand of Solomon, David's successor, the negative aspects of kingship were keenly felt by Israel. These negative perceptions of monarchy likely were retrojected upon Saul as a rival of David so that later judgments of his reign were unduly harsh.

THE FIRST KINGS: SAUL AND DAVID

As is apparent from the traditions of Samuel and Saul, the story of the early monarchies is complicated by the differing views of its interpreters. Likewise, the story of the reign of Saul is indissolubly linked with the rise of David. The tension between these two powerful leaders energizes the narrative and provides the drama that made it a classic story in Israel's self-understanding.

Saul: Charismatic Leader

Like the judges before him, Saul emerged as a charismatic figure in a time of crisis. Prior to his military triumph at Jabesh-Gilead, "the spirit of God came upon Saul in power" (1 Sam. 11:6), a familiar formula in the stories of the judges. Also like the judges, Saul functioned as a commander in battle, a warlord. His was not the elegant, sophisticated court of King Solomon. The rough-hewn pile of rocks unearthed by archaeology at Gibeah that may have served as Saul's "palace"/fortress—little more than a wall with a corner tower and a modest building—bears little resemblance to the later luxurious structures of Solomon in Jerusalem.

Saul's task was to battle a superior foe, the Philistines, and to drive them back to the sea. Only someone with great courage would have undertaken to defeat an army with superior experience, organization, and weaponry. But with "the spirit of God upon him," Saul moved against the Philistines. He was assisted by his cousin Abner, his son Jonathan, and whatever men he could recruit: "and when Saul saw any strong or valiant warrior, he took him into his service" (1 Sam. 14:52). Saul never seemed to have a large army. On one occasion he was said to have six hundred men (1 Sam. 13:15), probably a realistic estimate of the size of his army. In any case, the narrative places great emphasis upon the courage of the Israelites and the providence of God.

Saul won a major victory at Michmash (1 Sam. 13:5–14:46), but he was never able to win a complete victory over the Philistines. Apparently he was successful in stemming their advance and in regaining control of the Central Highlands. He also brought the tribes together in closer unity and won further victories against Moab, Edom, and the Amalekites. In spite of his accomplishments, however, he is depicted by the biblical writers as a failure. (Even in the New Testament, in the eleventh chapter of Hebrews, Saul is not listed in the heroic descriptions of God's faithful.)

Saul's rejection by God is described variously in two accounts. In one account (1 Sam. 13:8-15) Saul is said to have been rejected because he, not Samuel, offered a sacrifice (but later both David and Solomon did so [2 Sam. 6:12-19; 1 Kings 3:15]). In the principal account, however, his rejection is attributed to the fact that Saul did not "destroy utterly" all of the Amalekites, who were an especially hated enemy since they were the first to attack the Israelites in the wilderness after their escape from Egypt. "To destroy utterly" *(herem)* meant to kill all the enemy and their flocks, taking no spoils of war but "dedicating" them to God. But since Saul kept the best of the flocks—he said they were to be an offering to God—and spared Agag the king, the narrative says that God rejected Saul. Samuel, however, "hewed Agag in pieces before the Lord in Gilgal" (1 Sam. 15:33). The Amalekites proved to be a troublesome enemy for David and that was not forgotten in the principal account of Saul's rejection (likely written during the latter part of the United Kingdom period), since they were blamed for his downfall.

The tragic end to Saul's life came upon the battlefield against the Philistines. Three of his sons were killed, and in the fierce fighting Saul was badly wounded by archers. Saul asked his armor-bearer to kill him lest the Philistines find him helpless and "make sport" of him. When the armor-bearer refused in fear

Figure 7.1. Ruins at Beth-shan. In the background is the tell, or mound, containing the ruins of several ancient cities built on the site. (The ruins in the foreground are from the Hellenistic and Roman eras when the city was known as Scythopolis.) The Philistines hung the bodies of Saul and his sons on the city wall of Beth-shan (2 Sam. 31:8-12). *(Photograph by Mitchell G. Reddish)*

of God, Saul fell upon his own sword and died. The Philistines then cut off his head, stripped him of his armor, and nailed his body to the city wall of Beth-Shan. But, in a poignant note, the men of Jabesh-Gilead—the city Saul rescued at the very beginning of his career—courageously traveled all night and took the bodies of Saul and his sons from the wall and buried them with honor in Jabesh (1 Sam. 31:8-13). This narrative makes it clear that not everyone in Israel held Saul's memory in low esteem.

The Glory of David

As dark as the story of Saul is, the rising star of David looks even brighter by contrast. From the beginning David is portrayed as a hero. It is important to remember that much of this source material was produced as an apologetic for David—that is, to justify some of David's more questionable actions. Nonetheless, as we shall see, these accounts describe David with surprising candor.

Little is known about David's beginnings other than that he was the youngest of eight sons of Jesse of Bethlehem (1 Chr. 2:13-15; 1 Sam. 16:8-11). His initial encounter with Saul is obscure. As in the stories of the anointing of Saul, three main accounts are given of David's introduction to the court of the king:

1. One tradition shows Samuel, at Yahweh's direction, choosing David as Saul's successor while Saul was still living (1 Sam. 16:1-13).
2. Another tradition says that David was a musician skilled with the lyre who was brought to Saul's court to soothe his fierce rages and dark depressions (1 Sam. 16:14-23).
3. The famous story of the slaying of Goliath, a giant warrior of the Philistines, by the "youth" David locates the first meeting of Saul and David upon the field of battle (1 Sam. 17). Additional references describe David as an experienced warrior who served as Saul's armor-bearer (1 Sam. 16:21) and as captain of Saul's bodyguard (1 Sam. 22:14).

It is likely that each of these texts incorporates part of the extensive tradition that surrounded such a dynamic figure as David: skilled musician and writer of psalms, brave youth devoted to Yahweh worship from childhood, courageous and crafty soldier. All of these elements are to be found in the narratives of David's long and remarkable career. But in the story of David, as in the stories of all the notable persons in Hebrew Scripture, the ultimate focus is not upon the biography of the person but upon the God of Israel and the understanding of Yahweh revealed by those narratives.

Once David is established in Saul's court, three events lead him to the throne of Israel: he becomes the closest friend of Jonathan, Saul's son; he is named commander-of-a-thousand and is adored by the populace, who chant, "Saul has killed his thousands, and David his ten thousands" (1 Sam. 18:7); and he marries Michal, Saul's daughter (1 Sam. 18:20-27). Each of these events dramatically elevated David's prominence in Israel. But they also increased Saul's paranoia and jealousy toward David concerning David's designs on the throne (whether real or imagined). The expected rift was not long in coming. After Saul made attempts on his life, David fled the court into the wilderness of Judah, where he became the leader of a band of fugitives like himself.

In the eyes of the court of Saul, David was an outlaw. But he was regarded quite differently by others. Like Robin Hood of English tradition, David and his band of men (who were likely not "merry") lived off the wealth of the land. First Samuel 22:2 describes them: "Everyone who was in distress, and everyone who was in debt, and everyone who was discontented gathered to him; and he became captain over them." They also shared their loot—if not directly with the poor, at least with the elders of Judah (1 Sam. 30:26-31). David thereby endeared himself to the leaders in the south. His generosity was much more, however, than a simple payoff to the village leaders. The power of the chiefs of such bands as David's depended upon redistribution of captured wealth to the people who sheltered and supported them. The more they gave, the more they got in manpower, services, and general goodwill. As more fighters joined them, more wealth could be seized and distributed. The chief thus gained a larger army; David was said to have four hundred men (at one point, Saul only had six hundred men in his "national" army). David's skill as a raider/warrior would not escape the notice of the nation, either. The days of his coronation were not far away.

David also represented to the common person something closer to the heart: he was one of them, not a descendant of the royal family. Furthermore, with his band in the wilderness, he was a classic example of a Habiru chieftain. He led a group of outsiders, those on the fringes of society who had escaped or been driven out from the inner circles of society. Israel obviously remembered its own wilderness days, and its sympathy was so great that even David's stint as a mercenary with the Philistines—at the very time Saul was killed in battle, although the Philistines had not insisted on David's presence in that battle—was recorded without prejudice. Additionally, among David's followers were Abiathar (a descendant of Eli the priest) and Gad the prophet. The presence of these religious figures signals a different note in the makeup of David's group. This band was not simply a gang of malcontents; it was a group representing the true heritage of Israel—free, daring, and faithful to Yahweh. David's strong commitment to Yahwism was thereby underscored again.

Following the death of Saul, David moved his family and followers to Hebron in Judah and there was crowned king of Judah (2 Sam. 2:2-4).

Meanwhile, in the north, Ishbosheth (also called Ishbaal), son of Saul, was made king of Israel. These actions made final a situation that had long existed: Judah and Israel were two separate states. David, plainly desirous of unifying both states under himself, quickly moved to solidify his strength in Israel. He made contact with Jabesh-Gilead in the Transjordan, hoping to bring those previous supporters of Saul to his side. Ishbosheth was angered, and fighting raged between the two sides for about two years. Ishbosheth was subsequently assassinated, and though David clearly had much to gain from his death, it never was attributed to his instigation.

Israel then moved to join David, and David made a covenant with the elders of Israel at Hebron, where "they anointed David king over Israel" (2 Sam.

Figure 7.2. This stepped structure in Jerusalem was part of the city during the time of David. *(Photograph by Mitchell G. Reddish)*

5:3). Although David was king of both Israel and Judah, he was king of *each*; Israel and Judah remained separate states. (Apparently this separation continued even under Solomon.) Nonetheless, the Philistines could not ignore the threat of this union, and they struck twice against the central hill country but were defeated both times. With these defeats, their effort to expand westward across Palestine ended.

David next attacked Mount Jebus, home of the Jebusites, a Canaanite stronghold that had never been taken, and there established Jerusalem as his new capital city. In another shrewd decision, he then had the Ark moved to this "City of David," which made Jerusalem the united religious center of Yahwism for both Israel and Judah. Furthermore, to ensure that none of the descendants of Saul would threaten his reign, David allowed the Gibeonites to take vengeance on Saul's five grandsons and two of his sons. Only the life of one crippled son of Jonathan was spared. With his hold on Israel and Judah solidified, David turned his attention toward the competing nations to the east. First, the remaining Canaanite city-states were incorporated into the empire. Then, in a series of battles, David won victories over the Transjordanian states of Moab, Edom, and Ammon. The Ammonites were supported by powerful Aramean (later Syrian) forces to the north, but David also defeated them and stationed troops in Damascus. His kingdom then extended from the Red Sea in the south to the "Great Bend of the Euphrates" in the north. By controlling the major trade routes, David enormously enriched the national treasury (which principally benefited the court and its powerful patrons).

Directing this far-flung empire required much more bureaucracy than the simple family court that was used under Saul. Complex political, military, and religious units were established, some of them almost exact duplicates of Egyptian systems. Centralization was foremost in David's administrative plans and required at least two programs that were vigorously opposed: a census of the people (likely for purposes of taxation and conscription) and the building of a central temple in Jerusalem. The first of these projects was accomplished, accompanied by much complaint. But building the temple remained for Solomon's day. Only a site was purchased and an altar erected upon it during the time of David (2 Sam. 24:18).

David's Domestic Problems

David's success in consolidating an empire was far greater than his success in unifying his own family. A hallmark of this portion of the biblical narrative is its unblinking focus on the story of David's domestic intrigues. Perhaps the full humanity of this classic figure in Israel's history drew him even closer to his people, in spite of some of his treacherous conduct.

From the beginning David had engaged in multiple political marriages to strengthen bonds between himself and needed allies. In time, however, that sword cut both ways as his wives and offspring contended for political advantages of their own. Central to these intrigues was David's affair with Bathsheba, wife of Uriah, a Hittite who was away in David's army: "It happened, late one afternoon, when David rose from his couch and was walking about on the roof of the king's house, that he saw from the roof a woman bathing; the woman was very beautiful" (2 Sam. 11:2). David brought Bathsheba into his palace and she subsequently became pregnant. He then ordered her husband home from the battlefield so that it might appear that he had fathered the child. But Uriah frustrated David's plan by refusing to break the tradition that required sexual abstinence during warfare. Even after David had gotten Uriah drunk, he still slept outside with the servants (2 Sam. 11:6-13). David then sent Uriah back to the battlefront with a sealed message that ordered him to be abandoned in the thick of battle, and he was killed. After a period of mourning, Bathsheba became David's wife and gave birth to a son. "But the thing that David had done displeased the Lord" (2 Sam. 11:27).

One of the most dramatic encounters in the Bible follows. Nathan the prophet is sent by God to David, and Nathan tells David a story about two men, one rich and the other poor. The rich man had flocks and herds, "but the poor man had nothing but one little ewe lamb," a pet that he fed from his table and carried in his arms. When a visitor came to the rich man's house, he was unwilling to take one of his own flock for the banquet, so he killed the poor man's lamb. David became enraged: "The man who has done this deserves to die." Nathan then thundered against David, "You are the man!" Because of his sin, Nathan said, God would punish him: "Thus says the LORD: I will raise up trouble against you from within your own house" (2 Sam. 12:1-15).

These words could stand as an epitaph for the last years of David's life. One bitter episode with David's children followed another. The child born to Bathsheba died. David's son Amnon raped Tamar, his half-sister; another son, Absalom, murdered Amnon in revenge. Then Absalom plotted an insurrection against David and was forced to flee for his life. But as he rode under the thick branches of an oak tree, his head was caught in the branches and he was murdered by Joab, the general of David's army, as he hung from the tree. David, however, wept bitterly and cried, "O my son Absalom, my son, my son Absalom! Would I had died instead of you, O Absalom, my son, my son!" (2 Sam. 18:33).

To the end of his life David was never without intrigues and conflicts within his family. He should have been succeeded by his son Adonijah, but Bathsheba persuaded David to make her son Solomon king while David was still living. After forty years on the throne, the aged David died and "Solomon sat on the throne of his father David; and his kingdom was firmly established" (1 Kings 2:12).

THE REIGN OF SOLOMON

David's career was spent in wars to create an empire; Solomon's career was spent in efforts to develop it. First, however, he had to consolidate his hold on the empire by eliminating opposition from Adonijah, David's eldest living son, and his supporters, Joab, captain of the army, and Abiathar the priest (1 Kings 1–2). Once that was achieved, Solomon moved to reorganize the bureaucratic structures of the kingdom. And although no wars troubled his reign, he greatly expanded the military defense of the nation. Trade and commerce also flourished under Solomon, so that his wealth became proverbial; Jesus said that the flowers of the field were so beautiful that not "even Solomon in all his glory" was their equal (Matt. 6:29). His wisdom was just as proverbial (Matt. 12:42). Many of his actions were at best questionable, but he was a shrewd politician and a skilled manager. Solomon was equally renowned as a builder. Besides the construction of the famous Temple in Jerusalem, he also built a royal palace, various public buildings, and fortified walls and cities. Nevertheless, with all his achievements, Israel never remembered Solomon as an enduring inspiration, which was how they remembered David.

The Throne Succession Narrative

These stories of Solomon's rise to power are contained in 2 Samuel 9–20 and 1 Kings 1–2 and sometimes are called the "Succession Narrative" or "Throne Narrative." Although the narrative was previously believed to have been written by a single unbiased author who described the good and bad alike within David's house, both its unity and objectivity have become a matter of scholarly debate. By any standards, however, this account of the events that led to the enthronement of Solomon is truly remarkable.

The final episodes of this narrative describe Solomon's brutal suppression of any threats, real or imagined, to his right to the kingdom. (Even though he is said to be acting on the advice of the dying David, the single-minded brutality and ambition of Solomon is evident.) These events clearly signal the despotic nature of the future rule of Solomon. Israel had gained wealth and power, but it had also gained an absolute monarchy with virtually limitless power over its life. For no matter how flattering the description, the portrait of Solomon nonetheless reveals his tyranny.

Expansion and Change

The national boundaries changed little between the kingdoms of David and Solomon, but internally great changes took place. These developments may be summarized in four areas: governmental organization, military development, trade and commerce, and construction.

Governmental Organization. Solomon appears to have been an able organizer, although overly given to expansion of bureaucracy. He enlarged the royal cabinet, giving it some features common to Egyptian government. The northern part of the kingdom, Israel, was also divided into twelve administrative districts, each with its own governor appointed by the king. Each district was responsible for providing for the expenses of the royal court one month a year. (Judah seems to have been one separate district and exempt from this requirement.) These administrations also looked after general taxation, handled conscription for the military, and possibly recruited workers for the public labor projects.

Military Development. Solomon built extensive passive defenses, such as strategically placed walls and fortified cities (Hazor, Gezer, and Megiddo). Likewise, he modernized the weaponry of the army. Previously chariots had heavy armor and were not extensively used by David; one account mentions one hundred chariots during his reign. The exact number of chariots built by Solomon is unclear, but at least ten times as many—and possibly more—were constructed. He also imported horses from Cilicia. To house and maintain this chariot corps, Solomon built chariot garrisons around the land that contained stables for the horses, as well as barracks for the charioteers and miscellaneous supply buildings.

Trade and Commerce. With the luxury of peace, Solomon broadened trade in all directions. Spice caravans crossed the Arabian Desert. Copper and iron mined in the Arabah were traded in North Africa for such exotic products as gold, peacocks, and apes (perhaps for a royal zoo?). Wheat and olive oil were exchanged in Phoenicia for wood of cedar and pine. The most ambitious of these trading plans involved an agreement between Solomon and Hiram, king of Tyre. Solomon built a seaport and a fleet of ships at Ezion-Geber on the Gulf of Aqabah, an arm of the Red Sea, and the Phoenicians contributed their maritime skills. This joint endeavor expanded trade to North Africa and southwestern Arabia. Solomon's visit from the Queen of Sheba (or Saba, an area of great wealth in southern Arabia) may have involved issues regarding this commerce (1 Kings 10:1-10).

Construction. The Temple of Jerusalem was Solomon's most renowned building accomplishment, but he constructed many other notable buildings. His palace, for example, took thirteen years to build (interestingly, the Temple only took seven years, indicating that the palace was considerably larger). He built other royal buildings, all made with such fine materials as cedar, gold, bronze, and

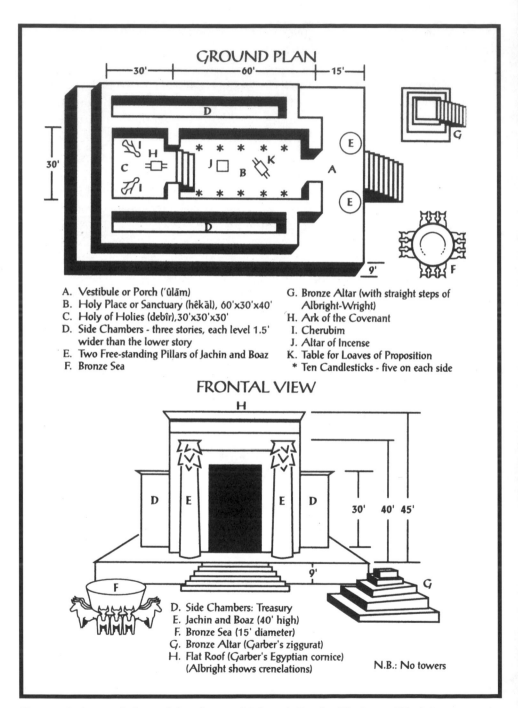

GROUND PLAN

A. Vestibule or Porch ('ûlām)
B. Holy Place or Sanctuary (hêkāl), 60'x30'x40'
C. Holy of Holies (debîr),30'x30'x30'
D. Side Chambers - three stories, each level 1.5' wider than the lower story
E. Two Free-standing Pillars of Jachin and Boaz
F. Bronze Sea

G. Bronze Altar (with straight steps of Albright-Wright)
H. Ark of the Covenant
I. Cherubim
J. Altar of Incense
K. Table for Loaves of Proposition
* Ten Candlesticks - five on each side

FRONTAL VIEW

D. Side Chambers: Treasury
E. Jachin and Boaz (40' high)
F. Bronze Sea (15' diameter)
G. Bronze Altar (Garber's ziggurat)
H. Flat Roof (Garber's Egyptian cornice)
(Albright shows crenelations)

N.B.: No towers

Figure 7.3. A ground plan and frontal view of Solomon's Temple. (*The Jerome Biblical Commentary*, by Brown/Fitzmyer © 1968. Reprinted by permission of Pearson Education, Inc., Upper Saddle River, N.J. 07458.)

cut stone. The construction of military buildings and various fortified cities with casemate walls (parallel walls joined with cross walls for strength and utility) places Solomon among the greatest of ancient builders. But for Israel, nothing compared in significance with the building of the Temple. Solomon's Temple was the first of a succession of temple structures on the same location in Jerusalem. This first Temple was destroyed when Israel fell to the Babylonians in 587 B.C.E. It was rebuilt following the return of the Jewish exiles from Babylon and later elaborately enlarged under Herod the Great (37–4 B.C.E.). Our information about Solomon's Temple comes from 1 Kings 6–8 and 2 Chronicles 2–4. (Whatever archaeological evidence remains of the Temple lies beneath the Dome of the Rock in Jerusalem, a Muslim mosque, where no excavation is permitted.)

The dimensions of Solomon's Temple were more modest than might be imagined. Even so, it was larger than Canaanite and Phoenician temples, which it resembled, that have been discovered. As nearly as can be determined, the Temple was 105 feet long, 35 feet wide, and 52 feet high. On the outside of the Temple in a courtyard stood the "molten sea," an enormous bronze basin fifteen feet across that perhaps symbolized the watery chaos of creation (Gen. 1:6-10) and was used for ceremonial purposes. Across from it stood the great altar on which animal sacrifices were made. The entry door to the Temple was flanked on either side by two freestanding, ornate bronze columns approximately thirty-three feet high and seventeen feet around. The congregation worshiped outside near the altar; the limited size of the Temple suggests that only priests and perhaps the royal family entered the Temple proper.

The Temple consisted of two rooms entered through a "porch" or vestibule that may have had no exterior door or roof, resembling the courtyards of private dwellings in that region. The sides and back of the Temple were surrounded by an adjoining storage building. Once inside the vestibule, the priests entered the central room, or Holy Place, through an elaborate cypress wood door overlaid with gold. This room was sixty feet long and thirty feet wide. It contained a small incense altar, ten golden lampstands, and a table for twelve loaves of "the bread of the presence," an unleavened bread offering.

At the end of the Holy Place a few steps led up to an elevated room with a lower ceiling: the Holiest Place, or Holy of Holies. It was a perfect cube, 30 feet by 30 feet by 30 feet, without windows. Its walls were of cedar and its floor of cypress, as in the Holy Place. In the impressive darkness of this sacred chamber stood two winged cherubim—guardian figures, imaginary animal/human beings associated with deity—fifteen feet tall, made of olive wood overlaid with gold. Beneath their wings stood the Ark of the Covenant. Originally carried about by the Israelites in their wanderings, it contained the tablets of the Law and represented the presence of God. Once in Solomon's Temple, the Ark was regarded as the throne of God.

THEOLOGICAL DEVELOPMENTS DURING THE MONARCHY

The political, social, and economic changes during the United Kingdom were matched by far-reaching developments in Israel's understanding of its relationship to God. Royal theology and Zion theology would alter forever Israel's expectations about God.

Royal Theology (also called "Davidic Theology")

As a theocratic state, Israel needed assurance that God endorsed the perpetual succession of a dynasty of kings. That assurance was provided by the oracles of Nathan to David (2 Sam. 7), which promised David that God would "make you a house [dynasty] . . . and . . . your throne shall be established forever" (2 Sam. 7:11, 16). The "royal psalms" (for example, Pss. 2, 72, 110) used at coronations also associated the reign of the king with the favor of Yahweh. The king was regarded as God's representative; as such, he was the administrator of justice within Israel. Later, messianic anticipations would be attached to his reign so that the future "Golden Age" of Israel, it was promised, would be led by one of the house of David.

Zion Theology

Royal theology assured David that his line would continue forever; Zion theology assured Jerusalem that it would exist forever. (Zion was likely the name for the fortified citadel atop Mount Jebus that comprised the pre-Israelite city of Jerusalem.) Numerous psalms refer to Zion as a holy mountain, as the dwelling place of God, and as the place of God's sanctuary; as such, it was indestructible (Pss. 46, 48, 76). In the New Testament, Zion is referred to as the dwelling place of God (Rev. 14:1).

Obviously royal theology and Zion theology were intertwined in meaning. What these theologies implied for Israel's future—particularly following the division of the empire and the captivity and destruction of Jerusalem—became a matter of ongoing conflict within the later institutions of Judaism.

THE YAHWISTIC HISTORY

One of the major strata in Hebrew Scripture is a lengthy body of material traditionally known as J and dated to the Solomonic era. This source has been identified in Genesis, Exodus, and Numbers (and perhaps in Joshua and Judges, though with much revision).

In an epic story, an unknown author or authors describes Israel's early history from the creation of the world to the entering of Canaan. The writer shows close attachments to both Judah and the court circles in Jerusalem. The once-prevailing belief that J was composed from premonarchical material during Solomon's period (ca. 961–922 B.C.E.) has been strongly challenged, however. Some scholars would not attribute these narratives to a single source, and they would date them to the exilic or postexilic period. Others tend to view J as a theological or editorial processing of earlier traditions over a considerable period of time. In any case, few would deny that much of the material found in J dates to the period of Israel's settlement in Canaan, prior to the monarchy.

The varied experiences of the ancestral period were originally remembered and recited orally: narratives of adventure, of heroes, of dangers met and overcome; songs of triumph, of praise, of mourning; poetic and proverbial expressions of wisdom; and etiologies (for example, the Tower of Babel story explains the origins of different languages). Nor did this oral period end when the literary period began; each continued, side by side. Unquestionably, however, the gradual unifying and centralizing of the tribes that intensified with the monarchy led to a pooling of these early traditions. This eventually resulted in what has been termed "an all-Israelite epic." This epic narrative interpreted Israel's experience from the creation through the wanderings of the ancestors to the settlement and monarchy. Parallel traditions of this epic developed in the north and the south: J presents the emphasis of Judah, in the south; E (for Elohim, the name used for God in this tradition) developed in the north. Eventually these traditions were fused together and united with P, the Priestly version of this epic. Israel saw these traditions, in spite of their clear differences, as enriching each other in presenting the story of the followers of Yahweh.

The themes in J are wide-ranging. Yahweh is portrayed in intensely realistic, anthropomorphic terms (having the characteristics of a human being). As such, the God of J is personal yet clearly different from humankind. In Genesis God walks in the garden of Eden ("plain" or "desert") in the cool of the evening or visits with Abraham at his tent. But this God is no local deity; indeed, J presents a God who is the creator of the entire human race. Most important, J understands the God of creation as the God who called and led Abraham according to a divine promise of blessings and obligations (Gen. 12:1-3). All of the primeval stories (stories of the earliest ages) in J anticipate this event, the participation of Israel in a divine plan for the nations. By emphasizing the theme of "all Israel" in the events of the early ancestral period, J sought to combat the divisiveness that always threatened the nation. The primeval narratives united the universal creation of humankind with the particular calling of one person—Abraham—and, through the promises to his descendants, eventually with a unified people of God: the nation of Israel.

Israel's Primeval Stories

Creation accounts were common in the ancient Near East. Parallels have been drawn between the creation story of the Babylonians (which dates even earlier than the Genesis story), *Enuma Elish*, and the biblical account. There are even closer parallels between the Genesis Flood story and the Gilgamesh epic of the Babylonians, which also has a flood and an "ark," a ship filled with all kinds of animals that finally comes to rest on a mountain. Gilgamesh even includes a raven, dove, and swallow that are sent out to search for land. Like the Hebrews, the Babylonians also attributed extremely long ages to their antediluvian ("before the flood") ancestors. Although it is apparent that the Genesis account draws on primeval tradition and uses a similar vocabulary, the differences in the stories are more striking than the similarities. The Yahwism that informs the Genesis story presents an entirely different view of the divine-human encounter. Unlike the other accounts in which humans are playthings of countless warring gods, the Genesis stories accord dignity to humanity rather than servile subjection, and even Yahweh's judgment is a moral consequence of evil.

From Creation to the Fall

The creation narrative of J (Gen. 2:4*b*–3:24) differs from the account of the Priestly tradition (Gen. 1:1–2:4*a*) in numerous ways. The creation of human beings, not the creation of the universe, is the principal focus of J. The first person (*'adam*, "human") is made from the soil (*'adama*—notice the play on words). But this human is not complete until a second act of creation, when the first woman (*eve*, possibly "life") is created (Gen. 2:23). They both come from one body; they both are animated by the breath of God; they both are drawn to one another as "one flesh"; and they both return to the dust from which they came.

They begin life in a garden, but their disobedience to God (the "fall" of humanity) ends this early paradise. They leave the garden to experience the hardships of toil and pain. Their two sons, Cain and Abel, engage in the first act of violence when Cain becomes jealous of Abel and kills him. In a note often sounded by J, God places a mark on Cain—not a curse, but a sign of gracious protection in spite of his sin. This motif of the God who will not allow wrongdoing but nonetheless cares for humanity is a persistent theme in J. The ancestral period and the monarchy will be marred by disobedience to God's ideal; nevertheless, God provides much more than could have been expected.

Among the multitude of observations that might be made about this creation narrative, one must not be ignored. This story does not focus on a scientific account of the origin of the universe but on the gracious provision of God for humankind. Even as God provided from the beginning, J says, so God

Figure 7.4. The step pyramid at Sakkara, Egypt (near Cairo), built in 2730 B.C.E., is the first pyramid in history. Its construction is similar to the ziggurats of Mesopotamia, although the ziggurats functioned as temples rather than as tombs. (*Photograph by Clyde E. Fant*)

provided through the wanderings of Israel and the stresses of monarchy. Modern readers should not allow issues of no consequence to the purposes of these early narratives to obscure their profound view of God and humanity.

The Flood and the Tower of Babel

Again, these ancient accounts often have been distorted by efforts to impose modern scientific categories upon a prescientific narrative. The message of the Flood story (Gen. 6:5–9:17), which is woven of both J and P materials, is one of penalty for sin and provision by God. In these accounts sin has become so far-reaching that humanity suffers the consequences. Yet God spares some—Noah and his family—along with some animals. Unlike the Babylonian accounts, it is no mere whim of the gods that destroys life (in one account, humankind was making too much noise and the older gods needed sleep!). The moral warning of the Flood in Genesis stands as a sign even to a prideful monarchy of the penalty for wickedness. Yet evil survives the deluge, and the rainbow is taken as a sign that God allows life to continue in spite of sin.

The story of the Tower of Babel, a story without parallels in other Near Eastern accounts, reflects a confrontation with another form of evil, the pride of cosmopolitan states. As people banded together, they grew in pride. To "make a name" for themselves, they sought to build a city with a pyramid-like structure, a *ziggurat* or step-temple, "with its top in the heavens." (The early dwellers in Mesopotamia worshiped the moon god in temples atop such structures.) In this story God then scattered them across the earth and confused their languages. The opposition of many people in the tribes of Israel to the encroachments of monarchy, and perhaps to the imperial ambitions of Solomon in particular, may be reflected in this narrative (Gen. 11:1-9).

Following the primeval stories of Genesis 2–11 lie the ancestral narratives of J, in which God makes of one family a "people." Emphasis is placed upon Abraham and the blessings offered to and through his descendants. Given promise and responsibility in covenant with God, they are the bearers of the purpose of God. Yet at the beginning of the monarchy with Saul and toward its conclusion with Solomon, Israel struggled to find meaning in the transition from a group of wandering tribes to a bureaucratic empire. In that process, Israel's understanding of God underwent far-reaching changes.

The Divine-Human Encounter and the Yahwistic History: A Profound View of God, Humanity, and Creation

The stories of Israel's tribal life were received by J from its earliest oral history and unified into a written interpretation of that life. For J, Yahweh's calling of Israel to be "one nation under God" goes back to creation itself. The scattered tribes and varied worship expressions of early Israel find unity in this all-Israel epic. Likewise, as a player in the international arena, Israel found a higher calling; it could not be God's child alone. Through Abraham and his descendants, it must be a blessing to other nations. In this way J preserved the founding traditions of Israel yet interpreted them to embrace the modern world of David and Solomon.

Nevertheless, this stratum of Pentateuchal literature clearly reflects the tension between the early freedom of the tribes under Yahweh alone and the later bureaucratic regimes of the kings. Apparently a segment of Israel chafed under the often heavy-handed and despotic regimes of the monarchy, particularly that of Solomon, and yearned for the "simpler" days of free tribal life. The early stories of Genesis—the Creation, the Flood, the Tower of Babel—reflect God's judgment on human wrongdoing and prideful, grandiose schemes but also reveal God's persistent love and care of Israel. It has been suggested also that David's sin and God's mercy are reflected in the Adam and Eve story in Eden.

Nonetheless, for J, Yahweh is Israel's God forever—not only a God of the early ancestors and covenant but also a God of the radical changes of monarchy. The excesses of the monarchy, however, stretched that confidence to the breaking point, as we shall see in the chaos of the coming Divided Kingdom.

Chapter 8

THE DIVIDED KINGDOM: ISRAEL AND JUDAH

Suggested Biblical Readings: 1 Kings 1:11–2:12; 11:41–12:20; 2 Kings 17:1-14; 24–25

The United Hebrew Kingdom that David and Solomon had built disintegrated after Solomon's death. The internal unrest that had plagued the latter part of Solomon's reign finally erupted into civil strife that resulted in the creation of two separate Hebrew nations. The Northern Hebrew Kingdom, Israel, existed as an independent nation for approximately two hundred years. Judah, the Southern Kingdom, survived as an independent nation for about 340 years. The fortunes of the two nations were tied both to the internal features of their individual development and to the changing politics within the Fertile Crescent. Although the two kingdoms were separate political entities, their histories are somewhat parallel and interrelated.

THE NATURE OF THE SOURCES

Our knowledge of Hebrew history from Solomon's death in 922 to the fall of Judah in 587 B.C.E. is dependent upon several types of sources: historical narratives, prophetic narratives and messages, and noncanonical records.

Historical Narratives

The Hebrew Bible contains two rather lengthy historical narratives covering the period of the Divided Kingdom. The first narrative, found in 1 Kings 12 through 2 Kings 25, is a portion of the work of the Deuteronomistic historian, completed during the Hebrew Exile in Babylon about 550 B.C.E. In constructing the history of the Divided Kingdom, the Deuteronomistic writer used several sources. Some of these sources are cited in the narrative but are no longer available as individual documents. They include "the Book of the Acts of Solomon" (1 Kings 11:41), "the Book of the Annals of the Kings of Israel" (1 Kings 14:19), and "the Book of the Annals of the Kings of Judah" (1 Kings 14:29). These sources were likely formal annals based on official court records. The Deuteronomistic historian probably also used popular stories about kings and prophets and records of the Temple in Jerusalem.

The other historical narrative that covers this period of Hebrew history, 2 Chronicles 10–36, is a portion of the work of the Chronicler, the name given to the writer/editor of the material in the books of 1 and 2 Chronicles, Ezra, and Nehemiah. Three features of this material render it less useful than the Deuteronomistic narrative: it repeats much of the information found in 1 and 2 Kings; it frequently alters the details of the earlier Deuteronomistic writing to serve specific theological purposes; and it displays an almost exclusive interest in the Southern Kingdom.

Prophetic Narratives and Messages

A second set of sources available to the student of the Divided Kingdom consists of the works of Hebrew prophets. The books of Amos and Hosea illuminate certain aspects of the history of the Northern Kingdom, while Micah, Isaiah, Nahum, Zephaniah, Habakkuk, and Jeremiah do the same for Judah. These texts shed considerable light on the social, economic, political, and religious conditions in Israel and Judah, although they often lack attention to historical details.

Noncanonical Sources

Although references to the Hebrews in noncanonical documents are rare before the end of the tenth century B.C.E., a large number of inscriptions and seals dating from the period of the Divided Kingdom mention them. Moabite, Assyrian, and Babylonian records mention aspects of Israelite and Judean history. These records have been especially helpful in dating certain events mentioned in the biblical texts and in establishing a timeline for the history of the two kingdoms. For example, the first siege of Jerusalem by Nebuchadrezzar, king of Babylon, is described by the Deuteronomistic historian in 2 Kings 24:10-17, but no precise date is given. Noncanonical sources are invaluable in this matter since records from Nebuchadrezzar's archives mention the Babylonian capture of Jerusalem on March 16, 597 B.C.E.

Features of 1 and 2 Kings

Of the various sources available, 1 Kings 12 through 2 Kings 25 is the primary source for our knowledge of the Divided Kingdom. If read with attention to its particular theological emphases, this narrative provides the best basis we have for reconstructing the history of the Divided Kingdom. Four main features characterize this Deuteronomistic narrative.

First, a theological assumption of the Deuteronomistic history provides a

Figure 8.1. The water tunnel at Megiddo, dated to the ninth century B.C.E., was dug through solid rock to allow residents to acquire water without leaving the protection of the city walls. *(Photograph by Clyde E. Fant)*

guiding principle according to which the story of the Divided Kingdom is constructed. This principle (which will be characterized more fully in chapter 11) centered on the belief that faithfulness to the Sinai covenant brought God's

157

blessings upon the Hebrew kingdoms while disobedience to the covenant resulted in national ruin. The history of Israel and Judah in 1 and 2 Kings is interpreted on the basis of this principle.

Second, this history focuses on the Hebrew kings. The historian generally follows a regular pattern in tracing the history of the kingdoms through their kings. Initially, basic facts are given about each king (Israelite and Judean), including the length of reign, battles fought, and certain elements of family history. (This information probably was obtained from the two basic sources of the Deuteronomistic writer, the "Books of the Kings of Israel and Judah.") The king's reign then is evaluated and a judgment of the king is pronounced according to the theological framework of the Deuteronomistic historian.

A good example of the style of reporting of the Deuteronomistic writer appears in the record of the reign of Azariah of Israel in 2 Kings 15:1-7:

> In the twenty-seventh year of King Jeroboam of Israel King Azariah son of Amaziah of Judah began to reign. He was sixteen years old when he began to reign, and he reigned fifty-two years in Jerusalem. His mother's name was Jecoliah of Jerusalem. He did what was right in the sight of the LORD, just as his father Amaziah had done. Nevertheless the high places were not taken away; the people still sacrificed and made offerings on the high places. The LORD struck the king, so that he was leprous to the day of his death, and lived in a separate house. Jotham the king's son was in charge of the palace, governing the people of the land. Now the rest of the acts of Azariah, and all that he did, are they not written in the Book of the Annals of the Kings of Judah? Azariah slept with his ancestors; they buried him with his ancestors in the city of David; his son Jotham succeeded him.

Third, the extent of this documentary of the kings of the Divided Kingdom is relatively brief when compared to the lengthy account of the reigns of David and Solomon earlier in the Deuteronomistic history. The historian's bias toward Judah is evident in that not a single northern king receives a favorable judgment. Indeed, only two Judean kings (other than David and Solomon), Hezekiah and Josiah, are given high praise in the history. These two rulers alone are judged to measure up to the standards of devotion to Yahweh established by the writer of 1 and 2 Kings.

A fourth characteristic of the Deuteronomistic narrative of the Divided Kingdom is its selective coverage of certain historical events believed to illustrate the theological theme of the larger history. That is, interspersed among the chronicles of the kings are treatments of events that were thought by the historian to be particularly demonstrative of the Hebrews' fidelity or infidelity to the covenant. For example, the stories of the fall of the individual kingdoms are told to illustrate Yahweh's judgment upon wayward peoples (2 Kings 17:1-41; 24:18–25:21), and the details of the reform initiated by King Josiah of Judah are given to demonstrate the Yahwistic devotion of the king and his followers (2 Kings 23:1-30). This selective coverage of events left significant gaps in the history written by the Deuteronomistic historian. This is especially true with regard to the history of Israel, in which important kings like Omri receive slight treatment.

THE DIVISION OF THE KINGDOM

Upon the death of Solomon, Rehoboam, his son, became the king of the United Monarchy. According to 1 Kings 12, one of the new king's first acts was to call the northern tribes together at Shechem, the chief town in the northern part of the kingdom. Rehoboam expected to be affirmed as king by the northern tribes at this assembly, but their support was not forthcoming. The northern tribes had felt the brunt of Solomon's heavy-handed policies and requested relief from this oppression. Solomon had required forced labor in his building projects from the ten northern tribes, but not from the two southern tribes to which he and his family belonged. Their leader, Jeroboam, spoke to Rehoboam on their behalf, saying, "Your father made our yoke heavy. Now therefore lighten the hard service of your father and his heavy yoke that he placed on us, and we will serve you" (1 Kings 12:4). After consulting with "the young men who had grown up with him and now attended him" (1 Kings 12:8b), Rehoboam answered the request of the northern tribes: "Now, whereas my father laid on you a heavy yoke, I will add to your yoke. My father disciplined you with whips, but I will discipline you with scorpions" (1 Kings 12:11). When Rehoboam tried to enforce his new policy, the northern tribes withdrew and declared Jeroboam their king, leading to the division of the United Kingdom and further weakening the nation.

Causes of the Division

The breakup of the United Monarchy resulted from at least four causes. First, the Judean-based Davidic dynasty had replaced the Israel-based house of Saul. Some of the pro-Saul elements in the north were unhappy with the idea of Davidic kings and also objected to the notion of a hereditary monarchy. Saul, according to one tradition, had been made king by popular acclaim, and Jeroboam was selected in a similar manner. Apparently some in the northern tribes considered the conditions of oppression under Solomon to be a direct result of the policy of each king being automatically chosen from the same family.

Second, the oppressive policies of Solomon contributed to the breakup of the Hebrew kingdom. Solomon's harsh treatment of his subjects, especially those in the north, was etched deeply into the memory of the Hebrews. The heavy taxation and forced labor he instituted were especially difficult to bear, and the northern tribes complained that they paid double their dues in each of these areas. Solomon's economic and political suffocation of the north alienated that section of the empire from the monarch.

Third, the rising prominence of Jerusalem as a worship center and the consequent deemphasis of northern shrines led to the division. With the completion of the Temple during Solomon's reign, the primacy of Jerusalem as a worship center was established. The Ark of the Covenant, chief symbol of Yahweh's sovereignty over the Hebrews, now resided in the Temple, attended by priests who were under the direct control of the king. This emphasis on Jerusalem as the religious center of Yahwism placed the ancient worship centers in the north (for example, Shechem, Bethel, and Dan) in competition with the Judean capital.

Fourth, Rehoboam proved unable to keep the nation united. When he asserted his intention to bring stricter control to the kingdom and to increase the repressive policies of his father, the pent-up bitterness of the northern tribes burst into revolt.

For approximately two centuries after the end of the United Monarchy, Israel and Judah had a volatile relationship. They became adversaries and sporadic hostility erupted between them. The history of these two Hebrew nations is complex, and the next two sections of this chapter will offer a summary of the main features of that history.

THE NORTHERN KINGDOM (922–722 B.C.E.)

Seemingly conflicting experiences characterized the two-hundred-year history of Israel. On the one hand, Israel enjoyed times of significant national strength and international prestige. On the other hand, internal turbulence and instability plagued the Northern Kingdom. These contrasting aspects of the history of Israel can be illustrated by a treatment of Israel's most significant kings.

Jeroboam I

Israel's first king had served under Solomon's administration as a director of forced labor in the north. When Jeroboam opposed Solomon's policies, Solomon tried to kill him. Jeroboam then escaped to Egypt, where he sought refuge under Pharaoh Shishak. Shishak was the founder of a new dynasty in Egypt and was planning—even at the time of Jeroboam's residence there—an Egyptian offensive against the Palestinian nations. When Jeroboam returned to Israel during the revolt against Rehoboam, the northern tribes chose him as their king.

Jeroboam controlled the territory that had traditionally been occupied by ten of the twelve tribes. These northern tribes were led by the tribe of Ephraim, a name often applied to the Northern Kingdom by the biblical writers. The Deuteronomistic historian speaks of the Northern Kingdom as though it were roughly equal in size and strength to Judah. Actually, Israel emerged as the dominant kingdom in many ways.

For example, Jeroboam's kingdom was considerably larger than the Southern Kingdom, although both kingdoms lost to adversaries some of the territories that had been controlled by David and Solomon, especially in the region of the Transjordan. Israel not only dominated in land size over Judah but was also more strategically located for effective communication and commerce. North-south traffic through Canaan could bypass Judah but not Israel. Also, the plains of Dothan, Sharon, and Jezreel carried east-west trade through Israel. The presence of these trade routes meant that the Northern Kingdom shared in and profited from international commerce.

Jeroboam's kingdom was also militarily stronger than the armies of Judah. For several decades after the creation of the two Hebrew nations, there was intermittent warfare between them. Several times Israel had occasion to demonstrate its military dominance (2 Kings 14:8-14).

If Jeroboam's kingdom was comparatively strong in size, economy, and military strength, it was weaker than Judah in terms of political stability. Nineteen kings from nine different dynasties ruled over Israel during the course of its two hundred-year history, in contrast to the twenty kings of the family of David who reigned in Judah during a period lasting over three hundred years.

Much of the attention given to Jeroboam I by the Deuteronomistic historian concerns the reformation of worship that he instituted. Jeroboam and those who supported him based their reformation on a rejection of the increasing significance of the Jerusalem Temple. Renouncing the Zion theology that had claimed Jerusalem as the special city of Yahweh, Jeroboam proceeded to reform northern worship by reactivating several northern Yahwistic shrines (for example, Bethel and Dan), reviving the Aaronic priesthood, removing much of the authority of the Levites, and developing a new worship calendar. In these ways Jeroboam widened the religious gulf between Israel and Judah and asserted Israel's religious independence.

From the perspective of the Deuteronomistic historian, the renovation of the old northern worship centers and the reputed revival of idol worship at those sites were worthy only of rebuke. At Bethel and Dan, Jeroboam erected golden calves, probably representing thrones upon which the invisible Yahweh resided (1 Kings 12:28-29). Although intended to encourage Yahwism (and perhaps be equated with the Ark of the Covenant in Jerusalem), the calves were viewed by later Hebrew generations as objects of worship that evidenced the syncretism of Baal worship and Yahwism in the Northern Kingdom. As a result, the Deuteronomistic narrator condemned Jeroboam, calling attention to his rejection in words of judgment that came to be cited about each succeeding northern king: "He did what was evil in the sight of the Lord, walking in the way of Jeroboam and in the sin that he caused Israel to commit" (1 Kings 15:34).

Following the death of Jeroboam I in 901 B.C.E., Israel entered a twenty-five-year period of instability brought about by internal intrigue and external threat. None of the four kings who came to power during this time were able to stabilize the monarchy. Complicating this internal dissolution was the threat to Israel's northern borders by the rising power of Syria and Assyria. King Omri and his successors brought a much-needed stability to the kingdom, at least for a while.

The Omrid Dynasty

Omri was a military commander who led a successful coup and placed himself on the throne. Although the Deuteronomistic writer includes only eight verses (1 Kings 16:21-28) about Omri and includes the pronouncement that "Omri did what was evil in the sight of the LORD; he did more evil than all who were before him" (1 Kings 16:25), evidence indicates that he was undoubtedly a king of considerable ability.

Noncanonical sources indicate that Omri's successful administration not only brought internal stability to Israel but also improved the nation's standing with surrounding countries. One of his most significant accomplishments was moving the capital from the city of Tirzah to Samaria. (Shechem had been the first capital of the Northern Kingdom. During or shortly after the reign of Jeroboam the capital was moved to Tirzah.) Omri built this new city seven miles northwest of Shechem, and it remained the capital throughout the remainder of Israel's history. The well-fortified city of Samaria became the symbol of national strength for the Northern Kingdom, and its splendor was unrivaled in Palestine.

To enhance Israel's international standing, Omri entered into alliances with neighboring nations. The best example of his efforts in this regard was the marriage of his son, Ahab, to Jezebel, a princess of the Phoenician city-state of Tyre and a worshiper of Baal. This union would have dire consequences for the future of Yahwism in Israel, but it was a politically and economically astute move by Omri.

The Omrid dynasty continued in the accession of Ahab to the Israelite throne in 869 B.C.E. Ahab continued the work of strengthening Israel begun by his father. But in the eyes of the narrator of 1 Kings, the administrative and military successes of Ahab could not offset the serious challenge to Yahwism that occurred during his reign. The king and queen were blamed for a decline of Yahwism, which the writer believed contributed to the eventual downfall of the Omrid dynasty. The Deuteronomistic writer's perspective on the conflict is anachronistic and pro-Judean; that is, the writer projects back into earlier times concepts of exclusive Yahwism and the primacy of Jerusalem that were current in the middle of the sixth century B.C.E. There probably was a serious threat to Yahwism during the reign of Ahab, but it was one aspect of a number of conflicts between the Omrid rulers and the general populace. The growing socioeconomic injustices and heavy-handed administration of the rulers were also factors that fed popular unrest. The religious conflict became symbolic of all that was disliked about the Omrid rulers, and so the narrative focuses on this feature of the era.

To heighten the significance of the Baal-Yahweh conflict, the Deuteronomistic history includes numerous narratives that focus on the deeds of Yahwistic prophets who struggle against Baal worship. The Elijah stories (1 Kings 17–19; 2 Kings 1:2-16) and the Elisha stories (2 Kings 2; 4:1–8:15) are the most notable of these narratives (these stories are discussed in chapter 10).

The Jehu Dynasty

Jehoram, Ahab's son, was the last king of the Omrid dynasty. When he was wounded in battle while defending Israel against Syrian attack, he left Jehu, the head of his army, in charge. Jehu, urged on by the prophet Elisha, returned to Jezreel, where he assassinated Jehoram and the queen mother, Jezebel. The bloody coup continued until "Jehu killed all who were left of the house of Ahab in Jezreel, all his leaders, close friends, and priests, until he left him no survivor" (2 Kings 10:11).

Figure 8.2. Public grain silo at Megiddo built during the reign of Jeroboam II (786–746 B.C.E.). Note the steps leading down to the floor of the silo. (*Photograph by Mitchell G. Reddish*)

Jehu reigned over Israel for twenty-seven years, and four of his descendants ruled for another seventy years, making Jehu's dynasty the longest in Israel's history. But during the first half of this dynasty Jehu's lack of astute leadership sowed seeds that would eventually lead to Israel's downfall. Jehu's overthrow of the Omrids placed Israel in conflict with neighboring states, such as Phoenicia and Judah, with whom Ahab had encouraged friendly relations. Also, Jehu alienated Syria when he refused to unite with that country in a common Palestinian defense against the expansionist policies of Assyria, a Mesopotamian nation advancing toward Palestine. When Syria retaliated against Israel for this desertion, Jehu died in the battle and casualties reduced Israel's army to a fraction of its former size (2 Kings 13:7).

During the second half of the Jehu dynasty, especially during the reign of Jeroboam II (786–746 B.C.E.), Israel enjoyed a period of national restoration and expansion. Jeroboam II was a capable ruler who was helped by the fact that both Syria and Assyria were occupied with their own difficulties and therefore left Israel to its own development. One of Jeroboam's most important accomplishments was the extension of Israel's boundaries back to the limits of the old Davidic kingdom. The political stability under Jeroboam II provided the context for an economic boom in Israel. The prosperity of the kingdom exceeded anything that had existed in the Northern Kingdom since the days of Solomon. This economic advancement was not without its problems, however, as the prophetic books of Amos and Hosea testify. Both prophets attacked the social and economic injustices that characterized the Northern Kingdom during the pinnacle of the Jehu dynasty (the message of these prophets will be discussed in chapter 10).

The Fall of Israel

In the decade following Jeroboam II's death, five successive kings failed to keep Israel unified. There was extensive strife in the court, and two of the five kings were assassinated. Coupled with this internal disintegration was the renewed aggression of the Assyrian Empire and the reinvigoration of the kingdom of Syria. Taken together, these events spelled disaster. Tiglath-pileser III (sometimes called Pul in the Deuteronomistic history) ascended to the Assyrian throne in the year that Jeroboam II died. He initiated a well-planned program of expansion and consolidation. This program included the deportation and relocation of conquered peoples (in order to minimize rebellion) and the annexation of newly conquered territories into the Assyrian provincial government system.

From 745 to 722 B.C.E. the two small Palestinian states frantically tried to retain their independence in the face of this Assyrian imperialism. With the growing menace of Assyria in the northern Fertile Crescent, Syria and Israel (Ephraim) joined in an alliance to oppose the forces of Tiglath-pileser III. Rezin, the Syrian king, and Pekah, king of Israel, tried to persuade Ahaz of Judah to join this coalition. When Ahaz refused, they ordered their armies to lay siege to Jerusalem, although they "could not conquer him [Ahaz]" (2 Kings 16:5b). Syria and Israel hoped to replace Ahaz with a Judean ruler who would support the anti-Assyrian coalition.

This alliance was not strong enough to resist the Assyrians when the army of Tiglath-pileser III marched into Palestine in 732 B.C.E. Ahaz turned to the Assyrians for protection against the armies of Syria and Ephraim, resulting in Judah becoming a vassal state of the Assyrian Empire. The Assyrians then destroyed the Syrian capital, Damascus, and incorporated Syria into the Assyrian provincial system. Several small Transjordanian states (Ammon, Moab, Edom) also came under Assyrian control. Israel escaped destruction at this time primarily because some pro-Assyrian supporters gained control and placed a new king, Hoshea, over Israel. Hoshea paid tribute to the Assyrian king, and Israel became a vassal state with at least temporary security.

Several years later, around 725 B.C.E., Hoshea refused to pay the tribute to Tiglath-pileser III's successor, Shalmaneser V, and once again the Assyrians moved against Israel. Shalmaneser V captured and imprisoned Hoshea and put Samaria under siege. The siege lasted two years until Samaria's inhabitants surrendered either to Shalmaneser V or to his successor, Sargon II. With the fall of Samaria the Northern Kingdom came to an end in 722 B.C.E. Israel was then incorporated into the Assyrian provincial system.

Sargon II carried out the Assyrian program of deportation by resettling thousands of Israelites throughout Mesopotamia and replacing them with people imported from other areas of the Assyrian Empire. The new settlers brought their own culture and religious traditions to Samaria. They also probably joined in the worship of Yahweh, the god of the land in which they now lived, so that over the next several centuries the Assyrian province of Samaria was the scene of cultural and religious intermixing.

Second Kings 17:7-18 provides a theological explanation for the fall of Israel. Apostasy was the reason that "the LORD was very angry with Israel and removed them out of his sight; none was left but the tribe of Judah alone" (v. 18). Had Israel been faithful to the covenant, Yahweh would have saved them from destruction. Yahweh even sent to them his servants, the prophets, but "they would not listen but were stubborn, as their ancestors had been, who did not believe in the LORD their God" (v. 14). Although the harsh judgment of the Deuteronomistic writer was strongly expressed toward Israel, it was not absent from the narrator's treatment of the Southern Kingdom. The same standard of fidelity to the covenant relationship would be applied to Judah.

UNITED MONARCHY

Saul	ca. 1020–1000 B.C.E.
David	ca. 1000–961 B.C.E.
Solomon	ca. 961–922 B.C.E.

Israel (Northern Kingdom)	Judah (Southern Kingdom)
Jeroboam I (922–901)	Rehoboam (922–915)
	Abijah/Abijam (915–913)
	Asa (913–873)
Nadab (901–900)	
Baasha (900–877)	
Elah (877–876)	
Zimri (876)	
Omri (876–869)	
	Jehoshaphat (873–849)
Ahab (869–850)	
Ahaziah (850–849)	
Jehoram/Joram (849–842)	Jehoram/Joram (849–842)
	Ahaziah (842)
	Athaliah (842–837)
Jehu (842–815)	Jehoash/Joash (837–800)
Jehoahaz (815–801)	
Joash/Jehoash (801–786)	
	Amaziah (800–783)
Jeroboam II (786–746)	Azariah/Uzziah (783–742)
Zechariah (746–745)	
Shallum (745)	
Menahem (745–738)	
Pekahiah (738–737)	Jotham (742–735)
Pekah (737–732)	Ahaz (735–715)
Hoshea (732–723)	
Destruction of Samaria in 722 B.C.E.	
	Hezekiah (715–687)
	Manasseh (687–642)
	Amon (642–640)
	Josiah (640–609)
	Jehoahaz (609)
	Jehoiakim (609–598)
	Jehoiachin (598)
	Zedekiah (598–587)
	Destruction of Jerusalem in 587 B.C.E.

Note: Many of the dates given above are uncertain.

Figure 8.3. The Hebrew Kings

THE SOUTHERN KINGDOM (922–587 B.C.E.)

The Deuteronomistic treatment of Judah's history follows a pattern similar to that of the story told about Israel. The writer takes up each Judean king, dating his reign by reference to the contemporary ruler in Israel, giving pertinent information about his administration, and judging his accomplishments against the standard of Deuteronomistic theology. The significant difference in the treatment of the Judean kings as compared to Israel's sovereigns is that some of the southern rulers are positively evaluated. Two Judean kings, Hezekiah and Josiah, are lauded as faithful Yahwists, and a few others are given partial approval (for example, Asa, Jehoash, Azariah, and Jotham). The rest of Judah's kings, even though they were occupants of the Davidic throne, fall short of the Deuteronomistic expectations and are harshly condemned.

Rehoboam

The Deuteronomistic historian offers relatively few details about the administration of Judah's first king. Rehoboam inherited the prestige and honor of the Davidic dynasty. Although not as effective a ruler as his father, Solomon, Rehoboam held the Southern Kingdom together and strengthened it by fortifying cities in the southern hill country. Most of the emphasis in the narrative about Rehoboam is upon the events surrounding the division of the kingdom and the continuing conflict between the two nations. When Jeroboam and the northern tribes revolted, a period of hostilities between Israel and Judah began. Rehoboam was not able to subdue Israel, and the intermittent fighting continued well beyond Rehoboam's seventeen-year reign. The primary deterrent to Judah's prominence during Rehoboam's rule, however, was the imperialistic policies of Pharaoh Shishak of Egypt. In the fifth year of Rehoboam's reign, Shishak invaded Palestine, and though spared physical destruction, Judah became economically dependent on Egypt and became the weaker of the two Hebrew kingdoms. Judah's weakness continued through the reigns of several kings following Rehoboam. Then about the time that the Jehu dynasty reached its height in Israel during the reign of Jeroboam II, Judah also experienced a national recovery under King Uzziah.

Uzziah

According to the view of the Chronicler (2 Chr. 26–27), the Southern Kingdom reached its zenith of political and military power under Uzziah (also called Azariah). The accomplishments of Uzziah included victories over the Philistines, which allowed him to control important trade routes through Judah; the improvement of Judah's standing army by better equipping his soldiers;

numerous public building projects, especially the construction of defense towers on the walls of Jerusalem; and agricultural advancements.

Uzziah reigned in Judah during the period when Israel was experiencing the economic boom under Jeroboam II. Some of the same conditions that prevailed in the north and that led the prophets Amos and Hosea to pronounce God's judgment upon Israel also existed in Judah. For this reason the Deuteronomistic writer was able to give Uzziah only partial approval, saying that although "he did what was right in the sight of the Lord" (2 Kings 15:3), the king ultimately failed to keep the nation true to the covenant relationship because he permitted Baal worship to persist in Judah.

Ahaz

The national restoration that occurred under Uzziah was only temporary. Soon Judah entered a period of decline due to the weakness of the next several

Figure 8.4. This eighth- to seventh-century-B.C.E. bronze statuette of a man praying was found on the island of Samos, where it had been imported from Assyria. (*Photograph by Mitchell G. Reddish*)

kings and the rising power of Assyria, which placed external pressure on all the Palestinian states. The king who directed Judah through the early period of the Assyrian crisis was Ahaz. As mentioned earlier in this chapter, Ahaz was forced into conflict with his neighbors to the north, Israel and Syria, when he refused to join their alliance against Assyria. Instead, Ahaz became a vassal of Assyria and subjected Judah to military dependence and economic hardship.

The policy of appeasement that Ahaz followed also brought Judah under the influence of Assyrian religion. Ahaz permitted the construction of an altar in the Temple for the worship of Assyrian gods. This apostasy led the prophet Isaiah, who counseled the king, to condemn the foreign policy of Ahaz and advise him to avoid all foreign alliances. The condemnation of Ahaz also stands out in the Deuteronomistic writer's treatment of this period of Judean history. Ahaz "did not do what was right in the sight of the LORD his God, as his ancestor David had done, but he walked in the way of the kings of Israel" (2 Kings 16:2-3).

Hezekiah

Many people in Judah opposed the policy of appeasement that Ahaz followed. Among them was Hezekiah, the son of Ahaz. Hezekiah instituted wide-ranging reforms that began in the religious arena and affected the political, social, and military aspects of Judean life. The religious aspect of the reform focused on the eradication of foreign worship and the strengthening of Yahwism. In an effort to restore the significance of worship in the Temple, Hezekiah removed all the elements of Assyrian worship that had been added by Ahaz. He also destroyed the many local shrines that had been avenues for the intrusion of foreign religious practices. This attention by Hezekiah to the restoration of Yahwism led the Deuteronomistic writer to proclaim that "he trusted in the LORD the God of Israel; so that there was no one like him among all the kings of Judah after him, or among those who were before him" (2 Kings 18:5).

Hezekiah's religious reforms brought him into direct conflict with Assyria. The king was aware of the political implications of his religious program, and he led Judah to prepare for the possibility of Assyrian retaliation. He fortified some of the weaker towns of Judah, strengthened the walls of Jerusalem, and reorganized the army. An extraordinary accomplishment provided the city with its first source of fresh water. Hezekiah constructed the Siloam tunnel, an underground aqueduct from the spring of Gihon to the pool of Siloam. The tunnel was cut through almost a third of a mile of rock.

Although Hezekiah's reforms represented an anti-Assyrian stance, the king avoided open rebellion for several years. Eventually, however, Judah was drawn into direct participation in the Palestinian efforts to resist Assyrian advance. The first instance of open revolt during Hezekiah's reign occurred in

701 B.C.E. when Judah joined other southern Palestinian nations in a coalition against Sennacherib, the king of Assyria. Sennacherib inflicted destruction upon several of the alliance members and brought Judah into submission by taking some of Hezekiah's territory and increasing the tax that Judah was forced to pay. Again, about 688 B.C.E., Hezekiah participated in a wider rebellion against Sennacherib. In response, Sennacherib subdued several smaller states and numerous Judean towns and then laid siege to the city of Jerusalem. At the same time an Egyptian army arrived in Judah to assist in the battle against Assyria. Sennacherib defeated the Egyptians and then, for an unknown reason, withdrew to Assyria. At some point during the siege or during the Assyrian battle with the Egyptians, Hezekiah submitted to the Assyrians and Jerusalem was spared.

Sennacherib may have withdrawn from Judah because Hezekiah surrendered or because he returned to Mesopotamia to defend the Assyrian capital from attack by Babylon. The Deuteronomistic history provides an extensive narrative of the story of Hezekiah's conflict with Sennacherib and interprets the saving of Jerusalem as an act of divine intervention. The story told in 2 Kings includes a prophecy by Isaiah that Yahweh will not permit the destruction of Jerusalem and a record of the miraculous deliverance. "That very night the angel of the LORD set out and struck down one hundred eighty-five thousand in the camp of the Assyrians; when morning dawned, they were all dead bodies. Then King Sennacherib of

Figure 8.5. In this scene on an eighth-century B.C.E. stone slab from Hadatu in Syria, an Assyrian royal chariot is accompanied by guards. The Assyrians defeated the Northern Kingdom and made the Southern Kingdom a vassal state in the eighth century. *(Photograph by Mitchell G. Reddish)*

Assyria left, went home, and lived at Nineveh" (2 Kings 19:35-36). Writing from the perspective of several centuries later, the Deuteronomistic writer interpreted Sennacherib's withdrawal as an illustration of Yahweh's protection of Judah under faithful King Hezekiah.

Manasseh

The attempt of Hezekiah to revive Yahwism in Judah was apparently reversed during the long reign of his son, Manasseh (687 to 642 B.C.E.). Although very little is known about actual historical events in Judah during Manasseh's reign, it appears that he was not a devout Yahwist and that much of what Hezekiah had initiated religiously was lost.

The Deuteronomistic evaluation of Manasseh was harsh. In 2 Kings Manasseh is presented as probably the worst king ever to rule over either of the Hebrew kingdoms. The narrator believed his reign set the stage for the final destruction of Jerusalem. Consequently, nothing good is reported about Manasseh (2 Kings 21:1-18). The Chronicler, on the other hand, repeats the negative evaluation of Manasseh from 2 Kings but ends with a report of Manasseh's repentance and his leading a Yahwistic reform (2 Chr. 33:1-17).

Both biblical appraisals of Manasseh reflect the influence of centuries of tradition development. The Deuteronomistic material probably emphasizes the king's wickedness in order to contrast him with the good kings, Hezekiah and Josiah. The Chronicler probably reflects an idealization of Judah's past by developing a good ending for the story of a non-Yahwistic ruler. The truth is likely somewhere between these extremes. Manasseh's fifty-five-year reign, the longest in Judah's history, was undoubtedly a time of decline for Yahwism but certainly not as much of a "dark age" as the Deuteronomistic writer portrays.

Josiah

When Manasseh died, his son Amon succeeded him. During his two-year reign he continued his father's pro-Assyrian and non-Yahwistic policies. His successor, Josiah, is counted with Hezekiah as one of the greatest kings to rule over the Southern Kingdom. Given a positive appraisal by the Deuteronomistic writer in 2 Kings, Josiah was known as an ardent Yahwist, an effective reformer, and a devoted patriot. His sweeping reform program had political, economic, and religious impacts upon Judean life. This reform has been called the Deuteronomic Reform because it was based upon a portion of the book of Deuteronomy.

According to 2 Kings 22, in the eighteenth year of Josiah's reign (621 B.C.E.) "the book of the law" was discovered in the Temple by workers who were renovating the structure. After being verified as authentic by Huldah, a female prophet, this "book" became the basis for Josiah's Yahwistic reform of Judean life. Although the precise identity of the book is impossible to ascertain, it was an early form of a portion of Deuteronomy, most likely chapters 12–26.

The Deuteronomic Reform instituted at least four widespread changes in

Figure 8.6. A baked clay cultic stand, probably used for the burning of incense, found in Pella (in modern Jordan) from around the tenth century B.C.E. *(Photograph by Clyde E. Fant)*

Judean life. First, the Temple cult in Jerusalem was purified by the eradication of Assyrian and Canaanite elements of worship, including priests who conducted the idolatrous offerings, artifacts associated with the foreign traditions, and altars that had been constructed on the roof and in the court of the Temple. Second, the numerous local shrines around the Judean countryside were purged of both non-Yahwistic elements and aspects of Yahwistic worship not approved by the Deuteronomic Code, such as the burning of incense by Yahwistic priests at the local "high places." This move was essentially an effort to centralize worship in the Temple in Jerusalem. Third, the reform extended into the area of the former Northern Kingdom, although the Deuteronomistic historian probably exaggerates the extent of the reform. Fourth, the reform represented a virtual declaration of independence from Assyria since it threw off much of the cultural influence that the Mesopotamian nation had over Judah.

The Fall of Judah

At the time of Josiah's reforms in Judah, Assyrian power had declined. But as Assyria declined, another power was rising to dominance in the Fertile Crescent. Babylon, under the leadership of Nebuchadrezzar, conquered Assyria in 612 B.C.E. and almost immediately began to turn attention to the submission of Palestine. Then, while under the threat of Babylonian invasion, Judah was also brought into conflict with Egypt and lost King Josiah in a battle with the Egyptians in 609 B.C.E. at Megiddo.

The rise of Babylon was the beginning of the end for Judah. During the twenty-two years after the death of Josiah, three of his sons and one of his grandsons succeeded one another on Judah's throne. None of these kings was able to withstand the imperialism of Babylon, though in moments of Babylonian weakness they attempted to assert Judean independence. In 600 B.C.E. King Jehoiakim, son of Josiah, withheld the tribute payments from Nebuchadrezzar and prompted a Babylonian response. In 597 B.C.E. Nebuchadrezzar mobilized an army to deal with Judean defiance, then plundered Jerusalem and deported to Babylon many of the leading citizens of the Hebrew kingdom, including the new king, Jehoiachin, who had taken over when his father Jehoiakim died just before Jerusalem fell to the Babylonians. The Babylonians placed the youngest of Josiah's sons, Zedekiah, on the throne.

Under pressure from radical nationalists in his kingdom to break with Babylon, and encouraged by the spirit of rebellion among other Palestinian states, Zedekiah revolted in 588 B.C.E. In response, Nebuchadrezzar laid siege to the city of Jerusalem for almost two years. In 587 B.C.E., when the city ran out of food, its walls were breached and much of the city was physically destroyed, including the Temple. Nebuchadrezzar again deported many of the remaining citizens of Judah and settled them in Babylon. This fall of Jerusalem in 587 B.C.E. marked the beginning of an approximately fifty-year exile of the Hebrews.

The demise of Judah hardly stands out as a major event in world history. It is not mentioned in the records of Babylon. But in the history of the Hebrews it was an epochal event. The last of the Hebrew kingdoms had vanished. The people who had enjoyed political independence since the time of Saul were now without a political identity except as subjects of a foreign nation.

During the period of their national existence as separate kingdoms, the Hebrews had struggled politically to hold a place for themselves in the Near Eastern arena. They lost that battle. But, ironically, the period was one of the most creative and productive in terms of their religious development and their understanding of the divine-human encounter. The growth of Hebrew religious ideas during the period of the Divided Kingdom centers upon the work of the great prophets who spoke the message of Yahweh to kings and commoners within the Hebrew nations. The chapters immediately following will discuss how their work and their messages both influenced and were influenced by the historical events of the era of the Divided Kingdom.

Chapter 9

THE INSTITUTION OF PROPHECY

Suggested Biblical Readings: 1 Kings 17–19

Virtually every culture in the ancient world had individuals who were seen as a means of communication between the human and the divine. These persons, frequently called prophets, served as intermediaries between the world of the gods and the world of humans. They were believed to provide divine guidance and assistance for the king or the nation. Evidence for such individuals in the ancient Near East can be found as early as the eighteenth century B.C.E.

Since prophecy in some form was common among the neighbors of the ancient Hebrews, it is not surprising that it became an important feature of Israel's history. Hebrew prophecy seems to have had its formal beginning in the closing years of the period of the judges and to have reached its greatest heights during the preexilic and exilic periods. Although biblical texts refer to several early Hebrews—such as Abraham and Moses—as prophets, this title does not describe the primary function of these individuals. Later writers probably called them prophets in recognition of their farsighted leadership and the truth of their messages.

BACKGROUND OF HEBREW PROPHECY

Recent research has expanded our understanding of the forms of prophecy among the neighbors of ancient Israel. Noting similarities between certain behavior patterns of the ancient Hebrew prophets and their Near Eastern neighbors, some scholars have suggested that Hebrew prophecy was directly influenced by neighboring cultures. Other scholars doubt that direct links exist. In any case, Hebrew prophecy did not develop in a vacuum, and the similarities do suggest that religious and cultural exchanges between Israel and its Near Eastern neighbors may have influenced the development of Hebrew prophecy.

Since the discovery in 1933–35 of the "Mari letters" in the ancient city-state by that name on the Euphrates River, comparisons have been made between the early Hebrew prophets and certain religious functionaries there. These letters, which date between 1800 and 1760 B.C.E., tell of extensive prophetic activity in the Mesopotamian region. At Mari, as elsewhere in the area, prophecy was first connected with court prophets. These figures were frequently referred to as "prophets of peace" because they encouraged the rulers in times of warfare and invariably told them what they wanted to hear. (This term may lie behind the biblical criticism of those who say, " 'Peace, peace,' when there is no peace"; Jer. 6:14, Ezek. 13:10.)

Particularly significant at Mari were certain ecstatic prophets who entered trance-like states that appear to have rendered them temporarily incoherent or irrational and incapacitated. Parallels have been cited between these Mari prophets and the bands of prophets described in 1 Samuel 10. There Samuel tells Saul:

> You will meet a band of prophets coming down from the shrine with harp, tambourine, flute, and lyre playing in front of them; they will be in a prophetic frenzy. Then the spirit of the LORD will possess you, and you will be in a prophetic frenzy along with them and be turned into a different person.... When his [Saul's] prophetic frenzy had ended, he went home. (1 Sam. 10:5-6, 13)

In Israel, as in Mari, other individuals often interpreted these messages delivered by prophets during their altered states of consciousness.

Another example of prophecy among the neighbors of Israel has been found in Jordan. At Deir 'Alla, archaeologists discovered a fragmentary text that tells of a prophetic figure named Balaam, son of Beor, almost certainly the same person described in Numbers 22–23. In both accounts he is remembered as a "seer," someone who saw visions of events to come.

Ecstatic prophecy was nowhere more prominent than among Israel's nearest neighbors, the Canaanites. The Egyptian traveler Wen Amon vividly describes the Canaanites' practice of prophesying in an ecstatic trance. In an eleventh-century B.C.E. account of his journeys, Wen Amon tells of his experience with ecstatic prophets in the Canaanite city of Byblos. Likewise, in 1 Kings 18:20-29 several Canaanite prophets of Baal engage in frenzied activities that include cultic shouts, dancing, and cutting themselves with knives. Many of these ecstatic prophets joined guilds in which members were known as the "sons of the prophets." It is likely that some of Israel's early prophets also banded together into such groups.

THE NATURE OF HEBREW PROPHECY

Several terms in the Hebrew Bible clarify the role of the Hebrew prophet.

Seer. A seer was one who saw something that others did not see (Hebrew *ro'eh* or *hozeh*). That is, the seer was a specialist in communication with God by means of dreams, visions, or divination. Although references to seers appear in some later literature of the Hebrew Bible (2 Chr. 16:7, 10), the seer largely disappeared in the early monarchical period.

Sons of the prophets. In the Deuteronomistic history this term describes the prophetic groups or guilds that flourished between 869 and 842 B.C.E. The first mention of these groups is in 1 Samuel 10:5, in which they are called "a band of prophets." They were sometimes associated with Elisha and played a significant role in the overthrow of the dynasty of Omri.

Man of God. The term appears in various places in the Hebrew Bible, in which it is often interchangeable with "prophet." In Judges 13:6 the wife of Manoah, who seemed incapable of bearing children, was told by a "man of God" that she would bear a son. In fulfillment of the prediction of this messenger, Samson was born.

One who is called. By far the most common title for prophet in the Hebrew Bible is *navi*, which is found over three hundred times. It generally means "one who is called" or who "has a call" (from God), although in some contexts it may have other meanings. This term is used to describe many early leaders in Israel, including some not ordinarily thought of as prophets: Aaron (Ex. 7:1), Miriam (Ex. 15:20; Num. 12:1-15), the seventy elders (Num. 11:24-25), Eldad and Medad (Num. 11:26-30), Deborah (Judg. 4:4), and an unnamed prophet mentioned with the story of Gideon (Judg. 6:7ff.).

The term *navi* eventually superseded all other prophetic titles. This change resulted from the developing Hebrew notion that the prophet was a person called by Yahweh to speak God's message to the people. Whatever similarities Hebrew prophets may have shared with their non-Hebraic counterparts, the Hebrews transformed the office of prophet so that it always received its authority from the interaction of the proclaimer with Yahweh. Though they might have received their messages from God in various ways (divination, ecstatic vision, historical event), the *nevi'im* ("prophets") were believed to have spoken the message of God to Israel.

The English word "prophet" comes directly from the Greek word *prophetes*, meaning "to speak forth." Thus the modern word preserves the concept of the *navi* or speaker for Yahweh. The word "prophet" did not originally mean a predictor of the future (a "foreteller") but rather referred to one who offered a commentary on historical events based on a message from Yahweh (a "forth-teller").

Both the Hebrews and their neighbors had female prophets. Miriam, the sister of Moses, and Deborah, one of the Hebrew judges, were called prophets. When a previously unknown scroll of the Law was discovered in the Temple in the days of King Josiah, a woman prophet, Huldah, was consulted to verify it as an inspired part of the Law. She then delivered an oracle, which was precisely the same function performed by many male prophets (2 Kings 22:14-20). Other references to women prophesying, such as Ezekiel 13:17-23, suggest that more women may have been involved in prophetic activity than is usually believed.

FUNCTIONS OF THE HEBREW PROPHETS

The various terms for the prophets mentioned above express the nature of Hebrew prophecy and point to the primary function of the prophets as spokespersons for God. Some prophets also served as worship leaders, preservers of tradition, and predictors of the nation's future.

Figure 9.1. The Hebrew Prophets from the ninth to the sixth centuries B.C.E.

Israel		Judah
	9th century	
Elijah		
Micaiah		
Elisha		
	8th century	
Amos		
Hosea		Isaiah
		Micah
	7th century	
		Zephaniah
		Jeremiah (continues into the 6th century)
		Nahum
		Habakkuk
	6th century	
		Ezekiel
		Second Isaiah
		Haggai
		Zechariah
		Obadiah (6th or 5th century)
	5th century	
		Third Isaiah (late 6th or early 5th century)
		Malachi (late 6th or early 5th century)
		Joel (late 6th or early 5th century)

Spokespersons for God

The prophets served as intermediaries between God and Israel, interpreting for Israel God's work in nature and history. These interpretations took several forms.

First, prophets sometimes interpreted the meaning of a natural catastrophe in relation to Israel's history. Amos, for example, interpreted a drought as an occasion for communicating a message from God (Amos 4:7-12).

Second, they often announced moral judgment on behalf of God. Amos boldly condemned the king and the people of Israel and predicted the doom of the nation (Amos 5). The moral judgments of the prophets also included championing the cause of the powerless, such as widows, orphans, the poor, and others who were exploited (Deut. 16:11; 24:10; Isa. 1:17; 10:2; Jer. 5:25-28).

Third, acting on God's behalf, some prophets organized revolts against established dynasties. Such prophetic activity seems, however, to have been confined to the Northern Kingdom, where there was less respect for the kingship.

Fourth, prophets often served as counselors to the kings. Nathan gave David counsel from the beginning to the end of his reign (see 2 Sam. 7:1-17 and 1 Kings 1:11-27). The story of Micaiah suggests that often it was the custom of the kings of Israel, just as it was in Mesopotamia, to seek the advice of prophets when considering a military campaign (see 1 Kings 22:1-28). In fact, it seems likely that the earliest function of the prophet was to serve as a court prophet, someone located at the court or supported by the court. Only later did the role of prophet develop into the delivering of oracles to the people as a whole. With the passing of the institution of monarchy in Israel, the court prophet died out altogether and laypersons increasingly assumed the role of prophet.

Worship Leaders

Although conducting worship is generally regarded as the prerogative of priests, some persons referred to as prophets also performed at least two of the functions of worship. One priestly function was speaking to God in prayer for the people. Several prophets, including Samuel (1 Sam. 7:5), Elijah (1 Kings 18:36-37), Elisha (2 Kings 6:17), Amos (Amos 7:2), and Jeremiah (Jer. 42:4), are described as performing intercessory prayer. The second worship function normally provided by priests was offering sacrifices. On some occasions the prophets Samuel, Elijah, and Elisha offered sacrifices.

These incidents suggest that the distinction between prophet and priest was not always clear. Ordinarily, a priest was one who approached God for the people, while a prophet approached the people for God. Some prophets, however, were also priests (Jeremiah, Ezekiel, Zechariah). Others seem to have been attached to cultic sites or under the direction of cultic leaders (Amos 7:10-17; 2 Kings 2:3). But in time the distinction between the two roles seems to have become sharper, as the prophets criticized the merely formal and external observance of religion and the office of priest became more institutionalized and hierarchical.

Preservers and Reinterpreters of Tradition

The books of Chronicles and Deuteronomy closely relate the prophets to the priests at central places of worship, such as Shiloh. The priests of Shiloh apparently recorded traditions and preserved texts for centuries. The prophet Ahijah was from Shiloh, which may reflect the close relationship there between the priests and prophets as they shared in preserving and interpreting tradition.

Similarly, a close relationship between the prophets and priests existed at

Jerusalem and is reflected in the reformation of Josiah. It was a priest who found the copy of a book of the Law that became the basis of reform, and it was a prophet, Huldah, who was called upon to give her interpretation of the text.

Predictors of the Nation's Future

Although the prophets sometimes predicted the future of Israel, they are not to be understood as crystal ball gazers whose purpose was to reveal all secrets or predict all discoveries, scientific or historical, of the distant future. The future in which they were interested was the future of God's covenant people. By observing events in the present and interpreting the covenant demands of Yahweh, the *nevi'im* of Israel often predicted how God would deal with Israel in the future. In every case, these prophecies were based upon the degree to which Israel faithfully carried out God's will through the covenant.

REPRESENTATIVES OF PRELITERARY PROPHECY

The majority of biblical references to preliterary prophets are found in the Deuteronomistic history. The stories of these early prophets, who left no written collections of their proclamations, reflect the high degree of influence they wielded in the last years of the United Monarchy and the years of the Divided Kingdom. They also reflect the struggle that occurred between conflicting religious elements in Hebrew life, especially the conflict between the fertility religion of Baalism and the defenders of Yahwism, the traditional religion of Israel. The most notable of the preliterary prophets were Nathan, Elijah, and Elisha.

Nathan

Nathan was a court prophet for David. He played a significant role in the life of David on three occasions. The first occurred when David revealed to Nathan his plan to build a temple to house the Ark of the Covenant (2 Sam. 7:2-17). Nathan initially assured David of God's approval of his plan. Later he informed David that he did not need to build a house for God, since God had not needed a house during the years when the people of Israel were brought out of Egypt or during the period of the judges. On the contrary, Nathan assured David that God would build David a house. The use of the term "house," however, assumes a different meaning here. David meant a building; Nathan meant a "household" or "dynasty," indicating that the throne of David would continue after his death. (Recently a remarkable archaeological discovery at Dan, in northern Israel, revealed an inscription that mentions "the house of David," the first nonbiblical reference to David ever discovered.)

Nathan is mentioned again in the incident in which David committed adultery with Bathsheba and ordered her husband, Uriah the Hittite, killed by being abandoned to the Ammonites in battle (2 Sam. 11). Nathan announced God's judgment on David by means of a story that trapped him into admitting his own guilt (2 Sam. 12). His punishment was threefold: first, violence would plague his life (2 Sam. 12:10); second, his wives would commit adultery in view of the public (2 Sam. 12:11); and third, the son of David's adultery would die (2 Sam. 12:14).

Figure 9.2. Elijah defeated the prophets of Baal in a contest on Mount Carmel and afterward killed them. This statue on Mount Carmel depicts that scene. (*Photograph by Clyde E. Fant*)

Nathan played a significant role in David's life a third time, when David was near death. Nathan and Bathsheba influenced him to designate her son, Solomon, as his successor to the throne (1 Kings 1:11-27), even though Solomon was not first in the line of succession.

Elijah

While Ahab was king, the worship of Baal, whose popularity had been growing among some of the northern tribes, gradually replaced the worship of Yahweh. Jezebel, Ahab's wife, who was not a Hebrew, strongly advanced the cause of Canaanite worship. Into this situation came Elijah, who responded with a prediction of drought. Presumably to escape from the wrath of Ahab, Elijah hid for a time. But at the appropriate time he emerged from hiding and confronted Ahab with a challenge to assemble the tribes at Mount Carmel and ask them to decide between Yahweh and Baal. Ahab agreed to call the assembly. Elijah put the question to those assembled: "How long will you go limping with two different opinions? If the LORD is God, follow him; but if Baal, then follow him" (1 Kings 18:21). Their response was stony silence. Elijah, the one prophet of Yahweh present, challenged the 450 prophets of Baal to prepare one bull as a sacrifice to their god, while Elijah prepared one bull to sacrifice to Yahweh. Elijah and the prophets of Baal prayed to their different gods to ignite the sacrifices. The prophets of Baal prayed earnestly, but no fire came. Then Elijah poured water over his bull three times and prayed a brief prayer:

> Then the fire of the LORD fell and consumed the burnt offering, the wood, the stones, and the dust, and even licked up the water that was in the trench. When all the people saw it, they fell on their faces and said, 'The LORD indeed is God; the LORD indeed is God.' (1 Kings 18:38-39)

This dramatic story may well symbolize the breaking of the dominant strength of Baalism among the northern tribes. The victory at Mount Carmel, however, was followed by a sad ending. Elijah, who earlier had mustered great courage in challenging Ahab, fled in fear to the wilderness near Sinai after being threatened by Ahab's wife, Jezebel. God spoke to Elijah in the wilderness and told him things were not as bad as they seemed. Then God instructed him to return to Israel, to anoint Hazael king of Syria and Jehu king of Israel, to appoint Elisha as his prophet-replacement, and finally, to watch Israel's destruction (1 Kings 19:15-18).

Elisha

The prophet Elisha was the successor to Elijah. Subsequently, Elisha appears often with the "sons of the prophets" and sometimes travels with the Hebrew army on its military campaigns.

Figure 9.3. Ruins of Ahab's chariot city at Megiddo. Ahab fortified Megiddo to help protect his kingdom. *(Photograph by Mitchell G. Reddish)*

Perhaps the most dramatic event in the ministry of Elisha was his choice of Jehu to organize a revolt against the dynasty of Ahab. Previously, God had instructed Elijah to perform this task, but apparently he did not do it—and neither did Elisha. Instead, he sent one of the "sons of the prophets" to do it. Elisha told him simply to anoint Jehu and say, " 'Thus says the LORD: I anoint you king over Israel,' " and then leave immediately (2 Kings 9:3). It appears that this unnamed prophet took liberty with Elisha's instructions, for he told Jehu that God would kill everyone associated with the house of Ahab. Jehu, assuming that he was God's agent, killed every member of Ahab's family he could find, including Jezebel, Ahab's wife, seventy of Ahab's sons, and many other relatives and sympathizers. Then, pretending to be a supporter of Baalism, he assembled a large group of Baal worshipers, killed them, and turned their place of worship into a public latrine (2 Kings 10:18-27). Since Jehu is condemned in the Deuteronomistic history (which was influenced by the prophets), apparently the prophets disapproved of the lengths to which he went, though they likely approved of his opposition to Baalism.

Figure 9.4. This scene from the Black Obelisk depicts the submission of Jehu, king of Israel, as vassal to Shalmaneser, king of Assyria (841 B.C.E.) (© *The British Museum*)

THE DIVINE-HUMAN ENCOUNTER IN
THE PRELITERARY PROPHETS

The preliterary prophets assumed that the God who created the heavens and the earth had called Judah and Israel into being; the covenant at Sinai was the decisive event in their becoming an elect community of faith (Ex. 19). These early prophetic traditions express the belief that both Israel and Judah had violated the divine-human relationship by failing to live up to their covenant obligations. Their failures were reflected in their worship of other gods and in their practice of social injustices.

One of the principal functions of the prophets was to call Israel back to the covenant. The insistence of the preliterary prophets upon the maintenance of this covenant relationship would be refined and elaborated by the great writing prophets of the preexilic period, which will be the subject of the next chapter.

Chapter 10

THE PREEXILIC PROPHETS

Suggested Biblical Readings: Amos 2:4-16; 5:14-24; 7:1-9; Hosea 1:1-11; 3; 11; Isaiah 1; 6; 9:1-7; 11:1-9; Jeremiah 1:1-10; 7; 31:31-34

The eighth and seventh centuries B.C.E. brought a series of crises that ended in the downfall of Israel and Judah. Israel fell to the Assyrians in 722 B.C.E. and Judah to the Babylonians in 587 B.C.E. During the declining years of these kingdoms, a new group of prophets emerged to interpret these crises.

The preexilic prophets may be distinguished from their predecessors by the fact that their oracles were collected and preserved as independent literary works. These written records were preserved in the hope that their messages would be vindicated in the future (Isa. 8:11-16; Jer. 36:27-31).

The books studied in this chapter are collections of prophetic oracles along with editorial supplements, reinterpretations, and the application of the prophetic oracles to later situations. These oracles are often introduced with a formula such as "Thus says the LORD" or "Hear the word of the LORD." This introduction is followed by any one of several types of messages, including messages of judgment, calls to repentance, messages of comfort, and denunciations of violations of the covenant. These messages took the literary forms of laments, speeches, doxologies, or hymns.

This chapter will focus on the lives, messages, and historical situations of the prophets Amos, Hosea, Isaiah, Micah, Jeremiah, and Jeremiah's contemporaries Habakkuk, Nahum, and Zephaniah.

AMOS

Amos is among the latter prophets of the Jewish canon and is listed with the Minor Prophets in the Christian canon. Chronologically, the book of Amos is the earliest of the prophetic books.

Structure of the Book

The book of Amos contains three parts. The first part (1:1–2:16) includes a brief introduction and oracles against Israel and the surrounding nations. The first oracle is a list of judgments against the immediate neighbors of Israel: Syria, Philistia, Tyre, Edom, Ammon, and Moab (1:1–2:3). The second oracle is against Judah (2:4-5) and the third is against Israel. The second part of the book of Amos

(3:1–6:14) focuses special attention on the impending doom of the Northern Kingdom. The third section (7:1–9:15) reports a series of visions and also includes an account of the call of Amos, the close of his ministry, and an epilogue.

Political Background

The prophet Amos lived and worked during the reign of Jeroboam II (786–746 B.C.E.), the sixth king of Israel. Jeroboam reigned during a relatively stable period in the history of Israel. The Deuteronomistic history dismisses his long reign with a brief summary only seven verses long (2 Kings 14:23-29); additional information is available from the books of Amos and Hosea and from archaeological records. These sources point to several features of Jeroboam's rule. First, they show that Jeroboam restored the territories lost under Jehu and Jehoahaz, possibly even to the boundaries of the old Davidic kingdom. Second, he was supported in his efforts by a prophet named Jonah (2 Kings 14:25), possibly the person to whom the book of Jonah (which was likely written in the fifth century B.C.E.) was attributed. Third, they show that his reign was mostly peaceful, mainly because Israel's longtime foes, the Arameans of Damascus, had been subdued by the Assyrians, and the Assyrians themselves were preoccupied with internal disputes. Thus Jeroboam was able to achieve victory over most of his immediate neighbors and maintain peace among them.

Economic Background

Along with the political security of Israel came economic prosperity, especially for the rich and powerful, and the gap between the rich and the poor widened significantly. Scholars have debated the economic status of the prophet Amos. Some have argued that he was a poor shepherd keeping herds at Tekoa and had to have a second vocation as a keeper of sycamore trees (a tree that produced a figlike fruit eaten by the poor). Others have viewed Amos as a moderately well-to-do breeder of livestock who nevertheless suffered from the rampant injustices of that time. In any case, it is very clear that Amos's sympathies lay with the poor, who were cheated and exploited by the rich and powerful (8:5). By the time of Amos many people had lost their land and were at the mercy of those who dominated the economic power structure. Corrupt judges rendered decisions based on bribes rather than justice (5:10, 12).

Religious Background

During this time of economic prosperity in Israel, religious institutions also prospered. Many of those who controlled the political and economic power structures believed their prosperity resulted from their religious zeal: "Yahweh is with us," they claimed (5:14). In their worship at religious centers, especially at Bethel where King Jeroboam himself worshiped, great crowds gathered to celebrate God's blessings as a reward for their faithfulness.

The Visions of Amos

Amos certainly performed the work of a prophet, though his relationship with the prophetic movement is unclear. The book of Amos connects him with the other writing prophets by its account of his call: "The LORD took me from following the flock, and the Lord said to me, 'Go, prophesy to my people Israel'" (7:15). An account of his visions is given by an editor of the book, who explains that while Amos was delivering his oracles, Amaziah, the leading priest of Bethel, took two actions. First, he reported to Jeroboam that Amos was creating opposition to his rule. Apparently he saw the possibility that Amos's words might precipitate a revolution similar to those generated by earlier prophets. He quoted Amos as saying, "Jeroboam shall die by the sword, and Israel must go into exile away from his land" (7:11).

Second, he called Amos a seer and told him to go back to Judah to do his prophetic work: "Never again prophesy at Bethel" (7:13). This episode clearly shows the conflict between the priest of the royal sanctuary at Bethel, Amaziah, who represented the state religion of the king, and the prophet Amos, who was accountable to no one but Yahweh.

In a series of five visions (chapters 7 and 8), two facts about Amos's message seem clear. First, he was called to warn Israel against a false sense of security. Despite the prosperity and strength of Israel, Amos saw signs of danger. His first two visions (7:1-6) were of natural catastrophes that could bring an end to Israel's prosperity: a locust plague and a fire that threatened to destroy the land. However, the compassion of Amos was so great that after each of these visions he interceded for the people in prayer and the crises passed. These successful intercessions served to validate the role of Amos as prophet.

The next three visions of Amos reveal a second feature of his message, his warning of impending judgment. In the third vision (7:7-9) the LORD appeared as a building inspector with a plumb line, holding it beside a recently constructed wall. This vision interprets Israel as the LORD's building; like a wall too far out of line, it had to be destroyed. In the fourth vision (8:1-3) the LORD showed Amos a basket of summer fruit left over from the harvest festival and now spoiled; it had to be thrown out immediately. As is common in prophetic oracles, wordplay is involved in this vision. The sound of the Hebrew word for "summer fruit" (*qayitz*) suggests the Hebrew word for "end" (*qetz*). Thus the overripened fruit suggests the end of Israel. The message of both of these visions is in bold contrast to the first two visions, in which the crisis passed before catastrophe came; in visions three and four, judgment is imminent. Amos speaks for Yahweh, saying, "I will never again pass them by" (7:8*b*; 8:2*b*). The fifth and final vision (9:1-4) is the most terrible of all. None shall escape death, no matter where they attempt to run or hide, for God has become the enemy of wicked Israel. "I will fix my eyes on them for harm and not for good" (9:4).

Amos's Message to All the Nations

Amos appears to assume that there is a moral law by which God judges both Israel and its neighbors. In this regard Amos appears unique when compared to his predecessors. Earlier prophets condemned individuals and dynasties in Israel for violations of moral propriety, but Amos condemned other nations as well. One after another, he directs attention to the varied sins of Damascus and Syria, of the Philistines, of Tyre, of Edom and Moab. Their sins include unspeakable cruelty to one another, deporting whole nations into slavery, and endless cycles of revenge. Amos quotes God repeatedly as saying, "For three transgressions and for four, I will not revoke the punishment." Amos believed God would deal with these nations by allowing the moral law to run its course. Only two things could save Israel, Judah, and their neighbors from impending doom: their repentance and God's intervention.

In chapters 3–6 Amos outlines the reasons for the coming judgment upon Israel. First, the people had rejected the responsibility that comes with privilege (chapter 3). Israel had been given a unique relationship with God, but since it had violated that relationship its privileges would end. The people could no longer presume God's protection, which they had enjoyed in the past. Second, their special judgment would result from their perversion of morality. The oppression of the poor lay at the heart of their problem. In 4:1-3 Amos directs special condemnation to the women of Bashan—he calls them "cows of Bashan"—who were wealthy and greedy like their husbands who oppressed the poor and crushed the needy. In 4:4-5 he condemns the worship of the Israelites as a substitute for, rather than a stimulus to, ethical actions. They had disregarded justice and sold "the righteous for silver, and the needy for a pair of sandals" (Amos 2:6). Finally, Amos says God will make a special case of Israel because of its false sense of security coupled with its indifference to the needs of others (6: 1-7). Amos used the form of a funeral dirge to announce Israel's doom:

> Fallen, no more to rise,
> is maiden Israel;
> forsaken on her land,
> with no one to raise her up. (5:1-2)

Amos likewise condemned those who looked forward to "the day of the LORD," a term that first appears in the Hebrew Bible in the book of Amos. It is very likely that the phrase was in use by the time of Amos and recalled the early days when Yahweh was credited with victory in battles with the enemies of Israel. By the time of Amos "the day of the LORD" may well have come to symbolize the full victory of Israel over all its enemies. But since the Israelites had become God's enemy by their sins, on that day they would be victims rather than victors (5:18-20).

The concluding epilogue in the book (9:11-15) is likely the work of a later editor, who with these additional verses added a glimmer of hope to Amos's message of doom. These verses clearly indicate that their author linked judgment and salvation and saw hope in the future beyond the judgment about which Amos spoke. Some foundation for that hope may have been rooted in the language of Amos in chapter 5, in which he admonished his people to "seek the LORD and live" (5:6) and to

> Hate evil and love good,
> and establish justice in the gate;
> it may be that the LORD, the God of hosts,
> will be gracious to the remnant of Joseph. (5:15)

Grasping that slim hope, the editor wrote:

> I will restore the fortunes of my people Israel,
> and they shall rebuild the ruined cities and inhabit them;
> they shall plant vineyards and drink their wine,
> and they shall make gardens and eat their fruit. (9:14)

Nevertheless, the imperative upon Israel from the prophecy of Amos—quoted in recent years by Martin Luther King in the modern civil rights movement—is summarized in these words: "Let justice roll down like waters, and righteousness like an everflowing stream" (5:24).

HOSEA

Hosea is the only prophet of the Northern Kingdom whose words were preserved in a separate biblical book. (Amos did most of his prophetic work in the Northern Kingdom but was a native of the Southern Kingdom.) Though it is impossible to date his prophetic career precisely, it likely began in the last years of Jeroboam II (ca. 746 B.C.E.). It is uncertain whether he lived to see the downfall of the Northern Kingdom in 722 B.C.E.

Structure of the Book

The book of Hosea can be divided into two sections. The first section (chapters 1–3) describes Hosea's marriage and its impact on his understanding of Israel's plight. The second and largest section (chapters 4–14) is dominated by a long and varied series of prophetic speeches that describe Israel's unfaithfulness and the judgment soon to come. The final chapter reports Hosea's call to repentance and the promise of forgiveness and renewal that comes after judgment.

The literary composition of this book is unusually complex. Furthermore, the text itself is unclear in many places, making it second in difficulty only to the book of Job. Biblical translations of Hosea, therefore, are exceedingly varied.

Background of the Book

The background of Hosea is similar to the setting of Amos, but there are notable differences that are important to an understanding of Hosea's uniqueness. Hosea probably grew up during the prosperous and powerful reign of Jeroboam II and lived to see the rapid loss of political stability that followed the death of Jeroboam. Four of the last six kings of Israel were assassinated. The last kings of the Northern Kingdom established political alliances with numerous neighboring countries, including Syria, Assyria, Judah, and Egypt. All of these alliances failed to secure the nation.

Economically, the prosperity that characterized the reign of Jeroboam II, especially in the early years, came to an end as political stability declined. As a vassal state of Assyria, Israel suffered increasingly heavy economic burdens. The cruel taxes levied on the people for tribute to the Assyrians generally fell on the peasant tenants who worked the land of wealthy landowners. Smaller landholders were gobbled up by the powerful, and the numbers of the poor swelled. Conditions described previously in Amos became worse. Corrupt business practices and stealing, two forms of injustice that commonly increase in circumstances of economic desperation, became rampant.

Hosea reports that these desperate economic circumstances had destroyed compassion and moral stability. Murder, adultery, and drunkenness abounded. Religion was still popular, but it seems to have lapsed into new forms of syncretism with the religion of their neighbors. For example, cult prostitution, long a part of Canaanite Baal worship, seems to have revived in Israel. Even the priests were condemned as corrupt and immoral. Israel's covenantal relationship with Yahweh was severely compromised, if not forgotten altogether.

Marriage and Call

The book of Hosea reports that Hosea was called by God to take "a wife of whoredom and have children of whoredom, for the land commits great whoredom by forsaking the Lord" (1:2). Subsequently, Hosea married Gomer, with whom he had three children. He gave these children names that symbolized his understanding of God's judgment of Israel.

The first child was a son named Jezreel as a reminder of the cruelty of the house of Jehu. (Jehu had led a revolution against the house of Ahab and killed Ahab's son, Jehoram, and his wife, Jezebel, in the city of Jezreel almost one hundred years earlier.) The second child was a daughter named Loruhamah, meaning "not pitied," which symbolized that God would no longer have pity on Israel or forgive them. The third child, a son, was named Lo-ammi—"not my people"—to declare that the nation of Israel was no longer God's people.

The idea that God would order a prophet to marry a prostitute was so scandalous to early Jewish and Christian interpreters that they regarded the story as entirely allegorical. The story seems to deal with symbolic actions taken by Hosea to demonstrate the prophetic message God had placed upon him. Unfortunately, the details of those actions are not clear. Was the "wife of whoredom" (1:2) a cultic prostitute or an unfaithful woman involved with the practice of such a cult? If so, was she a prostitute prior to her marriage to Hosea or did she subsequently become unfaithful? In fact, is the woman of chapter 1 (Gomer) even the same person as the woman in chapter 3? Many interpreters do not believe so. The text is not specific. In any case, Hosea's experience led him to use the powerful imagery of unfaithfulness to symbolize Israel's relationship to Yahweh. In his marriage and in the negative names of his children, Hosea uniquely portrayed the pathos of the God who had been rejected by Israel.

Message of the Book

The message of Hosea centers around three closely related themes. The first of these themes is Israel's infidelity to the covenant. The term "covenant" appears five times in the book of Hosea; most of these references, following the analogy of the marriage covenant, emphasize the contrast between the faithfulness of Yahweh and the unfaithfulness of Israel. Just as Hosea's wife Gomer had been unfaithful to him, so Israel had been unfaithful to Yahweh. Their unfaithfulness took two forms. One form was religious apostasy, reflected in the revival of Baal worship and the embracing of other religions and their methods (2:8; 4:12ff.). The other form was immorality: "Swearing, lying, and murder, and stealing and adultery break out; bloodshed follows bloodshed" (4:2).

The second theme of Hosea is judgment and exile. Though less prominent in Hosea than in Amos, this theme is clearly present in the symbolic names given to Hosea's children (1:4-8). Hosea says that Yahweh will take Israel back to Egypt and the wilderness (8:13) or to Assyria (9:3) until they learn from their sins.

The third theme in Hosea, the steadfast love of Yahweh, is the heart of his message and provides the basis of his hope for the future. Hosea's presentation of divine pathos, the suffering of God, is a vital feature of the book (and is particularly described in chapter 11).

Since the book of Hosea, like Amos, was edited by later writers, statements of future hope that are to be attributed to the prophet himself are debated. The foundation for those hopes, however, may have been laid by Hosea himself. Despite Israel's disobedience, God's love for Israel, Yahweh's child, will not die (11:8). The day will come when those previously called "not my people" will be known as "Children of the living God" (1:10). The book ends with a plea for Israel to return to its God and the assurance that Yahweh will heal their faithlessness and love them freely again (14:1-4).

ISAIAH

Isaiah lived and did his work in Judah during its declining years, that critical period when the Northern Kingdom was defeated by the Assyrians and the

Figure 10.1. The Old City of Jerusalem as seen from the Mount of Olives. Jerusalem figured prominently in the messages of many of the prophets. *(Photograph by Mitchell G. Reddish)*

land was annexed to the Assyrian kingdom (approximately 740–701 B.C.E.). During most of that period, Judah was in constant danger and came very close to being destroyed by Assyria. Even though Judah escaped destruction, it was a vassal of Assyria much of the time. Isaiah and Micah sought to interpret the meaning of these events and the will of God for the people of Judah at this time.

Structure of the Book of Isaiah

The book of Isaiah in its present form consists of three books in one. The evidence for the three divisions of the book lies in the stylistic differences, theological content, and historical allusions of its various parts. Only the first thirty-nine chapters of the book of Isaiah are directly attributed to Isaiah of Jerusalem. (Even some of these materials are given later dates by many scholars.) This book is sometimes called First Isaiah. Chapters 40–55 belong to an unknown writer or writers of the exilic period, as evidenced by the references to Cyrus, the Persian king who lived during that period. This second book is often referred to as Deutero-Isaiah ("Second" Isaiah). Chapters 56–66 belong to the period following the Exile, as evidenced by references to events that reflect that period. This work has been called Third (sometimes Trito) Isaiah. How and why these three writings came to be put together is not known. One possibility is that a group of Isaiah's disciples produced the later material in the book to complete the story begun by Isaiah.

The first thirty-nine chapters of Isaiah are divided into four parts (the remaining chapters will be considered subsequently). The first part (chapters 1–12) reports Isaiah's call, his analysis of the sins of Judah and Jerusalem, and his prophecies against them. The second part (chapters 13–23) proclaims judgment against other nations. Part three (chapters 24–35) contains the "Apocalypse of Isaiah" (24–27) and prophecies concerning Judah (28–33) and the future of Zion (34–35). Part four (chapters 36–39) concludes the first book with a historical section on the Assyrian crisis.

Political Background

Throughout most of Isaiah's ministry, Assyria was the dominant power in the region. Many of the crises of this period are related to efforts by various groups to resist the advances of Assyria or throw off its yoke. Isaiah watched from afar as Assyria destroyed Samaria, the capital of Israel, and deported many of the leaders of the population in 722 B.C.E. During many of the crises that rocked the Northern Kingdom, Judah remained relatively stable and untouched. King Uzziah (783–742 B.C.E.), who died in the year Isaiah received his call, achieved fame almost comparable to that of David and Solomon. Under him Judah reached the summit of its power. This was possible partly because Egypt was in decline and Assyria was not yet at the pinnacle of its dominance. The situation changed dramatically, however, shortly after the death of Uzziah. Ahaz, his successor, formed an alliance with Assyria and Judah subsequently became a vassal of Assyria. Later, when Hezekiah was king, Assyria laid siege to Jerusalem but mysteriously withdrew, and Judah was spared.

Economic and Religious Background

The concentration of wealth in the hands of the rich and powerful in Judah followed a pattern similar to the situation in Israel earlier. Although they were wealthy in silver and gold, horses and chariots (2:7), fine garments and jewelry (3:18-23), and houses and property (5:8), they were guilty of oppression of the widows and the fatherless (1:17), of "crushing" the people and "grinding the face of the poor" (3:14-15). They indulged themselves to excess in food and wine at their feasts. Isaiah called them "heroes in drinking wine" and "valiant at mixing drink" (5:22). Furthermore, Isaiah said their corrupt judges "acquit the guilty for a bribe, and deprive the innocent of their rights!" (5:23).

Religion was thriving, but so was social injustice. Although the Temple attracted many worshipers, Isaiah compared them to cattle trampling the sacred courts of Yahweh. On behalf of Yahweh he thundered, "I reared children and brought them up, but they have rebelled against me" (1:2) and

> Your princes are rebels
> and companions of thieves.
> Everyone loves a bribe
> and runs after gifts.
> They do not defend the orphan,
> and the widow's cause does not come before them. (1:23)

Because of this inconsistency God said:

> I have had enough of burnt offerings . . .
> Trample my courts no more;
> bringing offerings is futile . . .
> I cannot endure solemn assemblies with iniquity. (1:11-13)

Isaiah's Call

Isaiah lived in Jerusalem and received his call to be a prophet in the year King Uzziah died (742 B.C.E.). While in the Temple he had a vision of Yahweh and heard a voice asking, "Whom shall I send, and who will go for us?" Isaiah answered, "Here am I; send me!" (6:8). Then he was given a strange challenge: Yahweh told him to speak to the people but also told him that the people would not listen. Judah was like a tree to be cut down; nevertheless, there would still be life in the stump (6:9-13). This call apparently signified that even though many would reject his message and judgment would follow, eventually God would bring new life.

Isaiah married and had at least two children. Like Hosea, he gave them names symbolic of the last days before captivity. One son he named Shear-jashub, which means "a remnant shall return," and the other he named Maher-shalal-hash-baz, which means "the spoil speeds, the prey hastens."

Phases of Isaiah's Ministry

In general, Isaiah's ministry may be divided into two broad phases. The first phase includes the beginning of his ministry, his effort to deal with the first major crisis of Ahaz's kingship (the war against Assyria by Israel and Syria), and his withdrawal from public life for a time. Isaiah had advised King Ahaz to trust in God and make no deal with anyone; he assured him that Judah would survive the crisis. Ahaz took only half of his advice. He did resist the efforts of Israel and Syria to force him into their campaign to stop the Assyrians, but he chose to make a deal with Tiglath-pileser, the Assyrian king. Ahaz may have sought to buy time with his deal with Assyria, thinking perhaps that Assyria would win and that it would be better to align himself with the victor.

The second phase came when the Assyrian crisis was at its height, during the reign of Hezekiah, the son of Ahaz. In 713–711 B.C.E. Hezekiah joined a coalition with Ashdod, Edom, and Moab in an effort to throw off the Assyrian yoke he had inherited from his father. Apparently some suggested bringing Egypt into the coalition. Isaiah advised against the revolt and also against getting assistance from Egypt (Isa. 20). According to the text, Isaiah walked around Jerusalem for three years "naked and barefoot" as a sign that Egypt would be taken captive by the Assyrians. Isaiah urged Hezekiah to trust in God and assured him, as he had his father earlier, that Jerusalem would survive the crisis. Whether due to Isaiah's advice or not, Hezekiah soon ceased participation in the revolt and was spared harsh punishment. Later, in 705 B.C.E., Hezekiah openly broke with Assyria and Sennacherib, king of Assyria, laid siege to Jerusalem. Isaiah again counseled Hezekiah not to accede to Assyrian demands. Hezekiah, however, paid a heavy tribute to Sennacherib (2 Kings 18:14-16), and Judah resumed its status as a vassal of Assyria.

Figure 10.2. Ruins of the ancient city of Lachish. One of the major fortified cities in Judah during the tenth to the eighth centuries B.C.E., Lachish was conquered and destroyed by the Assyrian king Sennacherib in 701 B.C.E. Later rebuilt, the city never regained its former glory. *(Photograph by Mitchell G. Reddish)*

Isaiah's Message

The message of Isaiah to Jerusalem and to Judah may be summarized around four themes. The first is the sovereignty of God as the Holy One. Whereas Amos emphasized justice and Hosea emphasized steadfast love and mercy, Isaiah emphasized the holiness of Yahweh. The "holiness" of Yahweh included justice and mercy but above all emphasized the distinctiveness, the "otherness," of Yahweh. This element is prominent in his call vision, reported in chapter 6.

The second theme of Isaiah's preaching is the judgment of God that would come upon the people of Judah for their rebellion against God. Symptoms of this rebellion included their pride (2:6-12), their indifference to the claims of justice (1:17, 21, 27), their attempt to hide behind their scrupulous religiosity (1:10-13), their moral instability (3:1-6), their lust for land (5:8), and their bribery (1:23). For Isaiah, the coming day of the LORD would be as it was for Amos, a day of darkness and not light, a day when God would judge the people for their sins (2:12, 17, 20).

The third theme of Isaiah is trust in Yahweh. This theme is made explicit in Isaiah's prophecies concerning the political events surrounding the revolt of Israel and Syria against Assyria. Isaiah assured the fearful Ahaz that the two kings of the rebel nations, who were the source of his fears, were like torches about to flicker out. He urged him simply to trust in God (7:4). Isaiah declared that God would give Ahaz a sign: a young woman would conceive (or was already pregnant—the text is not specific) and bear a son, and before the child would know right from wrong (possibly two years or so), the threatening nations would cease to exist. The child would be named Immanuel ("God with us"), a name that implied favor to the righteous and judgment on the wicked (7:10-17). Whether this woman who was to give birth was the wife of Isaiah or Ahaz or another is not specified. But Ahaz, for his own protection, betrayed his faith in Yahweh by sending gifts to the Assyrian king. Subsequently, as prophesied by Isaiah (8:5-15), both Judah and Israel fell.

The fourth theme of Isaiah is his faith in the Zion-Davidic tradition. Isaiah 9 and 11 (perhaps written later in Isaiah's career, or even by a later editor) foresee the coming of a wonder child who will perform the task not only of governing Israel properly but also of eventually ruling the whole earth. Either Isaiah or his disciples believed that out of Zion would come one who would bring peace and justice among many nations.

The nature of these "messianic" passages is much disputed. What was the original setting for these passages? Do they refer to a present person or a future person? Two things seem clear. In their biblical settings, these references point to specific, immediate situations to which the prophets sought to bring comfort, assurance, and hope; but beyond their immediate day, the prophets anticipated a coming ideal reign that would fulfill the promise of the ultimate kingdom of Zion. Both Judaism and Christianity have found in these words confirmation of their own deepest hopes and understandings of the promised peace of God.

Isaiah's faith in the protecting presence of God continued even with the invasion of Judah by Sennacherib. Isaiah had advised against revolt (Isa. 20) and viewed Assyria as the rod of God's anger (10:5-6). However, when Assyria's work as God's instrument was done, Assyria would be punished (Isa. 10:12; 14:24-27).

After the withdrawal of the Assyrians, Isaiah dropped out of public view. But his faith and the survival of Jerusalem throughout the Assyrian crisis made a lasting impact on his followers, as witnessed by the preservation and editing of his book by his disciples. One extrabiblical tradition says that he was martyred by Manasseh, a later king of Judah.

MICAH

In the midst of Isaiah's ministry, Micah appeared in Judah. He was from the small village of Moresheth, located in the southwestern foothills of Judah. The book of Micah falls into two parts, chapters 1–5 and chapters 6–7, both of which present oracles of judgment and oracles of hope. Only the first three chapters definitely date to Micah of Moresheth; the remainder contain prophetic sayings dating as late as the postexilic period.

Although his book is difficult to date with certainty, its introduction places it in the time of Isaiah. The book of Jeremiah says that "Micah of Moresheth . . . prophesied during the days of King Hezekiah," so it may be that his work was limited to the reign of Hezekiah (Jer. 26:18). The political, economic, moral, and religious background out of which Micah emerged was the same as that of Isaiah. He shared Isaiah's faith in God, his concern for justice, his belief in the judgment that would come because of Judah's failures, and his hope of salvation.

Micah's Message

Three themes are prominent in the book of Micah. First is the theme of judgment on both Israel and Judah. Micah is very explicit in announcing the fall of Jerusalem, a prediction that Jeremiah credits to him many years later (Mic. 3:12; Jer. 26:18-19). Jerusalem would fall because of exploitation of the poor by the rich and powerful (Mic. 2:1-4), indifference to the claims of justice (7:3), loss of integrity (6:12; 7:5), and the breakdown of the family (7:6).

The second theme of Micah is salvation. The book of Micah does not conclude with a word of judgment but a word of hope. In the future God will judge many nations, wars will cease, and everyone will enjoy economic security (4:1-4). A new ruler will come, born not in Jerusalem but in Bethlehem, the city of David, who will bring security to God's people (5:2-5).

The final theme of Micah is God's requirement of moral and spiritual responsibility. In his most noted statement, Micah says:

> He has told you, O mortal, what is good;
> and what does the LORD require of you
> but to do justice, and to love kindness,
> and to walk humbly with your God? (6:8)

JEREMIAH

The book of Jeremiah is the longest of all the prophetic books. It was likely the product of editing during the Exile and clearly follows the Deuteronomistic theology of covenant faithfulness as being essential for the life of Israel. But it modifies the absolute rewards and punishments motif of Deuteronomy by declaring the pathos of God—God yearning for Israel's return—as providing hope in spite of Israel's disobedience. The book also contradicts the Zion-royal theology that believed the monarchy and the Temple were indispensable to Yahweh and therefore immune to judgment.

It is uncertain whether the ministry of Jeremiah concluded with the fall of Jerusalem in 587 B.C.E., as the first chapter of the book seems to suggest (1:1-3), or if his prophetic activity continued for a while during the Exile (40:1; 43:8; 44:1, 24-25).

Political Background of Jeremiah

Jeremiah's prophetic activity began during the reign of King Josiah. The downfall of the Assyrian kingdom at the hands of the Babylonians and the Medes was taken by Josiah as an opportune time to expand his kingdom. Only three years later, however, Josiah was killed at Megiddo while trying to block Egypt's actions against the rising power of Babylonia. Subsequently, the Babylonians defeated the Egyptians (605 B.C.E.), and during the next years Judah desperately alternated its alliances between Egypt and Babylonia, always as a vassal paying heavy tribute. The nation consequently was torn internally by strife between pro-Egyptian, pro-Babylonian, and nationalistic factions.

Most of Jeremiah's career was profoundly affected by the political instability brought by the pressures of the Babylonians on Judah. Jeremiah saw several kings and one governor come and go. His book, however, connects his prophecies mainly with Josiah, Jehoiakim, and Gedaliah.

Religious Background

Two theologies struggled against one another during these tumultuous years. The survival of Jerusalem during the Assyrian crisis convinced many people of Judah that Jerusalem was invulnerable and that a king from the line of David would always be on the throne. This Zion theology seemed to be affirmed by certain of the words of Isaiah (Isa. 7:10-25; 28:1-22; 33:1-24). On the other hand, Deuteronomistic theology insisted that the election of Israel was conditional and required obedience to the Law; disobedience would be punished by exile and death. After the fall of the Northern Kingdom, this theology began to exert increasing influence in Judah. During the reign of Josiah, the Deuteronomic (or Yahwistic) reform furthered the influence of Deuteronomistic theology.

Jeremiah's Call

Jeremiah may have been descended from a priestly family, but he did not become a priest. Thus he could own land and was independent enough to have his own scribe (Baruch). Regarding his call, Jeremiah reports that the LORD spoke, saying, "Before I formed you in the womb I knew you, and before you were born I consecrated you; I appointed you a prophet to the nations" (1:5).

Jeremiah objected, saying that he was a mere youth and could not speak. But God ignored his excuses about his youth, warned him of the opposition he would receive, and assured him that though his enemies would fight against him, they would not win because God would be with him (1:4-19). In a vision Jeremiah saw a stick of almond wood (Hebrew *shaqed*), signifying that God would watch (*shoqed*) over the word given to him (1:11-12). In a second vision he saw a boiling pot tipped over toward the south, a sign that Judah would be attacked by an enemy from the north.

This entire account of the call of Jeremiah parallels the experience of Moses to a remarkable degree and thus signifies that Jeremiah is a Mosaic prophet—that is, one with whom the Lord had spoken directly (Num. 12:6-8). The overall effect of the narrative is to strengthen the authority of Jeremiah as a prophet.

Phases of His Ministry

The first phase of Jeremiah's ministry coincided with the period of Josiah's reform. In this phase, Jeremiah described Judah's sin (chapters 1–2), called for

Figure 10.3. The Jezreel Valley, also known as the Plain of Megiddo, was a strategic military location because it served as the pass through the Central Highlands mountains, separating Galilee from Samaria. Josiah died in battle at Megiddo. *(Photograph by Mitchell G. Reddish)*

national repentance (chapters 3–4), and warned of trouble from the north (chapters 5–6). He described the sins of Judah as degeneracy, sensuality, and double-mindedness. They forgot God (Jer. 2:32) but found themselves following the wrong leaders in desperation.

The consequences of Jeremiah's early preaching were discouraging. He was generally ignored and rejected in his hometown, though he may have caught the ear of Josiah. Strangely, the extensive reform of Josiah, given considerable attention in the Deuteronomistic history, is never directly mentioned by Jeremiah. Perhaps after being ignored, Jeremiah decided to withdraw from public life. Many scholars believe that Jeremiah was disappointed in the results of the reform—that he thought it was external and superficial and did not represent a change of heart on the part of the nation.

The second phase of Jeremiah's work took place during Jehoiakim's rule (609–598 B.C.E.). After his early ministry Jeremiah, like Isaiah, withdrew for a time. When Jehoiakim came to power in 609 B.C.E., Jeremiah broke his silence. Much of the material in chapters 7–20, though heavily edited in its present form, comes from this period. Jeremiah called the nation to repentance, and his life was threatened. He was first forced to hide, then later was imprisoned and narrowly escaped death. (Chapters 20–26, Baruch's memoirs, describe these events.)

At least some of the material in chapters 27–29, 32–34, and 37–39 comes from the third phase of Jeremiah's ministry, during Zedekiah's reign (597–587 B.C.E.). Jeremiah's statements during this period are pessimistic concerning the possibility of resistance to Babylon. On one occasion he wore a wooden yoke, such as oxen wore, to symbolize God's declaration that Judah must serve Babylon for a time and then Babylon itself would fall. The prophet Hananiah, however, took the yoke from Jeremiah and broke it, prophesying that God would break the "yoke" of Babylon upon their necks within two years. At the command of God, Jeremiah then reappeared in an iron yoke to emphasize the hard servitude to Babylon that would ensue. Hananiah subsequently died, establishing Jeremiah as a true prophet and himself as a false prophet (chapters 27–28).

Jeremiah also encouraged Zedekiah to cooperate with the Babylonians. For that advice he was accused of treason and imprisoned again. Instead of listening to Jeremiah, Zedekiah organized a revolt against the Babylonians. They then returned to Jerusalem, destroyed the city (including the Temple), captured Zedekiah, murdered his sons before his eyes, blinded him, and deported him to Babylon. The Babylonians released Jeremiah from prison and gave him the choice of going to Babylon, with the promise of good treatment, or of staying with the remaining people, over whom the Babylonians appointed Gedaliah as governor. Jeremiah chose to stay with "the poor of the land" who were left. Shortly thereafter rebels killed Gedaliah. Finally, a small group, against Jeremiah's advice, decided to go to Egypt and forced Jeremiah to go with them; it was probably there that he died.

Jeremiah's Message

Jeremiah's preaching is extensive and complex, but it may be summarized around three features. First, Jeremiah warned of the foe from the north that would bring destruction unless the people of Judah changed their ways (which foe Jeremiah had in mind is unknown). If they repented, he held out some hope that impending doom might be avoided. He described Judah as a piece of ruined clay that could still be remade in the hands of a skilled potter (18:4-6).

Second, after it became obvious that the people of Judah would not change, Jeremiah preached that they should surrender to Babylon. Yahweh had called Nebuchadrezzar his servant! According to Jeremiah, Nebuchadrezzar's triumph over Judah was Yahweh's means of punishing the people for their disobedience and idolatry (25:9; 27:6; 43:10). Jeremiah assured them that if they surrendered, they would continue to live on their own land. To demonstrate his sincere belief, he bought a piece of land while the Babylonians were besieging Jerusalem.

Third, Jeremiah held out hope to Judah (his own "complaints" notwithstanding—see below). Before Jerusalem was destroyed, he wrote to captives already in exile in Babylonia that the LORD would ultimately restore Jerusalem (chapter 29). But the captives must acknowledge their sins and repent of them. Then he predicted a new covenant (31:31-34), one that would be written on the heart. Knowledge of God would come from the heart, and God's part in the covenant would be the forgiveness of Judah's sin. The people of Judah were assured of restoration after the Exile and a new stage of harmony with God.

The conclusion of the book (chapter 52) served to support this hope. Since all of his oracles against the city had come to pass, Jeremiah could be accepted as a true Mosaic prophet whose promises would also be fulfilled. Likewise, his Deuteronomistic theology had been vindicated and could form the basis for the new nation to come.

The "complaints" of Jeremiah, found in at least five places (11:18–12:4; 15:10-21; 17:14-18; 18:18-23; 20:7-18), express Jeremiah's frustration at his enemies' seeming success, his own suffering (he was often beaten or imprisoned), and Yahweh's inaction. First retained because they marked Jeremiah's agonizing struggles, these laments later came to express the corporate agony of the people in their experience as exiles. Jeremiah thus became a symbol of endurance and fidelity in life's darkest hours.

ZEPHANIAH

Zephaniah was the first biblical prophet after Isaiah and Micah and the first prophetic voice following the dark days of Manasseh, the king who promoted idolatry. Though his activity is difficult to date with precision, Zephaniah may well have begun his prophetic career before Josiah's reform. Possibly he was among the reform prophets and Levites who shared responsibility for producing Deuteronomy.

The central message of Zephaniah is that the fire of God's wrath is about to burn the whole of the created order (1:2-3). He hoped the stinging judgment he announced would provoke the people of Judah to repent of their sins. The sins that justified his condemnation included their idolatry (1:4), their unethical actions (1:9), and their loss of faith in the God of Israel (1:12). According to Zephaniah, the "day of the LORD" would be a day of judgment on the Judeans and their neighbors. While he does not identify the immediate source of devastation (some think he may have had the Scythians in mind), he regarded God as the ultimate source of judgment. But beyond that judgment a faithful remnant would survive, and through them Yahweh would continue to work toward establishing the kingdom of God over all the earth (3:14-20).

NAHUM

Nahum was likely a temple prophet functioning within the cult at Jerusalem. His prophecy came near the time of the fall of Nineveh, the Assyrian capital, in 612 B.C.E. and may have been prompted by the nearness of that event. The revolt of Manasseh described in Chronicles may have been viewed by Nahum as a signal that the end was near for Nineveh. On the other hand, it is also possible that Nahum's message inspired Manasseh to revolt against Assyria. The focus of Nahum's message was the judgment of God on the capital of once-mighty Assyria, which had inflicted untold suffering on Judah. The subsequent destruction of Nineveh assured the place of Nahum in the canon. The poetry of the book is unexcelled in Hebrew Scripture.

HABAKKUK

Habakkuk, like Zephaniah, is difficult to date precisely, but most likely he lived either near the end of Assyrian dominance or near the beginning of Babylonian threats to Judah. The book is dominated by a strong challenge to a traditional view of God's justice. Unlike Isaiah, who readily accepted the use of Assyria as the rod of God's anger, Habakkuk asked how a just God could allow such violence and injustice. Why was wickedness not being punished?

Habakkuk did not answer this question fully. The answer he received from God and gave in his prophecy is that those who are not upright will eventually fall, and those who are righteous will live by faith (2:4). Perhaps fidelity will outlast injustice (2:1-4), for judgment will come on those who are dominated by covetous lust (2:6-8), economic pride (2:9-11), political corruption (2:12-14), drunkenness (2:15-17), and idolatry (2:19).

Habakkuk concluded his prophecy with the quiet affirmation that he would wait for trouble to come upon his enemies, and that no matter how bad things became, he would still trust and rejoice in God (3:16-19). This third chapter of Habakkuk is possibly a later addition; the commentary on the book produced by the Qumran community did not include it.

THE PREEXILIC PROPHETS AND THE DIVINE-HUMAN ENCOUNTER

Even in the darkest hours of the last years of Israel, the preexilic prophets never lost faith in the God of the Hebrews. Although they rejected the notion that the prime guarantee of the future of Israel was God's actions in the past (either in the Exodus or in the Davidic kingship), the preexilic prophets never really denied the importance of those events. They continued to believe that the God who called Israel into being was working in history and had not abandoned the people of Israel. They presented a reinterpretation of God's presence even in the catastrophes of history they experienced. These prophets interpreted the tragic events of their time not as evidence that God had abandoned Israel but as evidence of God's providence for them. Therefore they called their people to repent and learn from their mistakes.

In Jeremiah, particularly, new ground was broken in Israel's understanding of God. Jeremiah's agonized search for God in the pain of his experience contributed to the breaking down of the old assumption that the innocent are always rewarded and the unrighteous always punished. In its own long exile and slow recovery, Israel would cling to the endurance of Jeremiah as a model of fidelity to God.

The prophets of the Exile, who will be studied in the chapter that follows, continued to develop new interpretations of the past and provide new hopes for the future.

Chapter 11

THE EXILE, EXILIC PROPHETS, AND EXILIC HISTORIES

Suggested Biblical Readings: Ezekiel 1:1–3:15; 37:1-14; 47:1-12; Isaiah 40:1-11, 28-31; 42:1-4; 53; 55; Genesis 1:1–2:4; Joshua 23

The exilic period was both traumatic and creative. The Hebrews suffered greatly. They were stripped of all that gave them meaning—their holy city, the Promised Land, the Temple, and the Davidic monarchy. They reflected on their trauma in various ways. Two prophetic voices, Ezekiel and Second Isaiah, kindled sparks of hope with the promise of the restoration of Judah. Two interpretations of the past, the Deuteronomistic history and the Priestly history, attempted to make sense of the Exile in the light of Hebrew history. A new future and a new understanding of religion emerged from this difficult and creative time.

THE HISTORICAL SITUATION

Judah lay in ruins. The glue that had held the nation together—the Temple, symbol of religious unity; the Davidic monarchy, symbol of political unity; and the city itself, symbol of national vitality—was dissolved. Enormous human suffering followed. For about fifty years the future of the Hebrews seemed bleak, until the Persians freed the exiles in Babylon in 538 B.C.E. and permitted them to return to Judah to rebuild Jerusalem.

Responses to the devastation of Jerusalem and the Exile to Babylon varied among the deportees and the Hebrews remaining in Judah. One response was that of lament. The grief-stricken poets writing the book of Lamentations wailed over the loss of Jerusalem:

> How lonely sits the city
> that once was full of people!
> How like a widow she has become,
> she that was great among the nations!
> She that was a princess among the provinces
> has become a vassal.
>
> ....
>
> Enemies have stretched out their hands
> over all her precious things;
> she has even seen the nations

> invade her sanctuary,
> those whom you forbade
>   to enter your congregation.
>
> All her people groan
>   as they search for bread;
> they trade their treasures for food
>   to revive their strength.
> Look, O LORD, and see
>   how worthless I have become.
>
> Is it nothing to you, all you who pass by?
>   Look and see
> if there is any sorrow like my sorrow,
>   which was brought upon me,
> which the LORD inflicted
>   on the day of his fierce anger. (Lam. 1:1, 10-12)

A second response was that of anger toward their captors. Hebrew writers sought vengeance, picturing a future in which God would pursue and destroy the Babylonians (Lam. 3:64-66). In one of the most gruesome and troubling psalms thought to be from the exilic period, the sorrowing Yahwists cry out against the Babylonians:

> Happy shall they be who pay you back
>   what you have done to us!
> Happy shall they be who take your little ones
>   and dash them against the rock! (Ps. 137:8*b*-9)

A third response was that of hostility toward their neighbors who failed to support them in resisting the Babylonian invasion. The entire book of Obadiah, for example, seethes with anger against neighboring Edom.

A fourth response, influenced by the popular idea that the gods of the victor had proved their superiority over the gods of the defeated, gave up faith in Yahweh for devotion to Marduk, the chief Babylonian deity. In Judah, non-Yahwist cults flourished (see Jer. 44:16ff.).

A fifth response interpreted the Exile as the just judgment of Yahweh upon the unfaithfulness of the people of Judah. The oracles of Second Isaiah and Ezekiel present this view, as do the five poems of Lamentations.

> Jerusalem sinned grievously,
>   so she has become a mockery. (Lam. 1:8*a*)

> The LORD has trodden as in a wine press
>> the virgin daughter Judah. (Lam. 1:15*b*)

> The LORD gave full vent to his wrath;
>> he poured out his hot anger,
> and kindled a fire in Zion
>> that consumed its foundations. (Lam. 4:11)

The theme of exile as judgment included an emphasis upon the compassion and forgiveness of God. God's judgment was believed not to be utterly punitive. God disciplined so that the people would repent and return to the covenant. Again, Lamentations echoes this theme:

> For the Lord will not reject forever.
> Although he causes grief, he will have compassion
>> according to the abundance of his steadfast love;
> for he does not willingly afflict or grieve anyone. (Lam. 3:31-33)

Figure 11.1. The Babylonian Chronicle is a cuneiform text that describes the siege of Jerusalem by Nebuchadrezzar and the exile of Jehoiachin, king of Judah, to Babylon in 597 B.C.E. (© *The British Museum*)

While the situation of the deportees in Babylon was less than ideal, they apparently sustained themselves well. The Babylonians allowed them to live in a colony along the Chebar River and to maintain their social and religious traditions. Some of the people thrived. When Cyrus, leader of the Persians, permitted the Hebrews to migrate back to Judah fifty years later, only a portion returned. Of the remainder, some were absorbed into Babylonian society while others maintained Jewish traditions and identity.

THE EXILIC PROPHETS

During the Exile an extensive and important Jewish literature was produced. Among these writings are those of the prophets Ezekiel and Second Isaiah. Each writer contributed uniquely to the understanding of the divine-human encounter during the Exile.

Ezekiel

Ezekiel was sent from Jerusalem to Babylon in the first deportation in 597 B.C.E. with King Jehoiachin and other leading citizens. He received his call to prophesy about 593 B.C.E. in the village of Tel-abib along the Chebar River (Ezek. 1:1-3). He served as a priest and prophet from about 593 to 571 in Babylon, where he spoke to the exiles on behalf of God.

Scholars disagree about the location from which Ezekiel wrote. Although the audience of chapters 1–24 is the exiles in Babylon, the setting is Jerusalem after 597 B.C.E. Ezekiel's concrete knowledge of events in Jerusalem has led some to conclude that he had returned to Jerusalem for the period between the two deportations, but these arguments are not convincing. His reports of happenings in Jerusalem can be accounted for by considering his familiarity with Jerusalem and the possibility that he received news reports on events there.

The book of Ezekiel consists of three parts. Chapters 1–24 contain messages of warning and further judgment against Jerusalem that were uttered between 593 and 587 B.C.E. Chapters 25–32 include oracles of judgment against Judah's neighbors and derive from the same period. Chapters 33–48, which were written during the period following the second deportation of the Hebrews to Babylon in 587, turn from judgment to the hope of a restored Jerusalem.

Ezekiel 1–3 contains a record of Ezekiel's call to prophesy: "The word of the Lord came to the priest Ezekiel...and the hand of the LORD was on him there" (1:3). The call is punctuated by the startling throne chariot vision (1:4-28) and specifications of his message (2:1–3:11). In the vision a holy presence confronts the prophet. "The appearance of the likeness of the glory of the LORD" (1:28) arrives upon a throne chariot from the north. Surrounded by wind, cloud, and fire—

traditional indicators of the presence of God—and accompanied by four winged creatures that were composites of an eagle, a lion, and a man, the chariot appeared to move in any direction. Awed, Ezekiel fell upon his face and heard the voice of the LORD (1:28b). The LORD refers to Ezekiel as "son of man" (RSV) (NRSV: "mortal"), an address that occurs 93 times in the book. In Ezekiel it refers to the prophet as "a mere human" in contrast to the awesome holiness of God. God instructs Ezekiel to speak to the exiles, "a nation of rebels who have rebelled against me" (2:3). Several times (2:7, 3:11) God urges Ezekiel to speak for God regardless of whether the exiles listen.

Ezekiel's message of judgment (chapters 4–24) against rebellious Judah contains several themes. From an examination of the history of the people, Ezekiel finds that they have rebelled against God from the time of their captivity in Egypt. Unlike most prophets, who tended to idealize the Mosaic period, Ezekiel declares that from the earliest days the people had turned their back on Yahweh and sought other gods. According to Ezekiel, God called the people out of Egypt (20:5-7), "but they rebelled against me and would not listen to me . . . nor did they forsake the idols of Egypt" (20:8). For Ezekiel there was never a time of Hebrew innocence and purity. They continually and deliberately turned away from God to other gods, thereby defiling themselves and becoming spiritually unclean. God, whom Ezekiel depicts as holy, faithful, and pure, has regularly brought judgment upon them. During Ezekiel's own lifetime the same old rebelliousness had erupted. In chapter 16 he pictures Jerusalem and Samaria, the capitals of Judah and Israel, as harlots who have been unfaithful to God. Their rebellion has taken the form of infidelity to God; they have defiled the pure worship of God with the worship of foreign deities. They are also guilty of contracting political alliances with non-Yahwistic nations. Ezekiel believed that through judgment the people would come to "know" God—that is, acknowledge God's sovereignty over them as the covenant people (16:62).

Ezekiel dramatizes his prophecies of judgment through eight symbolic acts (4:1-11; 5:1-12; 12:1-20; 24:15-17). In Ezekiel 5:1-12, for example, he shaves his head and beard and divides the hair into three portions. He burns one third to indicate that a third of the citizens will perish in the forthcoming sack of Jerusalem. He chops another third with a sword to denote that a third of the people will be killed in the siege. He scatters a final third to the wind to prophesy the exile of a third of the population. Although Ezekiel's dramatic and somewhat bizarre actions are peculiar to him, they are not without precedent among the classical prophets. Several prophets named their children symbolically, and Jeremiah had declared a prophetic message in his purchase of a plot of ground in Anathoth. These behaviors, combined with spoken words, presented hearers with both a visual and an oral message.

Although the idea that the destruction of Judah was a just action of God

Figure 11.2. This ivory carving found at Nimrud (Calah, a city twenty miles south of ancient Nineveh) depicts "the woman at the window," likely a harlot. Ezekiel likewise depicts Jerusalem and Samaria, capitals of Judah and Israel, as harlots for their unfaithfulness to Yahweh. (© *The British Museum*)

against a rebellious and unrepentant people became the dominant interpretation of the Exile, Ezekiel also addressed the lingering belief of some exiles that their generation had been punished unjustly for the sins of previous generations. Their belief was expressed in the popular proverb, "The parents [previous generations] have eaten sour grapes, and the children's [present generation's] teeth are set on edge" (18:2). Although some Hebrew religious thought supported their belief (for example, Ex. 20:4-6), Ezekiel argued that "a child shall not suffer for the iniquity of a parent" (18:20). Those who commit wicked acts shall themselves be judged

(18:21-32). He thereby upheld the view that exile was a just punishment on the present generation.

Ezekiel 25–32 contains passages of judgment against Ammon, Moab, Edom, Philistia, Tyre, Sidon, and Egypt. These oracles reflect Ezekiel's understanding of God's sovereignty over other nations, not just the people of the covenant. They also suggest that the prophesied judgment will result from the failure of those nations to aid Judah. For example, Ezekiel declares that "because you [the nation of Ammon] said, "Aha!" over my [God's] sanctuary when it was profaned, and over the land of Israel when it was made desolate, and over the house of Judah when it went into exile; therefore I am handing you over" (25:3-4a). Nation after nation is declared guilty in a series of oracles that continue through chapter 32.

The theme and tone of Ezekiel abruptly change in chapters 33–48. These chapters appear to have been composed after the second deportation from Jerusalem in 587 B.C.E. (see Ezek. 33:21-22), which Ezekiel believes to have been God's final judgment against Judah. He then turns from oracles of judgment and enunciates the promise of the restoration of the nation. Ezekiel 34:11-15 is typical of the change in focus. In this passage God appears as a good shepherd to the exiles:

> For thus says the Lord GOD: I myself will search for my sheep, and will seek them out. As shepherds seek out their flocks when they are among their scattered sheep, so I will seek out my sheep. I will rescue them from all the places to which they have been scattered on a day of clouds and thick darkness. I will bring them out from the peoples and gather them from the countries, and will bring them into their own land; and I will feed them on the mountains of Israel, by the watercourses, and in all the inhabited parts of the land. I will feed them with good pasture, and the mountain heights of Israel shall be their pasture; there they shall lie down in good grazing land, and they shall feed on rich pasture on the mountains of Israel. I myself will be the shepherd of my sheep, and I will make them lie down, says the Lord GOD.

Ezekiel presents the restoration of the people of Judah in three images. First, in chapter 37 he reports his vision of an old battlefield that is littered with bones that have been bleached white in the desert sun. In the vision he hears the voice of God inquire, "Mortal, can these bones live?" In answer, God instructs him to say to the bones: "I will cause breath to enter you, and you shall live. I will lay sinews on you . . . and cover you with skin, and put breath in you, and you shall live; and you shall know that I am the LORD" (37:5b-6).

Ezekiel follows God's bidding and speaks to the dry bones. The bones become enfleshed—"breath came into them, and they lived." God then (37:11-14) interprets the vision to Ezekiel. The dry bones represent the barren and destitute people of Israel, into whom God will breathe new life. "I will put my spirit within you, and you shall live, and I will place you on your own soil; then you shall know that I, the LORD, have spoken and will act, says the LORD" (37:14). This powerful vision of the promised restoration of the covenant people should not be confused with the later Jewish and Christian idea of resurrection of the dead. Ezekiel's vision depicts the resuscitation of a dead nation rather than a belief in individual life after death.

Second, Ezekiel envisions the restoration of the spiritual center of Judaism, the Temple in Jerusalem, as well as the return of the people to Judah. It is no surprise that, as a priest himself, Ezekiel boldly locates the Temple and its rituals at the center of his restoration vision. The material in these chapters outlines a design for the new Temple, priestly rules for Temple sacrifice, and the distribution of the land to the immigrants, along with the division of that land.

Third, Ezekiel foresees the renewal of the faith of the restored people in Yahweh. He proclaims that God wishes to restore the people to a covenantal relationship, a covenant of peace (34:25) that is everlasting (37:26). Ezekiel 36:26-28 is illustrative:

> A new heart I will give you, and a new spirit I will put within you; and I will remove from your body the heart of stone and give you a heart of flesh. I will put my spirit within you, and make you follow my statutes and be careful to observe my ordinances. Then you shall live in the land that I gave to your ancestors; and you shall be my people, and I will be your God.

Ezekiel's vision in chapters 40–48 became a model to which postexilic Jews looked as they rebuilt Judah.

Second Isaiah

Second Isaiah, the unknown prophet who composed the elegant poems of Isaiah 40–55, also upheld the traditions of hope and restoration. When he wrote a few decades after Ezekiel, the political fortunes of Babylon had deteriorated and a mood of hope emerged among the exiles. A period of unstable political leadership followed Nebuchadrezzar's death (562 B.C.E.). As Babylon weakened, the Persians under Cyrus became the dominant power. Cyrus took control of the kingdoms of Medea and Lydia. Then, at the battle of Opis in 539, he crushed the last significant Babylonian resistance. He subdued Babylon without a battle and ended the exile of people the Babylonians had brought to the city. (The next chapter will take up the story of the return to Judah.)

Second Isaiah celebrates Cyrus as a servant of God who would deliver the Jews from bondage under God's leadership. Because the historical context of the content of Second Isaiah best fits this period, the book is dated to 540 B.C.E.

Chapter 10 has already discussed the stylistic, historical, linguistic, and theological reasons for deciding that Second Isaiah was not written by the eighth-century prophet Isaiah. Because the themes and language of First Isaiah bear some resemblance to those of Second Isaiah, scholars surmise that a "school" of prophets in the tradition of First Isaiah was responsible for assembling the materials in the book of Isaiah.

Beginning with chapter 40, hope permeates Second Isaiah's poems. He believes that the exiles' captivity will end very soon because their "penalty is paid" (40:2). Therefore, the prophet offers words of comfort to the people, promising that their misery and hardship are over (40:1-2). Many decades after the people last enjoyed the presence of the glory of God in the Temple, Second Isaiah reports a vision in which a new appearance of God is foretold: "The glory of the LORD shall be revealed" (40:5). God's awesome and reliable presence is contrasted to impermanent and vulnerable human life. "All people are grass... [which] withers... but the word of our God will stand forever" (40:6-8). God appears in the vision as a warrior-king (40:10) who has made possible the astonishing victories of Cyrus (41:2-4) and as a good shepherd who keeps the Jewish people safe (40:11). God appears as the source of all creation, including waters, heavens, and earth (40:12-28)—the Lord of history "who brings princes to naught, and makes the rulers of the earth as nothing" (40:23). God is the one who has "roused a victor from the east" (Cyrus) who will subdue the nations (41:2; 45:1). In the light of God's power over creation and history, Jerusalem should herald his coming (40:9) and the people should patiently expect his glory to be revealed (40:31).

Most of the central themes of Second Isaiah are present in chapter 40. Second Isaiah's hope for the exiles rests securely in God. In the face of what appears to have been a dispute about the power of God, the prophet seeks to establish God's incomparable nature by comparison to other gods. Through a series of rhetorical questions he asserts that God is the sole creator of the universe (40:12-14). (In all likelihood he was aware of the Babylonian creation myth, the *Enuma Elish*, which posed an alternative tradition from a mythical and polytheistic viewpoint.) For Second Isaiah, God is also the Lord of history (40:15-17). The nations are "like a drop from a bucket" (40:15). As Creator and Lord of history, God is unique. None can compare. In the light of the Holy One (40:25) the Babylonian gods are mocked as mere idols fashioned from wood and metal that cannot answer the prayers of a worshiper (40:18-20; 46). More boldly than any writer before him, Second Isaiah declares an explicit, radical monotheism: "I am God, and there is no other" (46:9*b*).

Based on this doctrine of God, Second Isaiah proclaims his message of hope. He declares a hopeful future by referring to important events from the past. First, he views the end of the Exile as a new Exodus. From their bondage in Babylon the exiles will be freed through the power of God working through

Figure 11.3. This glazed tile relief from the Ishtar Gate in Babylon (sixth century B.C.E.) shows a representation of a dragon, sacred animal of the Babylonian god Marduk. The dragon has a neck and head like a snake, front legs like a lion's legs, rear legs and talons of an eagle, and a body like snake skin. *(Photograph by Mitchell G. Reddish)*

Cyrus, just as they were freed from Egypt by the actions of God through Moses and Pharaoh (see 40:3; 43:15-21; 48:20-22; 51:10-11; 52:12). The hymn of 43:15-21 has close similarities to the hymn of praise that is sung at the Sea of Reeds (Ex. 15:1-18). The deliverance of the exiles from Babylon and their crossing of the desert to Jerusalem will be a new Exodus.

Second, he utilizes the Zion tradition. Jerusalem/Zion had come to represent the special dwelling place of God and the people of God. Although it lies desolate, he declares that a new Jerusalem will be built and populated (44:26; 45:13; 49:14-21; 54:1-3).

Third, a new Exodus and new Jerusalem are possible for Second Isaiah because God as Creator has already subdued chaos and brought into existence a created order. God is therefore capable of reconstituting the people in a new creative act. God's agent will be Cyrus, "whose right hand I have grasped to subdue [the] nations" (45:1). Astonishingly, Cyrus, who was not a Jew, is designated as God's anointed or messiah. The role of the exiles is to declare allegiance to the everlasting God and to wait patiently for the LORD to act, which will renew their strength (40:27-31).

The concept of the covenantal relationship between Israel and God lies at the heart of Second Isaiah's vision of hope. Although God has justly punished the rebellious citizens of Judah by means of the Exile, God's "everlasting love" and "great compassion" (54:7-8)—basic elements of the covenant—will lead to a reestablishment of the people and hence the covenant. God will act as Israel's redeemer. (In Hebrew a "redeemer" was a close relative who came to one's help in emergencies.) Second Isaiah makes use of the idea of God as the exiles' redeemer ten times, far more than any other prophet. God will act as redeemer to free Israel from bondage.

Central to Second Isaiah is another concept that is important for a proper understanding of the divine-human encounter in his writings. In four distinctive poems (42:1-4; 49:1-6; 50:4-9; 52:13–53:12) the figure of the Servant of God appears. Even though some scholars believe the Servant poems had a separate origin and were incorporated into Second Isaiah by the prophet or a later redactor, their arguments are not compelling. Both the style and theology of the poems fit integrally into Second Isaiah.

The foremost critical issue in interpreting the poems is the identity of the Servant. Is the Servant a corporate entity that represents a group of Jews or a specific individual? Strong arguments are made for both. On the one hand, the Servant appears in some passages in the poems as a corporate entity—that is, as a referent for the entire nation of Israel or faithful Jews within the nation. In passages outside the Servant poems—Isaiah 41:8-9, for example—the prophet refers to Israel as God's servant. In the first Servant poem, the Servant possibly refers to Israel, whose function (42:1-4) is to bring justice to the nations. The second Servant poem explicitly designates Israel as the Servant (49:3).

On the other hand, the Servant appears in other parts of the poems as an individual. In the second poem the Servant functions as a person who is to bring the nation back to God, "to restore . . . Israel," and to be "a light to the nations, that [God's] my salvation may reach to the end of the earth" (49:6). In the fourth poem, the servant also appears as a person.

No consensus has emerged over the identity of the Servant despite intense analysis of the Servant poems. Some scholars believe that the issue may be resolved if one recognizes that an individual can represent the entire nation and that the nation in Hebrew thought may be referred to as an individual. This reciprocity occurs in the stories of the ancestors and in the prophetic metaphors used to describe the relationship between God and Israel. If this is the case, one is not faced with a forced choice between the nation and an individual as Servant.

In any case, the role of the Servant is clear. The Servant represents God to all the nations for the purpose of declaring God's righteousness. Unlike Cyrus the powerful conqueror, another of God's servants, the Servant suffers humiliation in executing God's will. Indeed, the Servant suffers vicariously—that is, in the place of or on behalf of the nations. For the first time in the Hebrew tradition—and in contrast to the Deuteronomic theology—the element of righteous suffering on behalf of God's redemptive purpose enters Jewish thought. No longer could suffering be identified exclusively with infidelity. This theme became important to Jews later as a way of understanding their suffering at the hands of their enemies. The theme also became the basis for the Christian interpretation of the death of Jesus in the belief that he suffered death on behalf of others.

THE EXILIC HISTORIES

During the Exile the Hebrews reviewed their history as the covenantal people of God. From their reflections they produced two fresh interpretations of the past that both explained their present state and provided hope for the future.

The Deuteronomistic History

The Deuteronomistic history consists of books that interpret the history of Israel from the time of Moses to the Exile from the point of view of Deuteronomic theology. It includes Deuteronomy, Joshua, Judges, 1 and 2 Samuel, and 1 and 2 Kings. The material was brought into final form during the Exile in Babylon by an unknown Deuteronomistic writer/redactor.

Some scholars hold that the Deuteronomistic history is the product of a school of writers. The late-seventh-century reform movement of King Josiah, based upon an early version of Deuteronomy, had produced a tradition of thinking that lasted beyond Josiah's death into the Exile. These writers completed Deuteronomy by adding chapters 1–4 and 27–30. The existing preexilic traditions of Joshua and Judges were expanded. Few additions were made to 1 and 2 Samuel; 1 and 2 Kings, however, were composed by the Deuteronomistic authors. Working from the late–seventh century into the Exile, the Deuteronomistic writers completed their work shortly after King Jehoiachin was released from a Babylonian prison in 561 B.C.E. (2 Kings 25:27-30). Other scholars believe that the Deuteronomistic history is the product of two Deuteronomistic historians, one who worked shortly after Josiah's death in 609 and one who completed the Deuteronomistic history in Babylon around 550.

The Deuteronomistic history was written to give a religious interpretation of the history of the divine-human encounter from Moses to the Exile. In some ways it is one of the earliest theodicies—that is, an attempt to interpret national calamity to a people who believed they were chosen by God. The Deuteronomistic historians tried to understand why evil had befallen Judah and Israel. During this long period, these historians believed, the people were either blessed/rewarded or cursed/judged. If they remained faithful to the covenant with God, they enjoyed national security and prosperity. If, however, they mixed Yahwism with elements of Canaanite and Egyptian religion or abandoned Yahwism completely, they suffered judgment and material deprivation, usually at the hands of a foreign power such as Assyria, Egypt, or Babylon. In particular, the Deuteronomistic writers defined faithfulness to the covenant as keeping the Law of Moses as stated in Deuteronomy. Living by Torah brought blessing; disobedience brought curse.

At pivotal points in the people's history, their leaders had presented this option to them: Moses before the conquest (Deut. 28:1-68), Joshua in his farewell address (Josh. 23:1-16), Samuel at the inauguration of the monarchy (1 Sam. 12:1-18), and Solomon in his dedicatory speech upon the completion of the Temple (1 Kings 8:12-53). History was determined by the nation's response. For example, in 1 and 2 Kings the period of time from Solomon's accession (961 B.C.E.) to Jehoiachin's deportation (597 B.C.E.) is interpreted as a history determined by the obedience or disobedience of the kings of Israel and Judah. Only Hezekiah and Josiah are honored without qualification. Others, such as Jehoshaphat and Jotham, received reserved praise. Most, even Solomon (see 1 Kings 11:1-43), received harsh judgments. The Deuteronomistic writers used David as their model for a faithful king. For example, Solomon's infidelity to God is described in view of the fact that he "did not completely follow the LORD, as his father David had done" (1 Kings 11:6). Hezekiah, on the other hand, "did what was right in the sight of the LORD just as his ancestor David had done" (2 Kings 18:3).

The Priestly History

The Priestly history is one of the major literary traditions in the Pentateuch and includes large sections of Genesis, Exodus, Leviticus, and Numbers. The Deuteronomistic history focuses on Law; the Priestly history emphasizes worship and ritual. Priests associated with the Temple probably preserved the oral and written materials that provided its sources. Unknown writers brought this material into final literary form during the Exile. Although the material's relation to Ezekiel is obscure, it reflects ideas that are in keeping with Ezekiel 40–48. Some scholars surmise that Ezekiel himself influenced the focus of the Priestly history.

Like the Deuteronomistic history, the Priestly history was written in the wake of the devastating effects of the Exile. Its writers sought to present an interpretation of the past that would instill a way of life and worship in the exiles that would survive the devastation.

The Priestly history divides history into four periods. In each period God establishes an everlasting covenant with the people. The first period begins with Creation and continues to the Flood. The pinnacle of the Priestly creation account (Gen. 1:1–2:4a) is the appearance of human beings ('adam)—male and female—created simultaneously in the image of God (1:27). They are to be God's superintending representatives on earth. The creation account concludes with the

Figure 11.4. *Adam* by the French sculptor Auguste Rodin. *(The Nelson-Atkins Museum of Art, Kansas City, Missouri [Purchase: Nelson Trust] 55-70)*

institution of the Sabbath or a day of rest because the Priestly writers intended to establish an ancient precedent for the Sabbath observance. Creation's promise is thwarted, however, by humanity's continuing violence (see Gen. 3:1-21; 4:1-26; 6:11), and God responds by bringing judgment in the form of a flood.

The second period begins when Noah and his kin are delivered from the

Flood and they become the link to the future. After the Flood, God makes with Noah an everlasting covenant in which God promises never again to deliver the earth into chaos by a flood. The rainbow is a sign of this promise (Gen. 9:8-17). According to the Priestly historian, two new policies were instituted after the Flood: (1) humans were permitted to eat the flesh of animals (Gen. 9:1-4) for the first time and (2) the taking of human life was sanctioned (Gen. 9:6) under certain conditions.

The third period of history commences with Abraham and lasts until Moses. Genesis 17 reports the everlasting covenant God made with Abraham. God promises to Abraham that Canaan will belong to Abraham and his heirs forever and that Abraham's descendants will spread into many nations and receive great political status. Circumcision of males was the sign of this covenant (Gen. 17:9-14).

The fourth period of history began with Moses and continued to the Exile. At Sinai God reestablished with Moses the Abrahamic covenant (Ex. 6:1-9). The Priestly material in Exodus, Leviticus, and Numbers focuses directly on the proper worship of God. Regulations concerning the architecture of worship centers, the priesthood, sacrifices, and holy days are established. The sign of this period is the keeping of the Sabbath.

Several features are prominent in the Priestly history. One feature is the everlasting covenant. The emphasis that from the earliest days God had established an unbroken covenant with the people surely brought hope to the deeply grieving exiles. A second feature is that God appears by different names in the four periods of the Priestly history. In the first two periods God is called Elohim ("Majestic One"). In the third period God is termed El Shaddai ("God Almighty"). In the fourth period the name Yahweh is used of God, a name so sacred that only a few could utter it (Ex. 6:2-3). A third feature of the Priestly history is the use of genealogies that connect the people of the covenant in a unity that extends all the way back to Adam (see Gen. 5:1-32; 10:1-32; 11:10-32).

If the purpose of the Deuteronomistic history was to establish the exiles as an ethical community living in obedience to God's covenant, the primary intent of the Priestly history was to recreate the exiles as a worshiping community who observed the Sabbath and kept themselves ritually pure in response to God's everlasting covenant. Although Temple sacrifice could not be enacted during the Exile, the Priestly writers held firmly to the cultic tradition they brought from Jerusalem. Their intention was to kindle the flame of hope by explaining the past and preparing for a new future in a new Jerusalem Temple after the Exile.

Chapter 12

THE RESTORATION OF JUDAH

Suggested Biblical Readings: Ezra 1:1-4; 9:1–10:5

During the trauma of the Babylonian Exile, the Hebrew prophets Ezekiel and Second Isaiah provided a spark of hope for the exiles with their visions of a future return to Judah. The fulfillment of their visions seemed possible when the Persian conqueror Cyrus provided the opportunity for the Jews to restore Judah and to reconstitute a Jewish nation. The glowing dreams of the prophets, however, did not materialize, and the returning exiles faced great difficulties. In the midst of these problems, new religious developments occurred that were to shape future Judaism.

THE RESTORATION (538–424 B.C.E.)

The power Babylon enjoyed after conquering the mighty Assyrian Empire did not last long. It had only one outstanding king, Nebuchadrezzar (605–562 B.C.E.), who is remembered mainly for building the hanging gardens (if, indeed, they existed) and for carrying the Jews into exile. Most of the evidence available suggests that the Jewish exiles generally received humane treatment by the Babylonians. The last king of Babylon, Nabonidus (556–539 B.C.E.), was more interested in scholarship than in ruling. As a result, during his reign Babylon became vulnerable to an emerging and aggressive power in the ancient Near East—the country of Persia.

In 539 B.C.E. the forces of Cyrus of Persia took Babylon without a battle. The Persian Empire encompassed the entire Babylonian Empire, reaching from Greece to India and from Asia Minor to North Africa. Jewish exiles in Babylon and Egypt and the remaining Jews in Judah became subjects of Persia.

Persian policies regarding captured and exiled peoples differed sharply from the policies of the Babylonians. The Persians considered themselves benevolent rulers concerned for peace and order. They developed roads and communication systems and made the main travel and trade routes secure for safe passage. They also encouraged the preservation of local customs. Instead of imposing their religious beliefs on others, they allowed the rebuilding of the places of worship of their subjects and sometimes supported such procedures financially. The Persians also permitted local government under the watchful eyes of their own regional administrators. The attitude of Cyrus toward captive peoples is reflected in the Cyrus Cylinder, a clay artifact that describes Cyrus's defeat of the Babylonians. The inscription on the cylinder tells how Cyrus attributed his success to the aid of the Babylonian god Marduk and reports that Cyrus rebuilt worship places and returned exiles to their lands. The book of Ezra attributes Cyrus's victory to Yahweh instead of Marduk and contains a different version of the edict of Cyrus. Ezra's version includes provisions that the Temple in Jerusalem be rebuilt and refurbished with the vessels taken by the Babylonian ruler Nebuchadrezzar. Ezra states:

> Thus says King Cyrus of Persia: The LORD, the God of heaven, has given me all the kingdoms of the earth, and he has charged me to build him a house at Jerusalem in Judah. Any of those among you who are of his people—may their God be with them!—are now permitted to go up to Jerusalem in Judah, and rebuild the house of the LORD, the God of Israel—he is the God who is in Jerusalem; and let all survivors, in whatever place they reside, be assisted by the people of their place with silver and gold, with goods and with animals, besides freewill offerings for the house of God in Jerusalem. (1:2-4)

The return of the exiles to Palestine was a slow process. An entire generation of exiles had grown up in Babylon. Palestine was the land of their ancestors, but Babylon was home for most of them. Furthermore, the condition of the land of Judah—still mostly in ruins—was not attractive. These reasons, coupled with the benevolence of the Persians toward conquered peoples, led many of the Jewish exiles to remain in Babylon. The Jews who did return went back in four phases during the century following Cyrus's edict. According to Ezra, the first group of exiles returned under the leadership of Sheshbazzar, the son of exiled King Jehoiachin and a descendant of the royal house of David. Cyrus entrusted Sheshbazzar with the vessels that had been taken from the Temple at Jerusalem by the Babylonians and gave him instructions to rebuild the Temple. Under Sheshbazzar the returnees laid the foundation for the rebuilding of the Temple but did not complete its construction.

A second and perhaps larger group of exiles returned in the late–sixth century under the leadership of Zerubbabel, a grandson of Jehoiachin and also a descendant of the royal house of David. Zerubbabel was accompanied by Joshua the High Priest. With the encouragement and support of the prophets Haggai and Zechariah, who emerged around 520 B.C.E., the people resumed work on the reconstruction of the Temple. Haggai sought to motivate the people to work on the construction of the Temple. He answered the excuses of those who said that it was not a good time to rebuild the Temple by noting that they had rebuilt their own homes, while the Temple still lay in ruins. Haggai also assured them that if they would rebuild the Temple, God would bless them. Haggai prophesied to Zerubbabel that Yahweh was soon to establish the messianic kingdom and that Zerubbabel would be Yahweh's chosen one, the messianic king. Zechariah, a

Figure 12.1. The Cyrus Cylinder is a ten-inch-long, barrel-shaped cylinder made of clay that records the conquest of Babylon by Cyrus and his benevolence toward the conquered peoples. (© *The British Museum*)

contemporary of Haggai, shared Haggai's enthusiasm for the new Temple. Even more than Haggai, Zechariah inspired the people with visions of the glorious messianic age in which God's people would be led by two messiahs, a kingly messiah (Zerubbabel) and a priestly messiah (Joshua). With the urging of Haggai and Zechariah, the people established an altar in the midst of the Temple ruins, resumed the offering of sacrifices (Ezra 3:1-2), and completed the reconstruction of the Temple in 515 B.C.E.

Historians have suggested several reasons to account for the delay in rebuilding the Temple. First, Cyrus may not have provided the financial assistance he had promised. Second, the money and valuables collected from the Jews in Babylon for the Temple construction may have proved insufficient. Third, the returning exiles became discouraged; they were preoccupied with building their own homes and surviving under difficult circumstances. Fourth, the returning exiles encountered opposition from local groups when they resumed work on the Temple. Chief among those opposing the rebuilding of the Jerusalem Temple were the Samaritans (Ezra 4).

The Samaritans were a mixed cultural and religious group living in the area of Samaria, which was a center for Persian administration. Some were Mesopotamian colonists who adopted the religion of the land. They said to Zerubbabel, "Let us build with you, for we worship your God as you do, and we have been sacrificing to him ever since the days of King Esarhaddon of Assyria who brought us here" (Ezra 4:2). Before the exiles returned, the Samaritans had begun to encroach on land that was formerly a part of Judah. They probably considered the returning exiles to be outsiders and a threat to their territorial interests. Therefore the Samaritans questioned their motives for rebuilding the Temple. The Samaritans also reminded the Persians of the rebellious history of the people of Jerusalem during the time of the Babylonians and suggested that the Jews might be planning to revolt against the Persians. Perhaps they suspected that Zerubbabel and his people were considering revolt and were expecting a divine intervention that would bring them freedom (see Hag. 2:21-23). The Persians may have recalled Zerubbabel to Babylon to prevent such a possibility.

Sources say little about what happened in the fifty years after the Temple was rebuilt. Probably local groups continued to make trouble for the people of Judah (Ezra 4:4-23). Zerubbabel passed from the scene and the restored Temple with its priests and rituals became the center of Jewish life and worship.

One of the most difficult historical problems in biblical scholarship is the chronology of Ezra and Nehemiah, both of whom led groups of exiles back to Judah after the Temple was rebuilt. Nehemiah most likely arrived in Jerusalem in 445 B.C.E. The texts, however, are ambiguous concerning the date of Ezra's return. If he arrived prior to Nehemiah, as the present order of the materials in the books of Ezra and Nehemiah suggests, then he returned in 458 B.C.E. On the other hand, certain aspects of the career of Ezra are more understandable if one assumes that Ezra arrived after Nehemiah. If that was the case, then the date for Ezra's return would be either 428 or 398 B.C.E. Strong arguments can be offered for each of these positions. Since no consensus exists in current scholarship, the traditional chronology that holds that Ezra returned first in 458 will be accepted.

Ezra, a priest who has been called the "architect of Judaism," led a third small group of exiles who returned around 458 B.C.E. Subsequently, his work in Jerusalem focused on Jewish social and religious life. He introduced social customs that would ensure that Jews would remain insulated from foreign influence. Most radical was his prohibition against marriage with non-Jewish spouses (Ezra 9–10). Ezra had brought with him from Babylonia a copy of the "book of the law of Moses, which the Lord had given to Israel" (Neh. 8:1). Whether it included the full five books of the Pentateuch is not clear. Ezra held a public reading of this book of the Law, concluding with a covenant renewal ceremony during which representatives of the people signed a covenant binding the people to obedience to the Law. Ezra also brought a copy of a letter from the Persian ruler Artaxerxes that gave him considerable authority to enforce the Law. Under his leadership the Law became the center of Judaism.

A fourth group of exiles returned with Nehemiah, a Jew who was appointed governor of Judah and served from 445 until 424 B.C.E. Nehemiah rebuilt the wall around Jerusalem by forcing people to move into the city. He used his power as governor to improve the desperate economic situation in Judah by abolishing interest on loans and lowering the taxes that had been set by former governors. Nehemiah also initiated religious reforms in Jerusalem, including required observance of the Sabbath and payment of tithes to support the Levites, a class of Temple personnel subordinate to the priests. In addition, he fostered Jewish exclusivism by prohibiting intermarriage with foreigners and emphasizing pure Jewish ancestry.

THE LITERATURE OF THE RESTORATION

The primary literature of the restoration era includes parts of Isaiah (chapters 56–66), six books of the Latter Prophets (Joel, Obadiah, Jonah, Haggai, Zechariah, and Malachi), and seven books that are in the third section of the Hebrew Bible, the Writings (Ruth, Ezra, Nehemiah, 1 and 2 Chronicles, Esther, and the Song of Solomon).

The books of *1 and 2 Chronicles*, likely written during the fourth century B.C.E., provide an account of the history of David, Solomon, and the kings of the Southern Kingdom. Ezra, Nehemiah, Haggai, and Zechariah are the main historical sources for our knowledge of the restoration period of Jewish history. In the ancient manuscripts, 1 and 2 Chronicles comprised one scroll. The Chronicler drew heavily from parts of 1 and 2 Samuel and 1 and 2 Kings in telling his story of the history from David to the fall of Jerusalem. In agreement with Deuteronomistic theology, the Chronicler explains the misfortunes of God's people, including the Exile, as the result of their unfaithfulness to Yahweh. In the view of the Chronicler, the Jews are predominantly a Temple-oriented community of worshipers, and he places a primary emphasis on proper worship in a proper place (the Temple) led by religious leaders (the priests and Levites). Emphasis on the purity of the worshiping community pervades the work. The Chronicler, for example, stresses proper birth as a prerequisite for participation in the Jewish community. That meant that those with an ancestry mixed with non-Jews must be excluded from the community. (This emphasis on proper birth is the reason for the extensive genealogies in the opening chapters of 1 Chronicles.) The books of 1 and 2 Chronicles also present an exalted role for the priests and the Law.

The books of *Ezra* and *Nehemiah* were originally one work. Similarity in style and themes between Ezra-Nehemiah and 1 and 2 Chronicles has led to the widespread (though sometimes contested) opinion that the Chronicler was the author of this entire body of material. Ezra-Nehemiah continues the story begun in 1 and 2 Chronicles, describing the situation in Judah after the Exile. The Chronicler is intent on demonstrating that the postexilic community, devoted to the Law and the Temple, is the true continuation of the worshiping community established under David.

The book of *Haggai* consists of five short addresses to Zerubbabel, Joshua, and the people of Jerusalem intended to motivate them to complete the rebuilding of the Temple. The major theme of the work is the importance of the Temple and a purified community.

The book of *Zechariah* consists of fourteen chapters. Only the first eight belong to the prophet Zechariah, however. Chapters 9–14 consist of two oracles added by anonymous writers perhaps as late as the third century B.C.E. Zechariah 1–8 expresses his hope for a rebuilt Temple and restored Jerusalem by means of eight visions that come to him. These strange visions are very similar in form to apocalyptic literature, which became popular in some parts of Judaism during the Hellenistic period. Zechariah foresees a time when Jewish foes are subdued by God and a messianic age of Jewish fulfillment commences under the leadership of Zerubbabel and Joshua.

Joel, a short book of three chapters, is difficult to date because of the absence of references to events that can be dated from other sources. Nothing is known of the author except that his father was Pethuel. He may have been a cult prophet. The reference to the Greeks in 3:6 has led some scholars to date the book to the fourth century B.C.E. Others place the book in the late sixth or early fifth century B.C.E. The chief event in Joel is the story of a plague of locusts. It is unclear whether the author intended the story to reflect a historical event. The prophet presents the plague of locusts as a sign of the nearness of the "day of Yahweh," when God would judge the enemies of Judah, cleanse Judah, vindicate the righteous, and establish a universal kingdom.

Obadiah dates from the sixth or fifth century B.C.E. The book condemns Edom for its participation in the attack on Judah in 587 B.C.E. It describes the inevitable destruction of Edom by Yahweh (vv. 1-9), the sins of Edom against Judah when Edom participated in the plunder of Jerusalem (vv. 10-14), and the future restoration of Judah (vv. 15-21). Like Ezekiel and others, Obadiah condemns the pride of Edom and views its coming destruction as a warning about the future of all the nations that oppose the Lord.

The book of *Malachi* is an anonymous work; Malachi, which means "my messenger," is not a proper name. By the time this prophet wrote (between 515 and 445 B.C.E.), it was obvious that the rebuilding of the Temple had not brought the religious revival Haggai and Zechariah anticipated. Malachi reports that some people doubted the love of God, others were becoming lax in their worship habits, and divorce was becoming increasingly common. In response, the author first defends God's love for Judah by pointing to the recent devastation of the Jews' enemy, Edom, by the Nabateans as a sign of God's concern. Second, he criticizes the people for offering inferior sacrifices to God, sacrifices that they would not even consider offering to their governor. He urges that they take Temple worship seriously. Third, he is the first of the prophets to condemn divorce (2:16). It is uncertain whether he condemned divorce in principle or simply condemned the fact that it became too common among Jewish couples after the reforms of Ezra and Nehemiah, who urged divorce for those who had married foreign wives.

Third Isaiah (chapters 56–66 of the book of Isaiah) reflects the situation

Figure 12.2. This illustration, *Ruth and Boaz with the Reapers*, was taken from the *Maciejowski Bible*, from approximately 1250 C.E. (*The Pierpont Morgan Library/Art Resource, N.Y. [M. 638, f.17v]*)

after the Exile as viewed by several authors whose style and thoughts continued the tradition of First Isaiah. The Temple had been reconstructed, the sacrificial system renewed, and the priestly system firmly established. Much of this writing, however, reflects disappointment and disillusionment because the glorious restoration and unswerving faithfulness of the people foretold by Second Isaiah and other prophets had not materialized. No single unifying theme dominates these oracles. Some passages threaten judgment upon those who do not repent. Other passages exalt Jerusalem and the restored community. Still other sections reflect typical themes of the restoration: proper ritual, Sabbath observance, and reverence for the Law.

The book of *Ruth* is a romantic story set in the period of the tribal confederacy during the time of the judges. The book tells the story of the loyalty of Ruth, a Moabite widow in a Jewish family of Bethlehem, to her mother-in-law, Naomi. After living in Moab for a time, Naomi, who was also widowed, decided to return to her home in Bethlehem. On the way, however, Naomi wondered if it might be better for Ruth to return to her own people in Moab. In eloquent language, Ruth pleaded to remain with Naomi: "Do not press me to leave you or to turn back from following you! Where you go, I will go; where you lodge, I will lodge; your people shall be my people, and your God my God. Where you die, I will die—there will I be buried" (1:16-17). The remainder of Ruth tells how Naomi tactfully arranged a situation in which Boaz, a wealthy relative, took notice of Ruth and found himself under obligation to marry her, an obligation he freely accepted. The story ends with an account of the birth of Boaz's and Ruth's son Obed, the grandfather of David.

Although the account in Ruth was likely based on a very old story, the present work was composed in the period after the Exile to create a sympathetic attitude toward foreigners who believed in the God of Judah. Some scholars also believe that the story was told to soften the harsh decrees of Ezra and Nehemiah, who had required Jews to divorce their foreign wives and marry only within the covenant community. (Other scholars place this story and the book much earlier, in the transition period between the period of the judges and the monarchy.)

The book of *Jonah* is unique among the prophetic literature in that it is a single story instead of a collection of oracles. The story is connected to a prophet who supposedly lived in the Northern Kingdom at the time of Jeroboam II (786–746 B.C.E.). Almost certainly the book was produced after the Exile, when Judah's relations with its non-Hebrew neighbors were being debated.

The book tells the story of Jonah, who was called by God to preach to Nineveh, the capital of ancient Assyria. After a time of rebellion against God's call, during which Jonah was swallowed at sea by a great fish (the text of Jonah does not call it a whale) and then regurgitated upon the shore, Jonah repented and went to Nineveh. After calling the Assyrians to repentance,

Jonah was disappointed because God forgave them rather than destroy them.

Like the book of Ruth, the intent of Jonah may have been to correct the narrow exclusivism that was popular in some circles of Judaism during the period following Ezra and Nehemiah. Likewise, this story may have been an attempt to renew the Mosaic interpretation of God as gracious and merciful (Ex. 34:6-7), a concept that the author thought was in danger of being lost. Nowhere in the Priestly history, which was likely authored during this time, do the words "repentance," "forgiveness," or "loving-kindness" of God—*hesed* in Hebrew—appear. These concepts, much loved by the prophets, perhaps were omitted to strengthen the traditions of Temple and priests over against the prophetic traditions.

Figure 12.3. The scene of Jonah being thrown overboard prior to being swallowed by a big fish is depicted in this fourth or fifth century C.E. sarcophagus fragment from Istanbul. (*Photograph by Mitchell G. Reddish*)

The book of *Esther* recounts the dramatic story of how Jews averted persecution in Persia during the reign of Ahasuerus (Xerxes, 486–465 B.C.E.). Most scholars consider the book a work of historical fiction deriving from the late Persian period. Two versions of the story exist. A shorter version occurs in the Hebrew Bible and Protestant Bible. A longer version is in the Septuagint and Roman Catholic and Eastern Orthodox Bibles. Protestants place the additional material from the longer version, the so-called Additions to Esther, in the Apocrypha.

In the book of Esther two Jews, Esther and Mordecai, work together to avoid a pogrom (mass extermination) of the Jewish people. Through the courage of Esther, who approached the king uninvited to seek help for the Jews, her people were delivered. The Jewish festival of Purim celebrates annually the deliverance of the Jews described in Esther.

Like Esther, the *Song of Solomon* makes no mention of God or overtly religious topics. The book is a collection of love poems written in the postexilic period, although some of the material could be much older. The traditional belief that Solomon was the author of these poems has little support. In a frank and open manner these songs celebrate the physical desire and longing between a man and woman. Some scholars have suggested that the poems may have been recited in ancient Israel during wedding celebrations. Jews and Christians have traditionally applied allegorical interpretations to the poems. For Jews, they represent the love of God for Israel; for Christians, they speak of the love of God for the church. These interpretations probably stem from the notion found in Hosea of the divine-human covenant as a "marriage" and perhaps also from the attempt to find a more "spiritual" meaning for this book.

THE DIVINE-HUMAN ENCOUNTER IN THE RESTORATION

During the exilic and postexilic periods, the Jewish people gained new perspectives on their relationship with Yahweh. Building upon ideas that had surfaced during the Exile, the returning peoples developed a form of the Hebrew religious tradition that came to be known as Judaism. The following five components of the faith and practice of the Jewish people helped provide the enduring shape of Judaism.

Law

The Law, which was already an important component of Hebrew life, became a central element of Judaism in the postexilic period. In the absence of the Temple during the Exile, the Law had assumed new importance. Ezra was the chief promoter of the Law during the restoration. He returned to Jerusalem with "the book of the law" and made it the binding law of the land. The books of Ezra and Nehemiah emphasize that the Law became the main authority for Jewish religious and ethical practices. In the years ahead the Law was to continue its central role in the life of Judaism. Thus Judaism became a religion focused on living according to the statutes of the Torah, and Jews became a people of "the book."

Temple

During the preexilic period of Judah's history, the institutions of monarchy and Temple shared the power and authority over the land. In the absence of the monarchy during the restoration period, however, the importance of the Temple increased. The psalmists, the Chronicler, and the postexilic prophets placed great emphasis on the Temple as the place where God was especially present. The Torah provided guidelines for proper worship in the Temple.

With the dissolution of the kingship in Judah, the high priest became the dominant authority figure and the priests and Levites became more important than ever as those who managed Temple affairs.

Exclusivism

Jews also began to think of themselves as a singularly special people, the elect or chosen of God. Once they secured the borders of Judah and fortified the walls of the cities, they began to build a hedge around themselves to protect their new self-identity. They discouraged foreign influence, disassociating themselves socially, religiously, and politically from their neighbors. Their minority status as monotheists in a predominantly polytheistic world both isolated them culturally and at the same time strengthened their resolve to endure.

Universalism

Counterpoints to exclusivism also appear during the restoration. For example, in the literature of the restoration the heroine in the book of Ruth is a Moabite. In the book of Jonah the reluctant prophet carries the message of Yahweh's grace to a far-distant land. Likewise, Malachi notes that the sacrifices of non-Jews are acceptable to God. Jewish exclusivism sought to preserve a strong sense of a pure community of faith based on right conduct and right ritual; universalist tendencies provided an important counteremphasis. This openness to other peoples and traditions was an implication of the monotheism of the postexilic Jews, which extended God's presence and concern to all humankind.

Prophecy

Prophecy continued during the restoration, but much of its vitality was missing. The postexilic period produced only minor prophetic figures; no one of the caliber of Isaiah, Jeremiah, or Ezekiel came to prominence. Because the prophets of the restoration supported the Temple and its sacrificial worship system, prophetic functions may have been merged into priestly functions. Furthermore, the increasing importance of the Law in the postexilic period as the central authority for Jews may have diminished the influence of prophecy. Whatever the reasons might have been, prophets in the classical sense gradually ceased to appear. By the fourth century B.C.E., the production of prophetic literature came to an end among the Jewish people. The prophetic voice was not completely lost, however. In the Hellenistic age of Israel's history, a transformed prophetic voice—apocalyptic thought—would emerge to proclaim Yahweh's message to the people.

Chapter 13

THE PSALMS AND WISDOM LITERATURE

Suggested Biblical Readings: Psalms 1; 8; 22; 23; 106; Proverbs 7; 10;
Ecclesiastes 2:1-11; 12; Job 1–2; 40:6–42:17

Most of the Hebrew Bible describes the divine-human encounter in a narrative form that sets the story of God and the Hebrew people in the context of history. Events such as the deliverance from Egypt and the punishment of the Exile portray the "mighty acts of God" in Hebrew national history. The psalms and Wisdom literature, in contrast, focus more on individual matters and common human experience. Although they emerge out of the corporate history of Israel, they are responses to universal feelings and concerns—life and death, tragedy, disappointment, guilt, joy, and sorrow—that apply to all individuals regardless of their particular historical context. As a result, they are some of the best-known and most revered books of the Hebrew Bible. They will be studied together in one chapter because they have literary similarities, contain some common content, and in their final form come from the postexilic period.

PSALMS

Psalms was the songbook of the Second Temple, the Temple built by Zerubbabel and the returning exiles between 520 and 515 B.C.E. Psalms later came to have wide usage both in synagogue and Christian worship and continues to be used today.

Tradition claims that David is the author of Psalms. His association with music and poetry is strong: Amos 6:5 cites him as an improviser on musical instruments, he assigns roles in worship to musicians in 1 Chronicles 15, and several poetic passages outside of Psalms are attributed to him (2 Sam. 1:19-27; 22:1-51; 23:3-7; 1 Chr. 16:8-36). A noncanonical writing in the Dead Sea Scrolls credits David with 3,600 psalms and 500 songs. Claims such as these, however, have not led to a consensus that David authored the psalms. Ascribing authorship to a well-known person was common in the ancient Near East. Further, some psalms (73–85, 86–90) are ascribed to other authors, and many have no ascribed author. Although David no doubt composed some psalms and inspired others, he could not have been the author of the Psalter in its final form. Historical-critical and literary-critical studies have concluded that the psalms were authored over a period of several centuries. Although some are preexilic, most are postexilic and therefore could not have been composed by David. Numerous psalms contain the ascription "a psalm of David," but the Hebrew could just as accurately be rendered "a psalm to David" or "a psalm in the style or tradition of David."

Five separate collections compose the book. In all likelihood smaller collections of psalms were edited into one large volume for use in the Temple. Indeed, scribes provided numerous notes of instruction in the Hebrew text (like

Figure 13.1. A Palestinian woman caring for her sheep. The imagery of God as a shepherd occurs several times in the Bible, including the well-known Twenty-third Psalm. (*Photograph by Clyde E. Fant*)

"Selah") for Temple musicians and worship leaders. Although devout Jews surely read, chanted, or sung the psalms personally and privately, their primary use was for communal worship in the Temple. The fivefold division of Psalms is as follows:

   I.   Psalms 1–41
  II.   Psalms 42–72
 III.   Psalms 73–89
  IV.   Psalms 90–106
   V.   Psalms 107–150

Each division ends with a doxology or blessing of God (41:13; 72:18-19; 89:52; 106:48; 150).

Types of Psalms

Hermann Gunkel, an early-twentieth-century German scholar who wrote a form-critical study of the psalms, discovered that they were set in the context of public worship in the Second Temple. Gunkel further divided most of the psalms into major groups. Gunkel's classifications are helpful in understanding the book of Psalms. He found that about two-thirds of the psalms fit one of the following classifications: hymns, communal laments, personal laments, personal songs of thanksgiving, and royal psalms. He designated the remaining one-third as songs of pilgrimage, communal songs of thanksgiving, wisdom songs, Torah or prophetic liturgies, and mixed, which combined elements of the major classes. Although not all scholars use Gunkel's classifications, all recognize his contribution to understanding the psalms.

Hymns of Praise. At least twenty-four songs of praise to God are punctuated by the repetition of the phrase "Praise the Lord" ("Hallelujah" in Hebrew). A typical hymn of praise opens and closes with praise to God. The core of the hymn extols God for who God is and what God has done. Typical themes are God's creative activity, deeds of redemption, and steadfast love. Several hymns of praise sing the glories of Jerusalem (46, 48, 76, 87), and others celebrate God's kingship over the earth (47, 93, 95–100).

Psalm 8 is an example of a hymn of praise. It begins and ends with the same adoration: "O LORD, our Sovereign, how majestic is your name in all the earth!" (8:1, 9). Between these exaltations of praise, God is extolled for the glories of creation—the heavens, the moon and stars, and especially humanity (8:2-8).

The last hymns of the Psalter (145–150) also fit this classification. Psalm

146, for example, praises God at its beginning and end (146:1-2, 10*b*). Its core of grateful praise emphasizes God's protection of the righteous:

> The LORD sets the prisoners free;
> the LORD opens the eyes of the blind.
> The LORD lifts up those who are bowed down;
> the LORD loves the righteous. (146:7*b*-8)

Communal Laments. Israel expressed its deepest woes in song—a sort of Hebrew "blues." At least nine psalms focus on national difficulties.

Communal laments deal with national calamities caused by famine, defeat in battle, or epidemic. Communal psalms include a call to God, an assessment of the situation (which was often a complaint brought against God), an affirmation of faith in God's goodness, an appeal for help, and a concluding thanksgiving or vow.

Psalm 80 is an illustration of a communal lament. The people call upon God to "give ear" (80:1). Apparently an enemy had attacked Jerusalem and "broken down its walls" (80:12*a*). The people, however, believe God has allowed this disaster, and they complain: "Why?" (80:12*a*). Nevertheless, they appeal in faith to the "Shepherd of Israel...who lead[s] Joseph like a flock" (80:1*a*) to "restore us" (80:3, 7, 19), after which "we will never turn back from you" (80:18*a*).

Personal Laments. Personal laments constitute the largest category of psalms, about forty in number. They dealt with the problems faced by individuals and their structure is similar to communal laments. A number of these psalms (for example, 32 and 51) are traditionally identified with specific events in David's life, but their association with David is uncertain.

Psalm 22 exemplifies a personal lament. It speaks of one who is scorned and mocked to the point of death (22:6-7, 14-18). The tormented person cries out to God "by day...and by night" but receives no answer (22:2). Despite his consternation with God's silence, the maligned person recalls God's intercession for others (22:3-5) and asks God not to be "far away" and to "deliver my soul" (22:19-20). Once delivered, the person sings God's praises (22:22-31).

Personal Songs of Thanksgiving. In at least nine psalms, persons gratefully praise God on the occasion of their deliverance from difficulty. These psalms include an opening affirmation of praise, an account of the trouble and their deliverance by God, and grateful thanksgiving to God.

Psalm 32, a well-known illustration of a personal song of thanksgiving, is traditionally associated with David's deliverance from the guilt of adultery with Bathsheba. Although it fits the picture of David's situation, nothing in the psalm requires that it stem from that particular incident. The psalm universally applies to any worshiper of Yahweh plagued by guilt. The psalm opens with thanks to God in gratitude for forgiveness (32:1-2) and closes with a stirring affirmation of praise (32:10-11). The core recounts the festering sin that had remained unconfessed, the acknowledgment of the sin, and the deliverance of God (32:3-9).

Royal Psalms. At least nine psalms celebrate Israel's earthly kings. The king was God's chief representative among the people, and elaborate attention was directed to religious ceremonies involving the king. Psalms 18 and 21 sing of the king's victory over an enemy, Psalms 20 and 144 pray for the king's victory over a foe, and Psalm 45 appears to be from a royal wedding.

Psalm 110 is an example of a royal psalm. In it the king is welcomed to the sanctuary and invited to sit on the throne of God (110:1). The speaker, probably a priest, then recounts the power of the king near and far, enunciates the king's legitimate reign as an heir of the legendary Melchizedek, and proclaims the watchful presence of God over the king (110:2-7).

Other Psalms. Study of the psalms reveals several special minor categories that merit attention. One group (120–134) is a collection of "songs of ascent," which were used by pilgrims as they traveled to Jerusalem for sacred festivals. A second group (113–118) is associated with the feast of Passover. A third group, including Psalms 1 and 119, meditates on the Torah.

A fourth group is the imprecatory or cursing psalms (see 69, 109, 137) in which the Hebrews pray for God to destroy their enemies (sometimes even going so far as to describe the killing of their enemies' babies; see 137:9). For example, in Psalm 109 the author has been cursed and retorts with a curse of his own:

> May he be tried and found guilty;
>   may even his prayer be considered a crime!
> May his life soon be ended;
>   may someone else take his job!
> May his children become orphans,
>   and his wife a widow!
> May his children be homeless beggars;
>   may they be driven from the ruins they live in!
> May his creditors take away all his property,
>   and may strangers get everything he worked for.
> May no one ever be kind to him
>   or care for the orphans he leaves behind.
> May all his descendants die,
>   and may his name be forgotten in the next generation.
> May the LORD remember the evil of his ancestors
>   and never forgive his mother's sins.
> May the LORD always remember their sins,
> but may they themselves be completely forgotten!   (109:7-15 TEV)

These psalms, which could be considered a type of lament, shock contemporary readers when they read of the bitter hatred that leads to a call for God's vengeance. Knowing the context out of which the psalms came helps the reader to at least understand the bitterness. Psalm 137, for example, reflects the period of the Exile when the Babylonian military had devastated the Hebrews. They called upon God to vindicate them by doing unto the Babylonians as the Babylonians had done unto them. Another factor for the modern reader to keep in mind is that the Hebrews at the time had no concept of justice beyond this life. (Surprising as it may seem, the Jewish belief in the resurrection of the body to an everlasting life did not develop until about the third or second century B.C.E.) At this time the Hebrews believed justice had to be found within history, not beyond history. Therefore, they had an intense desire for vindication in the present.

Hebrew Poetry

The psalms were poems set to music. Hebrew poetry, which comprises about one third of the Hebrew Bible, is marked by parallelism and meter (or rhythm). Parallelism occurs when the thoughts of two parallel lines are related. In some instances the thoughts of the two lines are synonymous, such as in 107:32: "Let them extol him in the congregation of the people, and praise him in the assembly of the elders." In other cases two lines contrast with one another, such as in 1:6: "For the LORD watches over the way of the righteous, but the way of the wicked will perish." Two other types of poetic parallelism are formal parallelism and climactic parallelism.

Although English translations of Hebrew poetry can maintain parallel structure, it is difficult linguistically to represent the meter. Some meters indicated sadness, while others signaled excitement, depending upon the desired mood.

The Divine-Human Encounter in Psalms

In contrast to the psalms, which contain the psalmist's expressions of faith, thanksgiving, praise, and even doubt toward God, the Torah and the Prophets contain what purports to be direct revelation from God. In the Torah, Moses is the mouthpiece for God's truth; in the Prophets the oracles are regularly introduced with "Thus says the LORD." These writings declare the covenant and define the Hebrews' relationship to God and to one another in a religious community. Psalms are a different type of literature. Instead of stating how the Hebrews should relate theoretically to God, they describe how they actually did relate to God in worship. One may call the book of Psalms the practical theology of Judaism. In it one finds the ecstasy of praise and the lament of tragedy. It reflects the Jews' living out their beliefs in the God of the covenant in Temple ritual, kingly functions, and personal devotions.

Figure 13.2. Scribes in ancient Israel were responsible for the production and preservation of Wisdom literature. In this limestone statue an Egyptian scribe holds an open papyrus roll on his lap. *(Photograph by Clyde E. Fant)*

WISDOM LITERATURE

The Wisdom literature of the Hebrew Bible treats the practical question of the meaning of life. Unlike the speculative thinking of Greek philosophy, Hebrew wisdom was rooted in concrete, daily life. It focused on the practical activities that lead to a good life. The wise Hebrew was advised to follow the instructions of this literature.

Hebrew Wisdom literature includes Proverbs, Job, and Ecclesiastes. Wisdom also is found in other books, such as Psalms (1; 32; 34; 37; 49; 73; 112; 128). The Wisdom of Solomon and Ecclesiasticus are books of Wisdom literature in the Apocrypha.

The Hebrews did not invent Wisdom literature. Other Near Eastern cultures, especially the Egyptians, had wisdom traditions. Because wisdom was practical or common sense and not focally rooted in a particular theological tradition, much crosscultural interchange of wisdom occurred. The "thirty sayings" of Proverbs 22:17–24:22, for example, closely parallel the content of the Egyptian Instruction of Amen-em-opet.

The Wisdom literature in the Hebrew Bible is unusual because it does not focus on the dominant themes of the tradition, such as the Exodus, the covenant, and the Law. History or the acts of God are not important categories. Rather, the practical concerns of the individual receive its attention. Nevertheless, wisdom traditions lie deep in Hebrew history, going as far back as the beginning of the monarchy.

Scholars often distinguish between two types of Hebrew wisdom. Proverbs contains practical wisdom in that it conveys practical advice on how to live. Ecclesiastes and Job, on the other hand, reflect a skeptical wisdom that questions the value of practical wisdom.

Proverbs

The book of Proverbs is an anthology of seven collections that came into final form by 400 B.C.E. Each collection identifies the source of the material in it except for the final section of the book, which identifies its subject matter. The divisions are as follows:

1. Chapters 1–9: proverbs of Solomon
2. Chapters 10:1–22:16: proverbs of Solomon
3. Chapters 22:17–24:34: words of the wise men
4. Chapters 25–29: proverbs of Solomon
5. Chapter 30: words of Agur and numerical proverbs
6. Chapter 31:1-9: words of Lemuel

7. Chapter 31:10–31: the good wife described

Chapters 30–31 appear to be of foreign origin; the remainder are associated with Solomon. Solomon's precise connection, however, is unclear. Although the texts at 1:1, 10:1, and 25:1 read, "proverbs of Solomon," it is not certain whether this means that Solomon wrote or collected them or if they were collected by another and designated as Solomon's. Solomon possibly had a great influence on the proverbs, but it is unlikely that he authored them. In their present form they all derive from the postexilic period.

The practical wisdom of Proverbs falls into two classifications: instructions and wisdom sentences. Written in a parent-to-child format, instructions are commands usually followed by clauses that cite motives, predict consequences, or provide clarity. Some examples include the following:

> Listen, children, to a father's instruction,
>> and be attentive, that you may gain insight. (4:1)

> Do not withhold discipline from your children;
>> if you beat them with a rod, they will not die. (23:13)

Don't associate with people who drink too much wine or stuff themselves with food. Drunkards and gluttons will be reduced to poverty. If all you do is eat and sleep, you will soon be wearing rags (23:20-21 TEV)

A second classification of proverbs is the wisdom sentence. In contrast to the instructions, wisdom sentences are in the indicative mood and are similar in form to the modern English use of the word "proverb" as a "wise saying." Some wisdom sentences are "one-liners." Examples include the following:

The LORD hates people who use dishonest weights and measures. (20:10 TEV)

No wisdom, no understanding, no counsel, can avail against the LORD. (21:30)

Partiality in judging is not good. (24:23*b*)

Other wisdom sentences are "two-liners" in which the second line either repeats the meaning of the first line or contrasts with it:

> One is commended for good sense,
>> but a perverse mind is despised. (12:8)

> In the light of a king's face there is life,
>> and his favor is like the clouds that bring the spring rain. (16:15)

> The glory of youths is their strength,
>> but the beauty of the aged is their gray hair. (20:29)

> A good name is to be chosen rather than great riches,
>> and favor is better than silver or gold. (22:1)

Some two-line wisdom sentences are similes (figures of speech comparing two unlike things, often introduced by "like" or "as"). Numerous examples are found in chapter 26.

> Like a dog that returns to its vomit
>> is a fool who reverts to his folly. (26:11)

> Like somebody who takes a passing dog by the ears
>> is one who meddles in the quarrel of another. (26:17)

Other wisdom sentences are in the form of numerical proverbs, presenting lists of things that instruct in wisdom:

> Four things on earth are small,
>> yet they are exceedingly wise:
> the ants are a people without strength,
>> yet they provide their food in the summer;
> the badgers are a people without power,
>> yet they make their homes in the rocks;
> the locusts have no king,
>> yet all of them march in rank;
> the lizard can be grasped in the hand,
>> yet it is found in kings' palaces. (30:24-28)

Most of the proverbs belong to the classifications of instructions and wisdom sentences.

The book of Proverbs emphasizes four central themes. One theme is that of advice from parents to children. Indeed, much of the book concerns instructions to the young. Chapters 1–9 focus on this theme: "Hear, my child, your father's instruction, and do not reject your mother's teaching" (1:8). Many subsections of this collection begin with the address "Listen, children" or "My child" (see 2:1; 3:1; 3:21; 5:1, 7, 20). (Quite possibly, Wisdom literature derived from a school setting in which teachers called their students "my child.") In this collection youths are advised in righteousness, justice, equity, prudence, and discretion (1:3-4). Typical emphases include the value of wisdom over foolishness (2:1-22), the worth of self-discipline (4:20-27), and the danger of sexual activity outside of marriage (5:1-20; 7:6-23). In this

Figure 13.3. Several native animals are mentioned in the book of Proverbs, including the rock-dwelling coney or badger (actually the hyrax), described in Proverbs 30:26. *(Photograph by Clyde E. Fant)*

collection wisdom and foolishness are often personified as a wise woman or a foolish woman (9:1-18).

A second theme is the relationship of wealth to poverty. In agreement with the Deuteronomistic tradition (see, for example, 12:27), Proverbs teaches that honest labor produces wealth, while idleness and dishonesty lead to poverty. For example, it is "better to be poor and walk in integrity than to be crooked in one's ways even though rich" (28:6). At the same time, the poor are not to be abused (14:31) and the rich are to be generous. Under no circumstances does Proverbs teach that wealth alone provides the good life (15:17; 17:1). Further, "riches do not last forever" (27:24a). The "crown" of life is wisdom, not wealth (14:24a).

A third theme of Proverbs is personal self-control. The control of anger is the theme of 15:18: "Those who are hot-tempered stir up strife, but those who are slow to anger calm contention." The destruction wrought by words uttered in anger is emphasized in 15:1-7, and the devastation of gossip is detailed in 25:7b-10. Coupled with control of emotion and speech are warnings about excessive consumption of wine. A realistic passage from 23:29-35 merits quotation:

Show me people who drink too much, who have to try out fancy drinks, and I will show you people who are miserable and sorry for themselves, always causing trouble and always complaining. Their eyes are bloodshot, and they have bruises that could have been avoided. Don't let wine tempt you, even though it is rich red, and it sparkles in the cup, and it goes down smoothly. The next morning you will feel as if you had been bitten by a poisonous snake. Weird sights will appear before your eyes, and you will not be able to think or speak clearly. You will feel as if you were out on the ocean, seasick, swinging high up in the rigging of a tossing ship. "I must have been hit," you will say; "I must have been beaten up, but I don't remember it. Why can't I wake up? I need another drink." (TEV)

The value of seeking wisdom is perhaps the foremost theme of Proverbs. To seek wisdom is an act of obedience to God. Some refer to this theme as the theological wisdom of Proverbs. A child should be an avid, diligent learner, for sound wisdom "will be life for your soul" (3:22*a*). God grounded wisdom in the created order (3:19); therefore, a child is instructed to

> Trust in the LORD with all your heart,
>> and do not rely on your own insight.
> In all your ways acknowledge him,
>> and he will make straight your paths. (3:5-6)

The Divine-Human Encounter in Proverbs

Based on their belief that God created the cosmos, the Hebrews held that God authored their practical wisdom. They did not create it; they derived it from their experience of the world order God had created. Therefore, it supported covenant theology. The sages who gathered Israel's practical wisdom believed further that authentic knowledge of the Proverbs would enable a person to live confidently and harmoniously in God's creation. Acquisition of this practical knowledge would normally lead to health, wealth, and longevity—the same rewards promised by the Deuteronomistic theology. Rejection of practical wisdom by fools leads to sickness, economic poverty, and a brief life.

Job

The books of Job and Ecclesiastes are counterpoints to the common-sense philosophy of Proverbs. They represent skeptical wisdom that doubts the orthodox Deuteronomistic theology.

Job is one of the best-loved classics of Western literature. Tennyson and Carlyle highly commended it. Modern plays, such as Neil Simon's *God's Favorite* and Archibald MacLeish's *J.B.*, are based on it. The South American liberation theologian Gustavo Gutierrez has interpreted the situation of the poor in Latin America in the light of Job. Whenever the righteous suffer, the patience of faithful Job is often mentioned. Although Job is legendary for his patience, the poetic core of the book reveals an impatient and frustrated man.

The book of Job is structured as a sandwich: a prose prologue (chapters 1 and 2) and a prose epilogue (42:7-17) enclose a long poem (3:1–42:6). The prose sections tell the story of a man who was extraordinarily blessed by God with family, flocks, land, and stature within the community because he was righteous. His faith is put to the test by the "adversary" or "Satan," a member of the heavenly court who doubts Job's sincerity. (The reader should note that the

Satan is an angelic being who resides in the presence of God and not the archenemy of God who later struggles with God for human allegiance. The notion that Satan is the leader of the spiritual forces of evil arose later in Judaism.) The adversary questions Job's sincerity and inquires cynically, "Does Job fear God for nothing?" (1:9). With God's permission, the adversary tests Job's faith by systematically depriving him of wealth, children, and health. Job steadfastly holds to his integrity and faith and refuses to take his wife's advice to curse God and die. In the epilogue Job, while unable to comprehend the tragedy that has befallen him, submits to the sovereignty of God. Pleased with Job's perseverance, God restores to him more than what he had lost. The theme of the prose prologue and epilogue is that a righteous person who perseveres through adversity will be rewarded. The Deuteronomistic theology of punishment and rewards is tested in Job but survives the epic struggle as the heroic Job perseveres in faith and is justly rewarded.

The simplicity of the prose narrative that begins and concludes Job is qualified by the present structure of the book, which contains a long poetic section (3:1–42:6). Literary critics have studied the relationship between the prose and poetic sections. They surmise that the author of Job took an old folk legend about the ancient Edomite sage Job (Ezek. 14 mentions Daniel and Job as ancient wise and righteous men) and inserted the cycles of poetry into the prose. The poetry details the conversations between Job and three interlocutors (Job's so-called friends, Eliphaz, Bildad, and Zophar), follows with a speech of Job, and concludes with God's speech to Job and Job's submission to God. The book has the following outline:

     I. The prose introduction (1–2)
    II. The poetic core (3:1–42:6)
       A. Job prefers death to suffering (3)
       B. First cycle of poems
          1. Eliphaz and Job dialogue (4–7)
          2. Bildad and Job dialogue (8–10)
          3. Zophar and Job dialogue (11–14)
       C. Second cycle of poems
          1. Eliphaz and Job dialogue (15–17)
          2. Bildad and Job dialogue (18–19)
          3. Zophar and Job dialogue (20–21)
       D. Third cycle of poems
          1. Eliphaz and Job dialogue (22–24)
          2. Bildad and Job dialogue (25–27)
          3. Hymnic interlude (28)
       E. Job's final speech (29–31)

       F. The speeches of Elihu (32–37)

       G. God's speech and Job's submission (38–42:6)

  III. The prose conclusion (42:7-17)

Each cycle of exchanges follows the same pattern—Eliphaz-Job, Bildad-Job, Zophar-Job—creating a dramatic effect.

The author of Job is unknown, although he was probably a Hebrew scholar of wisdom who fashioned the book of Job into its present form sometime during or after the Exile. As with other Wisdom literature, knowledge of the author and date of composition is less important than for other books because the theme can be located in any place at any time.

The theme of Job can best be understood in the context of traditional Hebrew orthodoxy. It was widely believed that on the basis of the covenantal promises, God provided health, prosperity, and longevity to a righteous person, while an unrighteous person would reap sickness, poverty, and an early death. Thus, Job prospers because he "was blameless and upright, one who feared God and turned away from evil" (1:1). When Job's testing at the hands of the adversary comes, however, and Job is deprived of health and wealth, the dialogue between Job and his three interlocutors provides a tense test case for orthodox belief. On the one hand, "In all this Job did not sin or charge God with wrong-doing" (1:22), an assertion made in the prose narrative. In the poetic section he agonizes over his condition. His trauma is so great that he curses the day he was born (3:3) and wishes rather to be dead. He questions God's justice in that the same fate— death—befalls both the righteous and the unrighteous (9:22-24). He prays for a mediator who will renew his faith and bring his intense disenchantment with God to a resolution (9:33-35). He writhes in despair (16:18–17:16). The issue for Job himself is *why* he suffers when he has not been unfaithful.

On the other hand, Eliphaz, Bildad, and Zophar are mouthpieces for orthodox belief. In his first speech, Eliphaz insists that God is righteous and that justice is certain. He asks rhetorically, "Think now, who that was innocent ever perished? Or where were the upright cut off?" (4:7). All three "friends" berate Job because he considers himself blameless, when in fact he or his children must have sinned, else calamity would not have befallen him. They hold that Job's only recourse is to admit his fault and to humble himself before God; then he would find comfort.

Through the three cycles of poems, Job and the three questioners debate the validity of the orthodox theology. While Job admits that he is not completely blameless, his small faults do not merit the avalanche of crushing tragedies that have befallen him. Finally God speaks and chastises Job for questioning the divine intentions (chapters 38–41). God compares Job to other creatures and shows how limited and finite Job truly is. Job admits his ignorance of God's ways and submits himself to the divine will. He accepts his mortality. The poetic section ends at this point.

Many scholars view the canonical book of Job as the battleground for a fight over the close-minded Deuteronomistic theology of blessings and rewards. At the end of the poetic section Job has not been vindicated and the promise of the Deuteronomistic writer is not fulfilled. Many believe that the prose ending (42:7-17) that restores to Job twice what he had lost was added by scribes who insisted that he must be vindicated.

The Divine-Human Encounter in Job

The book of Job provides a provocative engagement of the divine-human encounter in Hebrew thought. First, Job pointedly contrasts God's transcendence with humanity's finitude. God is beyond human comprehension while yet remaining the sovereign, inexplicable power of the cosmos. God is both known and yet hidden (13:24). The God of Job is cloaked in mystery. Second, God's apartness creates an anxiety about meaning. When Job is troubled, he seeks meaning from his concept of God; but God is an enigma from which he can extract no sure meaning. Third, Job declares that a closed-minded orthodoxy of rewards and punishments is limited and even wrong. In the narrative conclusion God declares the three "friends" to be at fault. The book does not overturn orthodox belief, but it surely teaches that it is not beyond criticism. Fourth, Job seeks a mediator, a redeemer, who will be his advocate before God and reconcile him to God. In a new relationship meaning will be found and the gulf between Job and God will be bridged. Job, however, never finds such a mediator.

The presence of the book of Job in the Hebrew canon reflects the fact or suggests that the Jews engaged in a lively debate over the application of orthodox Deuteronomistic belief to every life situation. Since God enters into the dialogue of Job's quest to understand (chapters 38–41), one can infer that God welcomed the conversation. Ever since, the posture of faithful doubting has been encouraged in the Jewish and Christian traditions. Sadly, Qoheleth, another illustration of skeptical wisdom, questioned the seemingly meaningless scheme of creation and received only silence from on high.

Ecclesiastes/Qoheleth

The presence of Ecclesiastes in the canon is puzzling. How did a book that claims all searching for wisdom ends in vanity gain acceptance into the Hebrew canon? Historical sources indicate quite clearly that its value as Scripture was hotly contested among competing rabbinic schools. Several facts favored its inclusion in the canon. First, the book itself claims to be royal in origin. Although the Hebrew title of the book, Qoheleth, means simply "preacher" or "teacher," the writer designates himself as "son of David, king in Jerusalem" (1:1) and one who has been "king over Israel in Jerusalem" (1:12). Moreover, the writer is wealthy, has concubines, and loves proverbs (2:8; 12:9). These characteristics fit Solomon, and because of his authority the book was highly regarded. The second and closely related fact in its favor is that a majority of rabbis supported Solomonic authorship. Third, several passages in the book, such as 12:12 14, mute the abject skepticism of the bulk of the material, thereby making the book palatable to traditional wisdom. For these reasons the book, though disputed, was judged acceptable.

Recent scholarship denies Solomonic authorship for three reasons. The first reason is that a number of passages either could not have been written by Solomon or probably were not written by him. Ecclesiastes 1:12, for example, claims that the author had been king of Israel at an earlier time. This king could not have been Solomon, who died while on the throne. A second reason is that literary criticism indicates that scribes of traditional theology edited the book in order to bring it into orthodox acceptability. A redactor probably named Solomon as the author of the book to give it authority, a practice quite common in the ancient world. Third, literary critics have noted in the book several words of Persian origin and examples of Greek style and content, particularly in its sense of tragedy and determinism. For these reasons, in its canonical form the book doubtless is by an unknown writer and probably dates from the late–third century.

Although no clear structure organizes the text, several pertinent themes are clear. The first and central theme is the limit or even falsity of practical wisdom. Whereas the book of Proverbs outlines a path of wisdom that leads to a good, honorable, and satisfying life, Ecclesiastes laments the vanity of all human efforts (1:2; 12:8) and questions whether any sense can be made of life. Qoheleth says he has "applied my mind to seek and to search out by wisdom all that is done under heaven . . . and see, all is vanity and a chasing after wind" (1:13-14). The author details the experiences that have led him to these anguished conclusions: practical wisdom simply does not always prove to be true (8:16-17) or is inaccessible (7:23-24); the neat Deuteronomistic theology of practical wisdom (that the righteous prosper while the wicked suffer) is made false in experience (7:15); and injustice is rampant (4:1). Therefore Qoheleth concludes that practical wisdom is without value.

In a second theme, Qoheleth advises how one should live when wisdom is hidden or inaccessible. Even though God has not made known eternal truths that apply to daily life (6:10-12), some affirmations of God can be made and an appropriate way of life plotted. God remains supreme and sovereign, though distant and unfathomable (8:16-17). Instead of speculating about truths that cannot be attained with certainty, the faithful should accept and enjoy life. This advice becomes clear in 9:7-10:

> Go, eat your bread with enjoyment, and drink your wine with a merry heart; for God has long ago approved what you do. Let your garments always be white; do not let oil be lacking on your head. Enjoy life with the wife whom you love, all the days of your vain life that are given you under the sun, because that is your portion in life and in your toil at which you toil under the sun. Whatever your hand finds to do, do with your might; for there is no work or thought or knowledge or wisdom in Sheol, to which you are going.

Similar statements are pronounced in 2:24-26, 3:22, and 5:18-20.

A third theme of Qoheleth is the stark reality of death, which casts all humans into Sheol, the dwelling place of the dead (3:20). "For there is no enduring remembrance of the wise or of fools, seeing that in the days to come all will have been long forgotten. How can the wise die just like the fools?" (2:16). The only difference between the living and the dead is that "the living know that they will die, but the dead know nothing" (9:5*a*). Beset by futility, despair grips seekers of wisdom as they helplessly grope for the mystery of meaning in life. Even if they attain wisdom, it will perish with them (8:16–9:6). As explained earlier in the chapter, the Jews did not have a theology of rewards and punishment in the afterlife until later in their history.

The Divine-Human Encounter in Ecclesiastes

Proverbs and Job accept practical wisdom as a fact. Proverbs defined it and commended it; Job tested it. Ecclesiastes, on the other hand, unrelentingly questions practical wisdom. After an exhausting search, Qoheleth declares that searching for wisdom is vanity and a chasing after the wind. The book teaches that knowledge of God has limits and may be impossible. The search for wisdom accomplishes little and does not satisfy. According to Qoheleth, a wise person finds pleasure in food, drink, work, and marriage. The ending (12:9-14) cautions the reader that in spite of an unsatisfactory conclusion to the search for wisdom, one should "fear God, and keep his commandments; for that is the whole duty of everyone" (12:13*b*).

Chapter 14

JUDAISM IN THE HELLENISTIC AND ROMAN ERAS

Suggested Biblical Readings: 1 Maccabees 1–5

As the previous chapters have shown, the years following the Exile brought many changes to the Jewish people. Their understanding of God and the divine-human encounter was altered as a result of the theological and political crises associated with the exilic and postexilic periods. Furthermore, the people of Palestine no longer enjoyed political independence as they passed from the control of the Babylonians to the Persians. Political and religious changes continued beyond the time of the Persians as new political powers—specifically, Hellenistic and Roman rulers—began to dominate Near Eastern politics.

POLITICAL DEVELOPMENTS IN PALESTINE

Little is known about the political and historical developments within Palestine during the period from ca. 400–200 B.C.E. The historical information provided by the Chronicler ends with the restoration work of Nehemiah and Ezra during the fifth century B.C.E. The next major sources of information are 1 and 2 Maccabees, Jewish writings produced around 100 B.C.E. that describe the events in Palestine from ca. 180–132 B.C.E. During this "silent period" of Jewish history, a major change was taking place in Palestine and in much of the Near Eastern world. Hellenization, or the spreading of Greek culture and ideas, was occurring throughout the Near East. The person most responsible for this expansion of Greek culture was Alexander the Great.

The Beginnings of Hellenization

In 336 B.C.E. Philip II, king of Macedonia (a region in the northeastern part of the Greek peninsula), initiated an attack on Persian-controlled cities in Asia Minor. Assassinated before he could complete the invasion, Philip was succeeded by his son, Alexander III, later known as Alexander the Great. Alexander not only was victorious in Asia Minor but also extended his military conquests throughout much of the Near Eastern world. At the time of his death in Babylon in 323 B.C.E., his kingdom reached from Macedonia to Egypt and as far east as India. Palestine came under Alexander's control around 332 B.C.E.

Figure 14.1. Alexander the Great conquered much of the ancient Near East, spreading Hellenistic culture throughout the conquered territories. *(Photograph by Mitchell G. Reddish)*

Wherever Alexander marched, the spread of Hellenism rapidly followed. Much of the Near East had in fact already been affected by Hellenistic culture. The conquests of Alexander, however, hastened this process. Throughout the Near East, Greek style of dress became popular; theaters, gymnasiums, and stadiums modeled after Greek buildings were erected; and Greek became the common language of commerce and politics.

When Alexander died, his empire was divided among his generals, who fought over control of various territories. Of these claimants to Alexander's former empire, only two are of immediate concern to this study—Ptolemy Lagi and

Seleucus I. In the struggle for control, Ptolemy claimed Egypt, while Seleucus gained control over the Mesopotamian and Syrian regions as well as part of Asia Minor. Palestine was once again caught between competing powers. Eventually Ptolemy was successful in bringing Palestine under his control, and he and his descendants were able to maintain this control for the next one hundred years. During the Ptolemaic rule of Palestine, Hellenization continued but was not aggressively promoted. Many of the wealthy, aristocratic Jews seem to have freely adopted Hellenistic practices during this period. Ptolemaic control of Palestine ended in 198 B.C.E. when Antiochus III, a Seleucid, defeated the Ptolemies at Paneas (later called Caesarea Philippi). Antiochus III did not attempt to force Hellenization upon the Jews; in fact, he granted them certain privileges, such as recognition of the Torah as their national law and exemption from taxes for certain individuals. This situation changed radically, however, when Antiochus IV came to the throne in 175 B.C.E.

Antiochus IV was a cruel, despotic ruler. His self-proclaimed nickname was *Epiphanes*, "the manifest one," a title that implied divine status. In 167 B.C.E. Antiochus focused his attention on Jerusalem, seeking to eradicate Judaism and to Hellenize Palestine completely. Antiochus issued an order that effectively outlawed the practice of Judaism: circumcision was forbidden, Jewish sacrifices in the Temple were prohibited, possession of a copy of the Torah was outlawed, and the people were ordered to offer sacrifices to other gods. Anyone who failed to abide by these new measures was to be put to death. The most drastic assault on Judaism occurred in December of 167 when Antiochus ordered that the Jerusalem Temple become a temple to the Greek god Olympian Zeus and that an altar to Zeus be erected over the Jewish altar in the Temple. Some of the Jews, although probably only a small number, willingly accepted these Hellenistic reforms, but the majority of the people refused to comply. At first their resistance was passive. Second Maccabees contains stories of several individuals who became martyrs rather than violate their religious convictions. Soon, however, passive resistance gave way to active rebellion.

The Maccabean Period (164–142 B.C.E.)

In order to enforce his edict, Antiochus sent soldiers to the outlying villages to compel the people to make a sacrifice to Zeus. When the soldiers came to the village of Modein, northwest of Jerusalem, the villagers refused. When one young man finally stepped forward to make the required sacrifice, Mattathias, an elderly priest who lived in the village, killed him along with the king's officer. Mattathias and his five sons then fled to the mountains, where they began an armed revolt against Antiochus and his forces in 166 or 165 B.C.E. Mattathias died shortly thereafter, and Judas, one of his sons, assumed leadership of the revolt.

Judas was nicknamed Maccabeus, which means "the hammer." From this nickname came the term Maccabees, which was applied to Judas and his brothers and to the revolt itself, the Maccabean Revolt.

The Maccabees were soon joined in their guerrilla warfare by a group of devout Jews known as the Hasidim (the "pious ones" or "devout ones"). Judas and his forces successfully routed the Syrian army and quickly regained control of Jerusalem and the Temple. In 164 B.C.E., on the twenty-fifth day of the Jewish month of Kislev (which would have been in the month of December), Judas and his forces rededicated the Jerusalem Temple to the worship of Yahweh. The Jewish holiday Hanukkah, also called the Feast of Dedication or Feast of Lights, commemorates this important event in Jewish history (the Hebrew word "Hanukkah" means "dedication").

Judas continued his struggles against the Syrians, winning some battles and losing others. Eventually, due to political problems in Syria, the Syrians negotiated a peace settlement with the Jews that permitted the Jews to practice their faith legally and recognized Jewish control over the Jerusalem Temple. Although the Syrians still controlled Palestine politically, the fight for religious freedom had succeeded. Judas, however, was not content with religious independence; he wanted political independence as well. With that goal in mind, Judas and his supporters continued their struggles against the Syrians and the pro-Hellenistic Jewish High Priest who had been appointed by the Syrians.

When Judas died in battle in 161 B.C.E., his brother Jonathan took over as leader of the opposition forces. The death of the Jewish High Priest, coupled with the internal power struggles for the Syrian throne, led in 153 to Jonathan's being named Jewish High Priest (although he was not of the correct ancestry to be High Priest) and the official head of the Jewish people. By being a shrewd politician and aligning himself with first one rival to the Syrian throne and then another—along with continued military attacks against the Syrians—Jonathan increased his strength and enlarged Jewish territory. In 142 B.C.E. Jonathan was captured and killed by the Syrians and Simon, the only remaining son of Mattathias, was chosen by the Jewish people as Jonathan's successor.

The Hasmonean Period (142–63 B.C.E.)

During Simon's reign the Jews received exemption from paying taxes to the Syrians and gained political independence, a situation due more to internal weakness and turmoil in Syria than to Jewish strength. For the first time since Jerusalem had fallen to the Babylonians in the opening years of the sixth century, the Jewish people were free from foreign control. Simon's reign was one of relative peace and prosperity. In appreciation for all that Simon had accomplished, the Jewish people proclaimed him High Priest, prince, and military commander forever; that is, his descendants were to rule after him. Thus a new dynasty was begun, often called the Hasmonean dynasty. It was named after Hasmon (or Hashmon), an ancestor of the Maccabees.

When Simon was murdered by his son-in-law in 135 B.C.E., Simon's son John Hyrcanus became the leader of the Jewish people. Although the Jews were once again dominated by the Syrians for a brief period, Hyrcanus was able to regain Jewish independence and extend his territorial borders to include Samaria in the north, Idumea (Edom) in the south, and some regions of the Transjordan to the east. During the reign of Hyrcanus the names of two important groups within Judaism emerge for the first time, the Sadducees and the Pharisees, both of which will be discussed below.

Figure 14.2. Major Historical Events in Palestine 332 B.C.E.–135 C.E.

332 B.C.E.	Alexander the Great conquers Palestine.
301 B.C.E.	Ptolemy Lagi, ruler of Egypt, controls Palestine.
198 B.C.E.	The Seleucid king of Syria, Antiochus III, defeats the Ptolemies and gains control of Palestine.
175–164 B.C.E.	Antiochus IV Epiphanes, king of Syria, attempts to eradicate Judaism.
167 B.C.E.	Antiochus IV desecrates the Jerusalem Temple by turning it into a temple to Zeus.
166 B.C.E.	Maccabean Revolt
164 B.C.E.	Rededication of Jerusalem Temple by Judas Maccabeus
164–142 B.C.E.	Maccabean rule
142–63 B.C.E.	Hasmonean dynasty
63 B.C.E.	Jerusalem is captured by the Roman general Pompey.
37 B.C.E.	Herod (the Great) begins to rule as king of Judea.
4 B.C.E.	Herod dies. His kingdom is divided among three of his sons.
4 B.C.E.–6 C.E.	Judea, Samaria, and Idumea are ruled by Archelaus. After he is deposed, Roman procurators are appointed.
1 B.C.E.–31 C.E.	Philip rules area northeast of Galilee.
4 B.C.E.–39 C.E	Herod Antipas rules Galilee and Perea.
37 C.E.	Herod Agrippa I is appointed king of territory formerly held by Philip.
40 C.E.	Herod Agrippa I is given former territory of Herod Antipas.
41 C.E.	Herod Agrippa I is given former territory of Archelaus.
44 C.E.	Herod Agrippa I dies. Roman procurators are appointed to govern Palestine.
50–92/93 C.E.	Herod Agrippa II is given charge of the Jerusalem Temple, the right to appoint the High Priest, and various territories to govern.
66–74 C.E.	First Jewish Revolt against the Romans
70 C.E.	Destruction of Jerusalem and the Temple
132–135 C.E.	Second Jewish Revolt against the Romans is led by Bar Kokhba.

Palestine Under the Romans (63 B.C.E.–135 C.E.)

Following the death of Hyrcanus in 104 B.C.E., the Hasmonean descendants continued to rule over Palestine until 63 B.C.E., when Jerusalem came under the control of the Romans. Four years earlier, fighting had broken out between two Hasmonean brothers for the control of Palestine. Both men appealed to Rome for help in securing the Judean throne. Rome's answer to the squabble was to take control of Palestine for itself. Once more the Jews became subjects of a foreign power. Eventually the Romans named Hyrcanus II (a Hasmonean) as High Priest and ruler of the Jews. The actual power, however, lay with Antipater, an Idumean, who was named governor of Judea by the Romans. Antipater appointed two of his sons to help administer the country: Phasael was appointed governor of Jerusalem and Herod governor of Galilee. Antipater was the real power in Judea until his death by poisoning in 43 B.C.E. Shortly thereafter, Jerusalem was captured by a rival of Hyrcanus II. Phasael was killed, Herod fled to Rome, and Hyrcanus was captured. Instead of killing Hyrcanus, his enemies cut off his ears, thus rendering him incapable of ever serving as High Priest again, since the High Priest had to be free of any physical defects. In Rome Herod appealed to Antony and Octavius, who named him king of Judea. He returned to Palestine, but not until 37 B.C.E. was he able to drive out his opponents. Herod, later called "the Great," ruled over Judea from 37 B.C.E. until his death in 4 B.C.E.

In many respects Herod ruled Judea well. Due to his popularity in Rome, the size of Herod's kingdom was increased on several occasions until eventually he ruled a territory almost equal in size to that which Solomon had ruled. Herod was also an enthusiastic builder. He rebuilt the city of Samaria, renaming it Sebaste. Since the Judean coastline had few natural harbors, Herod created an artificial harbor for the newly constructed city of Caesarea, named in honor of Caesar. Several other cities were built and a number of fortresses were refurbished, including the fortress of Masada. Herod's most famous building accomplishment, however, was his reconstruction of the Jerusalem Temple. Deciding that the Temple was overshadowed by the more spectacular palace buildings nearby, Herod embarked on a major renovation of the Temple. When completed, the Temple was renowned for its splendor. A popular saying of the time proclaimed, "Whoever has not seen Herod's building, has never seen anything beautiful."

Although in the eyes of the Romans Herod was a respected and successful ruler, the Jewish people had a different opinion. The Jews disliked Herod for several reasons. For one thing, Herod was not regarded as totally Jewish. He was descended from the Idumeans, a people converted to Judaism at the point of the sword by John Hyrcanus. Another reason for his lack of popularity with the Jewish people was that his concern for Judaism was superficial, based more on political expediency than on religious commitment. Furthermore, Herod was a ruler with pronounced Hellenistic tendencies, building pagan temples in several non-Jewish cities, promoting Greek culture, and studying Greek philosophy and history. He was also a ruthless king. He did not hesitate to exterminate anyone he considered a threat to the security of his throne, including one of his wives, three sons, a brother-in-law, and a mother-in-law.

Herod died in 4 B.C.E. His will, ratified by the Romans, gave control of his kingdom to three of his sons, Archelaus, Herod Antipas, and Philip. Archelaus was given control of Samaria, Judea, and Idumea. Hated by the Jews, Archelaus was removed from office by the Romans in 6 C.E. Instead of replacing him with a native ruler, the Romans named a Roman governor, or procurator, to govern this portion of Palestine. The best-known of these Roman procurators was the fifth procurator, Pontius Pilate, who was responsible for the trial and execution of Jesus of Nazareth.

Herod Antipas was named ruler of Galilee and Perea, a position he held from 4 B.C.E. to 39 C.E. Antipas was ruler of Galilee during the lifetime of Jesus. He is named in the New Testament as being responsible for the beheading of John the Baptist. Suspected by the Romans of being overly ambitious, Antipas was banished to Gaul in 39 C.E.

Philip was given the territories to the north and east of the Sea of Galilee. This area was mostly inhabited by Gentiles rather than Jews. Although little is known of Philip, he apparently ruled well, maintaining his office until his death in 34 C.E., at which time his territory was added to the province of Syria.

The influence of the Herodian family on Palestinian politics, however, was not over. In 37 C.E. the Roman emperor Caligula granted the former territory of Philip to one of Herod's grandsons, Herod Agrippa I (son of Aristobulus), and gave him the title of king. After Herod Antipas was deposed in 39 C.E., the lands under his control were given to Agrippa, and in 41 C.E. Agrippa was also granted control of Judea and Samaria. Only three years later, he died. All of Palestine was then placed under the control of a Roman procurator. Beginning in 50 C.E. Agrippa's son, Herod Agrippa II, was given control over the Temple in Jerusalem, the right to appoint the High Priest, and also various territories in Palestine to govern. He died around 92 or 93 C.E.

The Jewish people were never satisfied with the Romans as their masters. Sporadic outbursts of violence occurred throughout the period of Roman occupation, but in 66 C.E. it erupted on a grand scale with open warfare against the Romans, sparked by the plundering of the Temple treasury by Florus, the Roman procurator. The Jewish fighters were initially successful, occupying the fortress at Masada and also gaining control of Jerusalem. The superior forces of the Roman army, however, soon began to crush the Jewish rebels. After conquering Galilee, the Romans marched on Jerusalem and placed it under siege.

Figure 14.3. Jerusalem fell to the Romans in 70 C.E. This house in the Upper City was one of the ones burned during that destruction. *(Photograph by Clyde E. Fant)*

The Jewish rebels, suffering from infighting among their various groups, were no match for the Roman army led by Titus. Jerusalem fell in 70 C.E., and the Romans burned the Temple and destroyed the city. Masada, the last Jewish stronghold, fell to the Romans in 74 C.E.

The defeat of the Jews was devastating. The Temple was destroyed, never to be rebuilt; the sacrificial system ended because sacrifices could be offered only in the Temple; and Jerusalem lay in ruins. After the war, Judaism had to redefine itself. The destruction of Jerusalem and the Temple led to the disappearance of the Sadducees and the Sanhedrin. Study of the Torah, which had always been an important part of Jewish life, was approached with even more zeal. The center of Palestinian Judaism shifted from Jerusalem to the city of Jamnia (Yavneh), where a group of scholars convened to interpret and implement the teachings of the Torah.

One final effort to throw off the yoke of the Romans was attempted in 132 C.E. when Bar Kokhba led a revolt against them. Kokhba proclaimed himself to be the long-awaited Jewish messiah, God's anointed, who would drive out the hated Romans and reestablish Israel as a mighty nation. Kokhba was supported in this claim by Rabbi Akiba, one of the leading rabbis of that time. The revolt ended in 135 C.E. with the defeat of the Jews, bringing to an end any Jewish control over

Palestine. No separate Jewish nation would exist again until the creation of the modern nation of Israel in 1948.

RELIGIOUS DEVELOPMENTS IN JUDAISM

Several significant changes occurred in Judaism during the Hellenistic and Roman periods. New institutions arose and new groups emerged that would play a major role in shaping the beliefs and practices of the Jewish people.

Institutions

Jewish life revolved around three institutions during the Hellenistic and Roman periods. One of them, the Temple, had already been an important part of Judaism for several centuries. The other two, the Sanhedrin and the synagogue, were recent developments.

The Temple in Jerusalem was the most important institution to all Jews, at least symbolically. Only in the Temple could sacrifices to God be offered. The Temple was the focal point for important Jewish holy days and festivals. Every devout Jewish male was expected to make a yearly journey to the Temple, although in reality many of those living outside Palestine would never have made the journey to the Temple even once during their lifetimes. The chief officer of the Temple was the High Priest, who was assisted in the administration of the Temple and in the performance of worship duties by a large body of priests and Levites, the latter being a lower order of Temple officials. Sacrifices were offered daily in the inner court of the Jerusalem Temple, and special offerings were made on the Sabbath and on special holy days. The layout of the Temple emphasized the holiness of Yahweh. Access to the holiest part, where Yahweh was thought to dwell, was restricted to the High Priest alone (see figure 14.4). Even the High Priest was allowed to enter this inner sanctuary only once a year, on the Day of Atonement.

Jewish literature, as well as the Gospels and Acts in the New Testament, speaks of a ruling council in Jerusalem called the Sanhedrin. Although scholars disagree over the exact composition and responsibilities of the Sanhedrin, this council of leaders seems to have served within Judaism as the supreme body responsible for judicial and administrative decisions. The Sanhedrin was composed of seventy-one members, presided over by the High Priest. Although lesser sanhedrins—or councils—existed in Palestine and elsewhere, the Jerusalem Sanhedrin was the supreme court of justice within Judaism.

Jews who lived outside Jerusalem, and particularly those who lived outside Palestine, seldom if ever were able to go to the Jerusalem Temple to worship. The synagogues arose in Judaism to provide alternative places of study

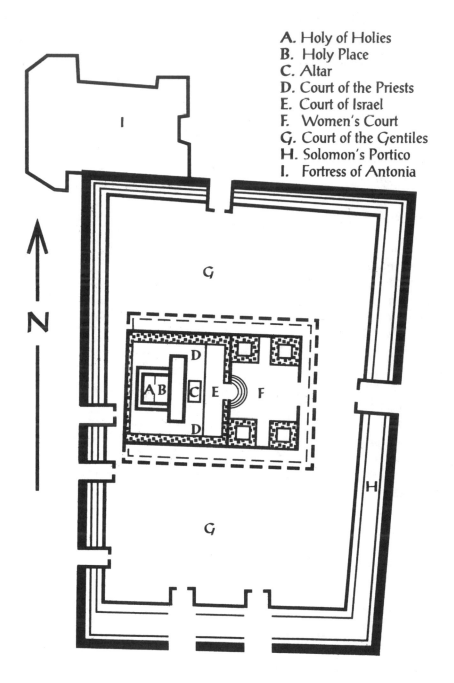

A. Holy of Holies
B. Holy Place
C. Altar
D. Court of the Priests
E. Court of Israel
F. Women's Court
G. Court of the Gentiles
H. Solomon's Portico
I. Fortress of Antonia

Figure 14.4. The Jerusalem Temple during the time of Herod the Great. *(Reproduced by permission of Elizabeth C. Clark)*

and worship. The origin of the synagogue is unclear. Some scholars have argued that its origins lie in the Babylonian Exile, while others look to the time of Ezra the scribe as marking the beginning of the synagogue. Whether exilic or postexilic in origin, by the first century C.E. the synagogue was a well-established institution within Judaism. Virtually every sizable community of Jews, both within and without Palestine, had a synagogue. In cities or towns where a large population of Jews existed, several synagogues might be found. These synagogues served several purposes within Judaism: they were places of worship; they served as religious schools; and, particularly outside Palestine, they were community centers for the Jews.

Worship in the synagogues differed from worship in the Temple. The synagogues were not governed by priests but by laypersons. Any Jewish male could be asked to read the Scripture or preach the sermon. Sacrifices, which were the central focus of Temple worship, were not offered in the synagogues. Worship in the synagogues consisted mainly of prayer, readings from the Torah and the Prophets, a sermon, and a series of benedictions. Later Christian worship was modeled after synagogue worship.

Figure 14.5. The only part of the Temple left standing after the Roman destruction was a portion of the Western Wall. The large stones in the lower part of the wall are of Herodian construction. *(Photograph by Clyde E. Fant)*

Groups

During the Hellenistic and Roman periods, several groups or parties arose within Judaism, including the Pharisees, the Sadducees, the Essenes, the Sicarii, and the Zealots. In addition, the Samaritans, a separate ethno-religious group, also were active in some parts of Palestine. Each group emphasized distinct ways of being Jewish.

The origin of the Pharisees, first mentioned during the time of John Hyrcanus, is unclear. They were likely an offshoot of the Hasidim, who arose in opposition to Antiochus Epiphanes during the second century B.C.E The major characteristic of the Pharisees was their strict observance of the Torah. Within postexilic Judaism a group of Torah scholars, called scribes, had arisen who devoted themselves to interpreting the Torah. These interpretations were preserved orally and transmitted from one scribe to another. For the Pharisees, these oral laws were as equally binding as the written Torah.

The name "Pharisees" means "the separated ones," a title apparently derived either from their separation from everything considered religiously unclean or from their separation from other people. Admired by the common people in Palestine, the Pharisees were in many ways the most devout individuals within Judaism. They sought to honor God by following God's laws as interpreted by the scribes, the majority of whom were probably Pharisees. In spite of their commitment to the Torah, the Pharisees were open to new ideas. They believed in the resurrection of the dead, rewards and punishments after death, and the existence of angels and spirits.

Unfortunately, the Pharisees have frequently been maligned because they were often portrayed as hypocrites or insincere individuals by New Testament writers. Although some Pharisees matched these descriptions (similar negative characterizations of certain Pharisees can be found in some Jewish writings), the Pharisees generally were devout people, zealous in their worship of God and meticulous in their observance of the requirements of the Torah. After the fall of Jerusalem in 70 C.E., the Judaism that survived was basically Pharisaic Judaism. The Pharisees were instrumental in preserving Judaism and in furthering the study and observance of the Torah. Their legacy continues in Judaism today.

The traditional view of the Sadducees understands them as being composed mainly of aristocratic and priestly families in Palestine. Their name is likely derived from Zadok, who was an important priest during the reigns of David and Solomon and whose descendants provided the majority of the High Priests in Judaism. The Sadducees were generally more inclined to accept Hellenization than were the Pharisees. As opposed to the Pharisees, the Sadducees rejected the oral interpretations of the Law. For the Sadducees, the only binding authority was the written Torah. Their conservative nature is seen in their refusal to believe in the existence of angels or spirits and in their rejection of the concept of resurrection and life after death. The Sadducees, so closely aligned with the Temple, did not survive as a potent force following the destruction of Jerusalem in 70 C.E. In recent years several scholars have strongly challenged this traditional understanding of the Sadducees due to the scarcity of reliable information about this group. Regardless of whether the traditional view of the Sadducees continues within scholarship, one can safely conclude that the Sadducees were a religio-political group within Judaism that was often in disagreement with the Pharisees over matters of biblical interpretation and religious practices.

A third group within Judaism was the Essenes. Unlike the Pharisees and the Sadducees, the Essenes are not mentioned in rabbinic literature or in the New Testament. Their beliefs and practices are discussed, however, by two first-century C.E. Jewish writers, Josephus and Philo, and by the first-century Roman scholar Pliny the Elder. Like the Pharisees, the Essenes possibly grew out of the Hasidim movement. The Essenes formed separate communities, held property in common, followed rigid rules for behavior, and shared common meals. Full acceptance into an Essene community came only after a three-year probationary period. Their daily schedule was strictly regulated and consisted of prayer, work (usually agriculture), ritual washings, and common meals. Some of the Essene groups apparently admitted only men and abstained from sexual intercourse. According to Josephus and Philo, Essenes could be found in many of the towns and villages throughout Palestine.

The best-known Essene community was the settlement at Qumran near the Dead Sea. (Some scholars, however, argue that the Qumran inhabitants were not Essenes but belonged to some other group within Judaism.) The Qumran community began around 140–130 B.C.E. when a group of Jews, led by an individual known as the Teacher of Righteousness, moved into the Dead Sea area to escape the "Wicked Priest" (possibly Jonathan, the Maccabean ruler) and to form a community that would practice a "pure" form of Judaism. They withdrew from Jerusalem and the Temple because they believed that Temple worship and the priesthood had become corrupt. The Qumran community produced a large body of literature that has come to be known as the Dead Sea Scrolls. This collection includes copies of writings now found in the Hebrew Bible, other Jewish religious literature, and original documents produced by the Qumran community itself. The Qumran settlement was destroyed in 68 C.E. by the Romans during the first Jewish-Roman War.

Josephus mentions four different groups or "philosophies" present in Judaism: the Pharisees, the Sadducees, the Essenes, and a fourth, unnamed group referred to as the "fourth philosophy." This last group, which first appeared in 6 C.E. and was founded by Judas of Gamala and Zadok the Pharisee, was extremely nationalistic and yearned for freedom from the Romans. Claiming "no lord except God," they called on the people to resist the Roman authorities. Although it is

Figure 14.6. Remains of the Qumran settlement where a community of Essenes lived. The Dead Sea is in the background. *(Photograph by Mitchell G. Reddish)*

unclear whether this resistance involved armed revolt or was simply a refusal to pay taxes, Josephus reports that Judas and his followers were willing to suffer torture and death for their beliefs.

During the 50s C.E. the Sicarii came into being. This group, which may have been a descendant of the "fourth philosophy," derived its name from the curved dagger or *sica* that its members carried with them to assassinate Roman sympathizers among the Jews. The Sicarii were active in the war against Rome, first in Jerusalem and then at Masada, where they committed suicide rather than be captured.

Another group, known as the Zealots, was also active during the first Roman war. Sometimes mistakenly identified with the Sicarii or the fourth philosophy, the Zealots were a separate group of extreme nationalists who were willing to fight and die for Jewish freedom. The Zealots apparently arose only shortly before the Roman war. In the New Testament one of Jesus' disciples, Simon, is called "the Zealot" (Luke 6:15). Since the existence of the Zealots as early as the time of Jesus is doubtful, it is unclear whether the phrase should be understood as a general description of Simon (the zealous one) or whether a later term is being applied anachronistically to Simon.

The term "Samaritan" describes any resident of the district of Samaria in Palestine, or it can be used in a narrower sense to describe members of a particular religious group centered around Mount Gerizim near Shechem. The latter use is the one that concerns us here. After Alexander the Great had conquered Palestine, the inhabitants of the city of Samaria rebelled. In retaliation one of Alexander's generals conquered the city, drove out the people, and founded a Hellenistic city on the site. The expelled Samaritans, who like their neighbors in Judea were worshipers of Yahweh, fled to Shechem and rebuilt that city, which had been in ruins for several hundred years. According to Josephus, during the fourth century B.C.E. a temple was built on nearby Mount Gerizim, which became the center of worship for the Samaritans. At this early stage the Samaritans probably understood themselves as a variant expression of Judaism rather than as a non-Jewish group separate from the Jews who worshiped in Jerusalem. Over time, however, tensions developed between the Samaritans and the Jews. The Jews came to despise the Samaritans and refused to consider them as part of the people of God. The extent of this hostility became evident in 129 B.C.E. when John Hyrcanus destroyed the Samaritan temple on Mount Gerizim.

The Samaritans continued as a religious group, having their own priesthood, religious practices, and canon (which consisted of only the Torah). During the Roman period and later, Samaritan communities also existed outside Palestine. A community of about five hundred Samaritans, led by a priest, continues today close to Mount Gerizim. Part of the future hope of the Samaritans is that the temple on Mount Gerizim will one day be rebuilt.

As is evident from the previous discussion, various expressions of Judaism existed during the Hellenistic and Roman periods, each claiming to express the true form of the Jewish faith. These groups, however, represented only a minority of the Jews of Palestine. Most of the people were not a part of any of these groups. Rather, they were the common people, known as "the people of the land." While they might have respected the authority of the Sadducees, admired the piety and devotion of the Pharisees, and been excited by the nationalistic fervor of the Sicarii and Zealots, most of the people of Palestine were too busy merely trying to eke out an existence to be concerned with the subtleties and distinctions of these various groups.

Diaspora Judaism

For the most part, our discussion of Judaism has dealt only with Palestinian Judaism. The Jewish people, however, were not confined to Palestine. The deportation to Assyria of the inhabitants of the northern kingdom of Israel in 722 B.C.E., the Babylonian Exile of the people of Judah in 597 and later in 587 B.C.E., and the voluntary migration of Jews to other lands resulted in a sizable

Jewish population outside Palestine. This scattering of Jews beyond Palestine is known as the Diaspora, a Greek term meaning "dispersion." Important centers of Diaspora Judaism during the Hellenistic and Roman periods were located in the cities of Babylon, Alexandria (Egypt), Rome, and several cities of Asia Minor.

One must not overemphasize the differences between Palestinian Judaism and Diaspora Judaism. The Jews who lived in the Diaspora were thoroughly Jewish, worshipers of the God of Israel and adherents to the teachings of the Torah. On the other hand, Palestinian Jews had also been affected by Hellenization. Many of them had adopted Hellenistic names and customs, and the Greek language was probably not uncommon even on the streets of Jerusalem. The difference was one of degree. Living in a world more thoroughly Hellenized than was Palestine, Diaspora Jews were more affected by Hellenization than were Palestinian Jews. As opposed to Palestine, where Aramaic remained the common language of the people, Greek became the normative language of much of the Diaspora, even among the Jews. This difference in language led to two important developments in Diaspora Judaism. The first was the production of a version of the Hebrew Scriptures in the Greek language. This translation, the Septuagint, will be discussed below. The second development was the infiltration into Judaism of Hellenistic concepts and modes of thought. Language shapes ideas, and as the Jewish faith began to be expressed in the Greek language, different nuances were given to old ideas. Greek literature and Hellenistic philosophy also reshaped Jewish thought.

The Jews of the Diaspora organized themselves into separate communities or associations. The center of these communities was the synagogue, which provided an important means of preserving and strengthening their Jewish heritage. Jews in the Diaspora were often granted certain privileges by the ruling authorities, such as the right to observe the Sabbath, the right to assemble, and the right to collect and send money to the Temple in Jerusalem. On the other hand, Diaspora Jews often suffered persecution and mistreatment from their non-Jewish neighbors, who saw them as different and failed to understand Jewish beliefs and customs. Diaspora Jews were forced to give a defense, or apology, for their faith and were often successful at converting to Judaism many Gentiles who were attracted to Judaism because of its high ethical standards, its monotheism, and its ancient traditions.

LITERARY DEVELOPMENTS IN JUDAISM

During the Hellenistic and Roman periods of Jewish history, Jewish literature proliferated. Although most of the writings that would eventually become a part of the Hebrew Bible had already been written, several other important writings were produced during this time.

The Apocrypha

The term "Apocrypha" refers to a collection of Jewish writings that are not a part of the Hebrew Bible but that are found in many early Greek and Latin copies of the Hebrew Scriptures. The Roman Catholic and Eastern Orthodox churches accept as a part of their canons most of the Apocrypha. These writings will be discussed in detail in the following chapter.

The Pseudepigrapha

The term "Pseudepigrapha" refers to a more loosely defined collection of Jewish literature, produced roughly between 300 B.C.E. and 200 C.E., that is a part of neither the Hebrew Bible nor the Apocrypha. The name "Pseudepigrapha" means "writings with a false inscription"; that is, many of these works were written under a false name, a pseudonym. Since there is no scholarly agreement on the exact boundaries of the Pseudepigrapha, the number of works considered to be a part of the Pseudepigrapha varies. Some of these writings were produced in Palestine, while others derive from Diaspora Judaism. In the form in which they now exist, many of the writings of the Pseudepigrapha show evidence of extensive Christian alteration or rewriting. Although the works of the Pseudepigrapha never became a part of any officially recognized canon, many of these writings were highly valued by both Jews and Christians. Several New Testament writers seem to have been influenced by some of the works in the Pseudepigrapha.

Included among the writings normally recognized as belonging to the Pseudepigrapha are legendary writings (such as the *Life of Adam and Eve* and *Jubilees*), apocalypses (such as *1 Enoch* and *2 Baruch*), testaments (such as the *Testaments of the Twelve Patriarchs* and the *Testament of Job*), and psalms (such as the *Psalms of Solomon*).

The Dead Sea Scrolls

Written roughly between the end of the third century B.C.E. and 68 C.E., the Dead Sea Scrolls are the literary product of the Jewish community at Qumran. The first scrolls from Qumran were found accidentally by a young Bedouin shepherd who discovered them stored in earthenware jars in a cave near the Dead Sea. Since that initial discovery in 1947, archaeologists and other scholars have conducted extensive research at Qumran. Contained among the nearly complete scrolls and thousands of fragments near Qumran were the writings of the Hebrew Bible, some of the Apocryphal and Pseudepigraphical works, and several documents originating from the Qumran community itself. Among the most important of the last category are the *Community Rule* and the *Damascus*

Document, both of which lay out rules and regulations for the community; the *War Scroll*, which describes the final battle between "the sons of light" (the people of Qumran and others like them) and "the sons of darkness"; the *Thanksgiving Hymns*, a collection of hymns expressing thanks to God; and various commentaries on portions of the Hebrew Bible.

The Dead Sea Scrolls were the most important archaeological find for biblical studies in the twentieth century. Not only did they provide information about the Jewish group that lived at Qumran, they also shed light on the history of the transmission of biblical manuscripts. Additionally, because Christianity had its origins in Palestinian Judaism, the Dead Sea Scrolls offered new insights into the background of the New Testament and the early Christian church.

Josephus

The most important Jewish historian during the Roman period was *Flavius Josephus*, born in Jerusalem ca. 37/38 C.E. Captured by the Romans during the first Jewish-Roman war, Josephus quickly won the respect and admiration of the Romans and was taken back to Rome, where he spent the rest of his life writing. His works include two histories of the Jewish people (*Jewish War* and *Antiquities of the Jews*), an apologetic work defending Judaism (*Against Apion*), and an autobiography (*Life*). Although biased and at times inaccurate, Josephus's writings are an extremely important source of information about Judaism during the Hellenistic and Roman periods.

Philo

Another important Jewish writer during this period was *Philo*, a wealthy Alexandrian Jew who lived from ca. 20 B.C.E. to 50 C.E. Trained in Hellenistic philosophy, Philo attempted to bridge the gap between Judaism and Hellenism by showing that the teachings of Judaism were consistent with the ideas of Hellenistic philosophy. In order to do so, Philo used a method of exegesis known as the allegorical method, in which allegedly hidden spiritual meanings are derived from biblical passages. This method of interpretation was to have a significant impact on the early Christian church. A prolific writer, Philo is a good example of one means by which Diaspora Jews attempted to accommodate their Jewish faith to Hellenistic culture.

The Septuagint

As more and more Jews moved outside Palestine and adopted Greek as their native language, a need arose for a version of the Hebrew Scriptures in a

Figure 14.7. The Arch of Titus in Rome, built to celebrate the Roman victory over the Jews in 70 C.E., depicts Roman soldiers carrying spoils taken from the Jerusalem Temple. This scene shows soldiers carrying the menorah, the seven-branched candelabrum. *(Photograph by Mitchell G. Reddish)*

language they could understand. Beginning in the third century B.C.E. the Hebrew Bible was translated into Greek in Alexandria, Egypt. This translation came to be known as the Septuagint, abbreviated by the Roman numerals LXX, because of the later tradition that seventy (or seventy-two) Jewish scholars collaborated on it. This Greek version of the Hebrew Bible became the standard version of the Scriptures for Greek-speaking Jews until the beginning of the second century C.E., when new Greek translations were produced. It also served later as the version of the Jewish Scriptures used by many of the New Testament writers and other early Christians. For Eastern Orthodox Christians today, the Septuagint remains the authoritative version of the Old Testament. One major difference between the Septuagint and the Hebrew Bible is that the Septuagint is a larger collection, containing all the works of the Apocrypha except 2 Esdras.

Rabbinic Writings

The word "rabbi" was originally a term of respect meaning "my master" or "sir." During the first century C.E. it became a title for teachers or other authorities, especially teachers of the Jewish Law. During the second and third centuries C.E. the term also began to be used in a technical sense to refer to certain individuals who devoted themselves to the study and interpretation of the Jewish Scriptures and who produced a large volume of literature as a result of their study. These rabbinic writings began to appear around 200 C.E. with the production of the Mishnah, a collection of legal instructions on various topics. Although these teachings were not put into writing until the end of the second century, many of them reflect ideas of much earlier Jewish scribes. Many of the oral interpretations of the Torah that had existed for more than a century are likely preserved among the writings of the Mishnah. After the Mishnah had been collected in writing, the rabbis began interpreting and commenting on its teachings. These commentaries were collected as the Gemara. Together the Mishnah and the Gemara compose the Jewish Talmud, which exists in a Babylonian and a Palestinian version, both of which were completed around 500 C.E.

In addition to the Talmud, the rabbis also produced other writings. Since many of the Jewish people could no longer understand Hebrew, whenever the Jewish Scriptures were read aloud in Hebrew in synagogue worship there was a need to have these readings translated for the people. In Palestine, Babylon, and several neighboring areas, Aramaic had become the common language of the people. When the Hebrew Bible was read in the synagogues in these areas, someone would give an oral translation of the Hebrew into Aramaic. Eventually, these oral translations of portions of the Hebrew Bible were collected and preserved in writing by the rabbis. These Aramaic translations or paraphrases came to be known as targums (which means "translations"). The rabbis also wrote commentaries on the writings of the Hebrew Bible. These commentaries were known as midrashim. Even though, like the Mishnah, these other rabbinic writings were not put into writing until the second century C.E. and later, they likely reflect ideas and interpretations that were common decades earlier.

In summary, the Hellenistic and Roman periods were among the most important periods of Jewish history. Historical events of major importance that reshaped Judaism occurred, new institutions and groups developed, literary activity flourished, and new religious ideas were forged. In the next chapter the literature and ideas of this period will be examined more closely. Special attention will be given to the book of Daniel, one of the last books of the Hebrew Bible to be written, and to the books of the Apocrypha.

Chapter 15

DANIEL AND THE BOOKS OF THE APOCRYPHA

Suggested Biblical Readings: Daniel 1–3; 7; 10–12; 2 Maccabees 6–7; Susanna; Prayer of Manasseh

Most of the materials included in the Hebrew Bible had been written by the end of the fifth century B.C.E. Literary activity within Judaism, however, did not cease at that time. The books of Daniel, Ecclesiastes, Job, Proverbs, and possibly a few other canonical works were produced or reached their final form between 400 and 100 B.C.E. In addition, as was discussed in the previous chapter, a variety of literary works that were not accepted into the Hebrew canon flourished between 300 B.C.E. and 200 C.E. This chapter will focus on some of the literature of that period—specifically, the book of Daniel and the works in the Apocrypha—and on some of the new developments within Judaism reflected in this literature.

THE BOOK OF DANIEL

The book of Daniel belongs to a distinctive type of literature known as apocalyptic literature. The word "apocalyptic" is derived from a Greek word meaning "revelation." Apocalyptic literature is revelatory literature; that is, the author of such literature claims to have received a special revelation from God, often mediated by angels, either through visions or direct speech. The contents of this revelation usually describe cosmological secrets or events of the endtime. Many apocalyptic writings arose during times of crisis as a way to offer comfort and encouragement to those whose present situation seemed hopeless. By pointing beyond this world to the heavenly world, apocalyptic writers told their readers that another world existed—another reality in which righteousness prevailed and evil was banished. By revealing scenes of the final judgment, when the wicked—including the current oppressors of the righteous—would be punished and the righteous would be rewarded, the apocalyptic writers offered hope to their readers.

The origins of apocalyptic thought within Judaism are complex. Many factors seem to have contributed to the development of these new ideas. Scholars have pointed to Hebrew prophecy, wisdom traditions, the Persian religion of Zoroastrianism, and Hellenistic ideas as shaping influences on Jewish apocalyptic thought. The teachings of the Hebrew prophets certainly influenced the writers of apocalyptic literature. Like the prophets, the apocalyptists were sure of God's ultimate control of the world and God's concern for the people of God. Prophets and apocalyptists alike spoke of God's intervention in the future and the salvation of the righteous; that is, both prophets and apocalyptists were concerned with *eschatology*, ideas about the "last days" or final period of history. A major difference occurs, however, in their understanding of history and how God will be involved in the world. The prophets were generally world-affirming, believing that, in spite of the sinful condition of humanity, God had not given up on the world. God would use human agents, they believed, to act within history to correct the evils of the world. Apocalyptic writers, on the other hand, were pessimistic toward the world and this present age. They believed the situation was so evil that God would not attempt to salvage this age; rather, God would use supernatural means to bring this age to a close and inaugurate a new age.

One literary technique adopted by most apocalyptists was pseudonymity, or writing under a false name. The author claimed to be some great figure from Israel's past, such as Enoch, Ezra, Abraham, Baruch, or Isaiah. The use of such pseudonyms served to give the writing more authority. A second technique used in some of the apocalyptic writings is known as *ex eventu prophecy*, or prophecy after the event. Writing from the perspective of an ancient figure, the author revealed coming events in world history, including the events of the endtime or last days. To the reader, it appeared that the ancient writer had accurately foretold the events of world history. In reality the actual author had simply recounted events of the past, cast in the form of predictions. This technique was a way of gaining credibility for the author's description of events that were truly future. The reader would conclude that if the writer had been correct in foretelling the events of world history up to the present, then the statements about events yet to occur must also be correct.

Jewish apocalyptic thought seems to have arisen after the Babylonian Exile. Its beginnings can be seen in some of the exilic or postexilic prophetic writings of the Hebrew Bible, works such as Isaiah 24–27, Second Isaiah, Zechariah, and Ezekiel. The first full-scale apocalyptic texts, however, are usually considered to be sections of *1 Enoch*, a composite work written between the third century B.C.E. and the first century C.E. The period from the third century B.C.E. to the second century C.E. saw the proliferation of apocalyptic writings within Judaism.

The only major apocalyptic writing in the Hebrew Bible is the book of Daniel, a work that purportedly derives from the sixth century B.C.E. during the time of the Babylonian Exile. Since at least the second century C.E., however, many readers of the book of Daniel have questioned an early dating because of the historical inaccuracies of the book. The opening verse of Daniel, for example, states that Nebuchadnezzar (a variant spelling of Nebuchadrezzar) captured Babylon in the third year of the reign of Jehoiakim (606 B.C.E.); this event actually took place in 597 B.C.E. In chapter 5, Belshazzar is called the son of Nebuchadnezzar; in fact, he was the son of Nabonidus, a later king. Moreover, Belshazzar was never actually king, as the book of Daniel claims, but only served in his father's absence. Later the writing states that Darius the Mede became the ruler of Babylon after the death of Belshazzar. Historians do not know a person by that name. Darius I Hystaspis did eventually rule over the old Babylonian territory, but he was from Persia, not Media. Furthermore, he ruled after Cyrus, not before, as Daniel states. The descriptions of early events contain more discrepancies than do the descriptions of later episodes. The closer to the second century B.C.E. one moves in the historical events recounted, the more detailed and accurate the descriptions become. Inaccuracies begin occurring once more in the author's description of the final campaigns and death of the "contemptible" king (Antiochus IV Epiphanes).

This sequence of historical inaccuracies has led scholars to conclude that, like most apocalyptic writings, the book of Daniel was written pseudonymously and used the technique of *ex eventu* prophecy. The book was not actually written by Daniel in the sixth century but was produced by some unknown person who lived during the time of the persecution of the Jewish people by Antiochus Epiphanes. The book should probably be dated ca. 166–165 B.C.E., after the beginning of the Maccabean revolt (the "little help" in 11:34 may be a reference to the Maccabean uprising) but prior to the death of Antiochus in 164 B.C.E.

Figure 15.1. Coin of Antiochus IV. The repressive measures of Antiochus IV were responsible for the outbreak of the Maccabean Revolt. The book of Daniel was written to offer hope and encouragement to the Jews suffering under Antiochus IV. *(Courtesy of The American Numismatic Society, New York)*

Contents of the Book of Daniel

Daniel is presented as one of the Jewish young men taken into captivity to Babylon by King Nebuchadnezzar. The first part of the book contains stories about Daniel and his three friends and their struggles to remain true to their Jewish faith in an alien land. Faced with persecution and even death, the four men never compromise their commitment to Yahweh, who preserves them from danger. In chapter 1, Daniel and his three friends are chosen for special training and service in the king's court. When given the rich food of the king to eat (i.e., food contrary to Jewish dietary law), Daniel and his friends courageously refuse to compromise their religious beliefs by eating the king's food. God grants them special wisdom and learning, with the result that the four are noticed and admired by the king.

The second story (chapter 2) reveals Daniel's skill in interpreting dreams. Troubled by a mysterious dream, Nebuchadnezzar calls together all of his wise men and asks them to explain the dream to him. The task is made even more difficult by the king's refusal to tell them the contents of the dream. Not only must his court diviners interpret the dream, they must also be able to surmise the contents of the dream. When none of the king's men are able to reveal the dream and its interpretation, Daniel, with the help of Yahweh, discloses the dream and its meaning to Nebuchadnezzar.

Chapter 3 focuses on Daniel's three friends, Shadrach, Meshach, and Abednego. Nebuchadnezzar erects a large golden image and orders that all people in his kingdom must bow down and worship the image. When the three men refuse, the king orders them to be cast into a fiery furnace. When asked about their refusal, the men reply, "O Nebuchadnezzar, we have no need to present a defense to you in this matter. If our God whom we serve is able to deliver us from the furnace of blazing fire and out of your hand, O king, let him deliver us. But if not, be it known to you, O king, that we will not serve your gods and we will not worship the golden statue that you have set up" (3:16-18). For the young men, martyrdom is preferable to violating their religious convictions. Their ordeal ends positively, however, because God protects them from the flames. Nebuchadnezzar is so impressed that he grants them permission to worship Yahweh and gives them a promotion in his court.

Chapter 4 further emphasizes Daniel's interpretive skills, describing how he interprets another troubling dream of Nebuchadnezzar's. In chapter 5, Nebuchadnezzar has been succeeded as king by Belshazzar, who arrogantly shows contempt for the Jewish people and their God by drinking from the sacred vessels taken from the Jerusalem Temple when it was captured by Nebuchadnezzar. Suddenly a hand appears, writing a mysterious message on the wall of the king's palace. When none of the king's advisers are able to decipher the message, Daniel is brought in. He interprets the message, warning that because of Belshazzar's arrogance his kingdom will be given to the Medes and Persians. That night Belshazzar dies and his kingdom is taken over by Darius the Mede. The final tale (chapter 6), like the one in chapter 3, is a story of divine deliverance. When Daniel is found guilty of worshiping the Hebrew God, he is thrown into a den of lions. God intervenes, however, and prevents any harm from coming to Daniel.

The tales in the first part of the book of Daniel were probably ancient stories that circulated in Israel. The author of Daniel used these stories to encourage faithfulness and offer hope. Daniel and his friends are examples of heroic faithfulness in the midst of a hostile environment. They were willing to die rather than violate their commitment to Yahweh. A similar situation faced the original readers of the book of Daniel. Antiochus IV was the living embodiment of Nebuchadnezzar or Belshazzar or Darius but was even more despicable. Confronted with persecution and tempted to compromise, the readers of Daniel were encouraged to emulate Daniel and his friends and remain loyal to Yahweh.

In the second half of the book, the apocalyptic portion, two significant

Figure 15.2. This scene from a fourth or fifth century C.E. sarcophagus fragment from Istanbul illustrates the story of Daniel in the lion's den. (*Photograph by Mitchell G. Reddish*)

changes occur. First, the Gentile (non-Jewish) kings are no longer simply misguided or uninformed leaders who might be reformed. Instead they are portrayed as rebellious monsters who must be destroyed. Second, Daniel is no longer an interpreter of dreams; now he is the recipient of dreams that must be interpreted for him by an angel. In chapters 7–12 Daniel receives four visions that reveal the course of world history and the events of the endtime. A careful reading of these chapters, informed by knowledge of political events in the ancient Near East, discloses that the author is describing actual historical events that had occurred. The idea that these visions contain mysterious references to events yet to occur is a misreading of the texts. Such an approach fails to take seriously the historical references in the texts and misunderstands the nature of apocalyptic literature.

In the first vision (chapter 7) Daniel sees four beasts arising from the sea, symbolizing the Babylonian, Persian, Median, and Hellenistic kingdoms. From the last beast arises a "little horn" who wages war against God's people and seeks to change their law. He is successful for a time, but then the "Ancient One" (God) comes and executes judgment against the little horn. God's everlasting kingdom is then inaugurated on earth, ruled over by "one like a son of man" (NRSV: "one like a human being"). The "little horn" is almost certainly a reference to Antiochus IV Epiphanes. Chapter 8 contains Daniel's vision of a fight between a ram (Media and Persia) and a male goat (Greece). Out of the victorious male goat comes forth a "little horn" who attacks even the heavenly beings. The good news from this vision is that the little horn (again, Antiochus) will eventually be broken through supernatural intervention. In chapter 9 Daniel puzzles over a prophecy in the book of Jeremiah. An angel comes to interpret the prophecy and foretells the future of Jerusalem and the eventual downfall of "the prince who is to come" (Antiochus). Chapters 10–12 present the longest vision of the book, a grand sweep of history that begins with the Persian Empire and concludes with the death of Antiochus. The death of Antiochus introduces the final events of world history in which God will send the archangel Michael to rescue God's people.

The message of these four visions in chapters 7–12 is that God is ultimately in control of history. Wicked rulers like Antiochus may reign for a period of time, but God will have the final word. Regardless of how difficult the situation may become, the faithful are not to give up hope; their God will prevail.

Two ideas appear in Daniel that will have an impact on later Judaism and on Christianity. Chapter 7 mentions the arrival in the last days of a mysterious figure. He is described as "one like a son of man" to whom is given an everlasting kingdom with dominion over "all peoples, nations, and languages." This "one like a son of man" in Daniel seems to refer either to the righteous remnant ("the holy ones of the Most High") among the Jews or to Michael, the patron angel of the

Jews (Dan. 10:12–11:1; 12:1). In later Jewish literature this "son of man" figure is identified with the Jewish messiah (in 4 Ezra and *1 Enoch,* for example). In the New Testament the term "Son of Man" takes on added importance because the Gospels portray Jesus as using this term as his favorite self-designation.

The second idea is the belief in individual resurrection. The ancient Israelites had no concept of individual life after death other than the idea of a shadowy existence in Sheol, the place of the dead. Daniel 12:2-3 is the only certain reference in the entire Hebrew Bible to the idea of resurrection of the dead. Even there, however, resurrection is apparently only partial, as it is limited to "some to everlasting life, and some to shame and everlasting contempt," likely the extremely righteous and extremely wicked. The idea of life after death occurs in several Jewish writings after the time of Daniel and by the first century C.E. was a popular belief among many of the Jewish people. The influence of this idea on Christianity can be seen not only in the belief in the resurrection of Jesus of Nazareth but also in the idea of a general resurrection of the dead in the last days.

THE BOOKS OF THE APOCRYPHA

The term "Apocrypha" is usually used to refer to the following Jewish writings that do not belong to the Hebrew Bible:

1 Esdras
2 Esdras
Tobit
Judith
The Additions to the Book of Esther
The Wisdom of Solomon
Sirach (or Ecclesiasticus)
Baruch
The Letter of Jeremiah
The Prayer of Azariah and the Song of the Three Jews
Susanna
Bel and the Dragon
The Prayer of Manasseh
1 Maccabees
2 Maccabees

In addition to these works, three other texts that are important to certain Eastern Orthodox churches are sometimes included under the category of the Apocrypha. These texts are 3 Maccabees, 4 Maccabees, and Psalm 151.

History of the Apocrypha

All of the writings in the Apocrypha except 2 Esdras are found in some ancient copies of the Septuagint. (Second Esdras first appears in several Old Latin versions of the Jewish Bible.) These works were read and used by many of the Jewish people until the end of the first century C.E., when an agreement that these works were not a part of Judaism's sacred texts was reached by leading Jewish teachers. Among the leaders of the early Christian church, the works of the Apocrypha were frequently quoted as authoritative writings. When Jerome made his translation of the Bible (known as the Vulgate) into Latin in the fourth century, he included the Apocrypha (with 2 Esdras). Although Jerome was careful to indicate in prefaces to the apocryphal books that these writings belonged in a category separate from that of the works in the Hebrew Bible, later copyists did not always include these introductory remarks. Even though some dissenting opinions were voiced, the consensus developed in the Christian church that the works of the Apocrypha were also to be read as Scripture.

When the Protestant Reformation occurred in the sixteenth century, the leaders of the Reformation decided not to accept the books of the Apocrypha as canonical. While these works were often considered valuable reading for inspiration and edification, they were not to be given authoritative status. In Protestantism today the books of the Apocrypha have no official authoritative status, although some Protestant groups do consider them worthy sources of spiritual insight.

In reaction to this dismissal of the apocryphal books from the canon, the Roman Catholic Church at the Council of Trent in 1546 declared all these writings, with the exception of 1 and 2 Esdras and the Prayer of Manasseh, to be "sacred and canonical." (The Prayer of Manasseh and 1 and 2 Esdras were placed in an appendix and continued to be printed in the official editions of the Vulgate. Eastern Orthodox churches today regard them as canonical.) Rather than call these writings apocryphal, the Roman Catholic Church referred to them as deuterocanonical, meaning "second canon," because they were added later to the canon. In Roman Catholic Bibles these writings are usually not grouped together but interspersed throughout the Old Testament. Furthermore, some of them are additions to other books rather than separate works: the Additions to the Book of Esther, as the name states, is a collection of supplements to the book of Esther; Susanna, Bel and the Dragon, and the Prayer of Azariah and the Song of the Three Jews are all additions to the biblical book of Daniel; and the Letter of Jeremiah appears as chapter 6 of the book of Baruch.

The Contents of the Apocrypha

The writings contained in the Apocrypha reflect a variety of historical settings, religious ideas, and literary genres. The literary genres include historical writings, historical fiction, Wisdom literature, prayers, letters, and an apocalypse.

Historical Writings. The books of 1 Esdras and 1 and 2 Maccabees are examples of Jewish historical writings. *First Esdras* (also known as Greek Ezra or 3 Ezra) was likely composed during the second century B.C.E., possibly in Egypt. The reader who is familiar with the biblical books of Ezra, Nehemiah, and 2 Chronicles will readily recognize the similarities between the contents of these works and the information contained in 1 Esdras. The book of 1 Esdras basically retells the events described in the book of Ezra, 2 Chronicles 35–36, and Nehemiah 7:73–8:13, adding extra material from unknown sources. The major addition in 1 Esdras not found in the biblical writings is the legend in 3:1–5:6 that describes a contest among three of the bodyguards of the Persian king Darius. As a reward for winning, Zerubbabel was allowed to return to Jerusalem and rebuild the Temple with considerable financial support from Darius.

The purpose for the writing of 1 Esdras is unclear. Several possibilities have been suggested: to honor and exalt Ezra; to strengthen the claims for the Jerusalem Temple as the only authentic Jewish Temple; or to promote the Law, Temple worship, or the priesthood.

The most important historical writing in the Apocrypha is *1 Maccabees*. Written at the end of the second century or the beginning of the first century B.C.E., 1 Maccabees describes the events in Palestine from the time of Antiochus Epiphanes (175 B.C.E.) until the beginning of the rule of John Hyrcanus (134 B.C.E.). This writing is the primary source for our information about this period of Judea's history. The account given in 1 Maccabees is rather straightforward and simple, with few supernatural or miraculous elements. The author takes a decidedly pro-Maccabean viewpoint; Mattathias, Judas, Jonathan, and Simon are praised highly. They are presented as being very pious and are classed with the righteous leaders of Israel's past. The work serves as a celebration and legitimization of the Maccabean rule.

The author of *2 Maccabees* states in chapter 2 that his work is an abridgment of a five-volume work by an individual named Jason of Cyrene. The present text of 2 Maccabees seems to be a composite work. The original part of the writing is contained in 2:19–15:39, whereas 1:1–2:18 contains two letters that were perhaps added later. The major portion of the work was likely composed ca. 125 B.C.E. The contents of 2 Maccabees cover the events in Palestine from roughly 180 to 161 B.C.E., describing in greater detail and often in contradictory ways many of the episodes mentioned in 1 Maccabees. Whereas 1 Maccabees is strongly pro-Maccabean, the author of 2 Maccabees appears intentionally to deemphasize the importance of the Maccabean leaders: Judas Maccabeus is the only Maccabean leader who plays a prominent role in the book. The focus of 2 Maccabees is on the Jerusalem Temple and the faithful Jewish martyrs instead. Also in contrast to 1 Maccabees, 2 Maccabees abounds with supernatural and miraculous elements demonstrating divine intervention in human history to reward righteousness and punish sinfulness.

Historical Fiction. This category, which is composed of fictional stories presented as history for the purpose of offering ethical and religious instruction, includes Tobit, Judith, Susanna, and Bel and the Dragon. The book of *Tobit* is a masterfully told story about a righteous Israelite and his family who were deported to Assyria after the fall of the Northern Kingdom in 722 B.C.E. The major theme of the work is the suffering of the righteous person. In spite of his exceptional piety, Tobit is the victim of much suffering and misfortune. At the end of the story, however, everything works out well for Tobit. He is healed of his blindness, his son returns home safely and marries a good wife, and Tobit recovers the money he had left elsewhere. In addition, the closing words of the book state that Tobit lived long enough to hear of the destruction of Nineveh, the capital of the wicked Assyrians. The message of the story is that God rewards the righteous and punishes the wicked. Possibly written in the third century B.C.E., the book of Tobit was likely meant to encourage Jews living in the Diaspora to remain faithful to Yahweh and Yahweh's commandments even in an alien and perhaps hostile environment.

One of the most popular writings in the Apocrypha has been the book of *Judith*. The work abounds with historical inaccuracies, including the description of its setting. (Nebuchadnezzar is presented as the ruler of the Assyrians and is said to be active after the time of the Babylonian captivity of the people of Judah.) Through his general, Holofernes, Nebuchadnezzar wages war against the people of Judea and many of their neighbors. Holofernes has been given orders to destroy native religions and compel everyone to worship Nebuchadnezzar as god. The plot of the story is how Judith, a devout Jewish widow, was able to kill Holofernes and save the people of her city from destruction. Many scholars would date the writing of Judith to around the time of the Maccabean revolt, when Antiochus IV (like Nebuchadnezzar in the book of Judith) sought to overrun Judea and eradicate Judaism. Judith is the female counterpart to Judas Maccabeus. The heroic example of Judith serves as a challenge to the readers to remain faithful to Yahweh and to resist the enemies of their faith.

The story of *Susanna* is one of the additions to the book of Daniel. Set in Babylon, Susanna is the story of a virtuous, beautiful woman who is falsely accused of adultery by two elders of the Jewish community. When the two men cannot convince Susanna by threat of blackmail to give in to their sexual advances, they falsely claim to have caught her in the act of adultery with a young man in her garden. As a result, Susanna is condemned to death by stoning. On the way to her execution, however, Susanna is saved by Daniel, who is able to prove her innocence and the conspiracy of the elders. Written prior to 100 B.C.E., the story of Susanna illustrates how God defends the righteous and is a call to obedience even in the face of persecution.

Bel and the Dragon, also an addition to the book of Daniel, is a collection of two stories about Daniel's defeat of false gods. In the first story Daniel, in true Sherlock Holmes style, proves that Bel, a large idol worshiped by Cyrus the

Figure 15.3. *Judith and Her Maidservant with the Head of Holofernes,* by the 17th-century Flemish painter David Teniers the Younger. *(The Metropolitan Museum of Art, Gift of Gouverneur Kemble, 1872 [72.2])*

Persian and his people, is simply a clay and brass figure and not a living god. The second narrative is similar, except that the false god is not an inanimate idol but a large serpent, or dragon. Daniel proves that the dragon is not a god when he kills it by feeding it a concoction made of pitch, fat, and hair. Afterward Daniel is thrown into the lion's den but is kept safe by Yahweh. The purpose of these stories was to demonstrate that all other "gods" are impotent and Yahweh is the only living God. Like Susanna, Bel and the Dragon originated sometime prior to 100 B.C.E. since the Septuagint version of Daniel, which included the additions, was translated ca. 100 B.C.E.

Wisdom Literature. Two books, the Wisdom of Solomon and Sirach, belong to the type of literature known as Wisdom literature. The title *Wisdom of Solomon* implies that it was written by King Solomon; in actuality, the work probably originated in Alexandria, Egypt, sometime between 100 B.C.E. and 40 C.E. In the Wisdom of Solomon, wisdom is personified and is praised highly. Wisdom is described as the source of guidance and strength for God's people, as evidenced in the examples that are given of individuals from Adam to Moses. The author is particularly concerned about the suffering of the righteous and promises that they will be rewarded—if not in this life, then in the next—because the righteous enjoy immortality. The wicked, however, have no hope for the future. The author issues a lengthy warning against idolatry, showing the foolishness of idol worship and the punishment of those, like the Egyptians, who worship idols. The themes of righteous suffering and idolatry perhaps point to the purpose of the Wisdom of Solomon: to encourage those Jews who are facing persecution and who are in danger of yielding to idolatry.

Sirach, or the Wisdom of Jesus Ben ("son of ") Sirach, derives its title from the reference to its author, who is named in 50:27. (This work is also known as Ecclesiasticus.) The major portion of the work was written in Hebrew in the opening decades of the second century B.C.E. by a Jewish scribe who taught in Jerusalem. Around 132 B.C.E. his grandson, living in Egypt, translated the work into Greek and added an explanatory prologue. Sirach is one of the finest examples of Jewish Wisdom literature. Its use of proverbs and the subjects it treats are similar to what is found in the book of Proverbs. The author emphasizes that wisdom comes from God and that the "fear of the Lord," meaning respect for and obedience to God, is the way to attain wisdom. Like the Wisdom of Solomon, Sirach personifies wisdom, even stating that "wisdom was created before all other things" (1:4). In addition to the praise of wisdom and the exhortations to obey God's law, Sirach also abounds with practical advice on how to have a successful life. The topics covered include friendship, relations between the rich and poor, arrogance and pride, responsibilities to family, proper behavior at a banquet, advice on lending money, and inappropriate speech.

Prayers. Two writings fit into the category of prayers. The *Prayer of Manasseh* is an example of a prayer of repentance. According to 2 Chronicles 33:10-13, Manasseh, one of the most wicked kings of Judah, was taken captive by the Babylonians. Feeling remorse for his wicked ways, he prayed for forgiveness and entreated God for mercy. Supposedly the Prayer of Manasseh is that prayer. Although the prayer does not actually come from Manasseh, it is an excellent piece of devotional literature. Suggested dates for the composition of the work vary widely. Many scholars would place its writing during the first century B.C.E.

The Prayer of Azariah and the Song of the Three Jews is one of the additions to the book of Daniel. This additional material contains two prayers that are included in chapter 3 of the book of Daniel in the Roman Catholic Bible. Azariah is the Hebrew name of one of the three young men described as companions of Daniel. When Nebuchadnezzar throws him and his two friends into the fiery furnace, Azariah offers a prayer of confession to God for Israel's sins, asking God to show mercy. An angel then comes down into the furnace with them and makes "the inside of the furnace as though a moist wind were whistling through it" (v. 27) so that they are not harmed. The second part of this work is a hymn by the three young men praising God for rescuing them from the fiery furnace. Like the other additions to Daniel, this supplement was added no later than 100 B.C.E.

Letters. One writing in the Apocrypha, the *Letter of Jeremiah*, claims to be a letter, although it reads more like a sermon. In some ancient manuscripts, this writing is added to the end of the book of Baruch. For this reason, the letter appears in some versions today as chapter 6 of Baruch. The Letter of Jeremiah is definitely independent of Baruch, however, and should be seen as a separate work. The writing claims to be a letter from Jeremiah to the Jews who were about to be taken into exile by King Nebuchadnezzar. The major theme of the work is the folly of idolatry: all idols are powerless because they are simply human creations. Scholarly estimates of the date of the writing range from the fourth to the second centuries B.C.E.

Apocalypses. Only one example of apocalyptic literature is found in the Apocrypha. The book of 2 *Esdras* (or 4 Ezra) belongs to the same type of literature as does the book of Daniel in the Hebrew Bible. In its present form, the book is a composite work. Chapters 3–14 claim to be written by Ezra the scribe and lament the destruction of Jerusalem by the Babylonians. The work actually dates from ca. 100 C.E., and the real crisis that the author is confronting is the destruction of Jerusalem by the Romans. The author struggles with the vexing question of why God allows the righteous to suffer. Part of the answer is found in apocalyptic eschatology: God will set all things right at the final judgment with the eternal rewards and punishments that follow. Chapters 1–2 and 15–16 are later Christian additions to this Jewish work.

Other Writings. Two writings in the Apocrypha that are difficult to categorize as belonging to a specific literary genre are the Additions to Esther and the book of Baruch. The *Additions to Esther* consists of six sections (105 verses) that were incorporated into the book of Esther in the Roman Catholic Bible. The book of Esther is an unusual biblical book because it contains no mention of God or religious practices. From a literary standpoint the supplementary verses enhance the dramatic appeal of the book, make the story more vivid, and add authenticity; from a theological standpoint they serve to enhance the religious dimension of the work. The contents of this addition include a dream of Mordecai's (Esther's cousin and adopted father) and its interpretation, prayers by Esther and Mordecai, a description of Esther's appearance before the king, and two letters containing the texts of two of the king's decrees. The additions are usually dated to the second or first century B.C.E.

The book of *Baruch* claims to be written by Baruch, the secretary of the prophet Jeremiah, during the Babylonian Exile. The work was supposedly read to the exiles, then sent along with a gift of money and Temple vessels to the people left behind in Jerusalem. The book is composed of four distinct sections, each probably with a separate origin. The first section (1:1-14) gives a narrative setting for the work and was likely composed as an introduction when the other three sections were joined together. The second section (1:15–3:8) is a corporate confession of sin and prayer for God's mercy. The third section (3:9–4:4) is a wisdom poem that asserts that the people were taken into exile because they turned away from wisdom, which is identified with the Torah. The fourth section (4:5–5:9) is a poem offering comfort to the people, assuring them that God will bring them home from the Exile and will punish their enemies. The book of Baruch is certainly a pseudonymous work; it was written long after the time of Baruch. Determining an approximate date for the writing of the work (or its various sections) is difficult. Scholarly estimates generally range from the second century B.C.E. to the first century C.E.

Three additional works, briefly discussed here, are not included in the Latin Vulgate and thus are not traditionally considered part of the Apocrypha. Some Eastern Orthodox Bibles contain these writings, however. For example, the Greek Orthodox Bible includes all three writings; the Slavonic Orthodox Bible contains Psalm 151 and 3 Maccabees and also includes 4 Maccabees in an appendix. Whereas the Hebrew Bible concludes with Psalm 150, Septuagint collections contain an additional psalm, *Psalm 151*. A somewhat different version of this psalm in Hebrew was discovered in one of the copies of the book of Psalms among the Dead Sea Scrolls. The contents of the psalm are a poetic summary of events in the life of David that are described in 1 Samuel 16:1-13 and 17:17-54. The first episode tells of God's selection of David to be king; the second story celebrates David's victory over Goliath, the Philistine warrior. The accounts are narrated in the first person, as if David himself is recounting the events. Although scholars are convinced the psalm was not actually written by David, the date of the psalm is uncertain. It likely was composed during the Hellenistic period.

The book of *3 Maccabees* contains two stories dealing with persecution of the Jews and the eventual vindication of the righteous. Although called 3 Maccabees, the work does not deal with the Maccabees or the Maccabean period. The villain of the writing is the Egyptian king Ptolemy IV Philopator, who reigned during the last decades of the third century B.C.E. In the first story, Ptolemy attempts to enter the inner sanctuary (the Holy of Holies) of the Jerusalem Temple but divine intervention prevents him. Angry over his failure, Ptolemy returns to Egypt and orders a census and enslavement of all Jews except those who agree to become devotees of the god Dionysus. Although some Jews do turn their backs on Judaism, most remain firm in their faith. The second story describes Ptolemy's attempt to kill the Jews of Egypt by turning a herd of drunken elephants loose upon them. Again divine intervention thwarts Ptolemy's plans and the Jews are saved. The setting of both stories in Egypt suggests Egypt as the location for the writing of this work. It was most likely written during the first century B.C.E. in order to encourage the Jews to remain faithful even during persecution and to promote trust in God's power to deliver them from danger. Although the work contains some accurate historical details, the author has clearly expanded a traditional story into a work of historical fiction.

Fourth Maccabees is a rhetorical and philosophical treatise that sets out to prove that "devout reason is sovereign over the emotions" (1:1). As proof of this thesis, the author retells the stories from 2 Maccabees of the persecutions inflicted by Antiochus IV on Eleazar and the seven brothers and their mother. All of these martyrdoms provide examples of the triumph of reason, faithfulness, and courage. Even in the midst of gruesome tortures, these faithful Jews demonstrate their loyalty to God and the Torah and serve as examples to the readers of this work. The date of composition of 4 Maccabees was probably between the middle of the first century and the early part of the second century C.E.

THE INFLUENCE OF THE APOCRYPHA

Many people, including some who come from a strong Jewish or Christian background, are unfamiliar with the writings in the Apocrypha. Indeed, many Protestants and Jews are completely unaware of the existence of the Apocrypha. Even though the religious authority of these works is disputed, they are still important writings. The person who wants to understand Judaism and

Christianity and their influences on society needs to be familiar with the works of the Apocrypha. The influence of the Apocrypha can be seen in several areas.

The Apocrypha and Judaism

Although all of the writings in the Apocrypha were eventually declared nonauthoritative for Judaism, several of them were read and admired within Judaism, both before and after their exclusion from the Hebrew canon. The best example of this is the book of Sirach, which was popular among later Jewish rabbis and was quoted often in the Talmud and other rabbinic writings. Portions of the books of Sirach, Tobit, and the Letter of Jeremiah have been discovered among the Dead Sea Scrolls, indicating their usage among the Jews living at Qumran.

The Apocrypha is important also for the historical information it provides. As mentioned earlier, 1 and 2 Maccabees are invaluable for the information they provide about the Maccabean period of Jewish history. For example, we learn about the origin of the Jewish celebration of Hanukkah in these works. The Jewish historian Josephus borrowed from 1 Maccabees and 1 Esdras in writing his histories of the Jewish people. In addition, the writings in the Apocrypha provide a glimpse of how Jewish individuals and Jewish ideas interacted with Hellenistic society. These works reflect Judaism's struggle to maintain its distinctiveness when confronted with political, military, and religious challenges. Although strident warnings against idolatry and pagan rulers are often voiced, the influence of Hellenistic ideas such as the belief in immortality can also be seen.

The Apocrypha and Christianity

Although the works of the Apocrypha are Jewish writings, their importance and status today is due primarily to their influence within Christianity. Several New Testament writers seem to have been familiar with some of the writings in the Apocrypha. For example, Paul and the author of Hebrews appear to have known the Wisdom of Solomon (cf. Rom. 9:20-21 and Wis. 15:7; Heb. 1:1-3 and Wis. 7:22-26), the author of Hebrews likely was familiar with 2 Maccabees (cf. Heb. 11:35 and 2 Macc. 6:18–7:42), and the author of James seems to draw from Sirach (cf. Jas. 1:13 and Sir. 15:11-12). Some scholars have even pointed to striking similarities between certain sayings of Jesus in the Gospels and passages from the Apocrypha that perhaps indicate his knowledge and use of this literature (cf. Luke 12:16-21 and Sir. 11:18-19). Among the leaders of the Christian church during the early centuries, writings from the Apocrypha were often quoted with the authority of Scripture. Although some dissenting voices were raised, the acceptance of this literature as authoritative was widespread.

The Apocrypha is obviously more important today for the Roman Catholic Church and Eastern Orthodox churches than it is for Protestant churches. For Roman Catholic and Eastern Orthodox Christians the Apocrypha serves not only as a devotional or historical source but also as a reference for doctrinal issues. For example, the Roman Catholic and Eastern Orthodox practice of offering prayers for the dead finds its major textual support in the Apocrypha, not in the Hebrew Bible or the New Testament. Some Protestants, however, even though they do not grant the Apocrypha canonical status, have found it to be a rich source for devotional reading.

The Apocrypha and Western Culture

Just as one cannot adequately understand Western civilization without a knowledge of the Bible and its influence, the same can be said for the Apocrypha. Aside from the religious importance of this literature, the writings of the Apocrypha have helped shape our culture in several areas, including literature, art, and music. In English literature, Chaucer mentions Holofernes and Judith in one of his *Canterbury Tales*. Allusions found in the works of Shakespeare appear to give evidence of his knowledge of at least eleven of the apocryphal works. John Milton's *Paradise Lost* is heavily dependent upon biblical literature, including works in the Apocrypha such as the Wisdom of Solomon.

Artists likewise have been fascinated with the themes and ideas of the Apocrypha. Scenes of Judith and Holofernes, Susanna and the elders, and episodes from the book of Tobit appear to have been the most popular of these portrayals. Well-known painters who have put on canvas their versions of these stories include Botticelli, Michelangelo, Titian, and Rembrandt.

The world of music is also indebted to the Apocrypha. The Apocrypha at least indirectly influenced the texts of several church hymns. For example, the idea expressed in the Christmas carol "It Came upon the Midnight Clear" that Jesus was born at midnight was derived from a misinterpretation of a passage in the Wisdom of Solomon (18:14-15). Several oratorios, including Handel's *Susanna* and *Judas Maccabaeus*, were based upon incidents described in the Apocrypha. German and Italian operas were based on Judith, and the Russian composer Anton Rubinstein wrote an opera entitled *The Maccabees*.

Judaism, Christianity, and Western culture in general have been greatly enriched by the writings of the Apocrypha. For the student of the Bible these works are especially important for bridging the gap in one's knowledge about the development of Judaism during the last two centuries B.C.E. and the first century C.E. The Apocrypha clearly demonstrates the creativity, flexibility, and diversity of Judaism during this period.

THE DIVINE-HUMAN ENCOUNTER IN THE HELLENISTIC
AND ROMAN ERAS

During the Hellenistic and Roman eras several new ideas concerning humanity's relationship to God and God's dealings with the world arose or were transformed within Judaism. These ideas are reflected in the writings produced

Figure 15.4. The Greek style of the carving on this Palestinian tombstone ornament from the first or second century B.C.E. gives evidence of Hellenistic influence in Palestine. The motif of friends bidding farewell to the departed was a popular one on tombs. *(Photograph by Clyde E. Fant)*

during this period, particularly in the Apocrypha, the Pseudepigrapha, and the rabbinic writings.

Life After Death

The belief in resurrection and individual life after death is almost nonexistent in the Hebrew Bible. In fact, the only clear reference is in the book of Daniel, likely the latest book in the Hebrew Bible. During the Hellenistic and Roman periods, however, this idea flowered within Judaism. Expressions of a belief in life after death can be found in several writings in the Apocrypha, the Pseudepigrapha, and the works of the rabbis. These works express a variety of views concerning the condition and location of the dead prior to the day of final judgment, the nature and location of the places of final reward and punishment, and the identity of those who would participate in the final resurrection. Some writings, influenced by Hellenistic ideas, even speak of the immortality of the soul instead of the more common Jewish belief in the resurrection of the body. By the first century C.E., the belief in resurrection and life after death was widespread

Figure 15.5. Masada, a nearly impregnable mountain stronghold fortified by Herod, was the last pocket of Jewish resistance to fall to the Romans in 74 C.E. The Romans captured Masada by building an earthen ramp up the western side of the mountain. (*Photograph courtesy of Educational Travel Services, Inc.*)

within Judaism, although it was not universal; the Sadducees, for example, refused to accept this idea.

Belief in Angels and Demons

Ideas about the existence of angels and demons can be found in the Hebrew Bible, but these ideas are not very developed. The situation changed, however, during the late–postexilic time, when belief in these supernatural beings became more detailed and more prevalent (see Tobit and 1 Enoch for examples of the growth of belief in supernatural beings). Good and bad angels were thought to exist, and many were given names and specific functions. Angels were thought to be active in the world, controlling natural phenomena (winds, seasons, stars) and serving as intercessors between God and humanity. The belief in demons and evil spirits also became highly developed in the postexilic literature. These hostile beings were believed to be responsible for death, mental illness, physical disease, natural disasters, and temptation to sin. They are led by the chief demon or evil angel, who is called Satan or the Devil or various other names. Satan and the army of demons are engaged in a cosmic struggle with God and the heavenly army of angels. The idea of Satan as an evil force independent of God and in opposition to God is also an idea that became prominent for the first time during the Hellenistic and Roman periods. Many scholars have suggested that the ideas about life after death, angels, and demons that proliferated in postexilic Judaism originated from or were strongly influenced by Zoroastrianism, the religion of Persia. As was discussed in chapter 12, the Jews were under the control of the Persians for over two centuries.

Messianic Hopes

In the Hebrew Bible the term "messiah" or "anointed one" is never used as a title for a future ruler who will usher in God's final kingdom. Rather, the term is applied to various individuals who are chosen as agents for God—kings, priests, and occasionally prophets. The term is primarily used to designate the reigning king, who was seen as God's special representative. The hope—as expressed in some of the prophets—developed among the Jewish people that one day God would raise up an ideal king of the line of David who would rule over Israel and restore it to prominence. Although the prophets never use the term "messiah" to refer to this future king, this concept is sometimes termed "messianic" in that it expresses the hope for a divinely chosen ruler to arise and bring peace and security for God's people.

This messianic idea underwent extensive development during the Hellenistic and Roman eras. Evidence for this development is found more in the

Pseudepigrapha than in the Apocrypha, although 2 Esdras in the Apocrypha does contain some important messianic ideas. Among these writings no consensus exists about the coming messiah; various views are expressed. The messiah may be of human or supernatural origin; he may even be described as being preexistent, hidden away until the right time for his appearance; he will come at the end of time to inaugurate a messianic age of varying lengths; he is sometimes described as a Davidic king and sometimes as a priestly figure; and in some writings the messiah is expected to crush Israel's enemies and judge the nations. The community at Qumran expected two messiahs, a kingly messiah and a priestly messiah. Some writings even speak of God's final rule, the "messianic age," without an individual messiah.

During the first century C.E., therefore, Jews held a variety of opinions about a messiah figure, including the belief in no messiah. The traditional view that most Jews anticipated the coming of a political and military messiah who would restore the throne of Israel and drive out their enemies is an overstatement. Certainly some Jews held to such a belief. Bar Kokhba in 132 C.E., for example, made messianic claims and found many people who were willing to believe and follow him. A careful examination of the evidence, however, reveals the diversity of messianic beliefs within Judaism.

This examination of the political, religious, and literary developments within Judaism during the Hellenistic and Roman eras has shown the importance of this time period. Even though the Jewish people were thwarted in their political ambitions, Judaism continued to thrive after this time primarily as a result of the Torah scholars and the Pharisees. Our study of Judaism will end here. We turn in the following chapters to explore the beginnings of another religious movement, one that emerged from and is heavily indebted to the vibrant, fertile Judaism of the first century C.E.

Part III
Origins and Early Development
of the Christian Tradition

Figure 16.1. View of "The Treasury" at Petra, capital of the Nabatean Kingdom, from the narrow entryway. *(Photograph by Clyde E. Fant)*

Chapter 16

THE LIFE AND TEACHINGS OF JESUS

Suggested Biblical Readings: Luke 1–3; 10:25–11:13; Mark 1; 2; 3:13-35; Matthew 5–7; 21:1-17

The impact of the life and teachings of Jesus on world history is so prominent that some knowledge of his life is important for anyone in modern society. As the twentieth century began to draw to a close, *Time* magazine stated that "it would require much exotic calculation . . . to deny that the single most powerful figure—not merely in these two millenniums but in all human history—has been Jesus of Nazareth" and that "a serious argument can be made that no one else's life has proved remotely as powerful and enduring as that of Jesus" (December 6, 1999, p. 86). Not long after his death, men and women who believed his message risked their lives to carry it to the Roman Empire whose representatives had ordered him killed. In the next three centuries the Christian faith spread across the Roman world until it toppled and replaced the old religions of Rome. Since that time various expressions of Christian faith have begun in virtually every nation on earth, so that Christianity now has twice as many adherents as any other religion.

Many symbols from the life of Jesus, such as the cross, and sayings of his—"A house divided against itself cannot stand" or "You will know the truth, and the truth will make you free"—are still familiar, even to those who do not know their origin. When more than one hundred consultants were asked to provide a list of names, words, and phrases that literate Americans today should know, many of their responses pertained to the life of Jesus:

Ask and it shall be given
Beatitudes
Blind leading the blind
Calvary
Consider the lilies of the field
Crown of thorns
Do unto others as you would have them do unto you
Get thee behind me, Satan
Golgotha
Good Samaritan
Gospel
Hearing, they hear not
A house divided against itself cannot stand
Incarnation
The Last Supper

Loaves and fishes
The Lord's Prayer
Love thy neighbor as thyself
Man shall not live by bread alone
Many are called but few are chosen
New wine in old bottles
No man can serve two masters
Pearl of great price
The prodigal son
Render unto Caesar the things that are Caesar's
Salt of the earth
The Second Coming
Sermon on the Mount
Strain at a gnat and swallow a camel
Throw pearls before swine
Turn the other cheek
Whatever you sow you will reap
You cannot serve God and mammon

But the life of Jesus has additional meaning for millions of Christians—that is, those who seek to follow the teachings of Jesus and, some would say, who trust or accept Jesus as both Christ (the anointed, or chosen one, of God) and Lord (having authority over life). As we will see, these impressions of Jesus occurred quickly in the young Christian community, and much of the New Testament reflects the view that Jesus was not simply a wise teacher or great healer, but the divine Son of God—indeed, the incarnation of God (the embodiment of God in the human form of Jesus). Their beliefs concerning the significance of Jesus are summed up in the words of the Gospel of John: "For God so loved the world that he gave his only Son, so that everyone who believes in him may not perish but may have eternal life" (3:16).

All of these assertions about Jesus, and more, fill the pages of the New Testament. They commingle with statements about his followers, the towns he visited, and the Romans who finally killed him. Some of this material is contained in the Gospels, the first four books of the New Testament, which tell of the life and death of Jesus; some of it comes from letters written by early disciples (followers; literally, "learners") of Jesus.

Some of these statements call for faith on the part of believers (Jesus was raised from the dead), while others are statements of historical fact (Jesus was a Jew who lived in Palestine in the first century). Efforts to separate the two have never been entirely successful and likely never will be. To get a historical view of Jesus, we must be as clear as possible about the early Christians' conclusions, which were based on faith, as distinct from conclusions based on modern historical investigation.

Figure 16.2. *The Return of the Prodigal Son* by the Spanish painter Bartolome Esteban Murillo is based on Jesus' parable of the prodigal son contained in Luke 15. (*The Return of the Prodigal Son*, Bartolome Esteban Murillo; Gift of the Avalon Foundation; © 2001 Board of Trustees, National Gallery of Art, Washington)

In order to do so, we first must examine the sources available to such a study and confront certain obstacles to obtaining a biography of Jesus. Then we will consider a portrait of Jesus from early tradition.

SOURCES OF INFORMATION

The primary sources of information concerning Jesus are the four Gospels of the New Testament, particularly the so-called Synoptic Gospels, Matthew, Mark, and Luke. ("Synoptic" means "to see together"; it refers to those Gospels that essentially view the ministry of Jesus in the same way. The Gospel of John follows a different chronology and approach to the ministry of Jesus and is therefore not one of the Synoptic Gospels.) Scattered references to Jesus also occur in Roman,

Jewish, and Christian literature of that period. Other Christian writings include both noncanonical literature (writings that were not accepted into the New Testament) and canonical literature, including the writings of Paul and others. The canonical Christian writings will be considered later in another section. The following are the noncanonical sources, Jewish, Roman, and Christian.

Jewish Sources

Considering the close connection between the early Christians and Judaism, it might be expected that Jewish writers would make significant mention of Jesus. After all, he was regarded as the fulfillment of Jewish expectations for a messiah by an ever-growing number of Jews as well as Gentiles, both in Palestine and in the larger Roman world. However, very few references to Jesus occur in Jewish writings. The works of Josephus, Jewish historian of the first century, say more about the Essenes than the Christians. But his writings do contain two references to Jesus, although one of these unquestionably contains Christian additions to Josephus's work.

The reference that is regarded as authentic—and the earliest Jewish reference to Jesus outside of the New Testament—is found in the *Antiquities of the Jews* by Josephus: "He [Ananus the High Priest] convened the judges of the Sanhedrin and brought before them a man called James, the brother of Jesus who was called the Christ" (20.9.1; Louis H. Feldman, trans.; Loeb Classical Library). The second reference is found in Book 18 of the same work. The recent discovery of an Arabic version of this text has authenticated the passage as a writing by Josephus, though it also contains some Christian alterations:

> About this time there lived Jesus, a wise man, if indeed one ought to call him a man. For he was one who wrought surprising feats and was a teacher of such people as accept the truth gladly. He won over many Jews and many of the Greeks. He was the Messiah. When Pilate, upon hearing him accused by men of the highest standing amongst us, had condemned him to be crucified, those who had in the first place come to love him did not give up their affection for him. On the third day he appeared to them restored to life, for the prophets of God had prophesied these and countless other marvellous things about him. And the tribe of the Christians, so called after him, has still to this day not disappeared. (18.3.3; Louis H. Feldman, trans.; Loeb Classical Library)

This passage contains several statements that could only be said by a Christian: "if indeed one ought to call him a man"; "he was the Messiah"; and "on the third day he appeared to them restored to life." Josephus plainly was not a Christian, so it is no surprise that these expressions are regarded as the later insertions of a Christian writer. Nevertheless, Josephus definitely refers to Jesus: he was wise and righteous, attracted Jewish and Gentile followers, was crucified by Pilate's orders, and his followers did not abandon his discipleship.

The few authentic references to Jesus in the Talmud refer to him as a rabbi from Nazareth who "practiced sorcery" (i.e., performed miracles) and led Israel astray, who mocked the words of the wise and taught Scripture in the same manner as the Pharisees, who had five disciples, who said he had not come to take away anything from the Law or to add to it, who was crucified as a false teacher on the eve of the Passover that happened on the Sabbath, and whose disciples healed in his name.

In summary, these Jewish sources certainly do not provide substantial information about the life of Jesus, but they do evidence some knowledge of his existence.

Figure 16.3. A thirteenth-century mosaic of Jesus Christ in Hagia Sophia in Istanbul, Turkey. *(Photograph by Mitchell G. Reddish)*

Roman Sources

Jesus lived in a Roman province and he was tried, sentenced, and executed by the Roman government. Furthermore, the early Christians carried the message of Jesus throughout the Roman Empire. Unfortunately, the only references to Jesus by Roman writers are in the context of their complaints about the new sect called "Christian," which they regarded as a mischievous superstition. Pliny the Younger, governor of Bithynia, wrote a letter to the emperor Trajan (about 112 C.E.) in which he described Christians as those who gathered together before dawn "to chant verses alternately among themselves in honour of Christ as if to a god" (*Epistles* 10.96; Betty Radice, trans.; Loeb Classical Library). He also reported that he had questioned certain persons in his province, regarded as loyalty risks, who testified that they had renounced their Christian faith some years before.

Tacitus, a contemporary of Trajan, wrote in his *Annals* that the emperor Nero (54–68 C.E.) put the blame for the spectacular fire that destroyed a large part of Rome (in the winter of 64–65 C.E.) on the Christians. Actually, the emperor made Christians the scapegoats for the disaster. Tacitus reports that Christians were followers of Christ, who "had undergone the death penalty in the reign of Tiberius, by sentence of the procurator Pontius Pilate" (*Annals* 15.44; John Jackson, trans.; Loeb Classical Library).

Suetonius (ca. 75–160 C.E.), another Roman writer, refers to the expulsion of the Jews from Rome by the emperor Claudius in 49 C.E. He said that "since the Jews constantly made disturbances at the instigation of Chrestus, he [Claudius] expelled them from Rome" (*Claudius* 25.4; J. C. Rolfe, trans.; Loeb Classical Library). If "Chrestus" means Christ, as is generally assumed, then Suetonius attributes these disturbances to the followers of Christ among the Jews. Such disturbances were possibly due to conflict in the Jewish community because of Christian preaching. Suetonius, just like Tacitus, says that "punishment was inflicted [by Nero] on the Christians, a class of men given to a new and mischievous superstition" (*Nero* 16.2; J. C. Rolfe, trans.; Loeb Classical Library).

Again, these Roman sources do not provide substantial information about the life and person of Jesus. But even in these passing references to the leader of a despised cult, at least two important facts emerge:

1. The Romans knew of a group known as Christians who were in Rome prior to 64 C.E., possibly prior to 49 C.E., and who held Jesus as an object of worship.
2. Jesus, the founder of this faith, was a historical person who was executed at the hands of the Roman procurator of Judea during the reign of the emperor Tiberius.

These broad statements confirm the New Testament picture of Jesus of Nazareth, who was crucified under Pontius Pilate and whose followers worshiped him as the Christ (anointed) of God. But we gain no additional information about him, nor do we obtain a sense of his life and work.

Christian Sources

Besides the twenty-seven writings that are contained in the New Testament, other early documents by Christians referred to the life and sayings of Jesus. These writings, however, were not admitted into the canon as Scripture. Their contents were often fanciful accounts or bizarre sayings reputed to be from Jesus. The early church rejected these writings, known as the New Testament Apocrypha, as unworthy of inclusion in the Christian Scriptures. Much of the New Testament Apocrypha consists of legendary stories that attempt to fill in details about the life of Jesus that are missing in the New Testament. For example, to supply details about the period when Jesus was taken to Egypt by his parents (Matt. 2:13-23), one apocryphal writing says that all of the animals met them as they entered Egypt and bowed down before Jesus. Another says that Jesus made clay birds, as did the other children, except that his flew away when he clapped his hands. And when Jesus' father, Joseph, who was a carpenter, was perplexed because he was asked to make a bed from two beams, one of which was shorter than the other, Jesus stretched one to make them of equal length. Other apocryphal writings add legendary details to the New Testament passion accounts (stories of the suffering and death of Jesus) and resurrection narratives.

Reputed sayings of Jesus that were not written into the four New Testament Gospels are known as "agrapha" (literally, "not written"). Most such sayings are found outside of the New Testament, either in the writings of the early church Fathers, such as Justin Martyr, Origen, and Clement of Alexandria, or in Egyptian papyri (documents written on papyrus, a paper made from rushes). One example of a saying of Jesus not contained in the Gospel narratives, however, is found in the New Testament (Acts 20:35): "It is more blessed to give than to receive."

The most prominent of the sources of these noncanonical sayings are the Oxyrhynchus Papyri and the *Gospel of Thomas* in the Nag Hammadi (Egypt) manuscripts. The *Gospel of Thomas* contains 114 sayings attributed to Jesus and is one of forty-five works in the thirteen papyrus volumes in the Nag Hammadi group. These writings in Coptic, an Egyptian dialect, probably date from the fourth century C.E. and are translations of earlier Greek manuscripts. In general, the apocryphal writings were written between the second and ninth centuries C.E. They include gospels attributed to Thomas, Mary Magdalene, Peter, and others; writings styled after the New Testament book of Acts, such as the *Acts of Paul*, the

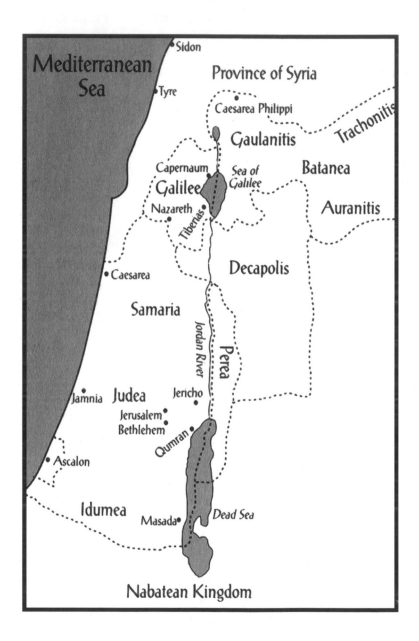

Figure 16.4. Palestine during the time of the New Testament.

Acts of Andrew, and the *Acts of John*; epistles, or letters, attributed to Jesus, Paul, and Titus; and apocalypses, such as the apocalypses of Peter, Thomas, and Paul.

Much of this material is so fanciful as to be preposterous; but recently, increased attention has been given to the sayings, a few of which have been regarded as possibly authentic or based on authentic sayings of Jesus. (The *Gospel of Thomas* in particular has attracted scholarly interest.) Although some of these may eventually prove to be useful to Jesus research, their greatest value seems to be in revealing the nature and doctrines of the groups that collected them.

In summary, research to this point in noncanonical sources of information has contributed little to our knowledge of the life of Jesus. We must depend upon the canonical sources in the New Testament for an understanding of his life, death, and message. But as we will see, even the New Testament sources do not provide answers that are as complete as we might desire.

OBSTACLES TO ACHIEVING A BIOGRAPHY OF JESUS

To achieve an understanding of a religion founded on the life of one individual, it would seem most logical to study first the biographical data (or, if possible, even the autobiographical data) and teachings of its founder. Then the writings of those followers who assisted in the beginning of the movement could be studied. Finally, later information from others who influenced the movement, but did not work with the founder, could be analyzed.

To some extent, that is the method followed in this study of the Christian movement and the literature that it produced. Unlike some presentations of the New Testament materials, this book attempts at least a minimal description of the life of Jesus before describing the writings and institutional development that resulted from his life. This approach has the advantage of acquainting the student with the thrust of the life of the founder of the Christian faith before examining the ideas that others developed later about that faith.

But there are some difficulties with attempting such an approach. First, Jesus left no autobiographical material. Second, none of our New Testament sources were written during the lifetime of Jesus. Third, the material on his life that does exist was not written in strict biographical form. Fourth, the four Gospels differ on some of his sayings, on the details of events, and, particularly, on the chronology of events in the life of Jesus. Finally, the sources that were written first—the writings of Paul—contain almost nothing about the life of Jesus; Paul's interest was in the risen Lord and his message.

In other words, the "primary" material on the life of Jesus—the Gospels of Matthew, Mark, Luke, and John—was written subsequent to and in the light of conclusions to which Christians had come after his death. This means that each of the Gospels is an interpretation of the life of Jesus as seen through the eyes of his followers, and each presents an interpretive portrait rather than a documentary account of his life. Furthermore, each of those portraits was written out of the particular needs and theological understandings of their religious communities (groups of Christians, in separate regions or areas, who had their own traditions concerning Jesus). Such portraits inevitably produce different perspectives. Memory, tradition, and theological reflection are united in these portrayals, and at this point it is not possible to separate them. The intent of the writers was to declare their faith in Jesus in a Christian theological writing, not a historical biography.

As a result, any effort to detail the exact words of Jesus' sayings or the specifics of his activities must recognize the obstacles to such an attempt. Some sayings of Jesus, for example, vary from Gospel to Gospel; other sayings are found in one Gospel but not in another. Likewise, in two or more Gospels some events differ in their particulars, while others are omitted entirely. Efforts have been made to unite all of these variations into one smooth "harmony" of the Gospels. Such attempts have never been entirely satisfactory. The earliest harmony, which was produced by Tatian in the second century, was rejected by the church. Obviously those who assembled the New Testament canon had no difficulty allowing the four accounts of Jesus' life to stand as they were written, without harmonization. Each narrative was judged to bear a significant witness of its own. When every saying and event in the life of Jesus is forced into a synthetic arrangement for purposes of agreement, such homogenization occurs that the original intent of the writers is obscured. The contribution to the picture of Jesus that was intended by the individual writers cannot be retrieved by blending four accounts into one.

In any case, every "life" of any historical figure—even modern ones—is a construction and an interpretation, a portrait, as seen through the eyes of someone. There are no completely "objective" biographies. A careful reader will try to discern the particular emphases or motifs of an author that may be prominent in the narrative. If, for example, a life of Thomas Jefferson devotes great space to Jefferson as a slaveholder but little to his role in framing the Constitution, we may guess that the question of slavery was the overriding concern of the author (particularly if the biography was written during the Civil War). In the same sense, each of the Gospels reveals something of both the life of Jesus and the particular concerns of the Gospel writer.

Nevertheless, with all of their differences, the Gospels are clear in their identification of Jesus of Nazareth with the Christ, or Messiah, God's anointed. As such, they present a Jesus who lived in history as well as a Christ to be believed through faith. God had acted, they believed, through Jesus of Nazareth. That Jesus lived was a historical fact; that God had acted through him was a statement of their belief. The Gospels were written to convey both fact and faith, not one or the other. Furthermore, at the deepest level of its experience, the early Christian church was driven by its conviction that Jesus not only lived and died but also had been raised from the dead by the power of God. That risen Christ, they believed, was also the historical Jesus. The proclamation of the church focused on that event. The Gospels grew out of that same proclamation and were themselves part of that proclamation. The Gospels, therefore, must be understood less as biographies and more as theological interpretations that proclaim faith in Jesus and what God did through him.

It is no surprise, then, that the several sources in the New Testament on the life of Jesus contain varying viewpoints and emphases. Each of the writers reflected images of Jesus' life and teachings that best conveyed the meaning of his life, death, and resurrection to them and the Christian communities they represented. For example, Mark presents a portrait of Jesus that differs in many particulars from that of John; and the interpretations of Paul and other New Testament writers are even more varied. Before looking at these distinctive emphases, however, attempts to establish "core" elements in the life of Jesus will be examined.

CORE ELEMENTS OF A LIFE SKETCH OF JESUS

Because of the complexity of the biblical sources and their lack of interest in a chronological or psychological presentation of the life of Jesus, it is not possible to present extensive details of his life. Nevertheless, the Gospels do present Jesus as a historical person of the first century, a Jew living in Palestine. From a study of these sources, a life sketch of Jesus, a minimal description, may be obtained by historical research. This material is necessarily less comprehensive than the fuller portraits of Jesus by the Christian community of faith, since it is information that might be gained by the methods of historical criticism.

A comparison might be made with the life of Muhammad. There are many assertions about Muhammad that a Christian might not be inclined to accept; Muslim believers, on the other hand, accept them as being consistent with their faith. But other information about his life story is available through accepted methods of historical investigation. Naturally, such a minimal outline of the life of Muhammad would not be satisfactory for Muslim believers, nor will a sketch of the life of Jesus suffice for Christian believers. That is, however, the beginning point for any study of Jesus' life.

Obviously the most objective data on the life of Jesus would be his original words and actions, without Christian interpretation. But since the only substantial material on his life is found in the remembrances of early Christians, no such independent data are available. Scholars, therefore, have used various criteria to arrive at the nearest approximation to such objectively assured data. Three criteria are frequently employed:

Dissimilarity. If reported words or actions of Jesus could not have been produced by traditional Jewish or early church practice, they are said to pass the test of "double dissimilarity." In other words, if something Jesus said or did could not have been derived from either Judaism or early Christianity, it may be regarded as original to Jesus.

This criterion, however, is too limited. It is unreasonable to assume that nothing Jesus said or did could have roots within Judaism, as close as Jesus' connection to the Jewish faith was. Likewise, it is not reasonable to assume that authentic sayings of Jesus would find no carryover into early Christian tradition. But this criterion is useful for establishing some sayings or actions that would be incredible as inventions of early Christianity or derivations from Judaism. For example, the baptism of Jesus by John the Baptist would find neither historical explanation in Judaism nor explanation in early Christian theology. Likewise, his so-called "cleansing of the Temple" was a scandal to historic Judaism and awkward, at best, for early Christianity. (In making such judgments, however, it should also be remembered that our knowledge of first-century Judaism and first-century Christianity is as indirect as our knowledge of Jesus himself.)

Independent attestation. This criterion gives strong historical probability to motifs, sayings, or actions of Jesus that occur in more than one of the sources underlying the Gospels, provided the sources are independent. For example, Mark, M, L, and Q are independent of other sources, while Matthew, Luke, and possibly John are not. If two of the independent sources agree, the historical probability of the citation is increased. Although this criterion has rarely identified individual sayings, it has helped to identify prominent themes in the activity of Jesus, such as his identification with outcasts of society, his regard for the Torah, his attitude toward the Sabbath observances (he ignored some regulations he regarded as trivial), and his expectations concerning the coming of the kingdom of God (or the reign of God).

This criterion also has its limitations. If a saying or event is not documented in more than one source, is it necessarily false? Obviously not. But independent attestation is regarded as increasing the likelihood of arriving at the original wording of a saying or the details of an event. (This criterion is in common use today to establish evidence in court testimony.)

Coherence. This third criterion, often used by scholars, utilizes the findings of the previous criteria. That is, once certain traditions have been accepted, other traditions that appear coherent or harmonious with them are also identified as authentic.

This criterion obviously involves more subjective judgment than the others, but it has been useful in recognizing persistent motifs or practices of Jesus.

For example, multiple episodes portray Jesus as being involved in Sabbath disputes and arguments over tradition with Jewish authorities. This material coheres with the strongly attested incident in the Temple when Jesus clashed with those who sold animals and exchanged money.

Since the criteria themselves vary among scholars, the elements in any sketch of the "unassailable" tradition concerning Jesus have varied also. It is interesting, however, to examine some of the lists of the "unquestionable" facts that have been proposed. One list includes the following items as being "indisputable" about the life of Jesus:

1. He was baptized by John the Baptist.
2. He was a Galilean who preached and healed.
3. He called disciples and spoke of there being twelve.
4. He confined his activity to Israel.
5. He engaged in a controversy about the Temple.
6. He was crucified outside Jerusalem by Roman authorities.
7. Following his death, the followers of Jesus continued as an identifiable movement.
8. At least some Jews persecuted at least some parts of the new movement.

A subsequent list by the same writer adds the following elements as being "certain or virtually certain":

1. Jesus shared "Jewish restoration eschatology"; that is, he expected a renewed Temple.
2. He preached the kingdom of God.
3. He promised the kingdom to the wicked, apart from the rituals of orthodoxy.
4. He did not explicitly oppose the Law.
5. Neither he nor his disciples thought that the kingdom would be established by violence. (E. P. Sanders, *Jesus and Judaism* [Philadelphia: Fortress Press, 1985], pp. 11, 326)

Another scholar's list of "unquestionable" facts about Jesus is similar:

1. Jesus was known in both Galilee and Jerusalem.
2. He was a teacher.
3. He carried out cures that were regarded as miraculous.
4. He was involved in controversies with fellow Jews over the Law of Moses.
5. He was crucified in the governorship of Pontius Pilate. (A. E. Harvey, *Jesus and the Constraints of History* [Philadelphia: The Westminster Press, 1982], p. 6)

Figure 16.5. According to the Jewish historian Josephus, John the Baptist was beheaded at the royal fortress of Machaerus, located atop this mountain in modern Jordan. *(Photograph by Clyde E. Fant)*

Such lists have the advantage of describing a relatively few clear-cut events or practices that characterize the ministry of Jesus. They have the limitation of being so specific, however, that they give little feeling for the life of Jesus. Lists of "authentic sayings" of Jesus, for many reasons, are even more problematic. Another approach, favored by a larger number of scholars, proposes to identify the main themes of Jesus' message, the kinds of things that he said and did. Furthermore, this approach suggests that we can be relatively certain of the ways he taught and, to some extent, the intention of his work and the meaning of his human life.

How can this be done? A careful study of the social world of Jesus—the institutions and customs of his day, both Jewish and Roman—provides a picture of the role of Jesus and his movement in its own setting. This broader social-world approach does not replace, but supplements and interprets, the findings of other critical methods. Against the backdrop of these wider patterns of life we are better able to draw proper historical inferences concerning the life and teachings of Jesus and the movement that continued in his name. In spite of the variations among the Gospels' reports of the life of Jesus and their silences at key points, they do present a coherent social world that yields attitudes, values, and assumptions about life. It is therefore possible to compare the statements in the Gospels about Jesus' actions and attitudes with the prevalent practices in his social world. Of course, the Gospels were written from a kerygmatic intent—that is, to proclaim the faith of the early Christians in Jesus—but they nonetheless locate Jesus solidly within the social world of his time.

His Early Life

Surprisingly little is known about the first thirty years of Jesus' life. Only two of the Gospels, Matthew and Luke, tell of his birth. He was born between the years 7 and 4 B.C.E. (not 1 B.C.E., due to variations in the ancient calendars) in Judea to a young Jewish girl named Mary and her husband Joseph, who was possibly a carpenter (the word *tekton* means "skilled laborer" and may refer to a carpenter or a stonecutter). Jesus grew up in Nazareth and may have followed the same trade. The only incident from his childhood reported in the Gospels was a pilgrimage to the Temple with his parents at the age of twelve, and even that incident has been questioned. There is no information about the "silent years" of Jesus' life (between the ages of twelve and thirty) prior to the start of his public ministry around the age of thirty.

Figure 16.6. The Jordan River is the most important river in Palestine. According to the Gospels, Jesus was baptized in the Jordan River by John the Baptist. *(Photograph by Mitchell G. Reddish)*

His Ministry

The Gospels are unanimous in attaching the beginnings of Jesus' ministry to his baptism by John the Baptist. This charismatic figure was an ascetic in the wilderness who preached repentance for sin, much in the tradition of the prophets. He believed that "the kingdom of heaven has come near" (Matt. 3:2). Those who heeded his call were baptized by John. He may have had an earlier association with the people at Qumran, but their water rituals were repeated (as were those of Israel also), whereas John's baptism was not. By going into the wilderness and submitting to John's baptism, Jesus identified himself with John's urgent call for the repentance of Israel. In preparation for the messianic age, the Israelites were to "flee from the wrath to come" (Matt. 3:7). Just as Israel was delivered from Egypt by passing through the sea, so baptism would symbolize their pilgrimage from the old life to the new kingdom. Jesus was therefore baptized to show his commitment to the coming reign of God and the need for a "new Exodus" by God's people (see Isa. 43:16-21).

The ministry of Jesus was centered in Galilee, which was noted for its tenuous connection with the Jewish leadership in Jerusalem. There he called twelve disciples, who probably represented the twelve tribes named for the sons of Jacob (a possible reason "the Twelve" were all men; Jesus was noted otherwise for having many female disciples). They were involved in an itinerant life with Jesus ("Foxes have holes, and birds...have nests; but the Son of Man has nowhere to lay his head" [Luke 9:58]). They were told not to carry even a minimum of goods or money ("no staff, nor bag, nor bread, nor money—not even an extra tunic" [Luke 9:3]). These requirements symbolized that the end of time was becoming a reality, that Jesus was involved in some way with the restoration of Israel in the last days. The mission of Jesus was a call to return to the prophetic vision of Israel as God's child, Israel obedient to God, Israel under the reign of God (perhaps a more accurate term than "kingdom of God"). Therefore his mission was to Israel; he did expect, however, the day when Gentiles would also follow (Matt. 8:11). Unlike others, Jesus did not believe in a kingdom of force but a reign of peace. Nevertheless, his movement was taken as a challenge to Roman rule as well as to the established religious hierarchy in Jerusalem.

The Gospels describe his daily work as preaching, teaching, and healing. His preaching proclaimed the impending reign, or kingdom, of God; his healing was a sign that this reign was already breaking into the present situation; his teaching showed an authority that was astonishing to his contemporaries, an authority derived from God rather than human teachers or traditions. His earliest recorded sermon (based on Isa. 61:1-2) was rejected by his fellow villagers at the synagogue in Nazareth. Jesus was forced to flee for his life after preaching that God's favor, on previous occasions, had been granted to foreigners while judgment had been visited upon Israel.

His healings, reported by all the Gospel writers, were the most prominent part of his miraculous works. Compassion and inclusion of the despised, such as ritually unclean lepers, were the dominant themes of his healing miracles. The earlier emphasis in Mark on exorcisms (the healing of persons afflicted with bizarre or psychotic-type behavior, known in the first century as "demon possession") was gradually broadened to include ailments of all kinds. "Nature" miracles—the stilling of a storm on the Sea of Galilee, the feeding of five thousand with a few loaves and fish—also show his concern for the needs of others, but they primarily declare his authority over even the physical elements of life. (Of course, there is no way to "get behind" these stories to determine their veracity, but they are as deeply embedded in the text as anything else about Jesus.)

Unlike other reported first-century miracle workers, Jesus used no magical formulas and rejected the notion that he had connection with demonic powers. Consistently his miracles were given for the benefit of others and the glory of God, not for display or his own benefit. The ethical dimension of his concern is prominent in these reports.

The length of Jesus' ministry is not certain. The traditional view that it spanned three years is based on the Gospel of John. The other Gospels, however, do not require more than a year or so for their events. In any case, the entire public career of Jesus took place in three years or less.

His Teachings

Jesus was most commonly referred to as "Teacher." He did not have the formal training of the teachers of the Law, nor did he teach exclusively in the synagogues. His teaching was directed predominantly to his disciples. Women and children also commonly attended his teaching, sometimes to the embarrassment of the disciples (Mark 10:13-16). All of his teaching methods were well known in that time. For example, Jesus used hyperbole, or exaggeration: "Woe to you, scribes and Pharisees. . . . You blind guides! You strain out a gnat but swallow a camel!" (Matt. 23:23-24). That same passage shows use of wordplay, or punning: "gnat" in Aramaic is *galma;* "camel" is *gamla.* He also made frequent use of simile ("be wise as serpents and innocent as doves" [Matt. 10:16]) and metaphor ("You are the salt of the earth" [Matt. 5:13]). Poetic forms are also present in Jesus' use of Hebrew parallelism (in which the second line is virtually synonymous with the first): "Ask, and it will be given you; search, and you will find" (Matt. 7:7-8). Jesus also used proverbs in his teaching: "Do not judge, so that you may not be judged" (Matt. 7:1); "For where your treasure is, there your heart will be also" (Matt. 6:21).

But it is parables, a type of extended metaphor or simile, for which Jesus is best known. One-third of his teaching in the Synoptic Gospels is in parables.

Approximately sixty parables of Jesus have been identified. Most of his parables teach something about human conduct or about God's nature. Some of the best-known parables include the Good Samaritan (Luke 10:30-35), the Prodigal Son (Luke 15:11-32), and the many parables of the kingdom (e.g., "the kingdom of God is like" a mustard seed that grows into a great tree, a pearl of great value, a seed growing secretly). The uniqueness of the parables of Jesus does not lie in their form (there were already many parables within Judaism) but in their predominant emphasis on the kingdom of God.

What was the message of Jesus' teaching? No brief summary can do justice to the diversity of his teaching. Some key themes, however, can be identified. Central to all of his teaching is the concept of the kingdom of God or reign of God. This kingdom is not geographical. Rather, it is the activity of God as ruler. According to the Gospel writers, that activity became manifest in the life and ministry of Jesus, but it has not yet fully come. As such, the reign of God has both a present and a future reality. Both of these dimensions are observable in the principal emphases of Jesus' teaching. The following themes identify his central concern with the reign of God.

Discipleship: The New Exodus. Discipleship, as Jesus envisions it, is to follow Jesus. By the very example of Jesus himself and the Twelve, who lead a life apart from home or possessions, the comfortable are challenged to new values. In many sayings the rich are warned against trusting in the security of wealth. The kingdom that Jesus envisions is the opposite of power and dominance; it is one of service and sacrifice. The disciples of Jesus must not be eager for authority over one another, for the one who would be greatest must be the servant of all (Mark 10:43-44).

In a curious way, the baptism of Jesus by John the Baptist further defined the nature of his call to discipleship. The new Exodus envisioned by Second Isaiah (43:16-21) for the exiles leaving Babylon was echoed by John in his call to repentance. By submitting to John's baptism, Jesus identified his movement with the coming reign of God. His disciples were to trust God to lead them away from "the wrath to come" (Matt. 3:7), for—according to Jesus—"the time is fulfilled, and the kingdom of God has come near" (Mark 1:15). (Jesus took up this message after John's arrest.) It was therefore time to "repent, and believe in the good news" (Mark 1:15). Baptism symbolized this new Exodus. Even as Israel left the threat of Egypt for the "land of promise" through the waters of the sea, so the followers of Jesus must renounce the evil of the present age and cross over to the shores of the kingdom of God. The presence of Yahweh, as promised by Second Isaiah (52:7-8), would return to Zion, and all of nature would rejoice (55:12-13). The discipleship of Jesus was therefore less of a lesson in wisdom and more of a march toward the reign of God.

Inclusiveness: The New Covenant. Another dominant teaching emphasis of Jesus, particularly noted in Luke, is the inclusiveness of the kingdom (Luke 3:7-9). Beyond the Exodus from Egypt lay the covenant experience at Sinai. Jesus follows the emphasis of Jeremiah: "The days are surely coming...when I will make a new covenant with the house of Israel and the house of Judah....I will write it on their hearts" (Jer. 31:31, 33). This new covenant will extend to the most unlikely, the outcasts of society, even those outside of Israel: "Then people will come from east and west, from north and south, and will eat in the kingdom of God"; likewise, "some are last who will be first, and some are first who will be last" (Luke 13:29-30).

This inclusiveness of outsiders and criticism of insiders was a provocation to the secular and religious aristocracy. Furthermore, Jesus' theme of God's universal care and the futility of riches was seen as an attack on the land (and those who possessed it) as symbol of the absolute favor of God. As seen in the reaction to his sermon at Nazareth, such inclusiveness was taken as a rejection of Israel's favored position. Even Jesus' own people, the Galileans (who were deeply attached to their land and agriculture), could not accept such judgment. But when asked by the imprisoned John the Baptist if he (Jesus) was the expected Messiah (since John saw no signs of the powerful, conquering messiah of popular expectations), Jesus replied that the blind and lame were being healed and the gospel ("good news") was being preached to the poor.

Likewise, Jesus' words reinforced his actions regarding the unclean, outsiders, and the marginal persons of society—women, children, Samaritans. All of these would find a new place in the kingdom preached by Jesus. For example, prior to entrance into "the community of Jesus," a woman had no possibility of being a disciple of a great teacher or of being a traveling follower of someone such as Jesus. But many women followed Jesus, including a group from Galilee who followed his ministry even unto his crucifixion (Mark 15:40-41). Furthermore, a woman would be the only one to anoint his head with costly oils, though it became an anointment of his body for death (Mark 14:3-9); a Samaritan was made the hero of Jesus' parable of "the Good Samaritan" (as explosive a phrase in first-century Judaism as the phrase "the good Communist" would have been during the days of the Cold War with Russia); and children were made role models of the kingdom ("whoever does not receive the kingdom of God as a little child will never enter it" [Mark 10:15]).

Testings: The New Wilderness. Israel wandered in the wilderness and struggled with its faith following its covenant experience, and Jesus warns of such dangers to his disciples also. Jesus himself is described as having undergone testings in the wilderness immediately following his baptism (Luke 4:1-13), and he warned his followers of such testings. A major emphasis in the teaching of

Jesus was placed on the trials awaiting those who seek to live under the reign of God. They must remain faithful in spite of those who will hate them and reject them, even as Jesus himself felt such rejection (Luke 10:16). The kingdom is imminent, and so is judgment. In some ways, Jesus taught, it has already begun. The Sermon on the Mount announces the ethic of the reign of God, and such ethical demands are present also in many other sayings. Jesus repeatedly emphasized the centrality of love and compassion as opposed to mere external observance of the Law. His disciples were even taught to "love your enemies, do good to those who hate you" (Luke 6:27), which was, as far as we now know, a teaching unparalleled in that time. The radical obedience required of his disciples will resist the conventional wisdom of land, possessions, and power; for when the judgment of God falls, it will be inescapable (Luke 17:23-30).

Reconciliation and Readiness: The New Kingdom. Since the kingdom, or new community under the reign of God, is open to all, those who would follow Jesus must join the "shepherd" in rejoicing over the finding of one "lost sheep" (Luke 15:3-7). As the waiting father receives the wandering son (Luke 15:11-24), so the disciples must receive others—and be received—in gracious love. They

Figure 16.7. The Gospels describe Jesus driving out money changers and animal sellers from the Temple's outer courtyard, which can be seen along with the inner part of the Temple in this model of Herod's Temple. (*Photograph by Mitchell G. Reddish*)

must not reflect the churlish attitude of the elder brother who is angry at the acceptance of the lost and unclean brother (Luke 15:25-32). Nor is purity merely a matter of ritual; at its heart are moral integrity, love of God, and a concern for human beings (Luke 11:37-41). The disciples also must not be indifferent. Preoccupation with the ordinary routine will be fatal. They must abandon security for the life of the gospel (Luke 17:22-37). They must be ready and watchful, unlike the lazy servant whose master returned unexpectedly (Luke 12:35).

Nevertheless, the disciples of Jesus do not need to live in anxiety, for God will care for their needs as God cares for the birds of the air and the flowers of the field (Luke 12:22-34). God gives these gifts by grace (Luke 12:32). The followers of Jesus, as the new Israel, will join the people of early Israel in the eschatological feast, the messianic banquet.

These teachings clearly identified Jesus with a radical critique of some prevailing interpretations of the Temple, the land, and the Law, though his criticisms of these were indirect. He himself faithfully went to the Temple, denied that he sought to destroy the Law, and claimed the land as God's. But he plainly gave a radically new interpretation to each of these concepts, which troubled the priestly aristocracy. If God cared for all universally, where was Israel's election, its promise of the land? If God gave unconditional forgiveness, was not the Temple system redundant or even altogether unnecessary? If he could directly reinterpret the Law, of what use was the scribal and priestly system? Land and Temple and Law meant social control. Furthermore, the ruling aristocracy of the Jews—including the High Priest—served only at the pleasure of the Romans. Any threat of a popular movement such as that of Jesus could result in brutal repression. To the ruling aristocracy, Jesus was clearly a danger. (Their fears of peasant leaders such as Jesus were borne out some thirty years later by the riots that broke out in Jerusalem when the peasants rioted against the upper priesthood and aristocracy.)

His Last Days

As long as Jesus remained in Galilee, he enjoyed relative safety. Judea, however, was a different matter. His disciples realized the danger to him in the regions closer to Jerusalem and attempted, unsuccessfully, to dissuade him from going there. In one dramatic journey, the so-called Triumphal Entry, Jesus entered Jerusalem to the cheers of the people. They waved leafy branches ("Palm Sunday") as did their ancestors, who celebrated the cleansing of the Temple by Simon Maccabeus in this way (1 Macc. 13:51), and threw their garments in Jesus' path as was done when Jehu was named king (2 Kings 9:13). In a highly symbolic move, Jesus rode in on a donkey—indicating his servanthood and humility—rather than on a warhorse. His followers in some sense regarded him as a king, but one who did not take up arms or advocate violent overthrow of the government.

Figure 16.8. The betrayal of Jesus in the Garden of Gethsemane is depicted in this mosaic in the Church of All Nations on the Mount of Olives. (*Photograph by Clyde E. Fant*)

Even more decisive for his fate was his symbolic move regarding the Temple, the so-called cleansing of the Temple. Jesus entered the outer court of the Temple, the only space where Gentiles were allowed to enter and pray, and found it a teeming oriental bazaar selling animals for sacrifice and exchanging foreign currency. This arrangement was made under the High Priest Caiaphas—in spite of the fact that two other such places in Jerusalem already existed—because it was so lucrative. Jesus overturned the tables of the money changers and animal sellers and drove them from the Temple area. Mark records that Jesus denounced these practices, saying that the Temple was to be "a house of prayer *for all the nations*" (Mark 11:17; emphasis added). In this symbolic action Jesus reacted against the corruption of the Temple and emphasized the accessibility of God to outsiders, the Gentiles, who had no place to approach God in the Temple system. Unquestionably, whatever the complete meaning of his action, the ruling authorities regarded it as an attack on the Temple.

By his words and actions, Jesus had challenged the traditional understanding of the three foundation stones of Judaism: the land, the Law, and the Temple. Just as the prophets (Isaiah and Jeremiah, for example) had suffered persecution at the hands of vested religious interests, so Jesus was rejected and finally killed for the threat he posed to existing authority. We cannot be sure of the full legal proceedings and trial of Jesus, but we do know he was tried, convicted, and crucified by the Romans. But why the Romans, when his conflicts seem to have been with the Jewish religious hierarchy?

First, authority for execution was in the hands of the Romans. Second, in spite of the hostility of the religious establishment, an adequate charge for execution was lacking. But when Judas, one of the Twelve, betrayed Jesus to the chief priests, they found an adequate charge. Likely what Judas betrayed was that the inner circle of Jesus in some sense thought of him as a king. It was possible for the Romans to hear such a concept in but one way—as a threat to *pax Romana*, Roman peace. Rome would not tolerate disorder in the provinces. The Roman governor, Pontius Pilate, having had difficulties already in governing the Jews, ordered the death of Jesus by crucifixion. He was crucified outside the city wall of Jerusalem and buried in a hillside tomb provided by Joseph of Arimathea, a member of the Sanhedrin and perhaps a follower of Jesus. The movement appeared to have ended at that point.

The witness of the New Testament writers, however, including all four Gospels, is that Jesus was raised from the dead by the power of God. Furthermore, they attest that he was seen by many eyewitnesses. This belief is central to the New Testament; indeed, it is the reason for the existence of the Gospels at all. For Christians, this was the gospel, the good news. Before the resurrection, the movement of Jesus seemed finished. After the resurrection, ordinary people risked their lives in Jerusalem and Rome for that faith.

Was Jesus raised from the dead by God? Regardless of the testimony of the New Testament, that conclusion requires faith. To the early church, the resurrection meant the vindication of the life of Jesus by God. Furthermore, it meant that the dominion of death was shattered for them as well and that the kingdom of God and its reign had begun. As the following chapters will show, every writer in the New Testament, from the Gospel of Matthew to the book of Revelation, regarded the resurrection of Jesus as the cornerstone of the Christian faith. And it is on this basis that each of them presents Jesus of Nazareth as the Christ.

Chapter 17

THE DEVELOPMENT OF THE GOSPELS: FROM ORAL TRADITIONS TO MARK

Suggested Biblical Readings: Mark 4:1–6:6; 8:1–11:19; 14:1–16:8

For many readers, the four Gospels—Matthew, Mark, Luke, and John— are the heart of the New Testament. These works present the story and teachings of Jesus of Nazareth, the central figure of the Christian faith. Contrary to popular belief, however, these writings are not firsthand, eyewitness accounts. The Gospels were written several decades after the time of Jesus and were based upon traditions that had been passed along orally. Rather than being mere recorders of historical information, the authors of the Gospels were creative theologians attempting to share their faith in Jesus as the bearer of God's salvation. The Gospel writers told their stories of Jesus in different ways, reflecting their individual understandings of the significance of this Galilean peasant who taught with authority, performed extraordinary acts, and challenged the religious establishment of first-century Palestine.

FROM ORAL TRADITIONS TO WRITTEN GOSPELS

As was the case with the Pentateuch and other writings in the Hebrew Bible, the four Gospels in the New Testament are the end product of a process involving both oral and written traditions. The Gospels not only reflect the events that they describe but also bear the stamp of the communities that preserved the traditions and the individuals who committed them to writing.

Early Oral Traditions

Following the death and resurrection of Jesus, his followers began to share stories about Jesus and his teachings with others. The New Testament, particularly the book of Acts, presents the early Christian church as a preaching community; that is, the early believers proclaimed their newfound faith openly to all who would listen. Convinced that God had acted in the life, death, and resurrection of Jesus to bring salvation to all people, the followers of Jesus wanted to share that good news with their neighbors. In addition to telling the stories about Jesus in order to win converts, the early Christians also used the Jesus traditions to enhance their worship, to teach new believers about the Christian way, to strengthen the faith of the church, to settle controversies within the church and without, and to explain to outsiders who they were. These oral traditions about Jesus, along with the Hebrew Bible, functioned as Scripture for the early church.

The Need for Written Records

While oral traditions about Jesus continued to be valued highly—even as late as the second century—within a few decades after the death of Jesus written records of the sayings and actions of Jesus began to be produced. Several factors likely contributed to the need for written documents. First, as the original followers of Jesus began to die, the need arose to preserve their memories and experiences. Second, the earliest believers expected Jesus to return soon and establish the kingdom of God in its fullness. Since in their belief the present world situation would not last long, there was no need to preserve permanently the Jesus traditions. When the Parousia ("coming") of Jesus did not occur as expected, the church began to preserve some of the traditions in written form. Third, as the

Figure 17.1. Fishermen on the Sea of Galilee near Capernaum. According to the Gospels, several of Jesus' disciples were fishermen. *(Photograph by Mitchell G. Reddish)*

church grew and expanded throughout the Mediterranean world, the need was felt for written records of Jesus' life and teachings to assist the church in teaching and preaching. Fourth, in the struggles over false teachings, authoritative sources were needed to help the church decide what was consistent with the words and actions of Jesus. The end result of this preservation of the activities and teachings of Jesus in written form was a literary work that came to be known as a gospel.

What Is a Gospel?

In the New Testament the word "gospel" is a translation of the Greek word *euangelion*, which means "good news." (The English words "evangelist" and "evangelism" are derived from *euangelion*.) Contrary to its use today, the word "gospel" did not originally refer to a literary document, such as the four Gospels contained in the New Testament. Rather, "gospel" meant the announcement of good news. The Septuagint used the verb form of *euangelion* when it translated passages from the Hebrew Bible describing the birth of a son (Jer. 20:15), a military victory (1 Sam. 31:8-10), and Israel's anticipated restoration after the Exile (Isa. 40:9; 52:7; 61:1). Ancient Greek writers used "gospel" to refer to the announcement of a military victory, a time for great celebration. The birth of the Roman emperor was on occasion described as "gospel," or "good news."

Among New Testament writers Paul uses the term "gospel" more than any other writer. The message of the saving nature of Jesus' death and resurrection was the "gospel" for Paul because it was good news that all people needed to hear. The writer of the Gospel of Mark began with the words, "The beginning of the gospel of Jesus Christ" (RSV). These introductory words in Mark should not be understood to mean the start of a literary work called a gospel; rather, they announce the beginning of the good news about the life, death, and resurrection of Jesus of Nazareth. The use of the word "gospel" in this introductory formula in the Gospel of Mark, however, probably contributed to the development of the use of "gospel" as a term for a distinct literary genre.

What type of writings are the Gospels? For many years, most scholars suggested that the Gospels were a unique literary genre, unlike any previous literary works. Recently, though, several scholars have argued that in many ways the Gospels are similar to ancient Greek and Roman biographies, which describe the lives and deeds of great individuals (philosophers, emperors, generals, and writers) as examples for others to follow. The Gospels certainly are not modern biographies. They have practically no interest in the early years of Jesus' life, his home and family life, his education, or his physical appearance; they are not concerned with Jesus' personality or the motivations behind his words and deeds. These are items one normally finds in modern biographies. The Gospel writers (or evangelists) were interested in presenting their interpretations of the religious significance of Jesus of Nazareth. They chose to include in their writings the events and teachings from the life of Jesus that supported their understandings of him. The evangelists, then, were not just collectors of stories about Jesus; rather, they were creative theologians. They took the information they had about Jesus and edited it in various ways to communicate their own understandings of who Jesus was. For this reason, the Gospels should be viewed as theologically interpreted history. They present the story of Jesus filtered through the faith of the early church.

The Production of the Gospels

A careful study of the Gospels reveals many similarities among Matthew, Mark, and Luke (the Synoptic Gospels) that are not shared with the Gospel of John. Two conclusions can be drawn from these comparisons. First, the origins of the Synoptic Gospels are interrelated. Second, the author of the Gospel of John probably had no direct contact with the other three Gospels; he wrote independently of the Synoptics. Therefore, in studying the origins of the four Gospels, the production of the Synoptics needs to be examined separately from the production of the Gospel of John.

When the contents and structures of Matthew, Mark, and Luke are compared, several facts become evident. First, the three Gospels are often very similar; indeed, in places their arrangements and wording are identical. Second, the Synoptics have major differences among them. Sometimes they tell the same story differently, sometimes their arrangement of material is different, and sometimes one Gospel includes material not found in one or both of the other Gospels. Third, when Matthew and Luke differ from Mark, they often do so in a similar way, either by adding material not contained in Mark or by recounting an event or saying in ways similar to each other but different from Mark. How can all these differences and similarities among the first three Gospels be explained? Did one Gospel writer copy from another Gospel? If so, which Gospel was written first, and which Gospels borrowed from it? The problem of determining the relationships among the first three Gospels is known as the Synoptic Problem.

The most widely accepted solution to the Synoptic Problem is what is called the Two-Source Theory. According to this view, the earliest Gospel written was the Gospel of Mark (ca. 70 C.E.). Matthew and Luke (each written ca. 85–90 C.E.) subsequently borrowed from Mark when they composed their Gospels. Several factors support the priority of Mark:

1. Mark is the shortest Gospel. Approximately 95 percent of the Gospel of Mark is reproduced in Matthew or Luke or in both. It is easier to understand why Matthew and Luke would have expanded what they found in Mark than why

Mark would have omitted so much material (especially major sections such as the birth narratives and the Sermon on the Mount).
2. Matthew and Luke seem to be following the order of Mark's Gospel. When Matthew and Luke diverge from Mark's outline to include other material, they always return to Mark's arrangement.
3. The variations between Mark and Matthew or Mark and Luke are usually more easily explained as changes made by Matthew or Luke rather than as changes made by Mark.

The use of Mark as a source by Matthew and Luke explains similarities found among all three Gospels. What about instances in which Matthew and Luke are similar to each other, but the material is missing from Mark? The Two-Source Theory attempts to solve that part of the puzzle by positing the existence of a second source called Q (from the German word *Quelle,* which means "source") that was used by Matthew and Luke but not by Mark. The Q source is described as a collection of sayings of Jesus interspersed with a few narrative sections, probably in written form. Apparently Q contained no material about the death and resurrection of Jesus. The use of Q by Matthew and Luke explains material they have in common that is not in Mark (or is in a different form in Mark). Since no copy of Q has ever been found, its existence is hypothetical and is seriously questioned by some scholars.

In addition to using Mark and Q as sources, Matthew and Luke each would have had access to stories and traditions about Jesus that were known independently to them. Matthew's special material is designated M; Luke's special material is designated L. M and L may represent combinations of both oral and written traditions. Some scholars consider M and L to be specific sources and

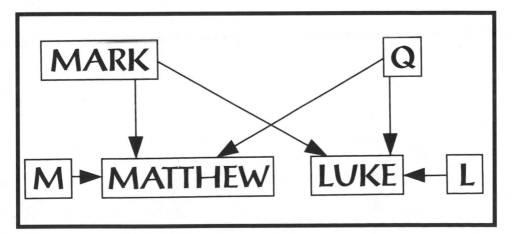

Figure 17.2. The Two-Source Theory.

prefer to speak of this solution to the Synoptic Problem as the Four-Source Theory rather than the Two-Source Theory. M and L, however, do not necessarily denote specific sources, like Mark and Q. The M and L material may simply reflect traditions and stories that circulated in different Christian communities. The relationships among the Synoptic Gospels can be illustrated by the diagram in figure 17.2 (the direction of the arrows is from source to user).

Other solutions to the Synoptic Problem have been proposed. One of the strongest alternative theories (although still held by only a minority of biblical scholars) argues that Matthew, not Mark, was the first Gospel written. This proposal, sometimes called the Griesbach Hypothesis (named for J. J. Griesbach, an eighteenth-century supporter), claims that Luke borrowed from Matthew and that both Luke and Matthew were then sources for the composition of Mark. One of the strengths of the Griesbach Hypothesis is that it does not require a hypothetical Q document to explain the material common to Matthew and Luke. According to this hypothesis, Luke derived the material from Matthew. Although the Griesbach Hypothesis answers some problems left unsolved by the Two-Source Theory, most scholars are convinced that it creates even more difficult problems. For example, if Matthew and Luke were sources used by Mark, why would Mark have omitted such important sections as the birth narratives and the Sermon on the Mount? No completely satisfactory answers to these questions have been given. For these and other reasons, most biblical scholars accept the Two-Source Theory as the best solution to the Synoptic Problem.

Unlike Matthew and Luke, the Gospel of John appears to have been written independently of the other Gospels. The evidence for this theory can be found by comparing the Synoptics with John. Much of the material that is central to the Synoptics is missing in John: the birth narratives, the baptism and temptations of Jesus, Jesus' emphasis on the kingdom of God, Jesus' use of parables, Jesus' ministry centered in Galilee around Capernaum, and Peter's confession at Caesarea Philippi. On the other hand, some of the most distinctive material in John is absent from the Synoptics: the visit of Nicodemus, the story of the Samaritan woman at the well, Jesus' ministry centered in Jerusalem, the "I am" sayings of Jesus, the raising of Lazarus, and the role of the Beloved Disciple. Also, even when similar material occurs in John and the Synoptics, it is often presented in different ways. For example, the Synoptics report that Jesus' so-called cleansing of the Temple occurred during the last week of his life. The Gospel of John, however, describes this event as one of the first acts of Jesus' public ministry.

These differences suggest that the author of the Fourth Gospel, although familiar with some of the same traditions that formed the writings of the other Gospels, did not have access to Mark, Q, Matthew, or Luke. The stories and teachings of Jesus came to the Fourth Evangelist through different channels. Figure 17.3 illustrates how, although the author of John and the authors of the

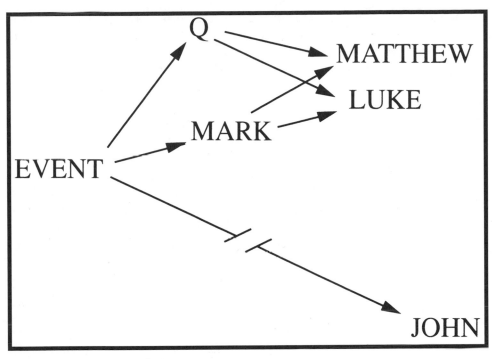

Figure 17.3. The Synoptics and John

Synoptics were often familiar with the same traditions about Jesus, those traditions reached them through independent means.

The simplicity of this diagram does not imply, however, that the Gospel of John is a direct reporting of events in the life of Jesus. The author of John, like the authors of Matthew and Luke, was likely dependent on various sources for information about the life and teachings of Jesus. Unfortunately these sources are not as easily identifiable for the Fourth Gospel as they are for Matthew and Luke. It must also be remembered that an oral period, during which time the teachings and stories of Jesus were told and retold in various settings, occurred between the actual events and their preservation in written form.

The Significance of Four Gospels

The presence of four different Gospels in the New Testament creates an interesting situation. In one sense, the reader would fare better if the New Testament contained only one Gospel. Then the problem of trying to explain or harmonize the many differences that occur among the Gospels would not exist. If only one version of the life and teachings of Jesus were present, then there would be no inconsistencies and variations. In the early church at least two attempts were made to have only one authoritative version of the story of Jesus. During the middle of the second century, Marcion, a Christian from Asia Minor who moved to Rome, decided that the only reliable Gospel was the Gospel of Luke (he even edited out portions of Luke). He rejected Matthew, Mark, and John and argued that the only works to be accepted as authoritative for the Christian church were his edited version of Luke and ten of the letters of the apostle Paul. The church rejected Marcion's position and in 144 C.E. formally excommunicated (excluded) him because of his false teachings, including his views on the Bible.

Later in the second century another attempt was made to have only one Gospel. Rather than reject any of the Gospels, Tatian attempted to bring uniformity to the Gospels by weaving all four of them into one continuous account. This work, known as the *Diatessaron*, was very popular in Syriac-speaking churches for several centuries until it fell into disuse. It never gained widespread acceptance elsewhere.

The preservation of all four Gospels in the New Testament was due to at least two factors. First, by the end of the second century all four Gospels were already very popular, some being more popular in certain churches than in others. Their widespread usage and acceptance would have made any attempt to discard them very difficult. Even more important, however, are the distinctive contributions each Gospel made to early Christianity's understanding of Jesus. Each Gospel had something different to say about Jesus. Realizing that no one Gospel could completely interpret the mission and message of Jesus, the church valued the multifaceted witness to Jesus presented through the four Gospels and wisely preserved all four writings. To appreciate the wisdom of that decision, the modern reader needs to study each Gospel separately, looking for distinctive themes, emphases, characteristics, and structures.

THE GOSPEL OF MARK

According to the Two-Source Theory, Mark was the first Gospel written, and the authors of Luke and Matthew borrowed extensively from Mark. Because of its chronological priority and its importance as the primary source for Luke and Matthew, we shall consider it first.

Historical Context

Although the Gospel of Mark itself makes no claim for authorship (the titles of all the Gospels reflect later church tradition and are not original to the writings), early church tradition identified its author as John Mark, who accompanied Paul on one of his missionary journeys and later became an interpreter for Peter in Rome. Supposedly John Mark based his Gospel on the preaching of Peter. Several factors

Figure 17.4. This synagogue at Capernaum from around the fourth century C.E. was built over the foundation of a first-century C.E. synagogue. According to Mark 1:21 and John 6:59, Jesus taught in the synagogue at Capernaum. *(Photograph by Mitchell G. Reddish)*

argue against this tradition, however. First, form-critical studies have suggested that the material in the Gospel is derived not from one source (the preaching of Peter) but from various traditions that circulated orally in early Christianity. Second, the author of Mark seems to be unfamiliar with Palestinian geography. The most glaring example of this occurs at 7:31, which states, "Then again he went out from the region of Tyre and came through Sidon to the Sea of Galilee in the midst of the region of the Decapolis" (authors' translation). The Sea of Galilee is south of Tyre, yet Mark has Jesus go approximately twenty-five miles north to Sidon on his way to the Sea of Galilee. Furthermore, the Sea of Galilee is not "in the midst of the region of the Decapolis" (English translations often obscure this discrepancy); at best it borders the edge of the region. Third, the author seems at times to be unfamiliar with Palestinian or Jewish customs. For example, the statement on divorce in 10:12 reflects Roman rather than Jewish custom. Although these problems do not prove that John Mark could not have been the author of this Gospel, they certainly call such a belief into question. The best approach is to assume that the writer of the Gospel is anonymous. For the sake of convenience, however, we will continue to refer to the writer as Mark.

The Gospel provides few clues concerning the place or date of writing of the work. The unfamiliarity with Palestinian facts mentioned above would point to its place of composition being outside Palestine. The strongest early tradition claims that the Gospel was written in Rome. This is probably still the best option. Other suggestions have been Alexandria in Egypt or Antioch in Syria. The only major clue for dating the work is the apocalyptic discourse in Mark 13, which presupposes the imminent destruction of Jerusalem and the Temple (which took place in 70 C.E.). Furthermore, if the Gospel was written in Rome, the emphasis in the Gospel on suffering and persecution would fit the situation of the late 60s, when Christians in Rome were suffering persecution at the hands of the emperor Nero. The most widely accepted date for the writing of the Gospel of Mark, then, is around 66–70 C.E. Because the author on several occasions explains certain Aramaic words and Jewish customs, the logical conclusion is that the Gospel was written for Gentile readers.

Literary Structure and Contents

In general terms, the Gospel of Mark seems to be divided into two roughly equal parts. The first part (1:1–9:50) describes Jesus' ministry centered in Galilee, whereas the second part (10:1–16:8) is focused on Jerusalem. The Gospel may be outlined as follows:

I. Jesus in Galilee (1–9)
    A. Introduction (1:1-13)
    B. The Galilean ministry (1:14–8:26)
    C. Events near Caesarea Philippi (8:27–9:29)
    D. Return to Galilee (9:30-50)
II. Jesus in Jerusalem (10:1–16:8)
    A. Journey to Jerusalem (10:1-52)
    B. The Jerusalem ministry (11:1–14:42)
    C. The arrest, trial, and crucifixion of Jesus (14:42–15:47)
    D. The empty tomb (16:1-8)

The Gospel opens with the baptism of Jesus by John the Baptist and the ensuing temptations of Jesus in the wilderness (1:1-13). This opening section contains several major themes that are important to Mark: Jesus is called Son of God (1:1), his identity is ratified from heaven (1:11), he is closely associated with John the Baptist (1:9-11), and he is in conflict with the forces of evil (1:13).

After this introductory section, Mark describes Jesus' activities in and around Galilee as a preacher, teacher, and miracle worker (1:14–9:50). Jesus begins his ministry in Galilee, proclaiming, "The time is fulfilled, and the kingdom of God has come near; repent, and believe in the good news" (1:15). The Gospel of Mark is a gospel of action. Mark portrays Jesus as being constantly in action, moving from one place to another, calling disciples, telling parables about the kingdom of God, healing the sick, and casting out evil spirits. Although Jesus gains a popular following, he also encounters growing opposition from the religious leaders, particularly over the violation of Sabbath laws. Jesus' identity is a major concern in this section. No one—neither the disciples nor the people who have been healed nor the religious authorities—fully understands who Jesus is or what his mission is.

The first half of the Gospel ends in 8:27-33 with Peter's confession near the city of Caesarea Philippi. In response to Jesus' question, "Who do people say that I am?" Peter replies, "You are the Messiah." Even this confession of Jesus' identity is insufficient, however, as evidenced by the remainder of the scene. After Peter's confession, Jesus warns his disciples to tell no one about him (this demand for secrecy will be discussed below). He then clarifies his identity and purpose by talking about the necessity of his suffering, rejection, and impending death, elements that were inconsistent with Jewish understandings of the messiah figure. For Mark, however, suffering is the key to a proper understanding of Jesus.

Figure 17.5. The Garden of Gethsemane on the Mount of Olives, seen from the Temple Mount. (*Photograph by Clyde E. Fant*)

The second half of the Gospel begins with chapter 10, which presents Jesus on his way to Jerusalem. As in the Galilean ministry, teachings, healings, and controversy occur on the journey. The remainder of this section (11:1–16:8) describes Jesus' final days on earth in Jerusalem. The shadow of the cross falls across the entire Gospel of Mark, but its outline is unmistakable in these final chapters. Opposition by the religious leaders increases until finally they plot to get rid of Jesus. One of Jesus' own disciples, Judas, agrees to betray his leader. Jesus warns his disciples of future suffering and persecution that they must endure and then shares a last meal (a Passover meal) with them. After agonizing in prayer over what lay ahead for him, Jesus is arrested, tried, and crucified. At the foot of the cross, a Roman centurion (army officer) proclaims what for Mark is Jesus' true identity when he says, "Truly this man was God's Son!" (15:39).

Jesus' body is wrapped in linen and placed in the tomb of Joseph of Arimathea, described by Mark as "a respected member of the council, who was also himself waiting expectantly for the kingdom of God" (15:43). On Sunday when three women come to visit the tomb of Jesus, they find it opened and his body missing. A young man dressed in white (an angel?) informs them that Jesus has risen and will appear to his disciples in Galilee. The women rush out of the tomb, "and they said nothing to anyone, for they were afraid" (16:8). The Gospel of Mark likely ended here at verse 8, since the earliest and best manuscripts of Mark that have been discovered end at this point. Furthermore, the Gospels of Matthew and Luke, which follow Mark closely to this point, have divergent accounts of postresurrection events, indicating that their copies of Mark ended at 16:8 also. Some ancient manuscripts do have additional verses in chapter 16 (found in many English translations), but these were likely added later to complete what seemed to be an abrupt ending for Mark's Gospel. The Gospel of Mark ends with an affirmation of the resurrection of Jesus, but with no accounts of appearances of the risen Jesus to his followers. For those accounts, one must turn to the other Gospels.

Characteristics and Themes

Through his selection, arrangement, and shaping of the material, Mark brought several issues into focus.

The Messianic Secret. Mark portrays Jesus as demanding secrecy about his identity throughout his ministry. Demons and unclean spirits are forbidden to reveal who Jesus is (1:25, 34; 3:12), and even his disciples are told to keep quiet (8:30; 9:9). Some interpreters hold that the commands for silence derive from Jesus himself. He did not want his role to be misunderstood because he was not the kind of messiah figure that was commonly expected. He prohibited premature disclosures of his identity until he could more clearly demonstrate his mission and purpose. This secrecy motif, however, probably owes more to the Gospel writer than to Jesus since most of the commands for silence are contained in Mark's transitional sections. For Mark, Jesus could never be correctly understood apart from his suffering, death, and resurrection. He was not just another miracle worker or teacher or prophet. Any understanding of Jesus that failed to comprehend him in light of his suffering and death for the sake of others would be an incomplete and inadequate understanding. That is why the fullest confession of Jesus occurs only at the foot of the cross (15:39).

Suffering. Suffering is a major emphasis in the Gospel of Mark. John the Baptist, the forerunner of Jesus, is imprisoned and executed. On three occasions Jesus predicts his own impending suffering and death (8:31; 9:31; 10:33-34). Even the disciples are warned that they too must expect suffering and persecution. As mentioned above, Jesus' life and mission cannot be accurately understood apart from his suffering. Furthermore, those who would be disciples of Jesus must be willing to suffer and even die for his cause. Jesus demands, "If

Figure 17.6. The Via Dolorosa, or "way of sorrows," traces the traditional path of Jesus' journey through the streets of Jerusalem to the site of crucifixion. The third station of the cross on the Via Dolorosa commemorates the place where Jesus supposedly stumbled for the first time. *(Photograph by Clyde E. Fant)*

any want to become my followers, let them deny themselves and take up their cross and follow me. For those who want to save their life will lose it, and those who lose their life for my sake, and for the sake of the gospel, will save it" (8:34-35). This emphasis on suffering in the Gospel of Mark is likely due to the historical situation of Mark's community. Faced with opposition and persecution, those early believers were likely tempted to compromise their faith or at least were questioning why they were suffering. Mark points them to Jesus, who himself suffered and died a martyr's death and who called them to follow in his path.

Son of Man. In the Gospel of Mark, Jesus never uses the title Christ (Messiah) for himself and only once accepts that identification from someone else (14:61-62). According to Mark, "Son of Man" is Jesus' favorite self-designation. The origin and meaning of the phrase "son of man" is one of the most stubborn problems in New Testament studies. Are any or all of the Son of Man sayings in the Gospels authentic sayings of Jesus? If he did refer to the Son of Man, was he speaking of himself or of another individual? Did the Gospel writers understand the term in the same way that Jesus did? The phrase "son of man" is used in Psalm 8 as a synonym for humanity: "What is man that thou art mindful of him, and the son of man that thou dost care for him?" (RSV). Some have argued that Jesus also used the phrase in this way, perhaps as a humble way of referring to himself. Perhaps because the phrase did not carry any specific connotations, Jesus could use the term and define it in his own way. Other scholars are convinced that in pre-Christian Jewish thought the title Son of Man was already being used of an apocalyptic figure who would bring about salvation and judgment at the endtime (a view based on Daniel 7). In using the title, then, Jesus would be referring to this future agent of God, either himself or someone else.

Even if the understanding of Jesus in regard to the Son of Man is not completely discernible, the meaning of the phrase for the Gospel writers is rather clear. For them, "Son of Man" is a reference to a glorious redeemer figure who will usher in God's final salvation. The evangelists were convinced that Jesus was that Son of Man. This apocalyptic notion is qualified in Mark, however, because the Son of Man is not only the one who "comes in the glory of his Father with the holy angels" (8:38) but also the one who must be rejected and killed.

Son of God. Although the title "Son of God" does not occur in Mark as frequently as does "Son of Man," the strategic locations in Mark where "Son of God" appears indicate its importance. Mark perhaps opens with this identification in the first verse of the Gospel. (Serious questions exist about the authenticity of the phrase "Son of God" in 1:1 because it is missing in several major manuscripts of Mark.) At both Jesus' baptism (1:11) and his transfiguration (9:7) a voice from heaven proclaims, "You are my Son, the Beloved." Finally, at Jesus' crucifixion,

Figure 17.7. This painting in the Church of St. Anthony in Veria, Greece, depicts the crucifixion of Jesus. *(Photograph by Mitchell G. Reddish)*

when his obedience to God leads to death, a Roman soldier recognizes the true identity of Jesus as he too proclaims Jesus to be God's Son (15:39).

In the Hebrew Bible the Davidic kings were seen as adopted sons of God. Chosen by God, the king was expected to serve faithfully as God's representative to the people, ruling with justice and righteousness. The Hebrew Bible also applies the phrase "sons of God" to the people of Israel, who are to obey God's call to faithful service. In Mark, the title "Son of God" should likewise be understood not as a declaration of physical descent but in terms of function. (The concept of divine sonship elsewhere in the New Testament, such as in the Gospel of John, seems to suggest the idea of physical descent.) Jesus is the Son of God because he responds obediently to God's call to self-sacrifice and service. For Mark, Jesus is indeed the Son of God who comes with power and authority; his Sonship is most clearly evident, however, in the cross.

Discipleship. At the outset of the Galilean ministry, Jesus issues a challenge—"Follow me"—to certain individuals, inviting them to become his disciples. Although the number and composition of Jesus' followers, which included both men and women, fluctuated throughout his ministry, Mark describes Jesus as appointing twelve men who formed an inner circle of followers (3:13-19). These twelve, the disciples, are noteworthy in Mark's Gospel more for their failures than for their successes. Mark presents the disciples as constantly failing to understand the teachings and mission of Jesus (4:10, 13, 41; 6:51-52; 8:14-21, 32-33; 9:2-13, 28-29, 32; 10:10, 13-16, 24, 35-45). Furthermore, their loyalty and commitment to Jesus waver and even fail: one of the twelve betrays him to his enemies (14:10-11); Peter, James, and John fall asleep during his time of agony in Gethsemane (14:32-42); they all desert him at his arrest (14:50); Peter denies him (14:66-72); and none of them is evident at his crucifixion (15:21-47).

This unflattering portrait of the disciples perhaps served at least two purposes for Mark. First, it was an encouragement to Mark's readers when they, like the first disciples, wavered in their commitment to Christ. Mark's Gospel reminded them that the way of discipleship was filled with difficulties, disappointments, and failures. Second, and more important, the disciples' failure to understand Jesus underscores Mark's emphasis that Jesus cannot be understood apart from his suffering and death. Prior to his death, all evaluations of Jesus are inadequate and partial. Only later would the disciples truly comprehend Jesus and his call to discipleship.

Mark and the Divine-Human Encounter

In the Gospel of Mark the divine-human encounter is centered in the cross and resurrection of Jesus. The cross represents the height of humanity's opposition to and rejection of Jesus and his message. It is the world's emphatic "No!" to God's offer of the good news of the kingdom of God about which Jesus—through whom the kingdom was being actualized—preached and taught. On the other hand, the suffering and death of Jesus is a divine necessity, according to Mark: "The Son of Man *must* undergo great suffering, and be rejected . . . and be killed" (8:31, emphasis added). The path to Jesus' exaltation and glory led through the valley of suffering. Although Mark gives no explanation, he is convinced that Jesus' death was the means of salvation for the world: "For the Son of Man came . . . to give his life a ransom for many" (10:45).

If Jesus' path included suffering, then those who would follow in his footsteps must expect suffering to be their destiny also. The message is plain:

> If any want to become my followers, let them deny themselves and take up their cross and follow me. For those who want to save their life will lose it, and those who lose their life for my sake, and for the sake of the gospel, will save it. For what will it profit them to gain the whole world and forfeit their life? Indeed, what can they give in return for their life? (8:34-37)

Consistent with the willingness to suffer for the sake of the gospel is the call for service and humility on the part of those who would be disciples. Jesus states:

> You know that among the Gentiles those whom they recognize as their rulers lord it over them, and their great ones are tyrants over them. But it is not so among you; but whoever wishes to become great among you must be your servant, and whoever wishes to be first among you must be slave of all. For the Son of Man came not to be served but to serve, and to give his life a ransom for many. (10:42-45)

The cross is the climactic example of Jesus' willingness to give of himself for the sake of others.

As important as the death of Jesus is in the Gospel of Mark, it is not the final word. Mark ends his Gospel with the discovery of the empty tomb, a testimony to the resurrection of Jesus. The cross served as humanity's response to Jesus; the resurrection was God's reply. The resurrection was a vindication of Jesus' life and teaching, turning the seeming defeat of the cross into a victorious triumph. Furthermore, the resurrection pointed to the future, as the risen Christ sent word to his disciples that he would meet them in Galilee (16:7). The fulfillment of this promise is not described in Mark. The Gospel is thus open-ended. For Mark, the divine-human encounter experienced in Jesus of Nazareth would continue in the community's experiences with the risen Christ.

The traditions about Jesus that Mark received were the raw materials for

Mark's story of Jesus. He took those traditions and shaped, edited, and arranged them in the manner that expressed his understanding of this man from Nazareth. The use of the traditions did not end with Mark, however. They continued to function in various ways in the early Christian communities. In the next chapter we shall look at the further development of those traditions.

Chapter 18

THE FURTHER DEVELOPMENT OF THE GOSPELS: MATTHEW, LUKE, AND JOHN

Suggested Biblical Readings: Matthew 1:1–3:23; 20; 27–28; Luke 7; 15:1–16:13; 18–19; 24; John 1–4; 7; 9:1–10:39; 11:1-53; 12:1-19; 13:1–14:19; 20:1-29

The previous chapter traced the development of the story of Jesus from oral traditions to written documents, a process that culminated in the production of the Gospel of Mark. The study of the development of the Jesus traditions continues in this chapter, focusing on the Gospels of Matthew, Luke, and John.

THE GOSPEL OF MATTHEW

The Gospel of Matthew, the first book in the New Testament, quickly became the most popular Gospel in the early church. It is also the most Jewish, showing Jesus to be the fulfillment of the Law and the hopes of Judaism.

Historical Context

The traditional view of the authorship of the Gospel of Matthew is that it was written by Matthew (called Levi in Mark 2:13-14 and Luke 5:27-29), the tax collector who became one of the twelve disciples of Jesus. Several reasons have led most scholars to doubt this view of its authorship. One of the biggest reasons is the difficulty of believing that one of the twelve disciples (who would have had firsthand knowledge of the life and teachings of Jesus) would have based his writing so heavily on the Gospel of Mark, which was written by someone who was not an eyewitness of the events. The identity of the author is best considered to be unknown, although we will follow the traditional practice of referring to the author as Matthew. He is often considered to have been a Greek-speaking Jewish-Christian scribe (13:52), thoroughly familiar with Jewish laws and traditions, similar to the scribes in Judaism. Some scholars have even suggested that he had formal rabbinic training.

Most scholars would date the writing of Matthew to about 85–90 C.E. This would allow time for the circulation and acceptance of the Gospel of Mark, from which Matthew drew heavily. It also coheres with evidence in the Gospel of

Matthew itself that seems to indicate that the Temple had already been destroyed (22:7) and that tensions between Judaism and Christianity had already passed the breaking point, which was the case in the closing decades of the first century. Because the earliest known references to the Gospel of Matthew have come from Antioch of Syria and the situation reflected in the Gospel matches that of Antioch at the end of the first century, the location for the writing of the Gospel is usually considered to have been in or around Antioch.

Literary Structure and Contents

The Gospel of Matthew follows the basic outline of the Gospel of Mark: John the Baptist, Jesus' Galilean ministry, journey to Jerusalem, Jerusalem ministry, death, and resurrection. Matthew has significantly altered the Markan pattern in several ways, however. First, he has added at the beginning of the Gospel the story of the birth of Jesus. Second, he has included much additional teaching material from Jesus that is not found in Mark. Most of these teachings are grouped together in five major blocks (chapters 5–7, 10, 13, 18, 24–25), each of which is preceded by a narrative section. That these sections are distinct and deliberate units of material is seen by the almost identical wording that ends each of the sections, "Now when Jesus had finished saying these things" (7:28; 11:1; 13:53; 19:1; 26:1). Third, he has included stories of Jesus' appearance to his disciples following his resurrection.

A simple outline of the Gospel of Matthew divides the book into three major sections. The second section contains the five blocks of teachings and narratives.

I.   The birth of Jesus (1–2)
II. The ministry of Jesus (3:1–26:2)
   A. A radical righteousness (3–7)
   B. Discipleship (8:1–11:1)
   C. The kingdom of heaven (11:2–13:53)
   D. Regulations for the Christian community (13:54–19:2)
   E. The end of the age (19:3–26:2)
III. The death and resurrection of Jesus (26:3–28:20)

The Gospel of Matthew opens with a genealogy of Jesus. By tracing Jesus' ancestry through David to Abraham, Matthew emphasizes Jesus' Jewish heritage and fulfillment of Jewish hopes and promises. He is Son of David and Son of Abraham. The final statement in the genealogy identifies Jesus as the one "who is called the Messiah" (1:16). One oddity about the genealogy is that Matthew lists, in addition to Mary the mother of Jesus, four women. Women were usually not included in Jewish genealogical tables. Furthermore, Matthew's choice of women (Tamar, Rahab, Ruth, and Bathsheba, who is simply called the wife of Uriah) is odd. In the first place there is something questionable or even scandalous about the sexual experiences of each of these women. Matthew's mentioning of these particular women, then, might be a way of preparing for the questionable circumstances of the pregnancy of Mary. Furthermore, by including these women Matthew might have been pointing out that God can use unusual means and unexpected persons to accomplish God's plans. In addition to being women whose characters were questioned, these women were all considered foreigners by Jewish tradition. Matthew's genealogy, then, which emphasizes Jesus as the fulfillment of Jewish hopes, also includes hints of the universality of the gospel.

Following the genealogy, Matthew tells the story of the birth of Jesus. The story of the virgin birth (actually, virginal conception) of Jesus emphasizes his special status. He is Emmanuel—"God with us"—the Son of God. Worshiped by foreigners (the wise men), he is rejected by Herod, the king of Judea. The story of Herod's attempt to kill the newborn Jesus and the escape of Jesus' family to Egypt and later return to Palestine is likely modeled after the story of Moses in the Hebrew Bible. Matthew presents Jesus in some ways as the "new Moses" who brings deliverance to God's people. Herod's actions in this story prepare the reader for the eventual rejection and death of Jesus in the Gospel.

The second section of Matthew discusses the ministry of Jesus. It begins with John the Baptist preaching in the Judean wilderness. After being baptized by John, Jesus goes into the wilderness, where he is tempted by Satan. Through all the temptations Jesus remains faithful to God. After his baptism and temptation, Jesus begins his activities of calling disciples, teaching, preaching, and healing throughout Galilee. The first major block of teaching material contains one of the most well-known parts of Matthew's Gospel, the Sermon on the Mount. This material, found in chapters 5–7, is a compilation of teachings of Jesus that were delivered on various occasions and not spoken all at one time. The first part of the Sermon on the Mount is a collection of nine sayings called the Beatitudes (from the Latin translation of the opening word, "Blessed," in each saying), which declare God's grace and favor upon those who seek to do the will of God. The major emphasis in the Sermon on the Mount is the radical righteousness that Jesus demands of his followers. In a series of six antitheses (5:21-48) Jesus contrasts the teachings of the scribes and Pharisees with his own teaching, highlighting the radical demands that he places upon those who would seek to live according to the will of God. Jesus declares, "You have heard that it was said to those of ancient times, 'You shall not murder'; and 'whoever murders shall be liable to judgment.' But I say to you that if you are angry with a brother or sister, you will be liable to judgment" (5:21-22). Again he states, "You have heard that it was said, 'You shall not commit adultery.' But I say to you that everyone who looks at a woman with lust has already committed adultery with her in his heart" (5:27-28). In a similar way, Jesus deals in the other antitheses with divorce, honest speech, revenge, and love for enemies. In all of these teachings Jesus exposes the core of the Law's intent. The righteousness that God demands is more than just correct actions. It involves right thoughts and right motivations as well. Matthew is careful to show that even though Jesus calls for righteousness more radical than that expressed in the common understanding of the Torah, Jesus does not abrogate the Torah. Rather, his life and teachings are the true fulfillment of the Torah.

The Sermon on the Mount is followed by a collection of the miracles of Jesus (chapters 8–9), emphasizing that Jesus is not only the Messiah of words but also the Messiah of actions. The second block of teaching material occurs in chapter 10. This section, known as the "missionary discourse," contains Jesus' instructions to his disciples before sending them out on a preaching and healing mission. After describing Jesus' conflicts and rejection, Matthew gives the third major discourse in the Gospel, which is a collection of parables about the kingdom of heaven (Matthew's phrase for the kingdom of God). The fourth discourse, contained in chapter 18, deals with regulations and discipline within the Christian community, whereas the final teaching block, chapters 24–25, contains apocalyptic teachings about the end of the world and the coming of the Son of Man.

Figure 18.1. The Church of the Beatitudes, on a hill overlooking the Sea of Galilee, is located on the traditional site of Jesus' Sermon on the Mount. *(Photograph by Mitchell G. Reddish)*

In the final section of the Gospel, Matthew follows Mark rather closely in the passion narrative, although he emphasizes more than Mark does that Jesus goes to his death in obedience to the will of God. Jesus' obedience is the supreme example of the radical righteousness that he demanded and that he himself lived out. The Gospel ends with two stories of the appearance of Jesus after his resurrection, first to the women at his tomb and then to his disciples on a mountain in Galilee. In the latter scene Jesus sends his disciples out into the world to make disciples, to baptize, and to teach. They can go with confidence, for the risen Christ assures them: "And remember, I am with you always, to the end of the age" (28:20).

Characteristics and Themes

Several characteristics and themes dominate Matthew's Gospel.

Jesus, the Fulfillment of Judaism. From the very opening of the Gospel, with its carefully structured genealogy, Matthew portrays Jesus as the one in whom the promises and hopes of Judaism find their fulfillment. This theme is reinforced in the Sermon on the Mount as Jesus claims, "Do not think that I have come to abolish the law or the prophets; I have come not to abolish but to fulfill" (5:17). Moreover, in several places in the Gospel, Matthew demonstrates how Jesus has fulfilled various prophecies or statements in the Hebrew Bible, stating, "All this took place to fulfill what had been spoken by the Lord through the prophet" (1:22; 2:5, 15, 17, 23; 3:3; 4:14; 8:17; 12:17; 13:35; 21:4).

Radical Righteousness. A major emphasis in Matthew is the demand for righteousness. Jesus calls for a deeper level of commitment, a radical obedience, from those who would live in accordance with the will of God. What he demands of others, he lives out himself, as seen even prior to his public ministry when he is baptized by John "to fulfill all righteousness" (3:15). His teachings, particularly the Sermon on the Mount, describe the demands of this new righteousness.

Son of God. As in Mark, the title "Son of God" is important in the Gospel of Matthew. In fact, Matthew adds the title in several places where it is not found in Mark's Gospel (4:3, 6; 14:33; 16:16; 26:63; 27:40, 43). Furthermore, the virgin birth story serves as another way of claiming divine sonship for Jesus. In Jesus, God is uniquely present, for he is Emmanuel, "God with us" (1:23). The Son reveals the Father (11:27), and through the Son salvation comes to the world (1:21).

The Teachings of Jesus. Although the Gospel of Matthew does not emphasize the title of teacher, by collecting and arranging the teachings of Jesus into five major blocks of material, Matthew has highlighted the teaching role of Jesus. Jesus is the teacher of a new way of righteousness who gives instructions for his disciples and the Christian community.

Matthew and the Divine-Human Encounter

In Matthew's Gospel, the encounter between God and humanity is focused in Jesus Christ, whom Matthew proclaims as God's Son. God's dealings with Israel, evidenced through history and expressed through the Torah, find their fulfillment in Jesus. Matthew's Jesus reinterprets the Torah and even goes beyond the requirements of the Torah, calling people to a radical righteousness that is demanded of all who would participate in the kingdom of heaven (the reign of God). In his preaching, Jesus invited people to become a part of this rule of God, saying, "Repent, for the kingdom of heaven has come near" (4:17). In his teachings, particularly in the Sermon on the Mount and in his parables, he described the nature and character of the kingdom of heaven. In his healings, he demonstrated that God's rule had already broken into history: "If it is by the Spirit of God that I cast out demons, then the kingdom of God has come to you" (12:28).

For Matthew the kingdom of heaven is manifested in the person of Jesus the Messiah, the Son of God. Those who have encountered Jesus have encountered the kingdom of God because God acts and speaks through the Son. For Matthew, Jesus is the unique revelation of God. This belief is most clearly expressed in the words of Jesus in 11:27-30:

> All things have been handed over to me by my Father; and no one knows the Son except the Father, and no one knows the Father except the Son and anyone to whom the Son chooses to reveal him. Come to me, all you that are weary and are carrying heavy burdens, and I will give you rest. Take my yoke upon you, and learn from me; for I am gentle and humble in heart, and you will find rest for your souls. For my yoke is easy, and my burden is light.

Jesus extends to people God's gracious offer of salvation. He acts and speaks on behalf of God. A person's response to Jesus, then, determines his or her relationship with God: "Everyone therefore who acknowledges me before others, I also will acknowledge before my Father in heaven; but whoever denies me before others, I also will deny before my Father in heaven" (10:32-33). For Matthew, the definitive divine-human encounter occurs in one's experience with Jesus the Messiah, the Son of God.

Figure 18.2. The evangelist Matthew is depicted writing his Gospel in this painting on the wall of St. Peter's Basilica in Rome, Italy. (*Photograph by Mitchell G. Reddish*)

THE GOSPEL OF LUKE

The Gospel of Luke is the first part of a two-volume work, Luke-Acts. Taken together, Luke and Acts form the largest writing in the New Testament. The following discussion will concentrate on the Gospel of Luke, and the next chapter will consider the book of Acts. Because the two writings are two parts of one narrative, the discussion of Luke will at times include references to Acts.

Historical Context

Traditions dating from the late second and early third centuries attribute authorship of Luke-Acts to Luke, a physician and occasional traveling companion of Paul (see Col. 4:14; Philem. 24; 2 Tim. 4:11). Some scholars still accept this view of Luke's authorship. Other scholars, however, conclude that Luke-Acts could not have been written by someone who traveled with Paul and knew him well, due to various discrepancies between material in Acts and information in the letters of Paul concerning Paul's life and theology. Furthermore, the author shows no indication of being aware of any of the letters of Paul. Since Luke-Acts itself does not name its author, it is best to consider the writer, whom we shall call Luke, to be anonymous.

Various locations have been suggested as the place of composition of the Gospel of Luke: Caesarea, Antioch of Syria, Rome, Asia Minor, and Achaea (southern Greece). Unfortunately, little evidence exists to support any of these claims. The original readers for whom the work was written were apparently Gentile Christians. Luke, for example, eliminates materials found in his sources that were of primarily Jewish interest (Mark 7:1-23). He also uses Greek instead of Hebrew or Aramaic names or titles ("Lord" or "teacher" instead of "rabbi"; "Skull" instead of "Golgotha"; and occasionally "lawyer" instead of "scribe").

Several considerations point toward an approximate date for the writing of the Gospel of Luke. If Luke used the Gospel of Mark, written ca. 65–70 C.E., then Luke could be no earlier than 70 C.E. As further support for the post-70 dating of the Gospel, Luke seems to have modified Mark's version of Jesus' prediction of the destruction of Jerusalem to make the prediction fit more closely with what actually did happen in 70 C.E. The latest date for the writing of Luke would be around 100 C.E. since Luke seems to have had no awareness of the letters of Paul, which apparently were circulating as a collection by the end of the first century C.E. Most scholars would date the composition of the Gospel of Luke (as well as Acts) sometime between 70 and 100 C.E. The most commonly accepted dating is about 80–85 C.E.

Literary Structure and Contents

Like Matthew, Luke adhered rather closely to Mark's outline of the story of Jesus while at the same time making several changes in Mark's version of the gospel message. He omitted some portions of Mark, reworded some passages, rearranged some sections, and added some material derived from Q and elsewhere. The major additions in Luke are a prologue, the story of the birth of John the Baptist, the story of the birth of Jesus, the episode of Jesus visiting the Temple at twelve years of age, the so-called Lukan travelogue (9:51–19:40), and stories of postresurrection appearances of Jesus. Luke's special material (material found only in Luke) contains some of the most admired and well-known passages in the Gospels: the Lukan version of the birth of Jesus, the story of Zacchaeus, the healing of the ten lepers, the story of the appearance of the resurrected Christ to the two disciples on the road to Emmaus, and several parables, including the two debtors, the good Samaritan, the rich fool, the prodigal son, and the rich man and Lazarus.

The Gospel of Luke can be outlined as follows:

Prologue (1:1-4)
  I. Infancy narratives (1:5–2:52)
  II. The period of preparation (3:1–4:13)
  III. The Galilean ministry (4:14–9:50)
  IV. The journey to Jerusalem (9:51–19:27)
  V. The Jerusalem ministry (19:28–21:38)
  VI. Passion narrative and resurrection appearances (22–24)

Luke begins his Gospel with a prologue, a common Hellenistic literary device, in which he states that his aim in producing this work is "to write an orderly account" (1:3) of the events "that have been fulfilled among us" (1:1). His work is dedicated to "most excellent Theophilus," who is otherwise unknown except for a similar mention in the preface to Acts. Luke composed this narrative for Theophilus (and his other readers) in order that "you may know the truth concerning the things about which you have been instructed" (1:4).

After the prologue, Luke begins his narrative with an account of the births of John the Baptist and Jesus. Only Luke provides information about John's family and his birth. The miraculous births point to both John and Jesus as being agents of God's salvation, although not equal agents. John is a "prophet of the Most High" (1:76) who will "give knowledge of salvation to [God's] people" (1:77), whereas Jesus is the "Savior, who is the Messiah, the Lord" (2:11). As in the other Gospels, John is secondary; his role is to prepare for the coming of Jesus. Luke's version of the birth of Jesus contains some of the most well-known elements of the Christmas story. Unique to Luke's version of the birth of Jesus are the journey of Joseph and Mary from Nazareth to Bethlehem due to a government census, the story of Jesus being born in a manger because there was no room in the inn in Bethlehem, and the announcement of the birth to the shepherds tending their sheep in a nearby field. At the end of the story of Jesus' birth and his family's return to Nazareth, Luke provides the only information in the New Testament about Jesus as a child when he describes Jesus as a boy of twelve visiting the Temple with his parents.

The next section of the Gospel of Luke (3:1–4:13) describes the preparation for the ministry of Jesus. This preparation consists of both the activity of John the Baptist (including the baptism of Jesus) and the temptation of Jesus. Additionally, in this section Luke presents the genealogy of Jesus, a listing that is considerably different from Matthew's account of Jesus' ancestry. Both genealogies have been constructed with theological concerns in mind. Whereas Matthew chose to emphasize Jesus' Jewish heritage (Son of David and Son of Abraham) in order to point to Jesus as the fulfillment of Judaism, Luke emphasized the inclusiveness of Jesus—he is Savior of all humanity. Luke accomplished this by tracing Jesus' lineage back to Adam, who is viewed as the ancestor of all humanity.

The Lukan account of Jesus' Galilean ministry (4:14–9:50) opens with Jesus preaching in the synagogue in his hometown of Nazareth. The text he reads is from Isaiah:

> The Spirit of the Lord is upon me,
>   because he has anointed me to bring good news to the poor.
> He has sent me to proclaim release to the captives
>   and recovery of sight to the blind,
>   to let the oppressed go free,
> to proclaim the year of the Lord's favor. (Luke 4:18-19)

Jesus claims that those words have now been fulfilled. In other words, Jesus is identifying himself as the bearer of God's salvation. In him, the kingdom of God has drawn near. Jesus further declares that God's salvation extends to those outside Israel, pointing to two examples in the Hebrew Bible in which God's grace is given to foreigners. At this declaration of the universality of God's salvation, the people in the synagogue become enraged and drive Jesus out of the city.

Throughout his ministry in Galilee, Jesus preaches, teaches, and heals. Luke gives a variant of Matthew's version of the Sermon on the Mount. In Luke, this collection of Jesus' teachings is more aptly called the Sermon on the Plain (6:17-49). Although similar to Matthew's version, the sayings in Luke are often worded differently, and much of the Matthean material is missing (some of the missing material is scattered elsewhere in Luke). Compared to Matthew's version, Luke's sermon puts greater emphasis on the poor and oppressed.

Although Matthew and Mark also describe Jesus' journey to Jerusalem, Luke has greatly expanded this section of his Gospel, stretching Jesus' journey over nearly eleven chapters (9:51–19:27). On the way to Jerusalem, Jesus is presented as continuing his ministry of preaching, teaching, and healing. This section emphasizes several of the special Lukan concerns (which will be discussed below) by Luke's inclusion of material not found in the other Gospels.

The Jerusalem ministry of Jesus is presented in 19:28–21:38. With a few variations, Luke's account follows the narrative in Mark, describing Jesus' entry into Jerusalem, the cleansing of the Temple, and various teachings of Jesus. Luke does not arrange this material into a daily scheme as clearly as does Mark. In Luke the Jerusalem ministry seems to have lasted more than one week (19:47; 22:53).

The final section of Luke's Gospel contains the passion and resurrection of Jesus (22:1–24:53). Again, Luke follows the Markan narrative closely. Luke emphasizes that the death of Jesus is, on the one hand, the fulfillment of the Hebrew Scriptures (22:37; 24:26-27, 44, 46) and thus part of the divine plan; on the other hand, the death of Jesus is due to the power of evil at work in the world (22:3, 53). Luke emphasizes the innocence of Jesus, who dies as a righteous martyr.

Like Matthew, Luke includes stories of appearances of the resurrected Christ to his followers, although Luke's stories are different from those in Matthew. Luke concludes his Gospel by telling of the ascension of the resurrected Christ into heaven, information contained only in Luke.

Characteristics and Themes

Several concerns and emphases dominate the Gospel of Luke.

Salvation History. Luke appears to understand God's saving activity in human history as occurring in three stages: the period of the Law and the prophets, ending with John the Baptist; the period of Jesus, ending with his ascension; and the period of the church, which will end with the return of Christ. The major concern of the Gospel of Luke is the second period, the period of Jesus, whereas the book of Acts describes the beginning stages of the third period, when the gospel is shared with all the world.

Universal Salvation. A major theme of Luke is the conviction that God's salvation is for all people. This emphasis on the universal nature of God's salvation

Figure 18.3. The Garden of Gethsemane, located on the Mount of Olives, was the place where Jesus was arrested. (*Photograph by Clyde E. Fant*)

is already evident in the Lukan account of the birth of Jesus. Luke sets the birth in the context of world history (2:1-2), implying that this event has universal significance. Furthermore, when Simeon sees the baby Jesus in the Temple, he proclaims that this child is God's salvation, which God had "prepared in the presence of all peoples, a light for revelation to the Gentiles and for glory to your people Israel" (2:31-32). As has already been mentioned, Luke's genealogy of Jesus, by tracing Jesus' lineage to Adam, underscores the inclusiveness of God's offer of salvation through Jesus. In the descriptions of John the Baptist and his preparation for Jesus, only the Gospel of Luke adds a universal dimension by quoting from Isaiah 40:5: "and all flesh shall see the salvation of God" (3:6). Jesus himself pointed to God's concern for all people in his sermon in the synagogue at Nazareth (4:16-30).

This concern for the inclusive nature of God's salvation in Jesus continues in Acts, the second volume of Luke's work. Acts shows the good news of God's salvation being carried to all parts of the world, embracing everyone, regardless of social, ethnic, religious, or national distinctions.

Concern for Outsiders. More than the other Gospel writers, Luke emphasizes God's compassion on the people who are social or religious outcasts. This is seen in the birth story with the announcement of Jesus' birth to the lowly shepherds instead of to more respectable members of society. Furthermore, the circumstances of Jesus' birth—being born in a manger—emphasize his connection with the poor and lowly. In quoting from Isaiah 61:1-2, Jesus identified his ministry as being the proclamation of good news to the poor, the recovery of sight for the blind, and the setting free of those who are oppressed. In Luke, Jesus tells the parable of the good Samaritan, in which a Samaritan, despised by the Jews, is the hero of the story. When Jesus heals the ten lepers, the point is emphasized that the only one who expressed gratitude to Jesus was a Samaritan (17:11-19). Only Luke includes the story of Jesus' compassionate dealing with Zacchaeus, who as a tax collector was a despised member of society (19:1-10).

Concern for Women. Closely related to the previous theme of concern for the outcasts is Luke's special emphasis on women, who in first-century Palestine were also marginal members of society. Luke's version of the birth of Jesus focuses on Mary, whereas Matthew's focuses more on Joseph. Only Luke contains the story of the two sisters, Mary and Martha, and Jesus' visit to their house (10:38-42). Luke emphasizes the presence and role of women throughout the ministry of Jesus (7:11-17, 36-50; 8:2, 42-48; 21:1-4; 23:27-31; 23:55–24:11). Only Luke records the parables of the persistent widow (18:1-8) and the woman with the lost coin (15:8-10). Jesus publicly associated with women (a practice discouraged in his time) and treated them with fairness and equality.

The Holy Spirit. The Holy Spirit, or Spirit of God, plays a major role in the Gospel of Luke. Luke emphasizes the Spirit of God at work in the events surrounding the births of John the Baptist and Jesus, at the baptism of Jesus, at his temptation, and several times during his Galilean ministry. The importance of the Holy Spirit is emphasized even more in the book of Acts, which mentions the Spirit more than fifty times. Especially significant in Acts is the coming of the Spirit of God upon the disciples on the day of Pentecost (Acts 2:1-4), which is a fulfillment of the words of Jesus at the end of the Gospel of Luke: "And see, I am sending upon you what my Father promised" (24:49).

Luke and the Divine-Human Encounter

According to Luke's understanding, the ultimate purpose of God is to bring salvation to all people, beginning with Israel. God's dealings with humanity, focused previously in the Law and the prophets, entered a new stage with the ministry of Jesus. A new era of God's saving act began with Jesus, who in his acceptance, forgiveness, and healing of people embodied God's salvation. Luke alone among the Synoptic writers calls Jesus "Savior" (2:11) and describes his mission as being "to seek out and to save the lost" (19:10). In his words and his actions Jesus brought forgiveness, healing, and salvation to a broken world. The work of proclaiming the good news to all people that was begun by Jesus is to be carried out by his disciples. They are to go "to all nations, beginning from Jerusalem," preaching repentance and forgiveness of sins in the name of Jesus (24:47).

Luke emphasizes that when the divine-human encounter occurs—that is, when salvation comes to the world—the proper response on the part of humanity is joy. The "Magnificat," the song of Mary celebrating the impending birth of Jesus, is a song of joy (1:46-55). The angel who announced the birth of Jesus to the shepherds stated, "I am bringing you good news of great joy for all the people" (2:10). On several occasions in Luke's Gospel joy and rejoicing are associated with salvation or the presence of God (8:13; 10:17; 13:17; 15:7; 19:37; 24:41). The final statement in the Gospel describes the disciples returning to Jerusalem "with great joy" after seeing the resurrected Christ (24:52).

The divine-human encounter in Luke, then, involves repentance and forgiveness, brings joy and salvation, and is inclusive of everyone. Through Jesus Christ, God reaches out graciously to all people—Jew and Gentile, man and woman, the poor, the sick, the oppressed, the outcast. Although some people choose to reject God's offer of salvation, God's purpose is that salvation be extended to all people.

THE GOSPEL OF JOHN

The Gospel of John is in many ways unlike the Synoptic Gospels, due to the evangelists' different theological viewpoints, their different historical and sociological contexts, and the different needs of the communities to which the Gospels were addressed. Above all, John's unique approach to the story of Jesus is due to John's independence and his use of sources different from those used by the other Gospel writers.

Historical Context

Like the other Gospels, the Gospel of John does not provide the name of the author of the work. The closest approximation to a statement on authorship is found in 21:24, in which the "disciple whom Jesus loved" (v. 20) is described as the one "who is testifying to these things and has written them, and we know that his testimony is true." Even this statement, however, does not identify the author. The Beloved Disciple, as described here, could not be the author of the Gospel in its final form (notice the plural pronoun "we," which indicates that more than one person is authenticating the message). At best, the Beloved Disciple was responsible for an earlier form of the Gospel or was the primary source for its material. Furthermore, the Beloved Disciple is never identified in the Gospel. Although the assumption is often made (following second-century church tradition) that the Beloved Disciple is John, the son of Zebedee and brother of James—and one of Jesus' twelve disciples—the Fourth Gospel itself does not identify this individual. Furthermore, the identification of the author as John raises several problems. Among them is the failure of the Fourth Gospel to include two of the major scenes described in the Synoptics in which the disciple John was present: the transfiguration and Jesus' agony in the Garden of Gethsemane. No convincing reason has been suggested to explain why John would have failed to mention these events. All attempts to identify the Beloved Disciple are purely conjectural. He remains an unknown figure.

A strong connection seems to exist between the Gospel of John and the three letters of John in the New Testament (1, 2, and 3 John), and a somewhat looser connection exists between all these writings and the book of Revelation. These connections are based on similarities in vocabulary, writing styles, themes, and theological outlooks. Traditionally, the disciple John has been considered the author of all five of these works. The differences among the works, however, argue against common authorship. An attractive option is to understand the Gospel of John and the letters of John (and possibly the book of Revelation) as originating from a group of individuals, all of whom were instructed and informed by one "teacher," perhaps the Beloved Disciple. The individuals in this group, sometimes referred to as the Johannine "school" or Johannine community (adopting the traditional name of John for the author), took the understanding of Jesus and the Christian faith that they received from "John" and applied this understanding to their own situations by writing the works associated with the name of John. For the sake of convenience we shall follow the traditional practice of referring to the author of the Fourth Gospel as John.

The writing of the Fourth Gospel is usually dated to the last decade of the first century C.E. The oldest surviving evidence of the Gospel is a small papyrus fragment (2.5 by 3.5 inches) containing portions of a few verses of the Gospel. This fragment, known as Papyrus 52, dates to the early to midsecond century. The beginning of the second century, then, would be the latest possible date for the Gospel. Furthermore, several passages in the Gospel (9:22; 12:42; 16:2) seem to indicate that the split between Judaism and Christianity had already occurred by the time of the writing of the Gospel. This irreparable rupture between church and synagogue apparently occurred during the last quarter of the first century. A date of around 90–100, then, for the final version of the Gospel of John seems the best choice. Traditionally, Ephesus has been claimed as the place of composition for this Gospel. More recently, some scholars have proposed Alexandria in Egypt or Antioch in Syria as the location of its writing. Available information does not permit a definite conclusion for locating the place of writing of the Gospel of John.

Literary Structure and Contents

One of the major differences between John and the Synoptics is that John did not arrange his material in the same way as the Synoptic writers. In the Synoptics, Jesus' ministry, which seems to have covered approximately a one-year period, is centered in Galilee. Only at the end of his ministry does he go to Jerusalem. In John, on the other hand, Jesus' ministry extends over approximately a three-year period, and Jesus travels back and forth between Galilee and Judea. The Gospel of John can be divided into four major sections:

I. Introduction (1)
II. Jesus' revelation to the world (2–12)
III. Jesus' revelation to his disciples (13–20)
IV. Epilogue (21)

One of the most memorable portions of the Gospel of John is the prologue (1:1-18), which presents Jesus as the "Word" of God. The Greek term *logos,* translated in the prologue as "word," has a rich heritage both in Jewish thought and in Hellenistic philosophy. In Jewish thought, the word was the creative power of God at work in the world. According to the account of

Figure 18.4. The Pool of Bethzatha (called Bethesda in some manuscripts) consisted of two pools divided by a portico and surrounded on each side by porticoes. John 5:2-9 relates that at this pool Jesus healed a man who had been sick for thirty-eight years. (*Photograph by Mitchell G. Reddish*)

creation in Genesis 1, creation occurred by the word of God, for God spoke, and the world came into being. Furthermore, the word of God informed and empowered the prophets of Israel ("The word of the LORD came to me saying"). Later Jewish traditions identified the word of God with the wisdom of God. In Hellenistic philosophy, particularly in Stoicism, the *logos* was the all-pervading principle by which the natural world was created and sustained. John used this concept of the *logos* as the creative, sustaining power of God to express his understanding of Jesus. This *logos*, John says, known to both Jews and Greeks, has entered history in a real person who revealed God to the world and provided for humanity the way to eternal life. As John 1:14 states, "The Word became flesh and lived among us." The remainder of John's Gospel is concerned with explaining the significance of that momentous event.

In chapters 2–12 John tells of the public ministry of Jesus, in which Jesus reveals his identity and his mission to the world. The major features of this section of the Gospel are the signs (or miracles) that Jesus performs and his conflicts with the Jewish leaders. This section, sometimes called the "Book of Signs," appears to be structured around seven major signs, which in John are intended to reveal the person and work of Jesus and to lead to faith in him.

These revelatory signs are interspersed with long discourses and dialogues, such as Jesus' dialogue with Nicodemus in 3:1-15. The miracles of Jesus, or their accompanying discourses, become the cause for conflicts between Jesus and the Jewish leaders, who refuse to acknowledge his authority and status. The final sign that Jesus performs, the raising of Lazarus from the dead (11:1-44), brings the conflict between Jesus and the Jewish leaders to a crisis that leads to the death of Jesus: "So from that day on they planned to put him to death" (11:53).

Chapters 13–20 focus on Jesus' private teachings to his disciples. The setting for the major portion of this teaching is the last meal that Jesus shared with his disciples. Two major differences between John's version of the Last Supper and the accounts contained in the Synoptics stand out. First, whereas in the Synoptics the meal is a Passover meal, in the Gospel of John Passover does not begin until the following evening. John may have shifted the chronology of the event to make a theological point. According to the Johannine arrangement, Jesus is crucified the afternoon before Passover begins, the same time that the lambs that were to be eaten for Passover were being slaughtered in the Temple. John would then be identifying Jesus as God's new Passover lamb. Second, John's description of the Last Supper does not mention the bread and wine and Jesus' interpretation of their significance. Instead, the major focus in John's Last Supper account is Jesus' washing of the disciples' feet, an action signifying Jesus' self-giving love (which points to his impending death) and illustrating the unselfish love and service that the disciples should render to one another.

John then records several farewell discourses in which Jesus prepares his disciples for his departure from them, offering them consolation and encouragement. After these private teachings, Jesus is arrested, crucified, and resurrected. Rather than a defeat, in John the crucifixion of Jesus is the culmination of his revelatory work. Through his death he is glorified (12:23) and is able to draw all people to himself (12:32). This section of the Gospel concludes with stories of the appearances of the risen Christ who fulfills his promise of sending the Holy Spirit to comfort and guide his followers (20:19-23).

The final chapter in the Gospel of John is an epilogue that was perhaps added later to the Gospel. This chapter describes an additional appearance of the risen Christ to his disciples, this time while they are fishing on the Sea of Galilee.

Characteristics and Themes

Several ideas appear prominently in the Gospel of John, indicating the major beliefs that the Gospel writer wished to convey to his readers.

Figure 18.5. This painting in the Church of St. Anthony in Veria, Greece, shows Jesus raising Lazarus from the dead, a story found in the Gospel of John. *(Photograph by Mitchell G. Reddish)*

The Identity of Jesus. In the Synoptic Gospels the identity of Jesus as Son of God and Messiah is certainly implicit, yet the disciples only gradually come to this understanding of Jesus and his mission. In the Gospel of John, on the other hand, Jesus is readily identified from the outset. In chapter 1, John the Baptist proclaims Jesus to be the Lamb of God (1:29, 36) and the Son of God (1:34). Immediately upon meeting Jesus, the disciple Andrew exclaims, "We have found the Messiah" (1:41). Nathanael, another disciple, is able after his first encounter with Jesus to say, "Rabbi, you are the Son of God! You are the King of Israel!" (1:49).

Even Jesus is very explicit about his identity. In speaking with a Samaritan woman, he tells her plainly that he is the Messiah (4:25-26). His favorite way of referring to himself in John is as "the Son," sometimes with the additional phrases "of God" (3:18; 5:25; 11:4) or "of Man" (1:51; 3:13-14; 5:27; 6:27, 53, 62; 8:28; 9:35; 12:23; 13:31). Jesus talks very candidly and at length about his relationship to God being a son-to-father relationship (5:19-47; 8:12-59; 10:22-39; 12:44-50; 14:1-13, 18-24; 17:1-26). Furthermore, Jesus' relationship with the Father is so close that Jesus can say, "The Father and I are one" (10:30), "Whoever has seen me has seen the Father" (14:9), and "I am in the Father and the Father is in me" (14:10, 11). From the opening words of the prologue ("In the beginning was the Word, and the Word was with God, and the Word was God") to Thomas's confession in 20:28 ("My Lord and my God!"), John leaves no doubt about the unique status of Jesus.

Realized Eschatology. The phrase "realized eschatology" has been used to describe the idea, prevalent in John, that the promised activity of God in the last days (the *eschaton*) is already fulfilled (or realized) in the present. In the Fourth Gospel, eternal life is not for the future only but has already begun for believers (3:36; 5:24). God's judgment of people, usually spoken of as one of the events of the "last days," is also a present reality in John (3:18-19; 9:39). Even the resurrection is in some sense a present reality for John (5:24). In contrast to the Synoptics, in which the idea of the Parousia of Christ is prominent, in John the Parousia is almost nonexistent (probably the Parousia, Christ's eschatological return, is the meaning of 14:3). In John the anticipated "coming" is the coming of the Holy Spirit or the Comforter to be with the disciples after Jesus' departure. The promise of this coming is fulfilled after Jesus' resurrection (20:19-23). John does not deny the future aspect of God's saving activity. The Gospel does include a future hope (6:39-40, 54; 12:25, 48; 14:3, 18, 28). John wants to emphasize, however, that the promised salvation is already present for those who believe in Jesus.

Symbolic Language. In the Gospel of John there is a rich use of symbolism: living water, bread of life, the true vine, the good shepherd, light/darkness, life/death, above/below. These terms are often used with both a literal and a symbolic meaning. For John, the symbolic meaning of these terms is primary. The light/darkness imagery is a good example of John's use of terms with a double meaning. In the Gospel those who live apart from God are in the dark; those who are children of God are in the light. Jesus, as God's Son, is the true light: "I am the light of the world. Whoever follows me will never walk in darkness but will have the light of life" (8:12). Understanding John's use of this light/darkness imagery helps one appreciate more fully the story of the man who is healed of blindness in chapter 9. The sight that the man receives is more than physical sight. Through Jesus, the light of the world, the man also receives spiritual sight.

Miracles as Signs. In the Gospel of Mark, and to a lesser extent in the other Synoptics, the miracles of Jesus are not seen as proofs of Jesus' identity. The miracles are intended not to induce faith but to serve as evidence of the inbreaking of the kingdom of God. In John, however, the miracles—usually called signs—reveal the identity of Jesus (10:37-38) and lead people to faith (2:23; 11:45). Yet the Gospel of John seems to have an ambivalent attitude toward faith based on signs (4:48; 20:29). Jesus' signs point to the truth and may lead to faith. Such faith, while better than unbelief, is immature faith. The most commendable faith, mature faith, is not dependent upon signs. As the risen Christ, after showing the skeptical Thomas the wounds in his hands and side, says, "Have you believed because you have seen me? Blessed are those who have not seen and yet have come to believe" (20:29).

John and the Divine-Human Encounter

In the Gospel of John, Jesus reveals the nature and power of God through the signs he performs and through his teachings. Jesus' revelation of his heavenly Father is reliable, for he and the Father are one (10:30). He knows the Father and the Father knows him (10:15). What he teaches is what he has received from the Father (8:28; 12:49). The Gospel of John states explicitly that the divine-human encounter occurs through Jesus Christ, who says, "I am the way, and the truth, and the life. No one comes to the Father except through me. If you know me, you will know my Father also. From now on you do know him and have seen him" (14:6-7).

The result of "knowing" God or "believing in" God or Jesus is eternal life (3:16; 6:40), a quality of life that begins in the present and continues beyond death. This new mode of living is so radically different that it can be described as a rebirth for the individual, a birth from above (3:3). The believer moves from darkness into light, from death into life. John is aware, however, that the divine-human encounter also has its dark side. For those who reject God, judgment and not salvation, death and not life, are what they receive (3:18, 36; 5:24).

The purpose of the writing of the Gospel of John, as expressed in the Gospel itself, was to facilitate the divine-human encounter, to help people come to know the God revealed in Jesus Christ and to experience the new life that God offers. This purpose is clearly expressed in the closing verses of chapter 20 (perhaps originally the ending of the Gospel): "Now Jesus did many other signs in the presence of his disciples, which are not written in this book. But these are written so that you may come to believe that Jesus is the Messiah, the Son of God, and that through believing you may have life in his name" (20:30-31).

BEYOND THE FOUR GOSPELS

Although the New Testament contains only four Gospels, these were not the only works that attempted to tell the story of the life and teachings of Jesus. Several other works, which were (or could be) called Gospels, circulated in the early years of the Christian church. Among these works were the *Gospel of Thomas*, the *Gospel of the Egyptians*, the *Gospel of Peter*, the *Gospel of the Hebrews*, the *Apocryphon of James*, the *Protevangelium of James*, and the *Infancy Gospel of Thomas*. These and other works are evidence of the power and appeal of the traditions about Jesus of Nazareth. Although none of these works is considered canonical today, some of them were highly popular among certain early Christian groups. Even though most of the materials in them are clearly fanciful, some authentic traditions from Jesus may be embedded in some of these writings. This is especially true of the *Gospel of Thomas*, which some scholars believe may contain otherwise unknown authentic sayings of Jesus. Even if they provide little or no reliable historical data about Jesus of Nazareth, these works are important for the information they provide about the development of the Jesus traditions in early Christianity. Although the study of these works is beyond the scope of this text, they are a valuable resource for a better understanding of the beliefs and teachings of the early Christian communities.

The story of Jesus did not end with his death and resurrection. His work and teachings continued in the followers who believed in him and shared this faith with others. The remaining chapters of this book will examine the beliefs, practices, and struggles of this new religious movement as they are reflected in the pages of the New Testament.

Chapter 19

THE DEVELOPMENT OF THE EARLY CHURCH: THE ACTS OF THE APOSTLES

Suggested Biblical Readings: Acts 1–2; 5:27–6:15; 7:54–9:31; 10; 15

The book of Acts—"the Acts of the Apostles"—continues one of the most remarkable narratives in ancient literature. Luke-Acts is the longest and most highly developed narrative in the New Testament. Most likely it was composed after the Jewish rebellion against Rome (66–73 C.E.), sometime during the last two decades of the first century. Originally Luke-Acts was composed as a two-volume work, each volume being approximately the length of a single papyrus roll. As the canon was assembled, however, Luke was separated from Acts to form part of the four Gospels' account of the life of Jesus.

Nevertheless, the unity of Luke-Acts is unquestionable. Both works are addressed to the same person, Theophilus, and both share a common language, literary style, and purpose. The language of Acts, like that of Luke, is a more polished Greek than that of the other Gospels. Its style has been compared favorably to that of the finest classical authors of ancient Greece. In Acts, Luke also shows the ability to write in various styles appropriate to the narrative. In the earlier sections, for example, his language and style are reminiscent of the Septuagint, upon which he depends so heavily as he seeks to unite the story of the emerging Christian church with the story of the Jewish ancestral faith. Later his writing is similar to a more contemporary Greek style, as he narrates incidents in the Greco-Roman world of his day.

But it is the purpose of Luke-Acts that reveals the true unity of these works. From the first chapter of Luke to the last chapter of Acts, one theme dominates. That theme is the implementation of God's purpose in the world: the inauguration of the inclusive kingdom of God, which embraces both Jews and Gentiles, insiders and outsiders, in God's salvation. There is tension in this narrative, however, because God's purpose encounters opposition in the world. Just as Israel was harassed and oppressed, so Jesus and his followers are misunderstood and persecuted. Ultimately Jesus is rejected as the Christ by the religious leaders of his own people, and his disciples who go forth to carry out his mission encounter similar opposition from the religious establishment. Yet many Jews do believe, and these believers form the nucleus of the early church. Luke portrays the refusal of the messianic kingdom by some Jews as the opportunity for the Gentiles to enter God's salvation, as the church shifted its primary mission activity from Jews to Gentiles. This turn of events underscores God's triumph over the opposition of the world—even rejection, suffering, and death cannot thwart God's purpose of inclusive salvation.

The plot of Luke-Acts is unified through the characters that are central to both narratives. Events centering on Jesus both conclude Luke (the resurrection appearances) and begin Acts (his ascension). Simon Peter, James, and John, who are prominent in the Gospel, are prominent in the first portion of Acts (chapters 1–12). Incidents in Acts also echo incidents in Luke. "Type scenes" in Acts, such as healings and conflicts with authorities, link Acts to Luke. Likewise, themes in Acts mirror emphases in Luke: the kingdom of God, the use of possessions, the work of the Holy Spirit of God, and the necessity for suffering among those who follow Jesus.

But the second portion of Acts (chapters 13–28) makes clear a critical turn. Paul, not Peter, is the dominant figure in the church. It is Paul's story that is followed, not that of any of the original apostles. Acts reflects tensions between the Jerusalem church of the original apostles and the newer Gentile churches of Paul (although as Paul's letters indicate, not nearly as much as was the actual case). The spread of the Christian movement, according to Acts, clearly was due more to the missionary efforts of Paul than to the work of any of the original apostles. Yet even in the second part of Acts, the story of Paul does not overshadow the larger purposes of its author, for when Paul reaches Rome (Acts 28:13-15), the gospel has somehow preceded him and the church is already established there. And Acts does not conclude with the death of Paul (which it never describes), though Luke implies that he knows of Paul's appearance before a Roman tribunal and his eventual martyrdom (Acts 27:24; 20:25, 38; 21:13; 25:11). Luke likely omits an account of Paul's death because his purpose is to present not a biography of Paul but a narrative of the mission of God that the followers of Jesus must fulfill. It is a mission beset with opposition and rejection, even as Jesus encountered opposition and rejection. But just as the resurrection and ascension signal God's vindication of the life of Jesus, so the final Greek word in the narrative of Acts signals the ultimate future of God's purposes: "unhindered."

Before this narrative is examined in some detail, three additional distinctive features of Acts should be noted:

1. Acts is marked by an unusual number of speeches. As much as 20 percent of its total content is given to speeches of various kinds: sermons or missionary addresses to both Jews (2:14-36; 3:12-26; 13:16-41) and Gentiles (10:34-43; 17:22-31); defenses before religious courts or civil rulers (4:8-12, 19-20;

Figure 19.1. According to Acts 27:8, the ship on which Paul was being transported as a prisoner to Rome stopped at this harbor at Fair Havens, Crete, on the way to Rome. *(Photograph by Mitchell G. Reddish)*

7:2-53; 22:3-21; 26:2-29); speeches to the churches (1:16-22; 15:7-21); and a variety of other kinds of address (20:18-35; 25:14-21).

2. Luke uses numerous summary statements, such as in Acts 2:43-47, to unite various episodes in his narrative and to present his understanding of the early church and its workings. Some of these summaries are quite brief, only one sentence or so (4:4; 14:1); others, such as 2:43-47, are more extensive.

3. Just as in the Gospel, Luke sets forth the material in Acts "in order." This phrase, however, does not refer to chronological order, but to an order of movement and direction that leads to an inevitable result. As such, Acts is not merely a history of the early church or a theological essay by Luke but a persuasive narrative designed to reveal God's purpose of inclusive salvation.

"BEGINNING IN JERUSALEM" (ACTS 1–6)

The first two chapters of Acts are foundational to the larger body of the book. In a series of events involving Jesus and his disciples, Luke establishes the theme and overall structure of the book. The gospel of Jesus is to be carried from Jerusalem to Judea and Samaria and finally "to the ends of the earth." These spreading, concentric circles of outreach of the new Christian movement form the structure of Acts. Besides this geographical design, another structure may be seen in the leadership patterns in Acts. In the first half of the book (chapters 1–12), which is set in Palestine, Peter is clearly the dominant figure; in the last half (chapters 13–28), Paul emerges as the leader of the westward movement of the church. Also, the latter part of the book, beginning at 16:10, is written in the first-person plural (this is the so-called "we" portion of the book). This may be Luke's way of indicating that he was present during these episodes, but what is perhaps more likely is that it may be a literary style common to ancient travel narratives.

The Climax of Salvation History: The Resurrection Faith

Acts opens by immediately referring to the Gospel of Luke, "the first book," which was also dedicated to Theophilus ("lover of God"). (Theophilus is otherwise unknown. He may have been a patron of Luke—perhaps an influential Roman or government official or a "God-fearer," a Gentile who, though not a proselyte to Judaism, regularly worshiped and prayed to the God of Israel and also "gave alms liberally" to the Jews.) In the Gospel, Luke says, he told all that Jesus said or did until "he was taken up." According to Acts (1:3), this ascension occurred forty days after his resurrection, during which time he taught them about the kingdom of God. In the Gospel of Luke, however, Jesus' only appearance is on Easter Sunday. (The number forty is used symbolically many places in the Bible: Moses' forty days on the mountain, Israel's forty years in the wilderness, forty days of Jesus' temptations, and so forth. It may refer to an indefinite or to an extensive period of time.) Acts seems to emphasize the preparation Jesus gave his disciples prior to his departure from them. They are told to wait in Jerusalem until the Spirit of God, which was promised in the Gospel, comes upon them. This Spirit will accompany them, even as Jesus had, and strengthen them. They should wait until they are baptized, or immersed, in this Spirit.

The disciples are understandably confused and uncertain about the future. They return to an old question: "Lord, is this the time when you will restore the kingdom to Israel?" (1:6). They show a continued misunderstanding of the nature of the kingdom—as did, no doubt, many people of Luke's own time (including, perhaps, Theophilus). Jesus' reply is intended to settle the matter once and for all. You are not to know such things, he says; you are to become witnesses to me, beginning in Jerusalem, unto the farthest reaches of the earth. After he has ascended, they are not to "stand looking up toward heaven" (1:11); they are told that Jesus would return even as he had departed. (An interesting misuse of this text occurred when the city fathers of Florence, Italy, sought scriptural grounds on which to ban Galileo's use of telescopes in the city square, a practice they regarded as blasphemous and in danger of bringing God's judgment. When the leaders could find no city laws to prevent him, the clergy supplied this text: "Why do you stand looking up toward heaven?")

The disciples then provide a replacement for Judas, who died a tragic death as a betrayer of Jesus. Matthias, who is otherwise unknown, is chosen by the group to be one of the Twelve. He meets the essential requirement: to have followed Jesus from his baptism by John until his ascension. The Twelve are once again constituted, and they, together with "the women"—a particular group that had followed Jesus continually from Galilee—and the mother and brothers of Jesus, form the inner circle of disciples. They, together with others, form a group reckoned at around 120 persons. They continue in prayer, waiting for the promised coming of God's Spirit.

Through this beginning, Luke accomplishes many things with few words: (1) he explains the absence of Jesus and the indefinite time of his return, which was a troubling question by Luke's day; (2) he establishes a connection between the historical Jesus and the ongoing mission of the disciples; and (3) he clarifies the nature of the coming of the kingdom of God, which is not limited to awaiting some particular day but means receiving God's Spirit and extending the message of the gospel of Jesus to all the earth.

The Early Church United: Pentecost and Common Life

The second chapter of Acts moves quickly to the fulfillment of this promise concerning the coming of God's Spirit. At Pentecost (a Jewish religious festival celebrating the harvest), fifty days after the first day of the Passover feast, all of the early followers of Jesus are together in prayer. Then they experience the phenomenon of something like "the rush of a violent wind" and "tongues of fire" that come upon them, and they are "filled with the Holy Spirit" and speak in languages understandable to the diverse group that surrounds them to learn the meaning of these events. Luke undoubtedly regarded this experience as a miraculous event, but it also fulfilled the promise of John the Baptist that the Messiah would baptize with fire. Likely both the purifying and consuming aspects of fire are symbolized in this event. In any case, Luke is principally communicating that in this miraculous event, people from many nations heard and understood the words of the disciples, who were all Galileans and presumably spoke no foreign languages.

This miracle at Pentecost has been interpreted as a reversal of the tower of Babel episode in Genesis (11:1-9), in which false worship led to a confusion of languages. Perhaps, but it surely is intended to indicate that the coming of God's Spirit makes possible the communication of the gospel to all people. In other words, the experience at Pentecost represents a furthering of Luke's purpose of presenting the inclusive nature of the gospel.

As the narrative continues, Simon Peter addresses the crowd to interpret what has happened. Some mock, saying that the disciples are merely drunk. Peter denies that charge (it is only 9:00 A.M., he says, which is too early for anyone to be drunk!), and beginning with the Hebrew Scriptures, he says that these events fulfill the promises of the prophet Joel (Joel 2:28-32).

These are the "last days," he says, when "your sons and your daughters shall prophesy." Likewise, he identifies Jesus as the "Lord" in Psalm 16:8-11 and 110:1 and as God's "Holy One." (This initial reference to the Hebrew Scriptures for proof that Jesus fulfilled prophecy would become a hallmark of New Testament missionary preaching.) God was acting through Jesus, Peter says, making an assertion that established the early Christian belief that Jesus was the fulfillment of Jewish expectations. But Jesus was misunderstood and unjustly killed. Furthermore, his disciples deserve no punishment; they should be believed. Peter concludes his sermon with an appeal to repentance (a characteristic motif in Luke) and belief. Baptism also was enjoined as an expression of commitment to the new Exodus into a new Promised Land, the kingdom of God, where Jesus is both "Lord and Messiah" (2:36). Many responded; about three thousand people believed Peter's words and were baptized.

This important chapter concludes with one of Luke's typical summary statements (2:43-47). The church is united, sharing goods in common according to the needs of the group. As necessary, they even sold possessions to meet needs. This does not appear to have been a complete or permanent communal life or a primitive "communism"; some texts indicate later the private ownership of property (for example, a house was owned by Mary, the mother of John Mark [12:12]). This generosity expressed the unity of the early Christians with those in need. There was also most likely the need to support the original apostles, all strangers in Jerusalem—no small undertaking for the Jerusalem church. Later, it is possible that others may have needed support because of persecution for their faith. But the overall intent of the text is to convey the joyful unity of the diverse followers of Jesus. It also continues Luke's theme of the proper use of possessions.

Furthermore, these early disciples, without exception, still regarded themselves as being a part of Judaism. Others doubtless saw them as an aberrant sect, but they believed that they represented true Judaism. In any case, they continued to worship regularly in the Temple while joining together in their homes in "the breaking of bread," an expression designating a meal of special fellowship (2:46). According to Luke, they were held in high regard by the people, and others joined their ranks daily.

To this point, the "church" was really a group of faithful Jews who believed that Jesus fulfilled Israel's ancient expectations for a messiah. They were not yet referred to as Christians ("belonging to Christ")—that would come later, at Antioch (11:26). No open division with Judaism had yet occurred. But this summary (2:43-47) is only a brief interlude in the tension that marks the Luke-Acts narrative. The very next incident (3:1-26) is followed by the arrest of Peter and John.

The Early Church Challenged: External Conflict, Internal Discord

Chapters 3–4 introduce the first conflict with authorities that was faced by the emerging church. Peter and John had gone up to the Temple at the hour of prayer, the ninth hour (about 3:00 P.M.). At the Beautiful Gate (perhaps on the eastern side of the Temple) they encounter a lame beggar, a man over forty years of age who sat there daily and was a familiar figure to those who entered. The man expects money but instead is healed by the apostles. Peter then addresses the astonished crowd of onlookers, telling them that the healing was not of their own doing but that the man had been healed in the name of Jesus by the power of God. Furthermore, it was God who had raised Jesus from the dead, the same Jesus whom they and their rulers had killed in ignorance. Peter calls them to repentance and faith in Jesus, who is the fulfillment of the Hebrew Scriptures; Moses is quoted (3:22-23) as promising a future prophet who must be obeyed. The sermon concludes with another of Luke's familiar themes, the inclusiveness of God's salvation: "In your descendants all the families of the earth shall be blessed" (3:25). The strong possibility that the Gentiles eventually would be included is suggested by the closing statement that when God raised up Jesus, he was sent to Israel *first* (3:26).

Opposition develops from the Sadducees and Temple authorities, who object to the apostles' preaching of the resurrection and order them arrested. (The Sadducees, who, contrary to the Pharisees, did not believe in the doctrine of the resurrection, would prove to be continuing opponents for Peter [Acts 5:17] and also Paul [Acts 23:6-10]). After the apostles are detained overnight, these authorities are joined in the hearing the next day by no less than the High Priest himself, Caiaphas, his father-in-law, Annas, and others of the family of the High Priest. (For reasons that are unclear, Luke refers to Annas as High Priest, but he actually held the post from 6–15 C.E. Caiaphas, who ruled from 17 to 36 C.E., would have been High Priest at this time.)

Peter again attributes the healing of the lame man to Jesus, and the apostles are forbidden to preach about Jesus. But the apostles refuse to agree to the order, signaling the determination of the early church to continue its mission even under persecution. The authorities are portrayed as being astonished by the boldness and eloquence of Peter and John, seeing that they are "uneducated" (not formally trained as rabbis) and "ordinary" men—nonprofessionals (4:13). Finally, after further threats, the authorities release them.

Another threat to the young church, however, came from its own internal problems, as narrated in Acts 5–6. Unlike the generous sharing of possessions of the early church (4:32-34)—particularly that of Barnabas (4:35-37), who will later become a missionary companion of Paul—one couple, Ananias and Sapphira, claimed to have given the church all the proceeds of the sale of their property, but lied. (The text implies that they did not have to sell their property; even then, they could have used the proceeds as they liked. Their sin, in the words of Peter, was in lying to God [5:3-4].) Both of them were confronted, and both fell dead. The church saw these events as a solemn warning against lying to the Spirit of God.

Even more troubling to the church, however, were complaints from some Hellenistic Jewish Christians who protested that their widows were being neglected, or discriminated against, in the sharing of food. Providing for widows was a Jewish custom that the early Christians continued. There were many widows in Jerusalem who were Hellenistic, or Greek-speaking, because they were not Palestinian but were from various countries of the Diaspora. Since all Jews attempted to make pilgrimages to the Temple, and most wanted to return to Jerusalem to die, there were many "Hellenistic" Jewish women who had been widowed in Jerusalem. A certain tension always prevailed between Hellenistic and Palestinian Jews, and that tension was carried over into the church by these converts to Christianity.

The solution to the problem was the appointment of seven men to "wait on tables" (to look after the practical matters of the church) so that the apostles could continue their work of preaching and teaching. (These seven men are frequently called the first deacons of the church, but no such formal designation is given them in the text.) This solution seems to have succeeded, and many others—including "a great many...priests" (6:7)—joined themselves to the church. Nevertheless, this text reflects the tensions between the Palestinian Christians and Christians from other lands, which later led to many issues of dispute for the young church.

"IN SAMARIA AND JUDEA" (ACTS 7–8)

As threatening as were the arrests of the apostles and the internal disputes of the church, it was another event that resulted in the scattering of the church and the subsequent mission outside of Jerusalem. That event was the death of Stephen, the first Christian martyr.

The Death of Stephen and the Scattering of the Church

Stephen was one of "the Seven" chosen by the apostles. Apparently these men did other things besides performing practical, daily duties for the church, since Stephen (and later Philip) also taught and preached. Stephen's preaching led to confrontation with those of the "synagogue of Freedmen" (former slaves) and other Jews from Asia (6:9). When they were unable to overcome his arguments, they employed false witness to charge him with blasphemy. Subsequently he was brought before the Sanhedrin and tried.

Stephen's defense consisted of a lengthy, powerful speech (7:2-53). There was nothing conciliatory about it. Even more than Peter, Stephen accused Israel of turning from the plan God intended and revealed through Moses and the prophets. Worse yet, he said that Israel rejected Moses even as it rejected Jesus and that the true habitation of God could never be a "house" (see Isa. 66:1-2)—in other words, the Temple. In saying this, Stephen, like Jesus, called Israel away from the cult of the Temple and back to Israel's earlier days under Yahweh, the days of the tribes and the prophets. His impassioned address concluded with these words: "You stiff-necked people, uncircumcised in heart and ears, you are forever opposing the Holy Spirit, just as your ancestors used to do. Which of the prophets did your ancestors not persecute? They killed those who foretold the coming of the Righteous One, and now you have become his betrayers and murderers. You are the ones that received the law as ordained by angels, and yet you have not kept it" (7:51-53).

Not surprisingly, at these words his listeners were enraged and took him outside of the city and stoned him to death (the Jewish punishment for blasphemy). In a significant aside by Luke, we are told that those stoning Stephen laid their outer garments at the feet of a man named Saul—later to be known as Paul, advocate for the Christian faith. At his death, Stephen, like Jesus, cried out, "Lord, do not hold this sin against them" (7:60). Whatever ultimate effect these words had upon the life of Paul, they had no immediate effect. A great persecution broke out against the church, and Paul (or Saul) "ravaged" the church, "dragging off both men and women" and committing them to prison (8:3).

The killing of Stephen marks a significant transition in the story of the early church. Prior to this event, all of the Christian witness is limited to Jerusalem. But after his death—true to Luke's concentric circles of witness as described in Acts 1—the church is scattered throughout Judea and Samaria (8:1). The apostles continue the work in Jerusalem, but the critical movement has been made; the gospel will now be preached "to the ends of the earth" (1:8).

Figure 19.2. During Paul's third missionary journey, according to Acts 17:22, Paul preached in Athens at the Areopagus (Mars' Hill), a hill near the Acropolis. *(Photograph by Mitchell G. Reddish)*

The Mission of Philip

According to Acts, the second member of "the Seven," Philip, is the first Christian missionary. Like others of the Jerusalem church, he fled the persecution but preached the message of Jesus wherever he went. He first moved northward and preached the gospel to the despised Samaritans, also performing acts of healing. These healings signal that God is with him and that the power of God, through the Holy Spirit, is now available to all disciples.

When the apostles in Jerusalem heard that the Samaritans had "accepted the word of God," they sent Peter and John there to see if it was true. After confirmation of that fact, Peter and John preached in numerous Samaritan villages. This is all the more impressive if we remember that it was John who wanted Jesus to call down fire on the Samaritan village that once refused them overnight lodging (Luke 9:51-56). Here Luke again shows the inclusiveness of a gospel that accepts even the despised Samaritans. (The story of the Good Samaritan is also found only in the Gospel of Luke [Luke 10:29-37].)

The second phase of the mission of Philip was equally significant. Instead of excluded Samaritans, this experience involved an excluded Ethiopian eunuch (eunuchs were castrated males who frequently were used as guards of royal harems). Philip traveled from Jerusalem toward the coastal region of Gaza, former longtime home of the Philistines. On that barren road he encountered an Ethiopian eunuch, the minister of finance of the Candace (queen mother) of Ethiopia (more accurately, Nubia, modern Sudan). This official was slowly traveling southward in a chariot, reading aloud from a scroll of Isaiah (reading aloud was the usual manner of reading in ancient times). When Philip asked if he understood what he was reading, the Ethiopian asked him to sit beside him in the chariot and explain the text. Acts says that Philip then "proclaimed to him the good news about Jesus"; he interpreted Isaiah 53:7-8 as referring to Jesus and undoubtedly made plain the inclusive grace of Jesus. (Eunuchs were excluded from Israel's sacred assembly [Deut. 23:1]. It is also interesting to speculate how this "God-fearer" obtained the scroll of Scripture, which was illegal for foreigners to possess. It could only have been purchased at great cost.) Seeing water (perhaps a pool standing in a wadi, or streambed), the Ethiopian asked if he might be baptized, and Philip baptized him. The story concludes as the Ethiopian—the first known black Christian—goes on his way in great joy.

Significantly, in this incident the gospel has been extended geographically not only to nearby Samaria and Judea but, through the eunuch, to remote Nubia, legendary for its invincibility (Isa. 18:1-2). It has also been extended racially to a black man and sociologically to an excluded outsider, permanently barred from the Temple by his physical deformities. Symbolically this incident dramatically portrays the fulfillment of another text in Isaiah 56:3-8, the very text that Jesus quoted in his "cleansing" of the Temple:

> Do not let the foreigner joined to the LORD say,
>> "The LORD will surely separate me from his people";
>> and do not let the eunuch say,
>> "I am just a dry tree."
> For thus says the LORD.
> To the eunuchs who keep my sabbaths,
>> who choose the things that please me
>> and hold fast my covenant,
> I will give, in my house and within my walls,
>> a monument and a name
>> better than sons and daughters;
> I will give them an everlasting name
>> that shall not be cut off.
>
> And the foreigners who join themselves to the LORD,
>> to minister to him, to love the name of the LORD,
>> and to be his servants,
> all who keep the sabbath, and do not profane it,

> and hold fast my covenant—
> these I will bring to my holy mountain,
>   and make them joyful in my house of prayer;
> their burnt offerings and their sacrifices
>   will be accepted on my altar;
> for my house shall be called a house of prayer
>   for all peoples.
> Thus says the Lord GOD,
>   who gathers the outcasts of Israel,
> I will gather others to them
>   besides those already gathered.

The joy of the eunuch reflects the fulfillment of this ancient promise that God would gather "others . . . besides those already gathered." The stage is now set for the preaching of the gospel to the Gentiles, and Luke's narrative turns toward the unlikely leader of this mission, none other than Saul of Tarsus, enemy of the church.

"TO THE ENDS OF THE EARTH" (ACTS 9–28)

Beginning with chapter 9, Acts traces in considerable detail the missionary activities of Paul, formerly known as Saul, whose life and times we will examine more closely in the next chapter. Since Acts is not a biography of Paul but a narrative that shows the fulfillment of the purpose of God (the inauguration of the inclusive kingdom of God), this chapter will follow the development of that story.

The conversion of Saul on the road to Damascus is one of the best-attested events in the New Testament; it is described three times in Acts (chapters 9, 22, and 26) and described or referred to by Paul himself in Galatians (1:11-17), 1 Corinthians (9:1; 15:8), and 2 Corinthians (4:6). Whatever the exact nature of the event, it brought about an amazing reversal in his life. Once known as a persecutor of the followers of "the Way" (as the early Christians were first known, perhaps from the saying of Jesus, "I am the way, and the truth, and the life" [John 14:6]), Paul became the "apostle to the Gentiles." (In his letters Paul later claimed the title "apostle" because he said that he had seen Jesus in his vision on the Damascus road, thereby becoming one of the "eyewitnesses" of Jesus.) He was confirmed in his experience by Ananias, a Jewish follower of "the Way" from Damascus who would have been one of Paul's intended prisoners. But Ananias had had a vision also, in which God had revealed several things about Paul: he was God's "chosen instrument"; he would witness "before Gentiles and kings," as well as before Israel; and he would suffer (Acts 9:10-19). All of these predictions proved to be true in the dramatic life of Paul.

Figure 19.3. A second century C.E. statue of the goddess Artemis. Paul's work in Ephesus touched off a riot led by silversmiths who suffered declining sales of miniatures of the temple of Artemis because of Paul's preaching. *(Photograph by Clyde E. Fant)*

In every respect, this calling of Paul parallels the call of the prophets. No doubt Luke intended it to certify the standing and message of Paul as part of the fulfillment of God's inclusive salvation. Even so, the early Christians were understandably wary of this conversion, which they doubtless saw as a ploy by the wily Saul to infiltrate their ranks and learn the names of Christians. It was only with the endorsement of the generous Barnabas that he was admitted to the circle of disciples at Jerusalem, in spite of his notable preaching at Damascus. But the beginning of the mission to the Gentiles is not to be in Paul's hands. The scene shifts to the seacoast, where the focus is again upon Peter and a vision of a different sort.

Peter and Cornelius: "No Partiality"

In an unusually detailed account for a single incident, Luke reports the experience of Peter with Cornelius, a Roman centurion stationed in Caesarea. (A centurion was an officer over a cohort, a unit of one hundred men. Centurions were chosen for their good judgment and steadfastness in battle.) Cornelius is a "God-fearer," a faithful Gentile worshiper of Yahweh, and he has had a vision telling him to send to Joppa for Simon Peter; no reason is given to him for this action. Meanwhile, Peter also has had a vision. At noon, on the flat rooftop of the tanner's house where he was staying, he saw a large sailcloth descending from the heavens, filled with all kinds of animals that, according to the Jewish dietary regulations, were considered unclean. He then heard a voice from heaven saying, "Get up, Peter; kill and eat," but he recoiled in disgust. A second time the voice ordered him to eat, telling him to call nothing unclean that God had cleansed (10:15). The same thing happened a third time, leaving Peter perplexed at its meaning.

Meanwhile the servants of Cornelius arrived at the house, and the Spirit of God instructed Peter to go with them without hesitation. When Peter asked why they had come, all they could say was that "a holy angel" had spoken to Cornelius and that they had come to fetch Peter at his request. By the time Peter arrived at Caesarea, the meaning of his rooftop vision had become clear to him: God was sending him a message, not about dietary laws, but about refusing to associate with "unclean" persons—Gentiles. Therefore, Peter did not refuse to enter a house filled with Gentiles (10:28-29). Peter then asked why he was summoned, and Cornelius said, "To listen to all that the Lord has commanded you to say" (10:33).

The point of everyone's baffled state in this narrative is to make perfectly clear that God was the instigator of everything that took place, so that no one could find any reason to object to this "inappropriate" visit to a Gentile by Peter. This became most important in Peter's later report to the Jerusalem church, which had demanded an explanation for his actions. This question (the relation of Gentiles to Judaism and Christianity) obviously remained a crucial one in Luke's day also, which explains the excessive repetition of the explanations of the visions of Peter and Cornelius in chapters 10 and 11. We must remember that there was not yet a clear sense of Christianity as a separate religion. From the standpoint of most Jews, Peter was admitting Gentiles to the Jewish faith without the necessary rituals of their religion.

At the request of Cornelius, Peter indeed preached the good news of "peace by Jesus Christ," declaring him to be "Lord of all" and that "God shows no partiality, but in every nation anyone who fears him and does what is right is acceptable to him" (10:34-36). While Peter was still speaking, the Spirit came upon the Gentiles (a sign of the initiative of God), even as it came upon the disciples at Pentecost, and they spoke in "tongues" and praised God, a sign in the early church of the presence of the Spirit (10:45-46). Peter then baptized them and they became the first Gentile converts. But back in Jerusalem, "the circumcision party," the conservative Jewish Christians who believed that a Gentile must undergo the rites of Judaism before becoming a follower of "the Way," demanded an explanation. Peter was able to assure them that, based on the initiative of God in all that was done, he had only been obedient to God. Even his critics then joined in praising God. But the matter was hardly over; the same issue led to numerous clashes within the church, as reported in Acts and particularly in Paul's letters (see Gal. 2). Acts 15 recounts the so-called Jerusalem conference (to which Paul likely refers in Gal. 2) in which the church met in considerable conflict over this very issue. The matter was settled in favor of the inclusion of Gentiles, but the stresses continued in many of the early churches.

In any case, the action of Peter toward Cornelius is presented in Acts as the pivotal event in the admission of Gentiles to the young Christian church. Not even the lengthy missionary work of Paul exceeds it in importance for the future direction of the church.

To Rome: Paul

The work of Peter at Caesarea was not the only early initiative toward Gentiles. Unknown men of Cyprus, also believers, on their own initiative went to Antioch and preached to the "Greeks" (although some sources say "Hellenists"), "[and many] turned to the Lord" (11:21). The Jerusalem church then sent Barnabas to Antioch, and when he ascertained the genuineness of their experience, he went to Tarsus to find Paul. They both returned to work in Antioch for a year, teaching the new believers, "and it was in Antioch that the disciples were first called Christians" (11:26).

The developing story of Paul is interrupted a final time to report the arrest of Peter and his miraculous deliverance from prison (12:1-17). His situation was all the more ominous because Herod had just put to death James, the apostle and brother of John, "with the sword" (12:1-2). But a sign of hope is given in the release

Figure 19.4. A modern mosaic in Veria (ancient Beroea), Greece, depicts Paul preaching to the citizens of the city. *(Photograph by Mitchell G. Reddish)*

of Peter and the subsequent death of Herod (12:20-23), which is followed by the words, "But the word of God continued to advance and gain adherents" (12:24).

These words might well summarize the subsequent missionary journeys of Paul. (Details of his life and journeys will be dealt with in the following chapter.) In three epic missionary voyages across the Mediterranean, Paul carried the gospel ever westward. Although believers had preceded him to Rome, Paul eventually reached Rome also—although not as he planned, but in chains. The subsequent narrative of Acts unfolds in four episodes (with the story of the Jerusalem conference described in 15:1-35):

1. The first missionary journey: Cyprus and eastern Asia Minor (13:1–14:28)
2. The second missionary journey: mainland Greece and western Asia Minor (15:36–18:22)
3. The third missionary journey: Ephesus and Greece (18:23–21:14)
4. Paul's arrest in Jerusalem and his journey to Rome (21:15–28:30)

These accounts are more than a detailed account of early Christian life; they are also fascinating narratives of ancient travels and perils. Throughout, Luke shows the indomitable progress of the purpose of God. Opposition, as expected, never ceases. At the end, Paul is under arrest in Rome, facing an uncertain fate.

But the fate of the gospel is certain: like the final preaching of Paul (28:30-31), it is "unhindered" in its westward march and "bold" in its inclusiveness. God's purpose of inclusive salvation has been proclaimed across the known world, and people of all nations are welcomed into the church of its Lord, Jesus Christ. Luke's lengthy narrative, Luke-Acts, has reached its end.

Figure 19.5. The Roman theater at Caesarea, located next to the Mediterranean Sea. Paul often used the port at Caesarea when leaving and returning on his missionary journeys. *(Photograph by Clyde E. Fant)*

THE *KERYGMA* OF THE EMERGING CHURCH AND THE DIVINE-HUMAN ENCOUNTER

The early church formed itself around the message and person of Jesus. Luke's epic narrative, Luke-Acts, shows that the center of the kerygma (literally, "proclamation") of Jesus was the kingdom of God, but the center of the kerygma of the early church was Jesus himself. This transfer of focus marked a change of emphasis in the biblical divine-human encounter and led directly to Christianity as a faith distinct from Judaism. The sermons of Acts, though really only summaries of the preaching of the emerging church, do reveal distinctive emphases, or themes, that give further insight into the early Christians' understanding of the divine-human encounter.

1. *Jesus as the fulfillment of the Hebrew Scriptures.* In one sermon after another, Peter (2:14-36 and elsewhere), Stephen (7:2-53), and Paul (13:16-43, among others) sought to show that all of the seemingly contradictory facts about the life of Jesus, such as his suffering and death, were really fulfillments of ancient Hebrew prophecy and belief. The psalms were employed to prove that David pointed to the coming messiah and that Jesus was the promised heir of David (Acts 2:25; 13:32). Even "the law of Moses" (Acts 28:23) was used as evidence to persuade Jewish audiences that Jesus was the Messiah. The story of Jesus, for the emerging church, was but the extension and completion of Israel's story.

2. *John the Baptist as the link between the old and the new.* That Jesus' ministry began at his baptism by John the Baptist is one of the unshakable conclusions of research into the life of Jesus. It also formed an integral part of early Christian preaching (10:36-38). This prophet, as the early church saw him, himself fulfilled Scripture and served as the link between David and Jesus (13:22-25).

3. *Jesus as a doer of good deeds and a healer.* The life of Jesus is not greatly developed in these early proclamations, but there is a distinct and repeated

Figure 19.6. The Fortress of Antonia, situated in the upper right in this model of Jerusalem, was built by Herod next to the Temple and housed Roman soldiers. When a riot erupted in the Temple over a mistaken belief that Paul had brought Gentiles into the Temple proper, soldiers from the fortress rushed down to squelch the disturbance. (*Photograph by Clyde E. Fant*)

emphasis on Jesus as one who "went about doing good" (10:38) and one through whom God did mighty works as signs (2:22).

4. *The death of Jesus as the result of human evil, but also as a part of the plan of God.* Jesus suffered and was crucified "by the hands of those outside the law" (2:23; 7:52-53) but also "according to the definite plan and foreknowledge of God" (2:23). In one sentence the dual explanation is given: Jesus was unjustly murdered, but his death was no surprise to God; indeed, God's plan for the inclusive salvation of all was accomplished even through such humiliation. Even the rejection of Jesus by some Jews opened the door for inclusion of the Gentiles (13:46).

5. *The resurrection and exaltation of Jesus as God's vindication of his life.* This crucified Jesus was exalted to "the right hand of God" (2:33)—the seat of honor—after he was raised from the dead by the power of God, a resurrection that his disciples had witnessed (2:32-33). He is now "Lord" (7:60) and "Savior" (13:23), the one whom Christians also refer to as the "Son of Man" (7:56), the fulfillment of apocalyptic expectations.

6. *Forgiveness of sins as being possible for "everyone who believes" (13:39).* Repentance from the wickedness done to Jesus allows sins to be "wiped out" (3:19); belief in the name of Jesus results in salvation (16:31). In the Gospels, it is first and foremost belief in the gospel of Jesus that is enjoined; but in the early preaching of the church, it is belief in Jesus himself that is urged. Exactly when such a change of emphasis occurred is uncertain, but in the emerging church—in Rudolf Bultmann's words—"the proclaimer became the proclaimed" (*Theology of the New Testament Vol. 1* [New York: Charles Scribner's Sons, 1951], p. 33).

As we examine next the life and teachings of Paul, we will see these basic themes repeated, developed, and expanded into a subtle and systematic understanding of the place of Jesus in Christian thought.

Chapter 20

PAUL AND HIS CULTURAL
ENVIRONMENT

Suggested Biblical Readings: Acts 16:1–18:17; 19:1-10; 22–28

Although Christianity began as a messianic movement within Judaism, by the end of the first century C.E. Gentile believers outnumbered Jews in Christianity. To a great extent this change in the composition and location of the church was due to the missionary work of the apostle Paul. His role in the rapid spread of Christianity to the Gentiles often brought him into conflict with Diaspora and Palestinian Jews, Roman officials, and groups within the Christian movement. Paul therefore emerges as a controversial figure in the Christian movement who nevertheless made an important contribution to the early growth of Christianity. To understand the work of Paul one must first understand the Greco-Roman world into which he carried the Christian gospel.

THE GRECO-ROMAN WORLD

The Greek cultural features of the Greco-Roman world of Paul's time largely stemmed from the influence of Alexander the Great, who before his death in 323 B.C.E. had succeeded in building an empire that stretched from Greece to India in the east and to Egypt in the south. Notwithstanding his remarkable military conquests, Alexander is best known for his promotion of Hellenistic (Greek) culture. The program of Hellenization that Alexander and his successors supported included emphases upon Greek philosophy, religion, customs, architecture, athletics, and, especially, language. (See chapter 14 for a fuller description of the beginnings of the Hellenistic era.)

When Rome conquered the remnants of Alexander's empire, it enhanced the cultural unity of the Hellenistic world with political and economic stability and ushered in the "Greco-Roman" period. The period of Roman peace and order, often referred to as the *pax Romana*, extended from 27 B.C.E. (the date of the crowning of Caesar Augustus) to 161 C.E. (the date of the death of Caesar Antoninus Pius and the beginning of the Parthian wars). Paul lived during the early part of this period.

The *pax Romana* brought immense benefits to the inhabitants of the Mediterranean world and provided an opportunity for the expansion of Christianity. During this period most of the empire enjoyed unbroken peace,

Figure 20.1. Paul, the important missionary of the Christian church, is depicted in this painting by the Dutch artist Rembrandt. (The Apostle Paul; *Rembrandt von Rijn; Widener Collection; Photograph © 2001 Board of Trustees, National Gallery of Art, Washington*)

although local conflicts occasionally erupted. Peaceful conditions promoted communication, travel, trade, a common law, and a common currency, all of which were enhanced by common languages (Latin in the West and Greek in the East). A unified and peaceful empire allowed Paul to travel safely and to communicate with ease through the common Greek language of the western part of the empire.

Religion in the Greco-Roman World

In the Greco-Roman world numerous religious movements and philosophical systems had found popular acceptance. Paul delivered his gospel in competition with a variety of alternative ideologies. Many of the alternative systems were syncretistic, blending elements from several religious or philosophical systems. Although this syncretism often blurred the distinctions between competing movements, a discussion of the features of several of the more important religions and philosophies will help provide an understanding of Paul.

The Roman Traditional Religion. The traditional religion of the Roman Empire resulted from the modifications the Romans made to the classical Greek Olympic religion. Greek and Roman deities had become largely interchangeable, and the Romans had adopted many aspects of the Greek religious rituals. The Roman traditional religion was intended to establish and maintain a proper relationship between humans and the gods. Performed under the authority of the state, these public rites were believed to guarantee the continuing welfare of the empire. Roman citizens were expected to revere and serve the traditional gods. They were permitted, however, to participate in other religions since Rome recognized the right of subject peoples to their own worship. Roman authorities monitored the extent of the worship of "foreign" deities so that such worship did not compete with the devotion to the traditional Roman gods. If worship of a foreign deity provoked scandal or threatened the prestige of the Roman gods, it would be suppressed. Customarily, then, other religions were tolerated as long as their adherents did not offend the traditional deities or commit social or political crimes.

Emperor Worship. The emperors came to play a significant role in the traditional religion since their participation set an example of the piety and virtue expected of all citizens. They also became objects of worship. Although Caesar Augustus refused to claim divine status for himself, his subjects elevated him to the status of divinity following his death. The degree to which the emperors after Augustus claimed divinity differed greatly, but by the end of the first century C.E., recognition of the divine status of the emperor had become an essential part of Roman religion. At times emperor worship became a test of loyalty to the empire. This requirement would bring Christians into conflict with the empire.

Neither the traditional Roman religion nor the emperor cult claimed the personal commitment of most of the people of the empire. These systems of formal rites had potent political significance, but many people sought a more personal expression of religion. The people additionally gave spiritual allegiance to one of the mystery religions or to one of the popular philosophies.

Mystery Religions. Most of the mystery cults were refinements of ancient nature rites that celebrated the growth and rebirth cycles of the changing seasons. Although each cult (for example, the Eleusinians, the Dionysiac mysteries, and the cult of Isis and Osiris) had a different myth from which it drew its basic elements, many of the mysteries worshiped a mother goddess and a male deity who was her consort or son. Initiates into these systems were promised victory over the chaos and negation of life by identification with the god or goddess.

These religions are called "mysteries" because of the secrecy imposed upon the adherents to their practices and beliefs. Especially secretive were the initiation rites through which an individual moved from being a "stranger" to becoming a participant in a knowledge that granted personal immortality. This hope for immortality is what made the mystery religions so attractive to many

Figure 20.2. This mosaic discovered at Sepphoris in Galilee depicts scenes from the life of Dionysus and the activities of members of the Dionysian cult. The Dionysian cult was one of the mystery religions of the ancient world. *(Photograph by Clyde E. Fant)*

people in the Roman Empire, including most of the emperors. Romans found in the mysteries the personal and emotional fulfillment that the public ritual of the imperial cult often did not provide.

Gnosticism. Gnosticism was another widespread religious movement that Paul encountered in the Greco-Roman world. Gnostics were those who possessed knowledge that granted personal immortality after death. The term "gnosticism" derives from *gnosis*, the Greek word for "knowledge." Gnosticism can refer to either a widely diffused movement in the Greco-Roman world that existed independently of Christianity or to a number of Gnostic variations of Christianity. The origins of Gnosticism remain obscure, but the scholarly understanding of Gnosticism has greatly advanced since the discovery of a library of fifty-two Gnostic books at Nag Hammadi in Upper Egypt in 1945. Among those works were the *Gospel of Truth* and the *Secret Teaching of John*, both of which contain themes that were common to many of the Gnostic sects. Most Gnostic sects affirmed four general principles.

First, Gnostics viewed the world as an imperfect and evil place, which led them to believe that it had been created by an inferior deity. Some Christian-oriented Gnostic sects identified this creator god with Yahweh of the Hebrew tradition in contrast to the God of the New Testament.

Second, Gnostics believed that humans consist of two related but ultimately independent realities: a physical body and a divine component called the soul, spirit, or spark. The spirit was trapped in the physical body and desired to be set free to return to its heavenly home.

Third, liberation of the spirit could be achieved through the acquisition of secret knowledge (*gnosis*), which was imparted in secret initiation rites. Liberating knowledge came through direct revelation from the spirit world (through a particular myth and its interpretation), or it might be brought by a redeemer figure. The redeemer was a purely spiritual being, uncorrupted by fleshly, human features. In Christian-oriented Gnosticism, Jesus was depicted as the cosmic redeemer who provided the secret *gnosis*. Thus, Gnostics understood Jesus as a being who only seemed to have physical qualities; he was in reality a divine spirit clothed in what appeared to be a human body.

Fourth, Gnostics believed they would eventually escape to the world of pure spirit, but while they lived in the physical world they must not be bound by it. This view led Gnostics to one of two attitudes toward the physical world and the body. On the one hand, some Gnostics promoted a radical asceticism in which they renounced the body and its passions and lived lives of physical deprivation. On the other hand, some Gnostics, believing that the material world could not harm them since their spirits were separate from it and invulnerable to damage or destruction to the body, lived radically sensual lives. Paul confronted both of these attitudes among early Gentile converts. In the second and third centuries Gnostic sects competed seriously with Christianity for people's allegiance.

Diaspora Judaism. The discussion of Diaspora Judaism in chapter 14 enumerated several of its important features. Two considerations must be noted with regard to Paul. First, Paul himself was a Diaspora Jew. This fact gave Paul a definite advantage in his missionary work with Gentiles. Second, Judaism had become a widespread and significant presence in most communities of the Mediterranean world. Jewish synagogues existed throughout the Diaspora. According to the book of Acts, these synagogues provided Paul with locations in which to present his views about Jesus. When he initiated work in a new community, he customarily began in the local synagogue.

Religious Philosophies

The Greco-Roman world also provided the setting for several philosophical systems that, while not possessing traditional religious beliefs and ceremonies, provided intellectual worldviews and emotional comfort for many individuals.

Epicureanism. Epicureanism, begun in the fifth century B.C.E. by Epicurus of Samos, declared that the root of all evil was fear—above all, fear of death and the afterlife. The gods, Epicurus believed, had little if any concern for the lives of humans. Epicurus also rejected the idea of immortality. The focus of life should be upon one's present existence, which was ruled by chance. The goal of human life was to avoid pain and to find happiness. Although often misunderstood today as a philosophy that promoted an easy sensuality, the Epicureans' aim was to achieve a freedom from disturbances that would bring a person inner harmony and peace.

Stoicism. Stoicism had much more influence in the Greco-Roman world than the way of Epicurus. Founded by Zeno of Cyprus in the fourth century B.C.E., Stoicism taught that a person could attain inner peace and virtue by living according to reason, for human reason was a part of the divine reason, the creative force that underlay all life. Believing that the universe was harmoniously balanced and rationally ordered, Stoics thought that any person, rich or poor, slave or free, could feel at home in the world because all persons participated in the same universal reason. Stoicism offered no hope of personal immortality. The Stoic goal of life was to achieve inner peace and happiness by maintaining an emotional detachment from physical pain and suffering.

Figure 20.3. Epicurus, from the island of Samos, was the founder of the school of philosopy known as Epicureanism. *(Photograph by Mitchell G. Reddish)*

Platonism. While both Epicureanism and Stoicism denied the possibility of a personal life after death, popular philosophies in the tradition of the Greek thinker Plato promised a positive afterlife. Plato (429–347 B.C.E.) believed that the foundation of the good life was a knowledge of the invisible world of perfect forms or ideas, of which things in the material world were imperfect copies. In Platonic thought, happiness was achieved when a person lived in conformity with the perfect ideas of justice, beauty, truth, and goodness. Through the apprehension of these perfect forms, humans could see how imperfect and transitory was life on earth and how perfect was the world of ideas that the human soul would ultimately enjoy. The goal of human life, then, was to become enlightened by this truth, to purify one's life of excessive material concerns, and to prepare for the soul's liberation. Optimistic in its appraisal of human nature and individual destiny, Platonism provided a basis of hope for many people in the Greco-Roman world.

Paul and the Greco-Roman World

Surveying the religious and philosophical currents in the Greco-Roman world provides valuable insights into Paul. First, understanding these various traditions helps to clarify some of the issues Paul addresses in his letters. Second, Paul himself was a product of Greco-Roman culture. His writings bear the signs of a person reared in a Hellenistic environment and familiar with the religious and philosophical ideas of his time. Tarsus, Paul's home, was the site of a famous school of Stoic philosophy. The extent to which these ideas influenced Paul is still debated. Some have argued that Hellenistic thought was the primary influence on Paul. Others have minimized that influence, pointing instead to the influence of his Pharisaical Jewish heritage. To understand the life and writings of Paul, it is best to see Paul as indebted both to his Hellenistic background and also to his heritage as a Jew of the Pharisaic tradition.

SOURCES FOR THE LIFE AND TEACHING OF PAUL

Several noncanonical documents, such as the *Epistles of Paul and Seneca* and the *Letter to the Laodiceans*, claim to be authored by Paul. None of the noncanonical material, however, was actually written by Paul and therefore provides no basis for our understanding of him. Only the authentic letters of Paul provide primary source material; the book of Acts serves as a secondary source.

Fourteen New Testament writings have been traditionally attributed to Paul. One of these, the book of Hebrews, is generally agreed to be non-Pauline. The authorship of six letters, 1 and 2 Timothy, Titus, Ephesians, Colossians, and 2 Thessalonians, remains debated. Because the authorship of the works is uncertain, they cannot be reliable sources for information about Paul. (Chapter 21 contains a summation of the status of this discussion.) The remaining seven letters are undisputedly by Paul. They include 1 Thessalonians, Galatians, 1 and 2 Corinthians, Philippians, Philemon, and Romans. These seven letters, then, are the primary sources for an understanding of Paul's life and thought. Still, because these writings are occasional letters addressing specific concerns of local Christian communities and individuals, details about Paul are limited. A basic outline of Paul's life can be sketched, but a complete biography cannot be constructed.

Acts serves as a secondary source for knowledge about Paul. Significant sections of Acts, especially chapters 13–28, concern the travels of Paul as a missionary to Diaspora Jews and Gentiles. Luke's presentation takes the form of a travel narrative with Paul as the chief hero. Like the letters of Paul, Acts does not provide a full biography. Luke's purpose in Acts was to include Paul's story in the larger story of the extension of the gospel to the Gentiles, not to tell all he knew about Paul.

Traditionally, Luke's version of Paul's life in Acts was the norm for understanding Paul. An effort was made to incorporate autobiographical material from the letters into it. This approach recognized considerable interrelation of the two sources; at many points they complement each other or are in direct agreement. Several problems, however, attend this use of the sources. One problem occurs in that it is difficult or impossible to reconcile the differences between Acts and the letters. For example, according to Acts, Paul visits Jerusalem at least five times (9:26-29; 11:29-30; 15:1-2; 18:22; 21:15-17). According to Paul's letters, however, he visits Jerusalem twice after his conversion (Gal. 1:18; 2:1) and mentions his plan to visit a third time (Rom. 15:25). These two chronologies cannot be perfectly harmonized in such a way as to allow each to stand as reported. A viable solution is to accept Paul's own report of two visits and to suggest that Luke has construed the visit of Paul to attend the Council of Jerusalem as three separate visits. A second difficulty in the synchronizing approach is that it does not give sufficient attention to Luke's theological and literary purposes in his selection of information on Paul. Luke wrote Acts to show how the gospel was inclusive of all people in the known world, not to tell the story of Paul's life. A third problem is that attempts to try to "correct" Luke's account of Paul in Acts with the autobiographical information in the letters do injustice to the literary function of Acts as a theological narrative of the progress of the Christian movement.

In using the primary and secondary sources to understand Paul's life and thought, then, it appears best to rely on Paul's letters as the primary sources where possible. Acts will be used to help fill out our understanding of Paul. As with all sources, they must be evaluated in terms of their intended purposes.

THE LIFE OF PAUL

The Early Years

Paul makes little reference in his letters to his early personal history, except to indicate that he was a Jew "of the tribe of Benjamin" and "a Hebrew

Figure 20.4. The Khazneh, or Treasury, was one of the many buildings carved out of the sandstone cliffs at Petra, the capital of the Nabatean kingdom. Aretas IV, king of Nabatea, attempted to capture Paul in Damascus. *(Photograph by Clyde E. Fant)*

born of Hebrews" (Phil. 3:5). The latter statement indicates that his family, though living in the Diaspora, was still speaking Hebrew or Aramaic. Luke presents Paul as a Hellenistic Jew from Tarsus, the capital of the province of Cilicia in Asia Minor (Acts 22:3). If Luke is correct, and there is no compelling reason to doubt him, this fact helps to explain the influence of Hellenism on Paul. Tarsus was heavily Hellenized in the period of Antiochus IV Epiphanes (175–164 B.C.E.) and exemplified a city of multiple cultures. Growing up as a Jew in Tarsus, Paul was likely exposed to the major religions and philosophies of his day. Luke also reports that Paul was born a Roman citizen, that he had a sister, and that he spent his youth in Jerusalem studying "at the feet of Gamaliel" (Acts 22:3; 22:28; 23:16).

A Student in Jerusalem

The claim that Paul was a student of Gamaliel is problematic for several reasons. First, in his letters Paul never mentions studying with the revered teacher Gamaliel, which is puzzling since he expressed pride in being Jewish. Second, if Luke were correct, Paul would have been in Jerusalem during the time of Jesus' ministry. Yet Paul never makes reference to any personal contact with Jesus during those days. Third, Gamaliel was a teacher of the liberal school of Judaism whose teaching was likely in opposition to Paul's strict view of obedience to the Law. Fourth, and perhaps most telling, when defending his authority as a Christian leader (Gal. 1), he never mentions study with Gamaliel among his credentials. Most scholars therefore believe that Paul, though educated in the Law (probably in Tarsus), was likely not trained in the rabbinical school of Gamaliel.

A Persecutor of Christians

As a young adult, Paul (or Saul) became a persecutor of Christians (Gal. 1:13-14, 23; Phil. 3:6; Acts 8:3). Although Paul implies that the extent of his persecution was limited (for example, he claims, "I was still unknown by sight to the churches of Judea that are in Christ" [Gal. 1:22]), Luke emphasizes this pre-Christian activity of Paul as background for the story of Paul's conversion to the Christian gospel.

Paul's Conversion to Christianity

Paul recounts the redirection of his life in Galatians 1:1-17, 1 Corinthians 15:8-10, and Philippians 3:5-16. (Acts narrates Luke's version in Acts 9:1-19, 22:6-16, and 26:12-18.) Paul had a profound personal experience as he traveled from

Jerusalem to Damascus with the intention of countering the Christian movement there. He clearly believed that he had "encountered" Jesus himself and communicated with him, which led him to believe that Jesus was the Messiah for whom the Jews had waited.

Luke emphasizes Paul's persecution of Christians as the background for his accounts of Paul's conversion. He reports Paul's conversation with the risen Lord: " 'Saul, Saul, why do you persecute me?' He asked, 'Who are you, Lord?' The reply came, 'I am Jesus, whom you are persecuting' " (Acts 9:4-5). Luke also adds several details that point to the miraculous nature of the event (a blinding light, voices, Paul's temporary blindness, and his sudden recovery of sight).

To refer to Paul's experience as a "conversion" may be misleading. As a result of his encounter with Jesus, he was not convinced to give up Judaism and turn to a new religion, Christianity; in fact, the division between Judaism and Christianity had not yet occurred. He continued to think of himself as a Jew, but he interpreted his Judaism in light of his encounter and his belief that Jesus was the Messiah.

Paul regarded this experience on the Damascus road as a turning point in his life. He reconstructed his Jewish beliefs based on his new belief in the resurrection of Jesus. He also believed that he had received a call like that received by the Hebrew prophets, but his was a call to take the gospel to the Gentiles.

Traditionally, Romans 7:7-25 was often used as a background for "explaining" Paul's conversion. In the Romans passage Paul laments his sense of unworthiness before the Law and reports that he found release from his burden of guilt through his faith in the risen Christ. To interpret this passage as though it represents Paul's guilt-ridden state at the time of his conversion, however, would be an error. Indeed, Paul believed that at the time of his conversion he was blameless before the Law (Phil. 3:4-6).

Joining the Christian Movement in Jerusalem

After his conversion Paul "went away at once into Arabia" (Gal. 1:17), probably the ancient Nabatean kingdom in what is now Jordan. Subsequently he returned to Damascus, began to proclaim the gospel there, and "after three years ... [went] up to Jerusalem to visit Cephas (Peter) and stayed with him fifteen days" (Gal. 1:18). (Paul could have meant "three years" from the time of his conversion or from his return from Arabia.)

This first visit of Paul to Jerusalem allowed him the opportunity to identify with the earliest Christian community and to receive firsthand from Peter and James, two of the apostles, the basics of Christian beliefs and practices. Following the Jerusalem visit, Paul left for "the regions of Syria and Cilicia" (Gal. 1:21), presumably to do missionary work.

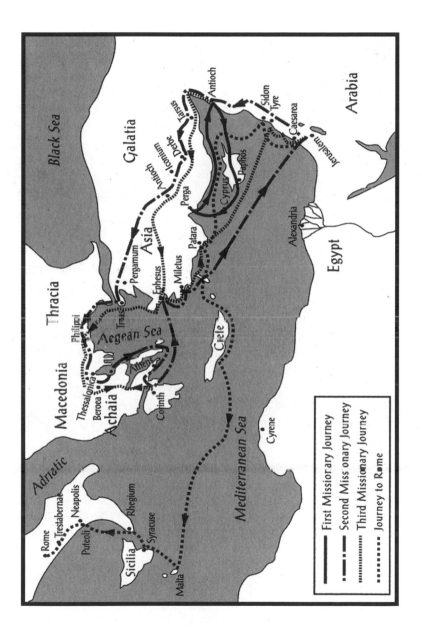

Figure 20.5. The journeys of Paul according to Acts.

Paul as a Christian Missionary to the Gentiles

Acts 13–28 portrays Paul as a Christian missionary who leads in spreading the gospel into Asia Minor and Europe. According to Acts, Paul undertakes three extensive journeys and at the end of each journey returns to Jerusalem and Antioch. Historians believe that Luke has recounted Paul's travels for the purpose of emphasizing the methodical expansion of the Christian movement throughout the Greco-Roman world. Luke has Paul returning to Jerusalem after each journey probably because Luke saw Jerusalem as the hub of the Christian missionary enterprise. Paul's letters do not present the journeys in as formal a fashion as does Luke, and at several points a harmony of the two accounts is problematic (note the earlier discussion regarding the number of Paul's visits to Jerusalem). Nevertheless, many of the details in Acts about the journeys are supported by the content of Paul's letters, and Paul doubtlessly traveled widely in the Roman Empire and was the primary bearer of the gospel to Asia Minor and Greece.

Taking the letters as the primary guide and using Acts as a supplement (where it does not contradict the letters), we may outline the missionary journeys of Paul as shown in figure 20.5.

Acts concludes with Paul under house arrest in Rome. It does not tell of Paul's death. Numerous traditions about Paul's last days have survived, including stories of a mission trip to Spain, a martyr's death under Emperor Nero, and his burial on the Ostian Way in Rome. None of these is verifiable, although the tradition of his martyrdom during Nero's persecution of the Roman Christians is widely accepted.

Paul's Ministry in the Greco-Roman World

Paul's experience on the Damascus road oriented him toward the specific task of carrying the gospel to the Gentiles. In response to that call Paul intended to carry the gospel to the known limits of the world. In the performance of that task he surpassed any other missionary of the early church. His ministry included four features that summarize his work:

1. Paul ministered primarily as an itinerant missionary. He began and nurtured Christian groups in Asia Minor, Greece, and Italy. Although he stayed for considerable periods in Corinth and in Ephesus, he worked principally as an itinerant teacher and preacher.
2. Paul attempted to establish a church in many of the towns and cities that he selected to spread the message of Jesus. He typically began his work in the

Figure 20.6. A Chronology of Paul's Life

Activity	Approximate Date (C.E.)
Paul is called (conversion experience)	32–33
Preaching in Arabia and Damascus	33–36
First visit to Jerusalem	36
Mission to Syria, Cilicia, and	
Galatia; returns to Antioch	36–49
Second visit to Jerusalem. Jerusalem Council	49
Mission to Asia Minor, Macedonia,	
and Achaia (including Corinth)	49–52
Paul in Corinth	50–52
Writes 1 Thessalonians	50
Returns to Antioch	52
Mission to Galatia, Ephesus, Macedonia,	
and Corinth	53–56
Paul in Ephesus	53–55
Writes Galatians	
Writes 1 Corinthians and	
portions of 2 Corinthians	54–55
(Writes Philippians and Philemon?)	55
Travels to Macedonia	56
Writes remainder of 2 Corinthians	
Travels to Corinth	56
Writes Romans	
Third visit to Jerusalem; arrested and sent to	
Caesarea as a prisoner	57
Travels to Rome for trial before Caesar	59
Imprisonment in Rome (house arrest)	60–62
(Writes Philippians and Philemon?)	

synagogue of the places he visited, attracting a group of Jews, God-fearers, and seekers to form a viable Christian congregation. The churches Paul established were relatively small groups of believing Jews and Gentiles. They lacked the structure and order that characterized later first-century Christian communities.

3. Paul encountered considerable opposition in his missionary efforts. His preaching in Jewish synagogues aroused the resentment of local officials who saw him as a threat to the stability of the local Jewish institution. He also encountered the anger of local governments and businesses upon whose interests he infringed.

Figure 20.7. The Parthenon on the Acropolis in Athens was built in honor of the goddess Athena. Paul preached in Athens during his journeys through Greece. *(Photograph by Mitchell G. Reddish)*

4. Paul maintained contact with the churches he had established through visits and letters. His letters show him to be one of the most creative and influential thinkers in early Christianity.

    The next chapter will examine those writings that are undisputed as letters of Paul.

Chapter 21

PAUL AND HIS WRITINGS

Suggested Biblical Readings: Galatians 1–3; 4:12-20; 5:1, 13-25;
1 Corinthians 1:1-25; 3:1-9; 7; 11:2-16; 12:12–13:13; 15:1-28;
Philemon; Romans 3:1-20; 4:13-25; 5; 8:1-39; 12

Chapter 20 discussed Paul's background and ministry in the Greco-Roman world. This chapter focuses on his writings. More than any other writer, Paul is featured in the New Testament. Paul composed at least one-fourth of the Greek text of the New Testament. He is a formative figure in the story of primitive Christianity. This chapter will describe the form of Paul's writings, that of the Greek letter, and then survey the content of Paul's seven undisputed letters. An extensive summary of Paul's beliefs and ethics concludes the chapter.

PAUL AS A LETTER WRITER

Scholarly consensus attributes to Paul seven authentic writings: 1 Thessalonians, Philippians, Galatians, Philemon, 1 and 2 Corinthians, and Romans. The other letters—1 and 2 Timothy, Titus, Ephesians, Colossians, and 2 Thessalonians—are either contested or rejected as Pauline.

Experts differ in their certainty concerning the letters not counted as Pauline. Most scholars agree that three of them are not Pauline (1 and 2 Timothy and Titus), the majority of scholars reject one letter (Ephesians), and some scholars contest two (Colossians and 2 Thessalonians). Several factors have led to doubts about the Pauline authorship of these letters: (1) their vocabulary and style differ from that of the undisputed Pauline writings, (2) their theology and concepts differ, and (3) the setting of each letter appears to reflect the situation of the late first century, long after Paul's lifetime. Questioning Paul's authorship of these letters does not, however, detract from the canonical authority of the documents. The following chapter will discuss these so-called deutero-Pauline—that is, "secondary Pauline"—letters, writings that were composed not by Paul himself but by individuals from his circle of followers.

Paul wrote more than the seven authentic letters listed above. Copies of these other letters have not survived, although portions of his other writings to Corinth probably appear in 2 Corinthians. Moreover, the texts of all of the authentic letters, except Philemon and possibly Philippians, appear to have undergone some editing. For instance, the ancient manuscripts of Romans diverge on the context and arrangement of chapters 15 and 16. Second Corinthians is likely a composite of several letters. Further, interpolations or later additions,

Figure 21.1. Head of Zeus, chief of the Greek gods. When Paul and Barnabas visited the city of Lystra, they were mistakenly acclaimed as Hermes and Zeus. *(Photograph by Mitchell G. Reddish)*

such as 1 Thessalonians 2:14-16 and 1 Corinthians 14:33*b*-36, have occurred in the transmission of the manuscripts. In addition, several of the authentic letters are composites of parts of other letters that have not survived. The obvious conclusion is that many of the canonical letters are not precisely as Paul wrote them.

Paul's letters were written to particular Christian churches about very specific topics. While they are rich with anecdotal, theological, and ethical substance, none of them individually or as a group will yield Paul's complete biography, theology, or ethics. They are occasional pieces, written for particular occasions to address specific situations. A study of the seven authentic letters, therefore, will not yield a comprehensive picture of Paul's thought.

Figure 21.2. Writings Attributed to Paul

Undisputed Letters	Letters Possibly by Paul	Letters Likely Not by Paul
1 Thessalonians	2 Thessalonians	Ephesians
Galatians	Colossians	1 Timothy
1 Corinthians		2 Timothy
2 Corinthians		Titus
Romans		
Philippians		
Philemon		

The Structure of Paul's Letters

Paul's writings generally follow the pattern of the Greek letters of his time. Typically, a Greek letter opened with a formal salutation and a statement of gratitude to the deities. Next followed the body or main content. A conclusion contained greetings to various persons and a prayer to the gods. The following letter, written in the second or third century C.E., is a good example of a Greek letter:

> Irenaeus to Apollinarius his dearest brother many greetings. I pray continually for your health, and I myself am well. I wish you to know that I reached land on the 6th of the month Epeiph and we unloaded our cargo on the 18th of the same month. I went up to Rome on the 25th of the same month and the place welcomed us as the god willed, and we are daily expecting our discharge, it so being that up till to-day nobody in the corn fleet has been released. Many salutations to your wife and to Serenus and to all who love you, each by name. Goodbye. (Addressed) To Apollinarius from his brother Irenaeus. (A. S. Hunt and C. C. Edgar, trans., *Select Papyri*. Vol. 1, *Non-Literary Papyri, Private Affairs* [Cambridge: Harvard University Press, 1932], p. 307)

Paul adapted this letter form to fit his religious purpose. He opens his letters by introducing himself (and often his coworkers) as the sender and he names his recipients. Then he greets his readers with a Christian version of the typical Greek greeting, "grace," with the addition of the Jewish greeting *shalom* or "peace." First Thessalonians 1:1 illustrates a typical Pauline introduction and greeting: "Paul, Silvanus, and Timothy, To the church of the Thessalonians in God the Father and the Lord Jesus Christ: Grace to you and peace." In place of a section thanking the gods, Paul regularly gives thanks to God for the church and mentions topics he will develop in the body of the letter. Again, 1 Thessalonians provides an illustration:

We always give thanks to God for all of you and mention you in our prayers, constantly remembering before our God and Father your work of faith and labor of love and steadfastness of hope in our Lord Jesus Christ. For we know, brothers and sisters beloved by God, that he has chosen you, because our message of the gospel came to you not in word only, but also in power and in the Holy Spirit and with full conviction; just as you know what kind of persons we proved to be among you for your sake. And you became imitators of us and of the Lord, for in spite of persecution you received the word with joy inspired by the Holy Spirit, so that you became an example to all the believers in Macedonia and in Achaia. For the word of the Lord has sounded forth from you not only in Macedonia and Achaia, but in every place your faith in God has become known, so that we have no need to speak about it. For the people of those regions report about us what kind of welcome we had among you, and how you turned to God from idols, to serve a living and true God, and to wait for his Son from heaven, whom he raised from the dead—Jesus, who rescues us from the wrath that is coming. (1:2-10)

Paul's content section deals with specific religious and ethical issues. In the conclusion he bids farewell to many people and pronounces a blessing, or benediction, on the recipients. The conclusion to 1 Thessalonians is typical:

May the God of peace himself sanctify you entirely; and may your spirit and soul and body be kept sound and blameless at the coming of our Lord Jesus Christ. The one who calls you is faithful, and he will do this.
Beloved, pray for us.
Greet all the brothers and sisters with a holy kiss. I solemnly command you by the Lord that this letter be read to all of them.
The grace of our Lord Jesus Christ be with you. (5:23-28)

THE CONTENTS OF PAUL'S LETTERS

1 Thessalonians

Paul, along with Silas and Timothy, wrote 1 Thessalonians, the earliest writing in the New Testament, from Corinth in 50–51 C.E. According to the contents of the letter itself, supplemented by information from Acts 17:1-15, Paul established a house church at Thessalonica during his second missionary journey. Paul and Silas had left Antioch and had traveled through Asia Minor to Troas, from where—now joined by Timothy—they sailed across the Aegean Sea. After a time of ministry and imprisonment in Philippi, they journeyed along the Ignatian Way (a major Roman road) to Thessalonica, the provincial capital of Macedonia. Paul visited the synagogue for three weeks and persuaded several Jews and God-fearers to begin a Christian group, probably in the home of Jason. The leaders of the synagogue incited a mob to storm Jason's home. Jason and others were brought before the local authorities, charged with treason, and fined. Paul and Silas slipped away to Beroea, where they started a church, only to be followed by Thessalonian critics who forced them to leave for Athens. Subsequently they went to Corinth, where Paul wrote 1 Thessalonians.

One of the difficulties in interpreting Paul's letters is that they contain answers to questions that can only be inferred from the content. From the content of 1 Thessalonians it appears that some local citizens were persecuting the Christians (1:6; 3:2-3). These may well have been the same Jews who had earlier harassed them. Other interpreters see them as Gentiles. The troublemakers also belittled Paul's religious authority (see 2:3-8).

To strengthen his readers, Paul defends his authority and sincerity by reminding them of his spiritual sincerity while in Thessalonica. He holds up the model of Jesus the martyr, who remained steadfast in the face of hostility and "who died for us, so that . . . we may live with him" (5:10). The Thessalonians should not flinch in the face of persecution and possible death. They should stand firm because the endtime is at hand. Jesus will return soon to raise the faithful dead to life and usher them and those still living into the messianic kingdom. Much like the Gospel source Q, 1 Thessalonians is saturated with the expectation of the Parousia.

Figure 21.3. The Roman Forum in Thessalonica, Greece. These buildings date from the second to third centuries C.E. Paul founded a Christian church in Thessalonica. (*Photograph by Mitchell G. Reddish*)

Galatians

Galatians propounds one of Paul's favorite themes, that of Christian freedom. The time and place of its writing are uncertain. Some believe Paul wrote from Ephesus while in prison or at least while a resident there. Others believe he wrote from Macedonia. The date of composition is between 52 and 56 C.E. Little is known of Paul's visits to the Galatian Christians. Acts reports that after the Jerusalem conference he traveled through their territory and then on into Greece. Later he returned to Galatia, but details of his visits are not recorded in the sources.

The specific location of the Galatian churches is disputed. Paul addresses his letter to "the churches of Galatia" (Gal. 1:2) and refers to the recipients as "Galatians" (Gal. 3:1). Originally, "Galatians" referred to the Celtic people who settled in northern Asia Minor in an area around modern Ankara, Turkey. The Roman province of Galatia, however, included a large area to the south. In Paul's day only the inhabitants of the traditional "Galatia" in the north referred to themselves as "Galatians." But Acts does not tell of Paul establishing any churches in the north. The only churches in Galatia mentioned in Acts are in the south (Lystra, Derbe, Iconium; Acts 14:1-23). This confusion has led to "North Galatian" and "South Galatian" theories of the destination of the letter. The churches could have been in the north central portion of Asia Minor, a region that had been settled by Celts (the North Galatian theory), or they could have been in an area to the south included in the Roman province of Galatia (the South Galatian theory). No compelling arguments settle the dispute. Wherever the locale, from the letter we know that Paul visited the region while suffering from an undisclosed illness.

The occasion for the letter was Paul's receipt of information that zealous opponents had followed him into the region and created theological chaos by disputing his interpretation of Christianity. Paul rebuked these opponents and their "different gospel." He defended himself and pleaded with the Galatians to support him. Paul disputed with his opponents over the role of the Jewish Law in Christianity. Paul's opponents demanded that all Christians undergo the Jewish rite of circumcision and keep the Jewish Law. Paul, on the other hand, argued that Christ had delivered Christians from such legal constraints into a remarkable freedom that touched on every area of life. Christian freedom transcended divisions based upon national origin, race, class, and gender: "There is no longer Jew or Greek, there is no longer slave or free, there is no longer male and female; for all of you are one in Christ Jesus" (3:28).

From the outset of the letter (1:1-9) Paul counterattacks his opponents. In the salutation he states his apostolic authority emphatically and briefly defines the gospel he preaches. Instead of offering a prayer of thanksgiving for the Galatians, he launches immediately into a tirade against his opponents.

The next section provides a defense of his authority and gospel (1:10–2:21). First he describes his conversion to Christianity and call to be a spokesperson, claiming to have divine credentials (1:10-24). Next he relates that the Christian leadership in Jerusalem had authorized him to evangelize the Gentiles (2:1-10). The Jerusalem conference (see Acts 15) decided that Paul would carry out his work among Gentiles, who would not need to undergo circumcision, while James, Peter, and John would focus attention upon Jews. Paul cites a confrontation at Antioch to emphasize his point. At Antioch Peter, Paul, and others were maintaining social and religious relations with converted Gentiles, contrary to Jewish regulations. Some Jewish Christian missionaries from Jerusalem arrived at Antioch and strenuously objected. Peter ceased the practice, but Paul defended himself against the charges and tried to persuade Peter to stand firm. For Paul, circumcision and the keeping of the Law were recommended but not necessary.

Paul defended his gospel in Galatians 1–2 by focusing on his personal history: his conversion, call, and authorization by the Jerusalem church. In the next section (3:1–4:31) Paul sought to show from the Hebrew Scriptures, the same source used by his opponents, that he was correct and his opponents were wrong. Throughout these two chapters he marshaled diverse arguments to show that faith in Christ brought a radical freedom that does not depend on the Law.

Paul's complex arguments contain two primary emphases. First, Paul draws on traditions about Abraham from the Pentateuch to argue that God counted Abraham righteous on the basis of his faith and not because he kept the Law. Thus he defends his gospel and rebuts his opponents. Second, he expounds his view of the Law. It served as a conscience and guide from the time of Moses but now has been reinterpreted. Adapting texts from Deuteronomy 27, Paul states, "Cursed is everyone who does not observe and obey all the things written in the book of the law" (Deut. 27:26 in Gal. 3:10). Since no one is able to keep the entire Law, it now serves only as a curse to those who follow it. Christ, however, took the Law's curse upon himself. Henceforth, the Law has no authority over humans who trust in Christ. No one should therefore fear the Law or those, like Paul's opponents, who would demand obedience to it.

In his letters Paul customarily followed doctrinal arguments with ethical admonitions. (For Paul, the conjunction of beliefs with a way of life indicates an important foundation of Christianity: what one believes should correlate with how one lives.) Thus Galatians 5:1–6:10 treats the practical aspects of faith. The basic faith of the Christian life resounds in 5:1: "For freedom Christ has set us free. Stand firm, therefore, and do not submit again to a yoke of slavery." One should not confuse Paul's idea of Christian freedom with several modern notions of the term. By "freedom" Paul does not mean (1) freedom of choice between options, (2) freedom from political or economic oppression, or (3) freedom from any external constraints, which enables one to master one's destiny. Rather, one is freed from the bondage of sin to life in the Spirit by freely submitting to the demands of Christ. Chapters 5 and 6 take up the implications of Christian freedom. Paul urges the Galatians to avoid returning to a Law-driven faith. They should instead embrace the life of the Spirit, by which they can avoid sinful entrapments and cling to Christ. Life in the Spirit entails certain activities: love of neighbor (5:13-15) and the attitudes of "love, joy, peace, patience, kindness, generosity, faithfulness, gentleness, and self-control. There is no law against such things" (Gal. 5:22-23).

The letter concludes (6:11-18) with a summary of its core content. Paul again rebukes his opponents, states his position on the gospel and the Law, and urges compliance with his position. He concludes with a blessing or benediction: "May the grace of our Lord Jesus Christ be with your spirit, brothers and sisters. Amen" (6:18).

1 Corinthians

When Paul traveled down the Greek peninsula to Corinth, he discovered a thriving seaport city that rivaled the cultural pluralism of any contemporary cosmopolitan center. After the Romans razed Corinth in 146 B.C.E., Julius Caesar erected a new city (44 B.C.E.), which became the capital of the province of Achaia prior to Paul's arrival (49–50 C.E.). Many different religions prospered in Corinth, including Judaism. According to Acts 18:1-17, Paul first declared his gospel in the synagogue. When opposition emerged, he established a house church of Jews and God-fearers in the home of Titius Justus, next door to the synagogue. After an extended stay of one and a half years, Paul moved on to Ephesus. From Ephesus he wrote several letters to Corinth. One letter preceded 1 Corinthians (see 1 Cor. 5:9) and several letters followed it. Second Corinthians is a composite of at least two and perhaps as many as five other letters.

Paul wrote 1 Corinthians in 53 or 54 C.E. in response to a report of problems in the Corinthian congregation brought to him by "Chloe's people" (1:11) and presented to him in a letter from Corinth (7:1). The structure of 1 Corinthians follows closely the pattern of a typical Greek letter. Following the salutation and thanksgiving (1:1-9), an extended body takes up the series of problems along with Paul's responses (1:10–16:18) and ends with a stylized conclusion (16:19-24).

Whereas the problems Paul addressed in Thessalonians and Galatians came from people outside the congregation, the issues at Corinth were internal. Once again the reader must infer the problems from the solutions Paul proposes. Apparently, some members held a distorted notion of life in the Spirit. Some understood that Christian freedom permitted the unbridled indulgence of the senses. They argued that salvation was completely spiritual and that one could indulge in sensuous living in which "all things are lawful" (10:23). Others took an opposite position, rigidly avoiding sensual activities. These ascetics followed a similar logic but drew an opposite conclusion. For them physical pleasure should be curtailed in favor of the cultivation of purely spiritual activities. Paul chastises both groups and points them toward a spiritual life based on *agape* or love.

In the first section (1:10–4:21) Paul addresses the problem of factions. The church had misdirected its loyalty away from Christ and had lodged it with leading Christians such as Apollos, Paul, or Peter. These figures may have been the ones who had baptized them. Each group believed its leader had a corner on the truth. Paul terms this "worldly wisdom" and contrasts it with the "foolish" wisdom of God, which is grounded not in empty rhetoric or esoteric knowledge but in "Christ crucified, a stumbling block to Jews and foolishness to Gentiles" (1:23). Paul criticizes reliance on human leaders and pleads for loyalty to God alone (3:5-11; 4:1-5). He condemns human pride (1:29; 3:18) and advises humility (1:27-29; 4:8-13). The wisdom of God must take precedence over human wisdom.

In 5:1–6:20 Paul discusses matters of moral conduct. He addresses a case of sexual immorality (5:1-13) in which a member of the congregation was living with his stepmother. Paul expresses shock and advises the church to expel the guilty party. In 6:1-11 he chastises Christians who take one another before the public courts. He counsels that Christians should settle legal disputes among themselves. In 6:12-20 he addresses the principle of mutual responsibility of Christians to one another. Against those who claim that "all things are lawful" (6.12), he upholds a morality of mutual concern and respect.

In chapter 7 Paul responds to the Corinthians' questions about marriage. Apparently the ascetic members of the congregation believed "it is well for a man not to touch a woman" (7:1). Although Paul prefers that the unmarried and widowed live the single life (7:7 8, 11, 27, 40), he heartily endorses marriage (7:2-5) and advises marriage for engaged couples if they cannot control their sexual urges (7:8). Against those who taught that even the married should live without sexual relations, he supports an active sexual relationship except for brief periods of abstinence for prayer (7:5). In response to ascetics who thought Christians married to non-Christians should divorce their non-Christian partners, Paul disagrees. Consistent with his preference for celibacy, he advises that the divorced should not remarry (7:10-11). Paul's apocalyptic expectation of the Parousia and the end of the "old age" permeates the entire chapter (7:20, 31). Thus, he advises single Corinthians to "remain as you are" so they can single-mindedly devote themselves to Christ in preparation for the "new age," unencumbered by entangling relationships.

The material from 8:1 to 11:1 expounds the relationship between

Figure 21.4. The Fountain of Peirene in Corinth. The church at Corinth was established through the efforts of Paul. Later, he wrote several letters to the church in Corinth. *(Photograph by Mitchell G. Reddish)*

Christian freedom and Christian obligations for others. Paul counters the position that "all things are lawful" with the constraint of a caring attitude based on the principle that all things are not helpful. One should use freedom not to destroy another but to enrich one another. Paul applies this principle to a dispute over food. Meat from sacrifices in non-Yahwistic temples was sold in the open market. Some Christians were horrified by other Christians who ate it (8:7). Those who ate it saw no problem because the other deities to whom the sacrifices had been made did not exist (8:4-6). Paul agrees with the partakers' principle (8:8, 10:26-30). He cautions them, however, not to offend the religious convictions of the abstainers (the "weaker" Christians). He sums up his position in 8:13: "Therefore, if food is a cause of their falling, I will never eat meat, so that I may not cause one of them to fall."

The next block of material (11:22–14:40) concerns conduct in worship. The first subsection (11:2-16) deals with the role of women in worship. Some Christian women had abandoned the traditional Jewish and Greek custom of covering their heads in worship. Paul sides with the traditionalists on this matter: "Judge for yourselves: is it proper for a woman to pray to God with her head unveiled? Does not nature itself teach you that if a man wears long hair, it is degrading to him, but if a woman has long hair, it is her glory? For her hair is given to her for a covering" (11:13-16). On the other hand, in the same passage Paul also affirms the role of women who pray and preach in public worship (11:5).

In the following subsection (11:17-34), which contains the earliest reference to the Christian observance of the Eucharist or Holy Communion, Paul warns the Corinthian Christians that when they meet to share a common meal and celebrate the Eucharist, they are to do so properly. Some of them were eating and drinking to such excess that nothing was left for others. Such behavior, typical at the banquets of the wealthy, violated the purpose of the communion meal.

Chapters 12–14 deal with worship practices that threaten the unity of the church. Some at Corinth were practicing religious ecstasy, which included trances or speaking in ecstatic tongues. Their enthusiasm had a disruptive effect. Paul appeals to his metaphor of the Christian community as "the body of Christ" (12:12-31) and to the principle of love (chapter 13) to repair the disunity that had resulted. He affirms diversity among the Corinthians by listing several spiritual "gifts" that the Corinthians should use for the building up of the group. According to Paul, all spiritual gifts, including speaking in tongues, have their place in worship and in the Christian community. They should, however, be controlled and used for the benefit of all. He limits their use on the basis of decency and order. All gifts should be exercised in accordance with *agape*, the principle of love.

First Corinthians concludes with the earliest canonical exposition of the early Christian belief about resurrection. Paul grounds his view of resurrection in tradition: "For I handed on to you as of first importance what I in turn had received" (15:3). He sees himself not as the inventor of resurrection theology but rather as its custodian. From Paul's extensive presentation we can infer that two misunderstandings had evoked his response. First, some Corinthians had difficulty thinking of life after death as embodied life. They conceived of a bodiless soul, cleansed of material aspects, as the essential self that survived death. (This was the basic premise of the Platonist and Gnostic view of immortality.) Paul, on the other hand, taught that the Christian afterlife was a state in which believers received a transformed or spiritual body. (This was the central point of the Christian view of the resurrection of the body.) Second, some believed that they had already entered the state of resurrection by having been raised with Christ in the rite of baptism. Paul counters this error by asserting that whereas the effects of eternal life already live in the believer by the indwelling of the Spirit, the fullness of resurrection comes later with the dawning of the new age. Paul not only counters these two errors, he declares that the basis for the Christian belief in life after death resides in the reality of Christ's resurrection (as Christ was raised, so shall we be). As Christ was embodied in his resurrection, so shall believers receive a transformed body that will be "imperishable."

Figure 21.5. The Library of Celsus in Ephesus, built in the beginning of the second century C.E., contained over 12,000 scrolls. Paul spent over two years in Ephesus and while there wrote several letters to the church in Corinth. *(Photograph by Mitchell G. Reddish)*

Paul concludes 1 Corinthians with ethical exhortations and material directed to specific individuals (16:1-18), closing with the affirmation that he has written the letter in his own hand (16:19-24).

2 Corinthians

Second Corinthians is a loosely edited collection of Paul's correspondence with Corinth. Scholars do not agree on the letter's literary structure or its precise intentions. Two views, however, are prominent.

One view holds that 2 Corinthians is composed of two letters: a letter of reconciliation and joy (chapters 1–9) and a "harsh" letter (chapters 10–13). Most scholars who take this position believe that Paul hurried to Corinth to deal with an emergency situation. He was, however, rebuffed and subsequently wrote the harsh letter contained in 2 Corinthians 10–13. Titus then brought word to Paul that the Corinthians had taken his counsel. In gratitude he wrote the letter in 2 Corinthians 1–9 to share his pleasure and to remind them of some important matters.

Other scholars find 2 Corinthians composed of the remnants of four letters. After sending 1 Corinthians and while still in Ephesus, Paul received word that some newcomers had entered the Corinthian church and claimed to be authoritative teachers of the Christian faith. Based on what he heard, Paul penned a letter (2:14–7:4, minus 6:14 to 7:1, which appears to be a non-Pauline addition) defending himself and criticizing his new opponents. In themes reminiscent of 1 Corinthians 1–4, Paul describes himself as a humble and sincere preacher of Christ, in contrast to the arrogant newcomers whose substance and sincerity are questionable. Paul then visited the Corinthians, only to find a strong segment opposed to him. He even suffered public humiliation. As a result, Paul sternly wrote "out of much distress and anguish of heart and with many tears" (2:4) a letter that chapters 10–13 preserve. Paul castigates his opponents as pride-ridden distorters of the gospel. They boast of "signs and wonders and mighty works" and their achievements in Christ's name. Paul reminds the Corinthians that he humbly submitted himself to the power of God. After he had fired off this "tearful letter," Paul left Ephesus and met Titus in Macedonia, where Titus told him that the Corinthians had repented of their ways. He then wrote his "thankful letter" (1:1–2:13; 7:5-16) in which he compassionately implored them to reconcile with one another just as they had reconciled themselves with Paul. In chapters 8 and 9, which were probably written from Macedonia, Paul commends his associate, Titus, to the Corinthians and encourages their financial support of the collection for the needy in Jerusalem.

Philippians

Punctuated by encouragements to rejoice and be joyful, Philippians is Paul's most positive letter. Acts 16 tells of the founding of the church at Philippi by Paul about 49–50 C.E. In response to a vision to carry the gospel to Macedonia, Paul and his associates crossed the Aegean Sea from Asia Minor to Neapolis. They next traveled to Philippi, a leading city of the region, where they spoke with several women. As a result Lydia, a businesswoman, converted, together with her household. Later, Paul and Silas were arrested. While in prison, they converted the jailer and his family, and upon their release they left for Thessalonica. We know little of Paul's later relationship with the church. He visited at least once (Acts 20:6) and perhaps several other times.

Since the second century scholars have maintained that Paul wrote Philippians from prison in Rome. References to "the whole imperial guard" (1:13) and "those of the emperor's household" (4:22) have been cited to support this claim. Neither citation is compelling, however, since both groups were present in other Roman cities. A recent theory suggests that Philippians may have been written during Paul's two-year imprisonment in Caesarea or during a hypothetical

Figure 21.6. The Via Egnatia in Philippi, Greece, a city where Paul established a church. The Via Egnatia, built in the second century B.C.E., was the major east-west Roman road through northern Greece. It ran from the Adriatic Sea eastward to Constantinople. *(Photograph by Mitchell G. Reddish)*

Ephesian imprisonment. Both arguments are plausible. There seems to be, however, no consensus about whether it was written from Rome, Caesarea, or Ephesus. Although some believe the letter is a composite of three letters, most hold to the integrity of the writing. As a unified document it follows the pattern of a Greek letter: salutation and thanksgiving (1:1-11), body (1:12–4:9), and conclusion (4:10-23).

In the body of the letter Paul takes up several topics. First, he offers thanks for the funds that the Philippians graciously sent to him. Second, he urges two women, Euodia and Syntyche, to cease their bickering. Paul urges the entire church to remain unified. Third, he warns against outsiders who would disrupt and distort the Christian faith. Fourth, he exhorts them to rejoice in Christ and to live in the pattern of Christ, Paul, Timothy, and Epaphroditus, all of whom have humbled themselves to God's purpose on behalf of the Philippians.

Philemon

Philemon is the only authentic Pauline letter written to an individual. In it Paul advises Philemon about Philemon's slave, Onesimus. Although Paul addresses the letter to an individual, it is not entirely private. Paul writes with Timothy and greets several individuals, probably those in Philemon's house church. Due to a reference to an Onesimus in Colossians 4:9, many believe Philemon lived in Colossae. This, however, is not certain. As with Philippians, one can make good arguments that Paul wrote to Philemon from Rome or Ephesus or Caesarea, although Rome is the traditional location.

Onesimus, a runaway slave, had made his way to Paul, who had converted him to Christianity. Onesimus had stayed with Paul and had become his aide. According to Roman law, Paul was now returning Onesimus to Philemon. He appeals to Philemon to receive Onesimus back without a spirit of vengeance, because Onesimus has become "much more than a slave: he is a dear brother in Christ" (v. 16 TEV).

The literary structure of the shortest of Paul's letters closely follows the Greek pattern. Following the salutation and thanksgiving (vv. 1-7), Paul makes his case for Onesimus to Philemon in the body (vv. 8-22) and concludes in typical fashion (vv. 23-25). Though brief, Philemon is a literary gem. The Greek text reveals a rich use of language punctuated by puns and wordplay. With subtle tact Paul gently makes a compelling plea for Philemon to deal kindly with Onesimus.

Contemporary readers frequently complain that Paul does not criticize the institution of slavery in Philemon or in other letters. In fairness to Paul, one should recall that he expected the endtime in his lifetime and perhaps for this reason made no overtures to restructure society. On the other hand, he argues in Philemon and elsewhere that culture must not determine the church's social fabric. He upholds the embodiment of a new community of brothers and sisters in Christ in which all are one in Christ.

Romans

Romans, Paul's most formal and theologically comprehensive letter, was written from Corinth as Paul contemplated a trip to Jerusalem to present the collection for the poor. Paul had no hand in establishing the Roman church; his knowledge of them came secondhand except for those he greets in chapter 16 (if chapter 16 is authentic to Romans). One can understand the focus and tone of the letter from this background. Paul wished to use Rome as a base for launching missionary work westward (15:24, 28, 32), perhaps as he had used Antioch as a post from which to carry out his three missions to Europe and Asia Minor. He therefore declared his position on doctrinal and ethical issues, perhaps to calm any anxiety they might have had about him and to enhance their support of his plan.

The body of the letter extends from 1:18 to 15:13. Paul enunciates the universality of his gospel in 1:16-17: "For I am not ashamed of the gospel; it is the power of God for salvation to everyone who has faith, to the Jew first and also to the Greek." The idea of righteousness or upright living before God is the key topic in the letter. In 1:18–3:20 he argues that all people—both Jews and Gentiles—are sinners who do not merit God's goodness: "All, both Jews and Greeks, are under the power of sin" (3:9). Sinners freely choose to be unrighteous by pridefully choosing to live in opposition to the Creator. Because "all have sinned" (3:23), God has revealed the nature of true righteousness in Jesus (3:21–4:25). The way of salvation is entirely the working of God, who by grace accepts the unrighteous as righteous. Paul points to Abraham, the spiritual parent of everyone who was "through faith . . . accepted as righteous by God." Abraham's experience is taken as the model for all people because "the words 'he [Abraham] was accepted as righteous' were not written for him alone." They were written also for us who are to be accepted as righteous, who believe in him who raised Jesus our Lord from death" (4:22-24 TEV). Righteousness, then, comes not by living obediently by following the Law, but by confessing one's inability to achieve righteousness and accepting God's gracious gift of righteousness offered in Jesus.

Chapters 5–8 explain the new life of those declared righteous by faith. The powers that controlled the old life—death, sin, and Law—have no power over the believer who lives in and by the Spirit. The old life of sin is overturned by God's gracious activity through Christ. "So then, as the one sin condemned all people, in the same way the one righteous act sets all people free and gives them life" (5:18 TEV). Since they are now "alive to God in Christ Jesus" (6:11), believers must "walk not according to the flesh but according to the Spirit" (8:4b) wherein they experience "life and peace" (8:6b).

Having exposed humanity's unrighteous condition, declared God's gracious provision for humanity's salvation, and explained the new life in the Spirit that salvation elicits, Paul pauses in chapters 9–11 to deal cautiously and sensitively with the fate of Jews who reject Jesus. Paul had acknowledged long before that God had chosen the Jews as the vehicle of God's saving purposes. Now God's saving power had been made manifest in Jesus. Thus, each person who believes in him becomes a true child of God, as Abraham had been. This remnant of believers in Jesus, chosen by grace, constitutes the "new" Israel. For the present Paul believes that most Jews are reluctant to affirm the messiahship of Jesus (11:25*b*). He hopes that soon "all Israel will be saved" (11:26*a*).

Paul continues in 12:1–15:13 to express additional thoughts about the nature of the new life in Christ. Whereas chapters 5–8 locate the foundations of this new life in the grace of God that enables one to lead a Spirit-filled life, this section depicts the practical and ethical implications of the spiritual life. Paul explores the believers' response to the declaration that they now have been declared righteous through God's grace, which is received by faith. Romans 12:1-8 sets the agenda for the remainder of the section. Christians are to offer their entire selves in obedience to God as "living sacrifices," submitting themselves to do

Figure 21.7. The Roman aqueduct at Caesarea. Paul was imprisoned at Caesarea for approximately two years before being sent to Rome. *(Photograph by Clyde E. Fant)*

God's will. The rest of the section explicates the meaning of the "will of God." Included are practical admonitions (12:9-21), proper attitudes toward the Roman Empire (13:1-7), the preeminence of *agape* (13:8-10), the impending endtime (13:11-14), and the relationship of the "strong" in faith to the "weak" in faith (14:1–15:13).

An extended closing to Romans explains Paul's philosophy of missionary work, announces his intentions to visit Rome and Spain, encourages generosity in the offering for the poor in Jerusalem, and sends greetings to many friends and acquaintances.

THE DIVINE-HUMAN ENCOUNTER IN PAUL

Paul's understanding of the divine-human encounter as contained in the seven authentic letters radically shaped early Christian belief and ethics. More than any other canonical writer, he shaped the theology of Augustine, Luther, and Calvin, all leading interpreters of Christianity. Paul's major ideas can be discussed under five headings: gospel, Christology, salvation, faith, and ethics.

Gospel

The gospel or "good news" about Jesus Christ is a word Paul uses forty-eight times, more than any other New Testament author. Sometimes it refers to missionary activity; more often than not, in Paul "gospel" refers to the message he preached and taught. He felt set apart at his conversion for the preaching of the gospel, of which he was "not ashamed" (Rom. 1:16). By "gospel" Paul meant several things. First, the gospel unveils a new age that heretofore had been cloaked in mystery. God's plan for all humanity, a plan that was previously hidden or only dimly perceived, has been made manifest in Christ. A new era had dawned, and Paul was its herald, both to Jews and Gentiles. Second, those who receive the gospel by faith become empowered by God to live righteously. The gospel comes "not in word only, but also in power and in the Holy Spirit" (1 Thess. 1:5). Third, Paul's gospel was both traditional and innovative. He frequently refers to beliefs and practices that had become established in the church as grounds for his advice. In 1 Corinthians, for example, he cites church tradition as a basis for his advice in 11:2, 11:16, and 15:3. Paul also developed early Christian views of the meaning of salvation, the role of the Law, the significance of Jesus' death and resurrection, and the apocalyptic expectation of the "new age" to come. Fourth, the message of the gospel sets the standard for Christian belief and practice. One is to believe it, obey it, and follow it.

If the gospel represents the message of Paul, Christology, salvation faith, and ethics sum up the content of his message.

Christology

"Christology" is a technical term referring to belief about Jesus of Nazareth as the Messiah or Christ. Paul uses three major titles for Jesus. One title is Son. The idea of "Son of God" was not new with Paul; it had a long history in both Judaism and the Greco-Roman world. First-century Judaism sometimes used it as a designation for the Messiah; in Greco-Roman thought it referred to a religious figure that displayed divine power. For Paul both of these ideas lie in the background of his use of "Son of God." As Son of God, Jesus was a divinely empowered deliverer. A second title is Christ. Paul uses the term 226 times. Although it designates Jesus as the Messiah, in Paul "Messiah" practically becomes identified as a proper name due to the frequent translation of the phrase "Jesus the Christ" as "Jesus Christ." In Paul's usage, Jesus as Messiah delivered humanity from the power of sin and death. A third title is Lord, emphasizing that Christ is worthy of human worship because of Christ's resurrection and exaltation.

According to Paul, the central event in Jesus' life was the crucifixion/resurrection. Christ died for humanity's sins and was raised so that people might be made righteous before God. The salvation of humankind depends on Jesus' death and resurrection.

Salvation

For Paul, the result of Christ's death and resurrection was the salvation of human beings. Here lies the heart of his gospel. Sin was the human problem that required salvation. Paul finds two ways of describing the human situation in which "all have sinned and fall short of the glory of God" (Rom. 3:23). Shockingly, Paul declares that sin arises from a mistaken attitude toward the Jewish Law as a guide to attaining righteousness. Paul claims that no one becomes righteous before God by living in obedience to the Law. Humans are "justified not by the works of the law but through faith in Jesus Christ" (Gal. 2:16a). He reasons that faith in God's mercy is the basis of attaining righteousness. Abraham first believed God, and God reckoned him righteous on the basis of his faith. The Law came later through Moses. Therefore, Paul argues, faith is prior to the Law. The purpose of the Mosaic Law was (1) to make manifest human sin—pride and selfishness—until the Messiah came, and (2) to provide a provisional guide for the faithful. That which was a good guide, however, proved to be a curse, for no one was able to keep the Law, as all have sinned. Moreover, even though the Law defined righteous living, human beings had proved themselves incapable of obeying the Law (Rom. 7:13-23). Paul believed that the human will was bound in sin, incapable of obeying the Law. He declares that the Law, which is good, had condemned him to death because of his human inability to obey it (Rom. 7:13-14).

Sin is an internal condition that dwells in humanity as an evil force, inhibiting one from keeping the Law—"For I do not do what I want keep the Law], but I do the very thing I hate" (Rom. 7:15b). Sin also manifests itself externally when one lives "according to the flesh" in opposition to God. "The wages of sin is death" (Rom. 6:23).

Paul speaks for all humanity when he asks, "Who will rescue me from this body of death?" (Rom. 7:24). His gospel contains an answer to that anguished question. God has provided a solution to humanity's problem through Jesus Christ's death and resurrection. In Paul the proclaimer of the kingdom of God in the Synoptic Gospels—Jesus—becomes the proclaimed. Rather than focusing on the teaching of Jesus as do the Synoptics, Paul makes Jesus himself the focus of his gospel. Paul uses at least seven images or metaphors to explain what has become possible for people through Christ's death and resurrection. They are justification, salvation, reconciliation, re-creation, expiation, redemption, and adoption.

Justification by grace through faith is Paul's favorite image. Basically a legal metaphor, it finds its roots deep within the Jewish belief that God is just or righteous. Humanity likewise is required to be righteous as defined by the Jewish Law. Each person, however, when standing before the tribunal of God's justice, is found guilty of violating God's standards and is therefore unjust and condemned to die. Christ, the Just One, has been "handed over to death for our trespasses and was raised for our justification" (Rom. 4:25). If we believe (the character of belief will be explained shortly), God declares us just on the basis of Christ's death/resurrection and our faith. Humans do nothing to earn this righteousness; it is a gift from God. Justification sets us right with God, then, by a purely gracious action of God.

Salvation is another metaphor Paul uses to explain the significance of the Christ event for humanity. A savior in both Jewish and Greek thought was one who rescued or delivered humanity from evil or harm. Christ as savior rescues believers from the power of sin and promises deliverance from death.

Reconciliation is a Pauline notion drawn from Greco-Roman thought that focuses on relationships. Before the Christ event, humans had a broken relationship with God. By Christ's death God has brought humans from a state of alienation from God to a status of friendship. "All this is from God, who reconciled us to himself through Christ, and has given us the ministry of reconciliation; that is, in Christ God was reconciling the world to himself, not counting their trespasses against them, and entrusting the message of reconciliation to us" (2 Cor. 5:18-19). As a result, people can be positively related to God.

Re-creation to a new life is a Pauline image that finds precedent in the Hebrew Bible's references to God's continuing creative and re-creative power. Paul states, "So if anyone is in Christ, there is a new creation: everything old has passed away; see, everything has become new!" (2 Cor. 5:17). The re-created person now shares a new life in Christ. The new life in Christ contrasts with the old humanity that derives from Adam.

Expiation is a Pauline metaphor drawn from the Jewish sacrificial system. Using the analogy of the sacrifice on the Day of Atonement, which ritually symbolized God's forgiveness of sin, Paul interprets Christ as the sacrifice whose blood (or life) has removed the sins of believers (Rom. 3:25).

Redemption is an image in which Christ "purchases" by his death the freedom of sinners who are in bondage to sin. Thus believers have been "bought with a price" (1 Cor. 6:20) "through the redemption that is in Christ Jesus" (Rom. 3:24). The key idea is freedom from slavery. Whereas the background of the idea lies in the notion of redeeming or buying goods or slaves, in biblical tradition the images of redemption are enriched by the memory of God's liberating activity in the Exodus and Exile.

Adoption as a child of God through Christ is the means by which humans, who by disposition and action have rejected God's parenting concerns, are brought into God's family as brothers and sisters in Christ (Gal. 4:5-7).

Alone, none of the images of the significance of Christ's death and resurrection suffice to capture completely Paul's understanding of its import. They all serve as portraits in a gallery, each depicting the event and its effects from different perspectives. In the Christ event God has acted through Christ to benefit humanity. For Paul, people receive these benefits through faith.

Faith

Faith has several elements. First, faith refers to one's comprehension of the gospel and one's assent to it. "So faith comes from what is heard, and what is heard comes through the word of Christ" (Rom. 10:17). Second, faith demands obedience to the gospel message. Faith therefore has a moral dimension. One not only assents to the truth of the gospel; one also commits to acting ethically. Third, faith for Paul involves a complete trust in the gospel. Persons must trust that God's actions in Christ have justified, reconciled, redeemed, re-created, and adopted them. Faith, then, involves three elements: assent or belief, obedience, and trust.

Upon a person's profession of faith, he or she was then initiated into the Christian community through the rite of baptism (1 Cor. 1:14-17; Rom. 6:1-11). The rite was administered by the immersion of the faithful in water. It represented identification with Christ's saving actions on one's behalf: "Therefore we have been buried with him by baptism into death, so that, just as Christ was raised from the dead by the glory of the Father, so we too might walk in newness of life" (Rom. 6:4).

Paul depicts life in the community of the faithful in the terms "body of Christ" and "walking in the Spirit." Although Paul used the traditional terms "saints" and "church" for the Christian community, his distinctive term was "body of Christ" (1 Cor. 12:12-31). It appears as a symbol of unity in 1 Corinthians, which addresses the issue of factions that had fractured the church at Corinth. Paul told them that the physical body had many diverse parts that yet worked together in harmony, so the members of the church should appreciate their differences, affirm the diversity of gifts among themselves, and work in harmony "for the common good" (1 Cor. 12:7), thus embodying the notion of the Body of Christ. The communion of the faithful with one another and with Christ was symbolically represented in the rite of the Eucharist (meaning "thanksgiving") or Lord's Supper (1 Cor. 11:23-34).

Ethics

How then should a faithful person live as a member of the body of Christ? Paul believed one should "walk by the Spirit." Before responding in faith to the gospel, one walked a path dominated by the power of sin. Now, "in Christ," one should live according to the Spirit in a life dominated by *agape* (Gal. 5:13). The new life included both freedom and obedience. Christ freed a person from the bondage of sin, death, and the Law by God's grace. But freedom was not a license to indulge the self. The transformed believer should do what was pleasing to God (Rom. 12:2). Out of gratitude to God for God's saving actions, one should submit willingly in obedience to the law of love. In Galatians 5:6 Paul describes it as "faith working [itself out] through love."

Chapter 22

THE DEVELOPING INSTITUTIONAL CHURCH

Suggested Biblical Readings: James 1–2; 1 John 1; 4; Colossians 2; Ephesians 3;
2 Thessalonians 2; 1 Timothy 4; Hebrews 8; 9:11–10:25; 11:1–12:2

Many of the later New Testament writings reveal the transition of the early Christian community from a loosely formed body into a more structured organization. With the passage of time, the developing Christian church was faced with new questions and problems. How should the earlier Jewish Christianity relate to the later Gentile Christianity? How should the church be organized? What qualifications should its leaders possess? How should Christians relate to the state? How should the church deal with those who leave it or deny its teachings? Why was the return of Christ delayed? Should the church expect such a return at all, or had the return already occurred? This chapter traces the struggles of the developing institutional church to maintain the community of faith in a changing world.

FROM CHARISMA TO INSTITUTION

In the latter part of the first century, the developing church faced issues that would have been totally unexpected by the earliest followers of Jesus. These can be summarized as three challenges that faced the church. First, conflicting theological and philosophical movements threatened the unity of the church. How could the church distinguish true belief from false doctrine? Second, with the passing of the earliest leadership of the church, Christianity had to structure a new organization and define the qualifications and duties of its leaders. Third, the church was faced with the question of the true worship of God. If Jesus is the head of the church, how do the life and death of Jesus relate to the High Priesthood and the Jewish sacrificial system?

Some of these questions had been considered before, but with the passing of time they became more acute as the church sought to stabilize its existence in a world caught in chaos and upheaval. In order to survive chaotic times, it became essential for the Christian movement to anchor itself in its ideals and practices. Two processes were essential if the movement was to survive: institutionalization, which provided permanence, and routinization, which provided predictability.

If the church was to survive more than one generation—something it had not expected, since it anticipated the return of Jesus within a generation—it had to institutionalize that which had been spontaneous. The early Christian movement was clearly a charismatic one; that is, it arose in response to a particularly gifted leader and functioned in a free, spontaneous manner. It had neither a formal constitution nor established officers. Its first followers abandoned conventional lives to follow Jesus in his wandering life of teaching and healing. After the departure of Jesus, however, the ever-growing number of followers and the multiplying interpretations of the meaning of his message forced the early church to define itself. Its beliefs, practices, and leadership had to be established for permanence.

Likewise, these elements, which evidently varied widely among the early Christian communities, had to be routinized: What were the rules, and who set them? When would they meet, and what would they do? Who was in charge? Who was responsible for what?

As important as institutionalization and routinization were to the new Christian organization, they bore within themselves the seeds of discontent. Once the spontaneous yielded to the predictable and the charismatic to the institutional, discontent with conformity and boredom with routine were likely to follow. The later church of the New Testament period found itself struggling to establish its identity through institution and routine, but at the same time it sought to preserve the dynamic forces that called it into being. The later New Testament writings clearly show both of these tensions.

SOURCES FOR STUDY

This chapter will consider those books of the New Testament that dealt with these issues. As was previously discussed in chapter 20, some of these writings have been attributed to Paul but are disputed: 2 Thessalonians, Colossians, Ephesians, 1 and 2 Timothy, Titus (these last three are also known as the Pastoral Epistles, or Pastorals), and the book of Hebrews. Of these, Hebrews is certainly not by Paul; on the other hand, scholars are not in agreement concerning the authorship of 2 Thessalonians, which may have been written by Paul. The same division of opinion exists (but to a lesser degree) regarding Colossians, while Ephesians is generally thought to be a writing from the Pauline circle but not from Paul himself. The great preponderance of scholarship rejects the Pastorals as writings of Paul.

These disputed Pauline writings are generally referred to as "deutero-Pauline." Likewise, the authorship of books attributed to Peter, James, John, and Jude has been disputed for centuries. First Peter may have been authored by the apostle, but many arguments have been advanced against that view. Second Peter is almost unanimously regarded by critical scholarship as pseudonymous. The letters of John were traditionally thought to have been written by the author of the Gospel with that name, but a number of factors argue against their common authorship. Furthermore, there is no agreement on the identity of John (most scholars do believe, however, that these letters were written too late to have been authored by the apostle John). Originally James and Jude were thought to have been written by brothers of Jesus but now they are regarded as pseudonymous.

What does the disputed authorship of these books say concerning their validity as source documents for the Christian faith? It is important to understand that the question of authorship in no way invalidates these books or contradicts belief in their teachings. If authorship by Paul or one of the original apostles of Jesus was essential to establish the divine inspiration of a biblical book, then surely the book would at least name its author. But Hebrews clearly does not do so, even though others later attached Paul's name to it. And although today we would regard attaching a famous person's name to the writings of another as at least dishonest, if not illegal, it was a familiar practice in the ancient world. Obviously this device was intended to attract readership and lend authority. But it was more than that. Most often such writings were authored by someone within the "circle" of the famous person—that is, by either an associate or a disciple of the person, one who intended to honor and further the work of the person

Figure 22.1. Theaters, like this one at Jerash in modern Jordan, were found in most important cities in the Roman world. (*Photograph by Mitchell G. Reddish*)

named. Such was likely the case with some of these later Christian writings. In any case, all of these books were accepted into the Christian canon—although acceptance did not come easily for some—and continue today to provide direction and inspiration for the church. Nonetheless, the scant usage of certain of these writings by the church over the centuries continues to show the church's decision-making process in canonization.

Regardless of their disputed authorship, this chapter will study the development of the institutional church as depicted in these sources. The authors of each of the books will be referred to by the name attached to the book.

THE CHURCH DISTINGUISHES RIGHT BELIEF
FROM FALSE TEACHINGS
(James; 1, 2, 3 John; Jude; 2 Peter; Colossians; 2 Thessalonians)

After Jesus was no longer among them, and after the death of many of the original followers of Jesus, the question of right belief became an urgent matter for early Christians. Was Paul to be believed, or were his detractors? Were Greek influences all bad? Should the church turn closer to its Jewish origins? Several of the later books of the New Testament are occupied with these questions. Because of the limitations of space, only the most prominent emphases of each of these writings will be presented.

Faith: Right Thinking or Right Living? (James)

One of the distinctive shifts from the writings of Paul to the later New Testament writings concerns the meaning of faith. For Paul, faith is the total committal of the person to God, specifically to God's act in Christ as proclaimed in the kerygma. It is also a committal to God's grace, which cannot be obtained by works (obedience to the Law, good deeds). Many passages in Romans (3:20-22; 9:30-32; 10:4-6; and others) are emphatic on this point, and the entire book of Galatians opposes the idea that faith must be supplemented by works of the Law for a person to stand justified before God. But it is apparent from the later New Testament writings that faith, at least in some circles, had come to mean an orthodoxy of ideas, a mental assent to a set of propositions. The book of *James* was written to counter just such a perversion of Pauline thought.

One of the problems in dating the book of James concerns the question of its relationship to Paul. Was it an early Palestinian Christian writing that preceded Paul and that came perhaps from the hand of James, a brother of Jesus? Or did it follow Paul's writings as a corrective to a one-sided understanding of his emphasis on faith? The latter appears to be the case. First, the Greek in which James is written appears to be much more polished and idiomatic than that which a Galilean peasant could have commanded, and second, it bears many characteristics of the Greek diatribe, a rhetorical style marked by questions posed to the reader. For these and other reasons the author of the book appears to be a Hellenistic (rather than Palestinian) Jewish Christian who wrote toward the end of the first century.

Is the thought of James in contradiction with that of Paul? James places considerable emphasis on deeds of compassion, particularly toward the poor (2:14-26) and orphans and widows (1:27). He also opposes favoritism toward the rich and discrimination toward the poor (2:1-7). These are the kinds of "works" James wants Christians to practice. He says that "faith by itself, if it has no works, is dead" (2:17), and he rebukes Christians who see a "brother or sister" who is "naked and lacks daily food" and say, " 'Go in peace; keep warm and eat your fill,' and yet [they] do not supply their bodily needs." He asks, "What is the good of that?" (2:14-16). James concludes: "For just as the body without the spirit is dead, so faith without works is also dead" (2:26).

When Paul speaks against the need for works, he is referring to such "works of the Law" as circumcision and sacrifices. He would agree that real faith results in works of compassion, "faith working through love" (Gal. 5:6). Paul's emphasis is on the faith-relationship required for right standing before God; James's emphasis is on the faith-actions required of living faith in contrast to dead faith.

The book of James is clearly a manual of Christian conduct, much of it resembling the book of Proverbs. It treats the subject of true wisdom for Christians (1:5; 3:17) just as Hebrew Wisdom literature urged God's wisdom for Israel. Its use of admonitions that urge action on Christians marks it as a sermon-treatise rather than a letter. As such, it continues to remind the church that belief and behavior, doctrine and ethics, belong together.

The Challenge of Gnosticism (1, 2, 3 John; Jude; 2 Peter; Colossians)

Three brief writings, *1, 2, and 3 John*, are presented as letters, although 1 John has neither the customary introduction nor conclusion of a letter. In several places, however, its use of the second-person form of address indicates that the author is writing to someone or someplace. Possibly 1 John was a catholic—or general—epistle, a letter circulated among several churches rather than only one. All three of the letters bear strong resemblance in vocabulary, theme, and style to the Gospel of John. The author of 2 and 3 John identifies himself as "the elder"; the author of 1 John does not. The authorship of all three epistles and the Gospel of John traditionally was assigned to the same person and dated sometime around the end of the first century. Although the person who wrote the letters of John is likely not the same person as the author of the Gospel of John, all four of these writings share similar traditions and possibly address the same community. As in the case of the Gospel, the author of these letters remains unknown.

First John clearly seems to be an attempt to clarify misunderstandings in the community concerning the human nature of Jesus as presented in the Gospel of John. The same controversy is addressed in 2 John; 3 John does not mention that issue but rather concerns itself with a specific issue of church government involving a man named Diotrephes.

The Gospel of John, as discussed in a previous chapter, presents Jesus in a way that is quite different from the Synoptic Gospels. In John, Jesus specifically offers miracles as "signs" of the messiahship and divine sonship he claims for himself. His humanity is affirmed by John—"the Word became flesh and lived among us"—but the greater emphasis is on his glory: "We have seen his glory, the glory as of a father's only son" (John 1:14). Apparently by the time of the writing of 1 John, some false teachers were asserting that Jesus was not human at all but only appeared to be so. So 1 John, in words reminiscent of the Gospel, says, "We declare to you what was from the beginning, what we have heard, what we have seen with our eyes, what we have looked at and touched with our hands"—in other words, the human Jesus (1:1).

What caused the need for such teaching? Certain forms of Greek philosophy taught that matter was evil and that only spirit was good. A similar dualism existed in some forms of Jewish thought in the first century. Good and evil, light and darkness, flesh and spirit—such concepts were part of the legacy of the Exile and also have been found to be particularly prominent in the Dead Sea Scrolls of the Qumran community. This same contempt for the material world characterized the Christian Gnostics, who believed that Jesus was divine, but not truly human because flesh was evil. Some kind of similar heresy seemed to be disrupting the churches in the community of John, although Gnosticism was not then fully developed. This teaching apparently was some form of docetism, the view that Jesus only appeared to be human. Because of its strong emphasis on the divine nature of Jesus, the Gospel of John was the favorite Christian writing of the Gnostics. Alarmed by their misunderstanding of the Gospel of John and their denial of the humanity of Jesus, John wrote to counter these false teachings by those he called "antichrists" (2:18, 22; 4:2-3).

John urged those to whom he was writing to "test the spirits to see whether they are from God. . . . By this you know the Spirit of God: every spirit that confesses that Jesus Christ has come in the flesh is from God" (1 John 4:1-2). The Gospel of John had indeed promised the Spirit to those who believed (John 14:26), but false teachers were claiming revelations from the Spirit that were inconsistent with the true nature of Jesus. Apparently some had followed these teachers and left the fellowship of the community: "They went out from us, but they did not belong to us" (1 John 2:19). John contrasts the conduct of the true children of God with the conduct of the children of darkness (3:1-2, 8-10). The principal difference is love: "Beloved, let us love one another, because love is from God; everyone who loves is born of God and knows God. Whoever does not love does not know God, for God is love" (4:7-8). Contrary to the Gnostic teachings, John reminds them that Christ will return. Those who live in God's love will have no reason to be ashamed (2:28). They should therefore love God and love one another: "Those who love God must love their brothers and sisters also" (4:21).

The same concern with error is present in 2 and 3 John. These are the shortest books in the New Testament, and both are clearly letters: 2 John is addressed to "the elect lady" (possibly a church, since some of her children were "walking in the truth" [v. 4]); 3 John is addressed to someone named Gaius. In 2 John "the elder" repeats the admonition to "love one another" (v. 5) and denounces those "who do not confess that Jesus Christ has come in the flesh" (v. 7). In 3 John the conflict centers upon a church leader named Diotrephes who refused to accept the authority of the elder and "who likes to put himself first" (v. 9). He refuses to welcome messengers from the elder and "even prevents those who want to do so and expels them from the church" (v. 10). Other New Testament writings reveal that such conflicts over authority were common in the developing institutional church.

The letters of 2 *Peter* and *Jude* apparently also deal with some form of early Gnosticism, although that is not as clear as it is in the letters of John. But whereas John urges love on the Christian community and seeks to assure them that they are God's children, 2 Peter and Jude attack their opponents, whoever they are, from all sides. Jude especially uses strong invective, calling them malcontents, grumblers, and passion-driven flatterers who try to take advantage of others (Jude 16). In only slightly gentler tones he calls them blemishes on the church's love-feasts; waterless clouds; fruitless, uprooted, twice-dead trees; wild waves of the sea, "casting up the foam of their own shame"; and wandering stars "for whom the deepest darkness has been reserved forever" (Jude 12-13). Whoever these opponents are, it is clear that they are insiders, members of the community. Jude warns the community against these false teachers who reject the church's leaders and urges the faithful "to contend for the faith that was once for all entrusted to the saints" (v. 3). An unusual feature of the book is that Jude quotes from two later, noncanonical Jewish apocalyptic writings, *1 Enoch* (Jude 6-15) and the *Assumption of Moses* (Jude 9). The author of Jude is unknown, though he calls himself "a brother of James."

Like Jude, 2 Peter is one of the latest New Testament writings. It seems to have been written after Jude because of its dependence on much of that letter. In fact, 2 Peter appears to be an expansion of Jude, adapted to the situation of the writer of 2 Peter. Although the name of Peter is attached to it, the book was produced by an unknown author and had great difficulty being accepted into the canon. Its situation and place of authorship, like those of Jude, are also unknown.

A striking feature of the book is its knowledge of other New Testament writings. The writer knows a collection of Paul's letters, which contain things "hard to understand," but he includes them among "the other scriptures" (3:15-16), probably meaning that he regards them as inspired. This in itself is strong evidence for a late date for the book. He also seems to have some knowledge of the Synoptics (1:17-18) and John (1:14). The principal emphasis of 2 Peter is on "scoffers" who questioned the return of Christ. The writer asserts that God is merciful, "not slow about his promise" in the delay of Christ's return, and that his return will be unexpected, "like a thief" (3:3-10). Like Jude—in fact, using many of his exact words—Peter reviles these opponents, adding invectives of his own as he calls them adulterers who are insatiable for sin, irrational animals, and slaves of corruption who have hearts trained in greed. He compares them to the proverbial dog that returns to its own vomit (2:10-22). In contrast, he urges the faithful to be "without spot or blemish" as they "wait for new heavens and a new earth, where righteousness is at home" (3:13-14).

Colossians is another book that is frequently described as opposing Gnosticism. Although it definitely centers upon heresy in the church, the nature of that heresy is unclear. Some "philosophy" or "tradition" (2:8) has arisen that urges certain Jewish ritual practices upon the church (circumcision, dietary laws, the observance of festivals and Sabbaths). But this emphasis on ritual and asceticism is coupled with the worship of angels and the exalting of "the elemental spirits of the universe" (2:18, 20). What is meant by that expression is uncertain, but it may imply that there were attempts to manipulate natural forces in the cosmos (the Greek word used here for universe). Colossians repudiates such efforts and reminds the church that in Christ "the whole fullness of deity dwells bodily" and that they "have come to fullness in him, who is the head of every ruler and authority" (2:9-10). In fact, Christ has triumphed over all such "rulers and authorities," stripping them of their powers and marching them (in the fashion of a Roman general's triumphal parade) in his own procession (2:15). The letter concludes with a lengthy section (2:16–4:6) on the ethical implications of this argument for the Christian life.

A major issue concerning Colossians is the question of authorship. Did Paul write it? Arguments are advanced on both sides. On one hand, the circumstances described in the letter correspond well with information in other Pauline letters regarding Paul's missionary work and imprisonment and could be fitted into the chronology of his life. On the other hand, the Greek language of Colossians differs significantly from that of the undisputed letters of Paul. Many terms unknown to Paul are used in Colossians, and many familiar terms and themes are missing. Overall, the letter seems to come from a later period in the

Figure 22.2. The area in the center of the photograph is the site of the ancient city of Colossae. The New Testament contains a letter to the Colossian church. *(Photograph by Mitchell G. Reddish)*

church than that in which Paul lived and worked, which suggests that someone within the circle of Paul wrote Colossians, rather than Paul himself.

The Question of the Return of Christ (2 Thessalonians)

Questions concerning the return of Christ surfaced quickly in the early church, apparently as soon as the first generation of Christians began to die without Christ having returned. What provision was made for them? Paul wrote 1 Thessalonians (likely his first letter) to reply to this question (1:9-10; 4:13-18).

The relationship of 2 *Thessalonians* to 1 Thessalonians, however, is not clear. It seems to have been written shortly after 1 Thessalonians, but the eschatology of 2 Thessalonians 2:1-12 does not correspond to 1 Thessalonians or, for that matter, to anything else Paul wrote. Apparently the Thessalonians have become agitated by the belief that the return of the Lord has already occurred rather than merely being delayed (as was the concern in 1 Thessalonians, which Paul wrote to encourage them about the certainty of Christ's return). Second Thessalonians urges them "not to be quickly shaken in mind" about Christ's return. In apocalyptic language they are told that a "rebellion" must come first and that the "lawless one," also called the "one destined for destruction," must be revealed; and "you know what is now restraining him, so that he may be revealed when his time comes." He will exalt himself above "every so-called god" and "[take] his seat in the temple of God, declaring himself to be God." This lawless one will display all powers and wonders, deluding those who refuse to love the truth, but "the Lord Jesus will destroy" him at his coming (2:2-12). Although interpreters have speculated on the identity of this "lawless one," the meaning of this passage remains obscure.

The authorship of this letter—more than that of any other letter of Paul— is hotly disputed by scholarship. Although some other smaller issues are debated, the question of the passage just cited is by far the key point of contention. Perhaps something Paul said in the first letter to the Thessalonians gave rise to their problem, or perhaps they were sent a deceptive letter by someone purporting to be Paul (2 Thess. 2:2). It is possible, of course, that Paul introduced such distinctive concepts (a rebellion, a lawless one, something restraining the lawless one) without any previous or subsequent allusions to them. But the apparent contradiction between the expectation of the sudden, imminent return of Christ expressed in 1 Thessalonians and the more structured scenario described in 2 Thessalonians (in which the Parousia must be preceded by certain apocalyptic events) has caused 2 Thessalonians to be disputed by many as a Pauline writing.

THE CHURCH ESTABLISHES ITS STRUCTURE
(1 and 2 Timothy, Titus, Ephesians)

The early fellowship of Jesus was noted for its lack of structure. In fact, the loosely gathered band of followers that traveled with Jesus may have served as an object lesson to contradict the hierarchical structures in Jerusalem—as a reminder of the twelve tribes of Israel, whose only leader was God alone. But questions of place and prominence among the disciples were not long in coming. Such matters were discussed among them, and James and John even asked Jesus for places of prominence at his right and left hands in his kingdom (Mark 10:35-37; in Matt. 20:20-21, it is their mother who asks it of Jesus). Mark reports that the remaining ten disciples became indignant at James and John when they heard of it (10:41). Jesus told them that such were the ways of the Gentiles, but it was not to be so among them; they were not to "lord it" over others as great ones. If they would be great, they must be servants (Mark 10:42-44).

Following the death of Judas, the disciples chose his successor. In the first church election they nominated two men, Justus and Matthias. Then they cast lots in the ancient manner of discerning God's will, and Matthias was chosen as an apostle (Acts 1:21-26). Subsequently the early church again was pushed toward organization, this time by complaints that there had been neglect of the Hellenistic widows in the church's charitable service. Seven men were chosen to tend to the distribution of food and other practical matters, allowing the apostles to devote their time to prayer and teaching. As subtle as these decisions were, they began the organizational process of the church. With the passage of time, however, the church faced many more complex questions of church structure.

Figure 22.3. This painting of Titus in the Basilica of St. Titus in Gortys, Crete, commemorates the tradition of Titus, a coworker with Paul, as a church leader in Crete. *(Photograph by Mitchell G. Reddish)*

The later writings of the New Testament reveal a focus on those issues.

The Organization of the Later Church (1 and 2 Timothy, Titus)

The three letters purportedly from Paul to his fellow workers Timothy and Titus are known as the Pastoral Epistles. As the name implies, these letters deal with pastoral matters in the church. Timothy and Titus are names known elsewhere in the New Testament. Paul first met Timothy in Lystra, where, according to Acts (16:1-3), he is already a Christian; both his mother and his grandmother are also Christians. He is portrayed as a trusted associate of Paul in his missionary efforts (1 Thess. 1:1; 1 Cor. 4:17; Phil. 2:19-24). Titus is nowhere named in Acts, but he is mentioned in Galatians as a Greek who accompanied Paul and Barnabas on Paul's second visit to Jerusalem (Gal. 2:1-10), and in 2 Corinthians he is described as a trusted figure in Paul's work in Corinth (2 Cor. 8:6; 7:5-16; 12:17-18).

At least four arguments have been raised against Pauline authorship of the Pastorals. First, the Pastorals were not included in the earliest canon of the church, nor are they present in the oldest manuscripts of the Greek New Testament (dating to the end of the second century).

Second, the language and vocabulary of the Pastorals are less typical of Paul's style than any of the other disputed New Testament writings sometimes attributed to him, including Colossians and Ephesians. More than 30 percent of the words in the Pastorals are not found in any of Paul's letters; only 5 percent are clearly Pauline.

Third, the circumstances concerning Timothy, Titus, and Paul described in the Pastorals do not correspond with events in the book of Acts.

Fourth, the theological perspective in the Pastorals is distinctly different from that seen in Paul's other writings. Paul's consistent use of faith as a relationship of unconditional commitment has shifted in the Pastorals to faith as doctrinal correctness. The practice of religious virtues or morality is indicated in the Pastorals by the use of the word *eusebia*. This term was commonly used by the Greeks to describe the worship of the gods but is unknown in the genuine writings of Paul, in which Paul consistently used *pistis* ("faith") and *agape* ("unconditional love") rather than *eusebia*. Those interpreters who still argue that Paul was the author of the Pastorals insist that these differences can be accounted for by the changed circumstances of these later letters, and that a chronology can be constructed that admits the additional events not mentioned in Acts. But the consensus of critical scholarship is that the Pastorals date to a period after the lifetime of Paul, possibly as late as the early second century.

Like other of the late New Testament epistles, the Pastorals combat false doctrine and urge proper conduct for Christians. They see proper behavior as resulting from correct understanding of doctrine and bad conduct as resulting from false doctrine (1 Tim. 1:3-10; 2 Tim. 3:2-8; Titus 1:15-16). The false teachers in the Pastorals insist on an asceticism that forbids marriage and certain foods (1 Tim. 4:1-3). This heresy was likely some form of early Gnosticism. Contrary to these teachings, the Pastorals affirm the goodness of creation: "For everything created by God is good, and nothing is to be rejected, provided it is received with thanksgiving" (1 Tim. 4:4). Christians are to live in this world as good citizens, obedient to government (Titus 3:1-2), "a model of good works" (Titus 2:7).

The distinctive emphasis of the Pastorals, however, is on the ministry of the church and the role and qualifications of officials in the church. Three titles are given to these officers, "bishop," "deacon," and "elder" (1 Tim. 3, 5), and their qualifications are described. "Bishops" (literally, "overseers") is always in the plural in the New Testament. They are said to need managerial ability (1 Tim. 3:4-5; Titus 1:5-9), but no description of their authority is given. Neither is there any indication of a single bishop presiding over a specific region. "Elders" are also said to "rule" in the church, and some of them, at least, "labor in preaching and teaching" (1 Tim. 5:17). In Titus (1:5-9) the titles of "bishop" and "elder" appear to be used interchangeably, denoting the same office. In any case, Titus was to appoint such leaders "in every town" (church) (1:5). "Deacons" serve the church (1 Tim. 3:10, 13), but how or in what capacity is not clear. In Greek usage the word originally meant a servant, one who waited tables, either a man or a woman; and in the later Greek religious observances it also had that meaning (on a pillar of a temple of Apollo, "deacons" were named among a list of temple attendants, following "cooks"). The roles of these officers undoubtedly underwent further development in the later church.

Guidance is given also to ministries for special groups in the Christian community, with considerable attention given to the needs of widows (1 Tim. 5:1-16). Furthermore, Timothy is admonished to "give attention to the public reading of scripture, to exhorting, to teaching"; whether "scripture" included more than the Hebrew Bible is not certain, though it is likely (1 Tim. 4:13). Timothy is to "put these things into practice," devoting himself to them.

The Pastoral Epistles, whatever their authorship, provide a rare and valuable glimpse into the needs and the ministries of the early Christian church.

The Unity of the Body of Christ (Ephesians)

The oldest manuscripts of the book of *Ephesians* do not designate Ephesus as its destination; it is addressed only to "the saints who are...faithful in Christ Jesus." This form of address designates it as a general epistle to all Christians rather than as one to a specific church. This fact would also explain its lack of

Figure 22.4. This 24,000-seat theater in Ephesus may have been the one into which Gaius and Aristarchus, Paul's companions, were dragged when a riot erupted over their promotion of the Christian faith (Acts 19). The road in the background led to the ancient harbor on the Aegean Sea. *(Photograph by Mitchell G. Reddish)*

references to specific local situations or persons. (The only name mentioned in Ephesians is Tychicus, a duplication of a reference from Colossians, which may be an indication of the dependence of Ephesians on Colossians; see Eph. 6:21 and Col. 4:7-8.) The contents of the letter are also general, making it more of a gathering of Pauline themes than a writing with specific intent.

Several features of the letter have caused Ephesians to be regarded as a writing by someone other than Paul. First, the other letters by Paul are all written to specific churches; they are not general epistles. Second, its vocabulary and syntax are markedly different from that of Paul. The sentences in Ephesians have an elaborate eloquence that is uncharacteristic of the sharp, impetuous sentences of Paul, which frequently become tangled or change thought abruptly in mid-sentence. Third, it is heavily dependent on Colossians; over one-half of Ephesians parallels passages in Colossians. (Some scholars have been convinced of the Pauline authorship of Colossians on that basis. In other words, the author of Ephesians must have regarded Colossians as Pauline to parallel it so closely.) Fourth, Ephesians displays a subtle but significant shift in certain of Paul's themes. For example, elsewhere in Paul Jesus Christ is the foundation of the church and the apostles are laborers who build on that foundation (1 Cor. 3:5-14), but in Ephesians they are the foundation of the church (Eph. 2:20). The overall effect of the writing implies a situation later than the time of Paul, when concerns of the church as an institution had taken center stage in the Christian movement.

Ephesians seems not to have an overall theme, but clearly a major focus of the book is an emphasis on the unity of the church in Christ, "the unity of the Spirit in the bond of peace" (4:3). That unity is the product of a divine plan, "the wisdom of God in its rich variety" (3:10), hidden from knowledge in ages past but now revealed to the church. Seven elements of unity are named: one body, one Spirit, one hope, one Lord, one faith, one baptism, and one "God and Father of all" (4:4-6). This unity in the church is "built upon the foundation of the apostles and prophets, with Christ Jesus himself as the cornerstone" (2:20). (Notice that the position of Christ is not lowered as the position of the apostles and prophets is emphasized.) Nevertheless, a subtle, incipient hierarchy is suggested by the order of these titles: apostles, prophets, evangelists [those who declare God's "good news"], pastors, and teachers (4:11).

The achievement of this unity requires two things of the church: "the knowledge of the Son of God" (4:13) and a life of "true righteousness and holiness" (4:24). A "new self" (4:24) has been granted to those who are in Christ, "created in Christ Jesus for good works" (2:10). The barriers between Jews and Gentiles have been broken down, and now a new person has been created in Christ, who "has made both groups into one and has broken down the dividing wall, that is, the hostility between us" (2:13-15). The result of this new reality for Christians should be a life consistent with their "new self, created according to the likeness of God in true righteousness and holiness" (4:24).

The latter portion of the book concludes with a series of ethical admonitions to the Body of Christ, the church, to "be imitators of God, as beloved children" and "to lead a life worthy" of their calling in Christ (4:1; 5:1). In anticipation of the long struggle in the world that the later church now awaited, Ephesians urges Christians to "put on the whole armor of God" to withstand the assaults of evil (6:10-17). The letter to the Ephesians undoubtedly contributed a strong word of encouragement and hope to the diverse elements in the church as they sought to find unity, harmony, and strength in a trying age.

THE CHURCH ENCOURAGES FIDELITY IN DIFFICULT TIMES
(Hebrews, 1 Peter)

Both Hebrews and 1 Peter are directed toward the fidelity of Christians in a difficult time. Outward circumstances have obviously become perilous for Christians. Hebrews and 1 Peter encourage Christians to hold fast their faith in spite of the hostility of the world. That encouragement primarily comes from the example of Christ as the true High Priest (Hebrews) and as the Suffering Servant (1 Peter).

Christ the High Priest (Hebrews)

The book of *Hebrews* is unique in its style, vocabulary, and argument. Although attributed early to Paul, the writing nowhere makes such a claim, and Hebrews is now almost unanimously regarded as pseudonymous. Except for Luke-Acts, the Greek style of Hebrews is superior to that of any other writing in the New Testament. Its ideas do not in the least resemble the other writings of Paul, not even as much as Ephesians or the Pastorals. The book is a tightly reasoned, complex argument unlike any other New Testament book. Its title is most likely a later addition based on inferences from the text. Its designated recipients are unknown. The book does not demand a Jewish audience to be understood, though it makes extensive use of Jewish customs and Scripture. Stylistically Hebrews is not an epistle at all, but a "word of exhortation" (13:22). Perhaps it is a sermon; more likely it is a theological treatise. The dating of the book is equally uncertain, though the circumstances seem to favor the latter part of the first century. (Since it does not mention the destruction of the Temple in 70 C.E., some would assign it an earlier date.) The author seems to indicate that he belongs to a later generation (2:3-4).

The structure of the book appears to follow a twofold division, with many complicated arguments along the way. The first portion of the book presents the superiority and finality of the High Priesthood of Jesus; the second portion consists of an exhortation to Christians to live lives worthy of the sacrifice of Christ. Apparently the Christians addressed by the author of Hebrews are tempted to give up their faith (2:3); they feel that they cannot hold out against the pressures upon them (3:14; 10:36-39). Some are "neglecting to meet together" (10:25), but they are enjoined to "hold fast...without wavering" (10:23). The book warns of the irreversible consequences of turning away from the faith (10:26-31).

The principal encouragement to those in this situation is the magnificent sacrifice of Christ on their behalf. Superior to that of angels or earthly High Priests, the sacrifice of Christ through his death on the cross provided a once-for-all offering. Unlike the offerings of earthly priests, this sacrifice need never be repeated (9:25-26). It provides a new covenant, a superior covenant that, as promised by the prophets, is written on the hearts of the faithful (8:8-13). The essence of the argument of Hebrews is captured in Hebrews 9:23-28, as the author of Hebrews uniquely blends Hellenistic terms and thought with Jewish customs and Scripture:

> Thus it was necessary for the sketches of the heavenly things to be purified with these rites, but the heavenly things themselves need better sacrifices than these. For Christ did not enter a sanctuary made by human hands, a mere copy of the true one, but he entered into heaven itself, now to appear in the presence of God on our

behalf. Nor was it to offer himself again and again, as the high priest enters the Holy Place year after year with blood that is not his own; for then he would have had to suffer again and again since the foundation of the world. But as it is, he has appeared once for all at the end of the age to remove sin by the sacrifice of himself. And just as it is appointed for mortals to die once, and after that the judgment, so Christ, having been offered once to bear the sins of many, will appear a second time, not to deal with sin, but to save those who are eagerly waiting for him.

Chapter 11, perhaps the best-known section of Hebrews, has been called "the roll call of the faithful." Many of the figures of the Hebrew Scriptures—Abel, Noah, Abraham, Moses, Rahab—and incidents from more recent Jewish history

Figure 22.5. This fourth-century C.E. mosaic from Antakya (ancient Antioch) in Turkey depicts a scene of a drunken Dionysus, the Greek god of wine. The cult of Dionysus was one of the popular mystery religions. (*Photograph by Mitchell G. Reddish*)

are presented as models of endurance under difficult circumstances. The chapter is a descriptive, colorful relief in the midst of a complicated intellectual argument.

The arguments of Hebrews might not be as persuasive to the modern reader as they were when they were written, but the encouragement of this book spoke a deeply provocative and supportive word to Christians—Jewish or Gentile—facing the overwhelming might of the Roman Empire.

Encouragement to Aliens: 1 Peter

The epistle known as *1 Peter* shares with Hebrews the encouragement of Christians in difficult circumstances. In this case, however, the author addresses himself to the church as a group of new converts, who no doubt were feeling estranged from their previous society as "aliens and exiles" (2:11). (This emphasis on those who are "born anew" [1:23], who are compared to "newborn infants" [2:2], and who are reminded of those in Noah's day who were "saved through water" [3:20] as "baptism . . . now saves you . . . as an appeal to God" [3:21] has caused some interpreters to regard this as a baptismal sermon. But its message appears to be broader than that.) They are urged to live in hope because of the resurrection of Christ (1:21). Christ is the cornerstone of the church, and his followers are described as "living stones" in the house of God (2:4-8). Moreover, they are called "a chosen race, a royal priesthood, a holy nation, God's own people" (2:9).

This encouragement is not to exalt them but to lead believers to the true worship of God and to proper conduct in the world. Surprisingly, perhaps, they are told to live in harmony with and obedience to their government, even to "honor the emperor" (2:17). Suffering may well be the result, but they have the example of Christ, God's suffering servant, before them (2:18-25; 3:9-17; 4:1-2, 12-16). In all their trials they are told to "cast all your anxiety on him [God], because he cares for you" (5:7). Though they suffer, they are promised that God will "restore, support, strengthen, and establish you" (5:10).

Like other of the later New Testament writings, the authorship of 1 Peter is uncertain. The elevated Greek in which it is written seems unlikely for an uneducated Galilean fisherman. Some interpreters disagree and credit its use to his secretary for the letter, Silvanus, or Silas (5:12). If he is the Silas in Acts (15:22), however, he also was a Palestinian unlikely to know such Greek. Furthermore, the letter gives no indication of first-person knowledge of Jesus, as we might expect from an eyewitness such as Peter. The letter may have been written from Rome, if "Babylon" is a cryptic reference to that city (5:13). In any case, it seems to be a circular letter directed to the churches of northern Asia Minor.

In spite of its disputed origin, 1 Peter is a writing that has held the respect

Figure 22.6. The region of Cappadocia in modern Turkey was the location of several Christian communities. The author of 1 Peter addresses his letter to Christians in five Roman provinces of Asia Minor, including Cappadocia. (Photograph by Mitchell G. Reddish)

and devotion of Christians from the earliest days of the church until today.

THE DIVINE-HUMAN ENCOUNTER: KEEPING THE FAITH IN LATER GENERATIONS

Jesus and his first followers led a wandering life of preaching, teaching, and healing. They had no organized religious system, no creedal agreements, and no hierarchy. In many ways their movement was a protest against the complex Jerusalem establishment and a call to a more direct, more intimate experience of God. Not surprisingly, the early church began as an unstructured charismatic movement, ever attracting more followers with its single-minded commitment to God and to one another.

But inevitably the church had to define itself, and in the process of refining its structure and its beliefs the young church modified its understanding of the divine-human encounter. The later church of the New Testament period produced a considerable body of writings to deal with these issues. Six emphases characterize these writings:

1. *A greater emphasis on faith as right doctrine.* Because of their opposition to early Gnosticism, the church felt a need to establish the right interpretation of the meaning of the life and teachings of Christ for his followers. For these later Christians, "faith" therefore came to mean right belief about God, whereas for Jesus it had meant right relationship with God. This change was exactly the same as that made by Israel after the Exile, when they felt the need to interpret the early experience of the Hebrews and the teachings of Moses. Like the intricate legal and cultic system developed by Judaism following the Exile, the later church also developed a more complex doctrinal and ecclesiastical system.
2. *A new emphasis on Christian writings as Scripture.* As the oral transmission of the gospel was supplanted by written documents, the concept of "Scripture" (inspired writings) began to be attached to Christian writings as well as to the Hebrew Scriptures. But this did not completely solve the church's problem of establishing correct teachings, because their need for correct interpretation of these Scriptures was just as great.
3. *A new emphasis on authority in the church.* In the writings of Paul, Jesus was always named as the foundation of the church. Later writings continued to acknowledge the headship of Christ (as the cornerstone of the "building" [the church] or the keystone in an arch), but a new emphasis called the apostles the foundation of the church. Furthermore, the need for a division of labor in the church introduced the offices of deacon (for practical duties) and elder/bishop (for administration, preaching, and teaching), which in subsequent centuries led to a complex hierarchy of offices.
4. *A renewed emphasis on the humanity of Jesus.* To counter the claims of docetism, which insisted that Jesus only "seemed" to be human, some later writings of the developing church renewed the church's insistence on the humanity of Jesus.
5. *A new emphasis on the superiority of Christ's sacrifice.* For the first time, Christ was presented as a High Priest (Hebrews), and the superiority of his once-for-all sacrifice was emphasized in contrast to the repeated sacrifices of other religions. The divine-human relationship was thereby rendered more stable than ever before. But Christians were also given warnings against the attendant danger of taking that relationship for granted and not living a life consistent with their faith.
6. *An increased emphasis on patient endurance in faith.* The church found itself facing unexpected years of waiting for the return of Christ. These later New Testament writings urged Christians to endure patiently in the face of internal strife within the church and external pressures from a hostile society. Those increasing pressures will be examined more fully in the following chapter.

Chapter 23

THE CHURCH IN CONFLICT

Suggested Biblical Readings: Revelation 1–7; 12:1–14:13; 19:1–22:5

The early Christian community faced internal and external struggles during the latter half of the first century in its attempt to define itself and its place in society. As the examinations of the New Testament writings in the previous chapters have already shown, internally the church was forced to deal with the issues of doctrine and church administration. Externally, as Christianity moved into the Greco-Roman world, conflict between Judaism and Christianity led to the complete separation of these two groups. Additionally, Christians encountered sporadic opposition from the Roman government. Chapter 23 will explore these external issues, giving special attention to the book of Revelation as a Christian response to the conflict between the church and the Roman Empire.

CONFLICT WITH JUDAISM

The first external struggles that confronted the early Christian church arose with the Jewish community. The Christian church was born and reared in Judaism. Jesus was Jewish, all his disciples were Jewish, the earliest converts to Christianity were Jewish, and Paul was Jewish. Most of the early Christians likely understood themselves as still being Jewish. Added to their Jewish faith was their belief in Jesus as the Messiah. At the outset, the Jewish people also seem to have accepted the Christians as another variation in the multifaceted Judaism of the first century C.E. The earliest Christians continued to worship in the Temple and the synagogues and to adhere to certain Jewish practices.

Developing Tensions

Despite the affinities between Christianity and Judaism, the letters of Paul and the book of Acts portray the conflicts and tensions that began to develop between them. Acts reports that Peter, John, and the other apostles were arrested, imprisoned, and stoned by the Jewish authorities due to their Christian preaching (3:1–4:22; 5:12-42). Violent action against the church also occurred when Stephen, after his denunciation of the Jews because of their rejection of Jesus, was stoned to death (Acts 6:8–8:1; whether his death was an official action of the Sanhedrin or simply the result of mob violence is unclear). According to Acts, the death of Stephen, the first Christian martyr, led to a great persecution of the church in Jerusalem. One of the individuals involved in this persecution was Paul

Figure 23.1. Vespasian (left) began the siege of Jerusalem (66 C.E.) and was named emperor of Rome (69 C.E.). His son, Titus (right), took over the siege and conquered Jerusalem. He was subsequently named emperor (79 C.E.). (*Photographs by Mitchell G. Reddish*)

(also called Saul), who later became one of the chief proponents of the Christian faith. Although Paul often preached in Jewish synagogues and as a result convinced some Jews of the validity of the Christian message, his preaching also on occasion angered the members of Jewish communities. The book of Acts reports several incidents in which Paul and his companions were imprisoned, stoned, or driven out of town by antagonistic Jews (see also 1 Thess. 2:14-16).

Sometime around 41 C.E. Herod Agrippa I initiated a persecution against some of the Christians in Jerusalem. Acts reports that James, the brother of John and one of the twelve disciples, was martyred by Herod Agrippa. (James is the only disciple of Jesus whose death is recounted in the New Testament.) The reasons for Agrippa's persecution of the church are unclear. Acts 12:3, however, reports that his actions pleased the religious authorities, which motivated him to continue his persecution.

James, the brother of Jesus and leader of the Jerusalem church, also suffered a martyr's death. Around 62 C.E. (or perhaps three or four years later) James was executed in Jerusalem. Two separate accounts describe his death. One comes from Josephus, the Jewish historian, who says that James, along with certain others, was stoned to death on the orders of Ananus, the new High Priest. The charge against James, according to Josephus, was that he had "transgressed the law." Josephus goes on to report that "the inhabitants of the city who were considered the most fair-minded and who were strict in observance of the law were offended" by the actions of Ananus (*Antiquities of the Jews* 20.9.1; Louis H. Feldman, trans.; Loeb Classical Library). The other account of the death of James comes from Eusebius, a fourth-century historian of the church who is dependent upon the work of Hegesippus, a second-century church historian. According to this version, James was killed by mob action led by the Jewish scribes and Pharisees after he declared Jesus to be the Son of Man. Although the two accounts do not agree in details (the account of Josephus is usually considered more accurate), they do concur that the death of James was the result of animosity between Jews and Christians in Jerusalem.

The effect of the Jewish-Roman War of 66–74 C.E. and the subsequent destruction of the Temple on Jewish-Christian relations is uncertain. Eusebius states that the Christians, being commanded by an oracle, fled Jerusalem prior to its fall and went to the town of Pella in Perea across the Jordan River. The historical reliability of this tradition is questionable. No evidence exists to confirm such a flight to Pella. The roles played by Jewish Christians during the Jewish Revolt probably were diverse. Some Jewish Christians, feeling a sense of loyalty and national obligation, likely fought alongside the Jews of Jerusalem against the Romans. Others certainly fled Jerusalem if they were able, some possibly going to Pella. The failure of some Jewish Christians to fight against the Romans probably heightened the tensions between Jews and Christians, for such behavior would have been interpreted as traitorous. Later Christian writers would interpret the fall of Jerusalem as divine punishment on the Jews for their rejection of Jesus or for the execution of James. Even the Gospels, with their apocalyptic predictions of the fall of Jerusalem, seem to imply that the destruction of Jerusalem and the Temple was part of the divine plan.

The Split Between Synagogue and Church

No single event can be cited as the cause for the final rupture between Judaism and Christianity. Likewise, no precise date can be given for this schism. Evidence from Jewish and Christian sources, however, yields the conclusion that by the end of the first century an irrevocable break was occurring. Within Judaism, one of the sections of the synagogue liturgy that was repeated three times a day was a prayer known as the Eighteen Benedictions. The twelfth benediction (in reality a malediction, or curse) asks that "the Nazarenes and the heretics perish quickly; and may they be erased from the Book of Life; and may they not be inscribed with the righteous" (Emil Schürer, *The History of the Jewish People in the Age of Jesus Christ Vol. 2.* Rev. and ed. by Geza Vermes, Fergus Millar, and Matthew Black [Edinburgh: T & T Clark, 1979], p. 12). (The term "Nazarenes" is likely a reference to Christians.) This curse is usually thought to have been added to the liturgy around 85–90 C.E. If that is true (and if it was truly aimed at Jewish Christians), then the existence of this public curse against Christians is a strong indication that the break between Judaism and Christianity was becoming a reality. No Jewish Christian could continue to attend worship in the synagogue for long when a part of the liturgy involved a public condemnation of Christians.

Other evidence of a definite schism is found in the Gospels, particularly in Matthew and John. Scholars have often noted the hostility in Matthew toward Judaism. On several occasions Matthew refers to the Jewish synagogues as "their" synagogues or "your" synagogues, thus distancing himself and the Christian community from Judaism (see Matt. 4:23; 9:35; 10:17; 12:9; 13:54; 23:34). Furthermore, the readers are warned against Jewish persecution (10:17-23). The Gospel of John is even more pointed in its treatment of Jewish-Christian relations. John 9:22 states that "the Jews had already agreed that anyone who confessed Jesus to be the Messiah would be put out of the synagogue" (see 12:42; 16:2). Virtually all commentators understand this remark as reflecting the situation of John's time rather than the situation during the time of Jesus. If, indeed, John accurately depicts the prevailing conditions in some synagogues during his time, then one can conclude that by the end of the first century, at least in some communities, the split between Judaism and Christianity was occurring.

Two primary factors contributed to the break between the two groups. The first was the Christian conviction that Jesus of Nazareth was the Christ, the Messiah of eschatological expectation. Through his life and death, they proclaimed, humanity was freed from the power of sin and reconciled to God. By proclaiming Jesus to be the Messiah, Christians had redefined the traditional Jewish concept of the Messiah. For Christians, the Messiah was no longer a political, military figure who would defeat the enemies of the Jews and reestablish Israel as a mighty nation. Instead, the Messiah was the one who had suffered and died in order to bring salvation to the world. Belief in Jesus and commitment to his teachings brought salvation and new life, both in this life and after death. The second factor was the inclusiveness of the Christian movement. The Christian faith was directly accessible to all people, both Jew and Gentile, apart from the rituals of Judaism. In Christ, all outward distinctions were abolished. God's covenant relationship was based on individual response to God's initiative of grace, irrespective of the circumstances of one's birth or one's faithfulness to the Jewish religious system. The decision made by the Christian church that a person did not have to be Jewish to be Christian rendered a rupture between the two groups inevitable.

From the Christian perspective, the Jews were guilty of rejecting God's offer of salvation in Jesus. From the Jewish perspective, the Christians were guilty of heresy by attributing divine status to one other than Yahweh and by violating the requirements of the covenant as described in the Torah. The split between Judaism and Christianity was a process more than an event. Given their different perspectives, however, the outcome was virtually unavoidable.

CONFLICT WITH ROME

For the first few decades of the Christian church, the conflicts it faced were internal disputes or struggles with Judaism. The Roman government took no action against Christians, who seemed to them to be only another sect within Judaism. In fact, the power and stability of the Roman government were great assets for the early Christians. Good roads, safer land and sea travel, and relative peace throughout the empire contributed to the rapid spread of the Christian message throughout the Mediterranean world. Paul, writing in Romans 13:1-7, urged his readers to respect and obey the government authorities because they have been appointed by God and act as God's servants to punish wrongdoers.

Peaceful relations between the church and Rome were not to continue for long, however. Although no concerted, empire-wide persecution of Christians by the government occurred during the first two centuries, sporadic, isolated incidents of persecution did endanger the church. Incidents from the reigns of four emperors illustrate the main conflicts between Christians and the Roman government during this period.

Claudius (41–54 C.E.)

Suetonius, a Roman historian, writing around 120 C.E. about the actions of the Roman emperor Claudius around 49 C.E., says, "Since the Jews constantly made disturbances at the instigation of Chrestus, he expelled them from Rome" (*Claudius* 25,4; J C Rolfe, trans.; Loeb Classical Library). The name "Chrestus" is usually understood as a misspelling of *Christus*, the Latin word for Christ. The situation described by Suetonius was apparently disturbances in the Jewish section of Rome due to the presence and spread of Christianity among the Jews Acts 18:2 refers to this expulsion of Jews from Rome: in Corinth Paul meets Aquila and Priscilla, who have recently come from Italy "because Claudius had ordered all Jews to leave Rome." This incident should not be viewed as government action against Christians, however. Claudius's edict was directed at Jews. Any Christians who were expelled were expelled as Jews, not as Christians. The Roman government does not seem to have made a distinction at this time between Jews and Christians. That step first occurred under Nero.

Figure 23.2. Roman Emperors during New Testament times

Augustus	27 B.C.E.–14 C.E.
Tiberius	14–37 C.E.
Gaius Caligula	37–41 C.E.
Claudius	41–54 C.E.
Nero	54–68 C.E.
Galba	June 68–January 69 C.E.
Otho	69 C.E.
Vitellius	69 C.E.
Vespasian	69–79 C.E.
Titus	79–81 C.E.
Domitian	81–96 C.E.
Nerva	96–98 C.E.
Trajan	98–117 C.E.
Hadrian	117–138 C.E.

Nero (54–68 C.E.)

Ancient Christian traditions claim that both Paul and Peter suffered martyrdom in Rome during the reign of Nero. Although the reliability of these traditions is uncertain, Nero's reputation as a persecutor of the church is well founded. In 64 C.E. a major fire ravaged a portion of Rome. According to the Roman historian Tacitus, Nero needed a scapegoat for the fire and so blamed the Christians, imposing cruel punishments on them in retaliation. Tacitus says that the Christians arrested by Nero "were covered with wild beasts' skins and torn to death by dogs; or they were fastened on crosses, and, when daylight failed were burned to serve as lamps by night" (*Annals* 15.44; John Jackson, trans.; Loeb Classical Library). The number of Christians affected by Nero's actions is unknown. Tacitus claimed that "vast numbers were convicted." Nero's actions are usually viewed as the earliest evidence of a distinction being made between Jews and Christians by the Roman government.

Domitian (81–96 C.E.)

Christian tradition remembers Domitian as one of the early persecutors of the Christian church. Eusebius, in his *Ecclesiastical History,* referred to Domitian as "the successor of Nero's campaign of hostility to God. He was the second to promote persecution against us" (*Ecclesiastical History* 3.17; Kirsopp Lake, trans.; Loeb Classical Library). Little evidence exists, however, to support this claim. The incidents of persecution by Domitian that are often cited are open to various interpretations. The most one can say is that ancient sources contain possible references to Christian persecution under Domitian, but certainty does not exist.

The best evidence for persecution of Christians during the time of Domitian is provided by the book of Revelation, which was most likely written during Domitian's reign. The author of the book has apparently been banished to Patmos on account of his Christian faith (1:9). The book itself is dominated by the idea of a life-or-death struggle between Rome and the church. Rome is the great beast that makes "war on the saints" (13:7). In another image, Rome is the great harlot, "drunk with the blood of the saints and the blood of the witnesses to Jesus" (17:6). One of

Figure 23.3. This head belonged to a colossal statue (perhaps twenty-five feet tall) in Ephesus of Domitian, Roman emperor from 81 to 96 C.E., who was viewed by the author of Revelation as the archenemy of the church. (Some scholars claim the statue portrays Titus, Domitian's brother.) *(Photograph by Mitchell G. Reddish)*

the major issues in the work is emperor worship. John describes the situation in Asia Minor as one in which participation in the cult of emperor worship was required. Those who refused were killed (13:15). Allowance should be made for John's use of hyperbole here. We have no evidence that emperor worship was required of all citizens. There was certainly social pressure to participate, and in cases in which Christians were brought before the local authorities on other charges, they may have been required to offer a sacrifice to the emperor or to the Roman gods. Those who refused may have been executed. The extent of persecution during the time of Domitian is unclear. It may have been limited to sporadic, local persecutions that were few in number. John saw in these few conflicts, however, the beginnings of an inevitable clash. The description of Domitian given by Roman historians is certainly consistent with the image of him as a persecutor of the church. He is portrayed as distrustful and suspicious, greedy for power, a cruel tyrant who ruthlessly persecuted his opponents and was a promoter of the emperor cult. One must use these sources cautiously, however. These Roman historians were biased against Domitian, and thus their descriptions of him may not be historically accurate.

Trajan (98–117 c.e.)

During the time of Trajan several instances of persecution occurred. Ignatius, bishop of Antioch in Syria, was arrested and transported to Rome, where he was executed. Even though Ignatius wrote letters to churches along the way from Antioch to Rome, he never mentions the reason for his arrest and persecution. The most revealing information about the persecution of Christians during Trajan's reign comes from correspondence between Trajan and Pliny the Younger, governor of Pontus-Bithynia in Asia Minor. Around 112 c.e. Pliny wrote to Trajan asking for guidance in the prosecution of Christians who were brought before him. Pliny's policy was that they were to be given a chance to renounce their faith and make an offering to the emperor. Anyone who refused was to be executed, because "stubbornness and unshakeable obstinacy ought not to go unpunished" (Pliny, *Epistles* 10.96; Betty Radice, trans.; Loeb Classical Library). Trajan's reply affirmed Pliny's practice and advised that Christians were not to be sought out but were to be punished only when brought to the attention of the authorities. Pliny's letter reports that in the past he had indeed executed some Christians who had stubbornly refused to renounce their faith, although no indication is given of how many Christians were involved.

Christians were often in a precarious position in the first century. Although being a Christian was apparently not in itself illegal, Christians were at times suspected of illegal activities by their neighbors. Misunderstandings of the Christian celebration of the Lord's Supper led to accusations of cannibalism. Misunderstandings of their love-feasts (or *agape* meals) and their custom of calling each other "brother" and "sister" led to accusations of incest. Their failure to participate in the worship of the various gods and goddesses commonly worshiped by their neighbors led to their being called atheists. Their failure to participate in emperor worship led to accusations of treason. Tacitus expressed

Figure 23.4. Trajan, Roman emperor from 98–117 C.E. Several instances of governmental persecution of Christians are mentioned during the time of Trajan. (*Photograph by Mitchell G. Reddish*)

the attitude of many people toward the Christians when he said they were "loathed for their vices" and were guilty of "hatred of the human race" (*Annals* 15.44; John Jackson, trans.; Loeb Classical Library). Suetonius calls Christianity a "mischievous superstition" (*Nero* 16.2; J. C. Rolfe; Loeb Classical Library). This apparently widespread belief in the criminal activities of the Christians, along with their stubbornness before the authorities, was perhaps reason enough for the sporadic instances of persecution against Christians in the first century. By the early part of the second century, as Pliny's letter to Trajan indicates, the situation had changed. Persecution for "the name" alone (that is, for simply being a Christian) had begun.

Besides the book of Revelation, which will be explored in some detail below, two writings in the New Testament seem to make reference to persecution by the government. In neither case is the date or circumstance of the persecution clearly discernible. Hebrews 10:32-39 exhorts the readers to endure present difficulties by remembering the times in the past when they suffered public abuse and affliction, imprisonment, and plundering of their property. In 1 Peter the motif of persecution and suffering is particularly strong. Throughout the letter the readers are warned about the persecution that is already present or is imminent (1:6; 3:13-17; 4:12-19; 5:9-10). The readers are encouraged to remain steadfast, rejoicing that they thus have an opportunity to share Christ's sufferings (4:13). The author exhorts the readers to live exemplary lives, so that if anyone is persecuted it will be because he or she is suffering as Christians and not as "a murderer, a thief, a criminal, or even as a mischief maker" (4:15). Earlier he even directs them to be subject to the governing authorities and to honor the emperor (2:13-17). Though the government was apparently persecuting some Christians, the author still encourages them to be obedient. His viewpoint is somewhat similar to the position of Paul expressed in Romans 13:1-7. This benevolent attitude toward the government and the social order is shattered, however, in the New Testament writing that deals most extensively with persecution and martyrdom: the book of Revelation.

A RESPONSE TO PERSECUTION: THE BOOK OF REVELATION

For most readers the book of Revelation, the last book in the Bible, is the most mysterious and enigmatic writing in the New Testament. It is also the most misunderstood. The images of grotesque beasts, cosmic warfare, and unexplained symbolism leave many readers puzzled about the message of this writing. In order to gain a better understanding of the work, one needs to examine its literary and historical contexts.

Figure 23.5. The island of Patmos off the coast of modern Turkey was the place where John, the author of Revelation, was apparently exiled. *(Photograph by Mitchell G. Reddish)*

Literary Context

What type of writing is the book of Revelation? Because it contains both a salutation (1:4-8) and a closing (22:21), which were common in ancient letters, and chapters 2–3 are composed of seven messages addressed to different churches, some scholars have classified the work as a letter. On the other hand, the work itself claims to be a prophecy (1:3). When viewed in its entirety, however, Revelation clearly belongs to the category of apocalyptic literature. In fact, the book of Revelation (also called the Apocalypse) provided the name for this type of literature because the term "apocalyptic" is derived from the first word in the Greek manuscripts of Revelation—*apocalypsis,* which means "revelation." Like the book of Daniel in the Hebrew Bible, then, Revelation is literature in which cosmic and eschatological secrets are revealed through visions to a human recipient by an otherworldly mediator. In common with other apocalyptic writings, the book of Revelation makes extensive use of symbolism and mythology. Also, like many apocalyptic writings, Revelation is crisis literature, written to offer hope and comfort to people who are struggling to remain faithful to their religious convictions in the face of intense opposition. The historical context of Revelation that precipitated this crisis will be discussed below.

One major difference, however, between Revelation and most apocalyptic writings is that Revelation is not pseudonymous. Its author, John, chose to write under his own name. Nothing is known about the author except what can be gleaned from the book of Revelation itself. John was a well-respected Christian leader, a prophet, among the churches in Asia Minor. He wrote with authority and expected his exhortations to be followed. Although later tradition identified the author with John, the disciple of Jesus, that identification is almost certainly incorrect. He never calls himself an apostle; in fact, his reference to the apostles implies that he is not one of them (21:14). He informs his readers that when he received this revelation he was on the island of Patmos "because of the word of God and the testimony of Jesus" (1:9). This statement is usually understood to mean that John had been exiled to the island of Patmos, one of a group of islands off the coast of Asia Minor, on account of his Christian faith. Some of these islands in the Aegean Sea were used by the Romans as penal colonies, where certain criminals were sent. To understand why John preserved and circulated this revelation he received on Patmos, the historical setting of the work must be closely examined.

Historical Context

The book of Revelation was obviously written in Asia Minor. Patmos, the island where John was exiled, lies off the coast of Asia Minor, and the seven cities to whose churches the prophetic messages are addressed (chapters 2–3) are all located in Asia Minor. The best evidence for dating the writing of the work comes from the comment of the second-century church leader Irenaeus, who stated that John had received this revelation at the end of Domitian's reign. The book is usually assigned a date, then, around 95 C.E.

The situation of John and his readers described in the book of Revelation is consistent with a date for the work during the reign of Domitian. One of the concerns of the author of Revelation was the threat of persecution of Christians by the government. The cause for this persecution was the refusal of Christians to participate in the cult of emperor worship (chapter 13). The refusal of Christians to participate appeared treasonous. To the Christians, however, to participate in emperor worship was to offer allegiance and obedience to Rome that belonged to God alone. Thus some of them refused to make an offering to the emperor and were persecuted. (The Jews also refused to participate, but they had been granted an exemption from emperor worship.) The extent of this persecution is unknown. As noted above, no evidence for a massive persecution of Christians during the reign of Domitian exists. The persecution that did exist was likely due to the desire of provincial governors or local magistrates to flatter and impress Domitian. They therefore promoted the emperor cult in their own areas. In Asia Minor during the

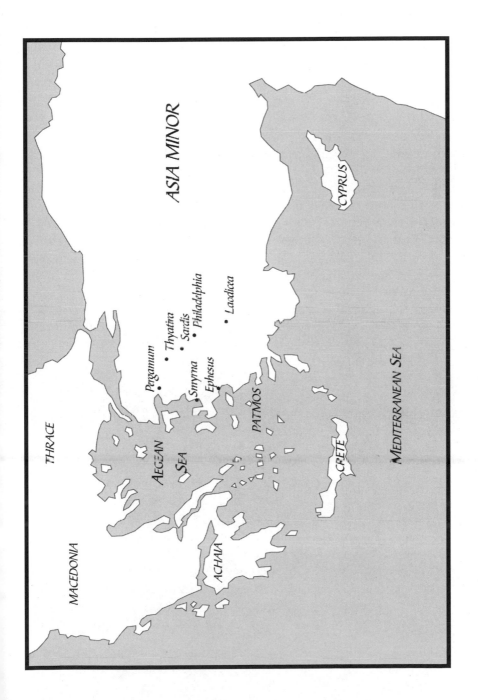

Figure 23.6. Locations of the island of Patmos and the seven churches addressed in Revelation.

time of Domitian the imperial cult was particularly strong. For example, the authorities at Ephesus were granted permission to build a temple to honor Domitian as a god. Even though actual persecution may have been sporadic and limited, from John's perspective the problem was a major crisis confronting the church and it needed to be addressed. John fears that some Christians will willingly compromise their faith under the pressure of persecution. John's revelation is addressed to this first-century situation of anticipated (and partially realized) persecution and martyrdom. He writes to exhort his readers to be faithful, challenging them to accept martyrdom, if necessary, for the sake of their beliefs.

Although persecution and emperor worship are major concerns for John, they are in essence specific instances of a larger concern in Revelation, that of cultural accommodation. How far could the church go in adapting and accepting the prevailing culture without losing its own distinctiveness and identity? The messages to the seven churches in chapters 2 and 3 demonstrate that some of John's readers already have been guilty of participating in the rituals or activities of some of the other religions of their culture, as well as of eating food that had been sacrificed to idols. Chapter 18 urges the Christians to separate themselves from Rome's extravagance and oppression. For John, cultural accommodation by

Figure 23.7. Restored bath-gymnasium complex from the second century C.E. at Sardis in modern Turkey. The church at Sardis was one of the seven churches in Asia Minor addressed by the author of Revelation. *(Photograph by Mitchell G. Reddish)*

Christians endangered their standing as a part of the people of God. Through the mysterious symbols and imagery of apocalyptic thought, John sought to encourage his readers to be faithful to God and to reassure them that, in a world seemingly dominated by evil, God would ultimately prevail.

Literary Structure and Contents

The contents of the book of Revelation are structured around groups of sevens: seven prophetic messages, seven seals, seven trumpets, and seven bowls. The book may be outlined as follows:

I. Prologue (1:1-8)
II. The prophet's call (1:9-20)
III. The messages to the seven churches (2–3)
IV. The heavenly vision (4–5)
V. The seven seals (6:1–8:5)
VI. The seven trumpets (8:6–11:19)
VII. The great conflict (12–14)
VIII. The seven bowls of wrath (15–16)
IX. The fall of the great city (17:1–19:10)
X. The victory of Christ (19:11–20:15)
XI. The new Jerusalem (21:1–22:5)
XII. Epilogue (22:6-21)

Through his visionary reports, John describes catastrophic events leading up to and including the final earthly conflict between good and evil, when Christ and his forces will be triumphant. John's arrangement of this material is not strictly chronological, however. John presents overlapping scenes of punishment, destruction, and triumph. His work has been compared to a well-orchestrated symphony in which the same musical theme is presented with several variations. The theme is explored from different perspectives, with each presentation adding a new dimension to the work. There is a chronological progression in John's material, but it is not a linear progression. Rather, the work advances in spiral fashion, recapitulating earlier themes as it moves forward.

The reader of Revelation needs to appreciate John's artistic imagination. His work is more impressionistic than descriptive, more akin to poetry than prose, overwhelming the senses with visual and auditory images. The total effect of those images is more important than the interpretive details of any one symbol. The message of the book can best be grasped, then, through a reading that, while sensitive to the first-century context of the work, is also open to the power of symbols to communicate and motivate. Any interpretation of Revelation that is chained to a literal reading of the text is certain to obscure rather than reveal the message of John's vision.

The prologue establishes that the revelation contained in the book originated with God and was mediated to John by an angel. Furthermore, the events that John describes are expected to take place soon, "for the time is near" (1:3). In common with many apocalyptic writers, John saw himself as living in the last days of history. The remainder of chapter 1 (vv. 9-20) details John's experience of being called to deliver God's message, which was similar to the call experiences of the Hebrew prophets. The exalted Christ ("one like the Son of Man") appears to John and directs him to write messages to seven of the leading churches in Asia Minor. (These prophetic messages are often called letters, but they do not have the literary form of letters in the ancient world. They are more like prophetic messages or imperial edicts.) The contents of these messages are given in chapters 2 and 3. The proclamations follow a similar pattern in which each church is praised for a particular virtue it possesses, followed by words of criticism and warning about failures in the church. Each prophetic message concludes with an eschatological promise for those believers who remain faithful to Christ. Chapters 2 and 3 reveal that John is not only concerned about the external threat of persecution facing the church but also anxious about the problems of false teachings and false teachers within the church.

Chapters 4 and 5 present John's spectacular vision of the heavenly throne room, where God is surrounded by various heavenly beings who continually offer up praise and adoration. God holds a scroll containing the divine purposes for the world. No one is able to open the seven seals on the scroll except the Lamb (Christ). When the first four seals are opened, four horsemen ride forth, symbols of worldwide destruction. The fifth seal offers a word of encouragement and patience for those who have been martyred. The sixth seal brings about cataclysmic destruction on the earth, followed by a promise of assurance for "the 144,000," a symbol of the group of faithful believers. The opening of the seventh seal introduces another series of seven, the blowing of seven trumpets.

The blowing of the first six trumpets brings about judgment on the earth in the form of destructive plagues, somewhat like the Egyptian plagues in the Hebrew Bible. These plagues symbolize God's punishment of the wicked. Before the seventh trumpet sounds, an interlude occurs, containing two visions that offer hope and comfort to the readers. The final trumpet blast provides a brief glimpse of God's consummation of history.

Chapters 12–14 portray the great cosmic conflict between God and the forces of evil. The first part of chapter 12 focuses on the heavenly aspect of this struggle. Adapting the widespread ancient myth of the struggle between chaos and creation, John describes the battle between the archangel Michael and the great red dragon (Satan). Defeated and thrown down to earth by Michael, the dragon continues his opposition to God by attacking the people of God. Chapter 13 sets the persecution of Christians in a cosmic context. Christians are not engaged in an isolated, minor struggle; rather, they are participating in the earthly manifestation of the cosmic conflict between God and Satan. Rome, and specifically the emperor, is depicted as "a beast rising out of the sea" (13:1) that demands to be worshiped. Those who refuse are killed. The beast from the sea is assisted by another beast that "rose out of the earth" (13:11). This second beast enforces the worship of the first beast.

The additional description of the first beast given later in chapter 17 makes certain the identification of this figure with Rome. For John, the beast who is the embodiment of evil and who wreaks havoc on God's people is not some future individual who is yet to appear. He is already present in the emperor with his demonic claims of divinity. One of the most intriguing symbols in Revelation is the use of the number 666 to refer to the first beast. The most likely explanation for this is the ancient practice of gematria, in which letters were assigned numerical values. By adding up the numerical values of the letters in a name, one could arrive at a number for that name. John tells us that "the number of the beast" is 666. The numerical value of the Hebrew letters for

Figure 23.8. In the book of Revelation, Armageddon (which means "Mount Megiddo") is the site of the final conflict between the forces of good and evil. Megiddo was the location of many important battles in Israel's history. (*Photograph by Clyde E. Fant*)

Nero Caesar totals 666. In cryptic fashion, John is stating that in Domitian the evil of Nero has been reborn.

After the scenes of conflict and persecution in chapters 12 and 13, chapter 14 offers an interlude containing three visions. The purpose of these visions is to reassure the church that God will punish the wicked and reward the faithful. Chapters 15 and 16 present another series of seven events, this time the pouring of seven bowls on the earth. The emptying of these bowls "of the wrath of God" (16:1) unleashes six additional plagues of destruction on the earth (again modeled after the Egyptian plagues). The sixth plague leads to the final battle between God and the evil kings. This battle is to occur at Armageddon, a term derived from Hebrew, meaning "Mount Megiddo." Megiddo was the name of an ancient city in northwestern Palestine and also a variant name for the Esdraelon Plain, in which the city was located. The Megiddo Plain was the site of several important ancient battles. John envisions this location as the site of the climactic earthly battle, but he does not describe this final battle. Instead, when the seventh bowl is emptied, a heavenly voice announces, "It is done!"

The destruction of Rome is the topic of chapters 17:1–19:10. Rome is called Babylon by John because Rome is the new Babylon. Just as in ancient times Babylon had oppressed the people of Judah and destroyed the Temple and Jerusalem, so now Rome, who had also destroyed the Temple and Jerusalem, is playing the role of the oppressor of God's people. Portrayed as a drunken harlot riding a scarlet beast, Rome finally suffers complete destruction.

In another depiction of God's conquest over evil, John portrays Christ as a mighty warrior on a white horse who, with his heavenly army, defeats the kings of the earth, the dragon, and the two beasts. The dragon is then imprisoned in a bottomless pit for a thousand years. This thousand-year period, the messianic kingdom, is the millennial reign of Christ and the martyrs. Only the martyrs share in this reign with Christ. This is their reward for giving the ultimate sacrifice of their lives for Christ. At the end of the millennium Satan is loosed and once more attacks God's faithful. The final conflict results in God's complete victory. Satan is thrown into "the lake of fire and sulfur," where he "will be tormented day and night forever and ever" (20:10). The final judgment of all the dead follows, with the wicked being cast into the lake of fire.

The conflict is finished. The first heaven and earth have passed away, and a new heaven and earth have appeared. John describes the new Jerusalem coming down from heaven (21:1–22:5). This city will be the dwelling place of God and the community of the faithful. John's description of the new Jerusalem—a city made of gold and precious jewels—is rich with imagery and symbolism. The new Jerusalem symbolizes eternal life lived in the presence of God, where "death will be no more; mourning and crying and pain will be no more, for the first things have passed away" (21:4).

This dramatic writing, the Revelation of John, sought to encourage beleaguered Christians to remain faithful. The book is a call to endurance, a challenge to Christians not to give in to the demands of the emperor cult. In spite of how the world might appear, John wants his readers to know that God is still in control and that God, not the emperor, is the one worthy of worship and praise.

The presentation of future happenings in the book of Revelation should not be understood as a literal prediction of future events. To turn this grand poetic vision into a system of charts and timetables does grave injustice to the book of Revelation and its author. John is not presenting a detailed forecast of endtime events. Rather, his apocalyptic scenario of the future offered hope to his readers by showing them God's final victory over evil and the eventual rewards for the faithful.

The Book of Revelation and the Divine-Human Encounter

For John, the divine-human encounter places absolute demands upon those who would be a part of the people of God. In the book of Revelation there is no place for shared loyalties, for ultimate allegiance to other gods or even to the emperor. God demands faithful witnesses who by their patient endurance contribute to the overthrow of the forces of evil. Even if such faithfulness leads to the ultimate sacrifice of martyrdom, the people of God are to persevere.

If the Christian's encounter with God places ultimate demands on an individual, it also offers immeasurable rewards. Throughout the book John depicts the final blessings awaiting "those who keep the commandments of God and hold fast to the faith of Jesus" (14:12). Although John primarily emphasizes eschatological rewards, he is also aware that there are present benefits for the faithful. The God "who was and who is to come" (1:8) is also the God "who is." God reigns now over history and creation. By holding before his readers the reminder that God is indeed sovereign over the universe, John provides for them an alternative vision of reality, one that recognizes that the power structures of the world are illusory and transitory. This new understanding of reality gave hope and meaning to life for a people who were oppressed and whose faith was severely challenged.

In John's understanding, the justice of God demands that the divine-human encounter also include God's judgment on the wicked. Those who have joined forces with the great dragon in its opposition to God and God's people will share in the punishment inflicted upon the dragon. Evil may appear triumphant, but ultimately God will reign supreme. Creation will triumph over chaos; light will triumph over darkness. Then, all God's people will join the heavenly court in exclaiming, "Hallelujah! For the Lord our God the Almighty reigns" (19:6).

SELECTED BIBLIOGRAPHY

The following works are recommended for the student who would like to pursue further study of the Bible.

Study Bibles

The HarperCollins Study Bible, New Revised Standard Version. New York: HarperCollins, 1993.

The New Oxford Annotated Bible with the Apocryphal/Deuterocanonical Books, New Revised Standard Version. 3d ed. New York: Oxford University Press, 2001.

The Revised English Bible: Oxford Study Edition. New York: Oxford University Press, 1992.

The New Jerusalem Bible, Regular Edition. New York: Doubleday, 1985.

Dictionaries and Encyclopedias

Achtemeier, Paul J., ed. *Harper's Bible Dictionary*. San Francisco: Harper & Row, 1985.

Bromiley, Geoffrey W., ed. *The International Standard Bible Encyclopedia*. 4 vols. Rev. ed. Grand Rapids, Mich.: William B. Eerdmans Publishing Co., 1979–1988.

Buttrick, George F., ed. *The Interpreter's Dictionary of the Bible*. 4 vols. Nashville: Abingdon Press, 1962; Supplementary Volume, ed. by Keith Crim, 1976.

Encyclopaedia Judaica. 16 vols. New York: Macmillan, 1972.

Freedman, David Noel, editor-in-chief. *The Anchor Bible Dictionary*. 6 vols. New York: Doubleday, 1992.

Mills, Watson E., gen. ed. *Mercer Dictionary of the Bible*. Macon, Ga.: Mercer University Press, 1990.

Neusner, Jacob, Alan J. Avery-Peck, and William S. Green, eds. *The Encyclopedia of Judaism*. 3 vols. New York: Continuum, 1999.

English Concordances

A Concordance to the Apocrypha/Deuterocanonical Books of the Revised Standard Version. Grand Rapids, Mich.: William B. Eerdmans Publishing Co., 1983.

Metzger, Bruce, ed. *New Revised Standard Version Exhaustive Concordance*. Nashville: Thomas Nelson, 1991.

Morrison, Clinton, ed. *An Analytical Concordance to the Revised Standard Version of the New Testament*. Philadelphia: Westminster, 1979.

Strong, J. *The New Strong's Exhaustive Concordance of the Bible*. Nashville: Thomas Nelson, 1984. (Based on the King James Version. This is a revision of the original 1894 work. Several editions have been published by various publishers.)

Young, Robert. *Analytical Concordance to the Bible.* Grand Rapids, Mich.: William B. Eerdmans Publishing Co., 1970. (Based on the King James Version. Available in several editions from various publishers. All recent editions are based on W. B. Stevenson's 1922 revision of the original 1873/1881 edition.)

Commentaries

One-Volume Works

Black, Matthew, and H. H. Rowley, eds. *Peake's Commentary on the Bible.* London: Thomas Nelson and Sons, 1962.

Brown, Raymond E., Joseph A. Fitzmyer, and Roland E. Murphy, eds. *The New Jerome Biblical Commentary.* Englewood Cliffs, N.J.: Prentice-Hall, 1990.

Laymon, Charles M. *The Interpreter's One-Volume Commentary on the Bible.* Nashville: Abingdon Press, 1971.

Mays, James L., ed. *Harper's Bible Commentary.* San Francisco: Harper & Row, 1988.

Mills, Watson E., and Richard F. Wilson, gen. eds. *Mercer Commentary on the Bible.* Macon, Ga.: Mercer University Press, 1995.

Newsom, Carol A., and Sharon H. Ringe. *The Women's Bible Commentary.* Exp. ed. Louisville: Westminster John Knox, 1998.

Commentary Series or Sets

Ackroyd, Peter, James Barr, Bernhard W. Anderson, and James L. Mays, gen. eds. *The Old Testament Library.* Philadelphia: Westminster.

Albright, W. F., and David N. Freedman, eds. *The Anchor Bible.* Garden City, N.Y.: Doubleday.

Anderson, Bernhard W., ed. *The Books of the Bible.* 2 vols. New York: Charles Scribner's Sons, 1989.

Chadwick, Henry, gen. ed. *Harper's New Testament Commentaries.* San Francisco: Harper & Row.

Clements, Ronald E., and Matthew Black, eds. *The New Century Bible.* Grand Rapids, Mich.: William B. Eerdmans Publishing Co.

Cross, Frank Moore, Jr., et. al., eds. *Hermeneia: A Critical and Historical Commentary on the Bible.* Philadelphia: Fortress.

Harrington, Wilfrid, and Donald Senior, eds. *The New Testament Message.* Wilmington, Del.: Michael Glazier.

Hubbard, David A., and Glenn W. Barker, gen. eds. *Word Biblical Commentary.* Nashville: Thomas Nelson.

Keck, Leander E., ed. *The New Interpreter's Bible: A Commentary in Twelve Volumes.* Nashville: Abingdon Press.

Krodel, Gerhard, ed. *Proclamation Commentaries.* Philadelphia: Fortress.

Mays, James L., ed. *Interpretation: A Bible Commentary for Teaching and Preaching.* Atlanta: John Knox.

Stuhlmueller, Carroll, and Martin McNamara, eds. *The Old Testament Message.* Wilmington, Del.: Michael Glazier.

Atlases and Geographies

Aharoni, Yohanan. *The Land of the Bible: A Historical Geography.* Rev. and enlarged ed. by Anson F. Rainey. Philadelphia: Westminster, 1980.

Aharoni, Yohanan, and Michael Avi-Yonah. *The Macmillan Bible Atlas.* 3rd ed. New York: Macmillan, 1993.

Baly, Denis. *The Geography of the Bible.* Rev. ed. New York: Harper & Row, 1974.

May, Herbert G. *Oxford Bible Atlas.* 3rd ed., rev. by John Day. New York: Oxford University Press, 1984.

Pritchard, James B., ed. *The Harper Atlas of the Bible.* San Francisco: Harper & Row, 1987.

Introductions

Introductions to the Bible

Harris, Stephen L. *Understanding the Bible: A Reader's Introduction.* 5th ed. Palo Alto and London: Mayfield, 1999.

Hauer, Christian E., and William A. Young. *An Introduction to the Bible: A Journey into Three Worlds.* 4th ed. Englewood Cliffs, N.J.: Prentice-Hall, 1997.

Hayes, John H. *Introduction to the Bible.* Philadelphia: Westminster, 1971.

Thompson, Leonard L. *Introducing Biblical Literature: A More Fantastic Country.* Englewood Cliffs, N.J.: Prentice-Hall, 1978.

Introductions to the Hebrew Bible

Anderson, Bernhard W. *Understanding the Old Testament.* 4th ed. Englewood Cliffs, N.J.: Prentice-Hall, 1986. See also abridged and updated 4th edition, 1998.

Childs, Brevard S. *Introduction to the Old Testament as Scripture.* Philadelphia: Fortress, 1979.

Eissfeldt, Otto. *The Old Testament: An Introduction.* New York: Harper & Row, 1965.

Gottwald, Norman K. *The Hebrew Bible: A Socio-Literary Introduction.* Philadelphia: Fortress, 1985.

Selected Bibliography

Hayes, John H. *An Introduction to Old Testament Study*. Nashville: Abingdon Press, 1979.

Kaiser, Otto. *Introduction to the Old Testament*. Minneapolis: Augsburg, 1975.

Introductions to the Apocrypha/Deuterocanonical Literature

Harrington, Daniel J. *Invitation to the Apocrypha*. Grand Rapids, Mich.: William B. Eerdmans Publishing Co., 1999.

Metzger, Bruce M. *An Introduction to the Apocrypha*. New York: Oxford University Press, 1957.

Introductions to Noncanonical Jewish Literature

McNamara, Martin. *Intertestamental Literature*. Old Testament Message. Wilmington, Del.: Michael Glazier, 1983.

Nickelsburg, George W. E. *Jewish Literature Between the Bible and the Mishnah*. Philadelphia: Fortress, 1981.

Schiffman, Lawrence. *Reclaiming the Dead Sea Scrolls*. New York: Doubleday, 1995.

Schürer, Emil. *The History of the Jewish People in the Age of Jesus Christ (175 B.C.–A.D. 135)*. Vol. 3, in 2 parts. English version revised and edited by Geza Vermes, Fergus Millar, and Martin Goodman. Edinburgh: T & T Clark, 1986 (Part 1), 1987 (Part 2).

Stone, Michael E., ed. *Jewish Writings of the Second Temple Period: Apocrypha, Pseudepigrapha, Qumran Sectarian Writings, Philo, Josephus. Compendia Rerum Iudaicarum ad Novum Testamentum*. Section Two: *The Literature of the Jewish People in the Period of the Second Temple and the Talmud*. Vol. 2. Philadelphia: Fortress, 1984.

VanderKam, James C. *The Dead Sea Scrolls Today*. Grand Rapids, Mich.: William B. Eerdmans Publishing Co., 1994.

Introductions to the New Testament

Brown, Raymond E. *An Introduction to the New Testament*. New York: Doubleday, 1997.

Childs, Brevard S. *The New Testament as Canon: An Introduction*. Philadelphia: Fortress, 1985.

Ehrman, Bart D. *The New Testament: A Historical Introduction to the Early Christian Writings*. 2nd ed. New York: Oxford University Press, 2000.

Kee, Howard Clark. *Understanding the New Testament*. 4th ed. Englewood Cliffs, N.J.: Prentice-Hall, 1983.

Koester, Helmut. *Introduction to the New Testament.* Vol. 1, *History, Culture, and Religion of the Hellenisic Age.* 2nd ed. New York: Walter de Gruyter. Vol. 2, *History and Literature of Early Christianity.* 2nd ed. New York: Walter de Gruyter, 2000.

Kümmel, Werner Georg. *Introduction to the New Testament.* 17th ed. Nashville: Abingdon Press, 1975.

Perrin, Norman, and Dennis C. Duling. *The New Testament: An Introduction. Proclamation and Parenesis, Myth and History.* 2nd ed. New York: Harcourt Brace Jovanovich, 1982.

Spivey, Robert A., and D. Moody Smith. *Anatomy of the New Testament.* 4th ed. New York: Macmillan, 1989.

Histories and Background Studies

Histories and Background Studies of Israel and Judah

Albertz, Rainer. *A History of Israelite Religion in the Old Testament Period.* Trans. John Bowden. 2 vols. Louisville: Westminster John Knox, 1994.

Ahlstrom, Gosta. *The History of Ancient Palestine.* Minneapolis: Fortress, 1993.

Bright, John. *A History of Israel.* 3rd. ed. Philadelphia: Westminster, 1981.

Coogan, Michael D., ed. *The Oxford History of the Biblical World.* New York: Oxford University Press, 1998. (This work covers the entire biblical period, not just that of the Hebrew Bible.)

de Vaux, Roland. *The Early History of Israel.* Philadelphia: Westminster, 1978.

Hayes, John H., and J. Maxwell Miller, eds. *Israelite and Judaean History.* Philadelphia: Fortress, 1977.

Lemche, Niels Peter. *The Israelites in History and Tradition.* Edited by Douglas A. Knight. Library of Ancient Israel. Louisville: Westminster John Knox, 1998.

Miller, J. Maxwell, and John H. Hayes. *A History of Ancient Israel and Judah.* Philadelphia: Westminster, 1986.

Noth, M. *The Old Testament World.* Philadelphia: Fortress, 1966.

Rogerson, John, and Philip Davies. *The Old Testament World.* Englewood Cliffs, N.J.: Prentice-Hall, 1989.

Sasson, Jack M., ed. *Civilizations of the Ancient East.* 4 vols. New York: Simon & Schuster/Macmillan, 1995.

Shanks, Hershel, ed. *Ancient Israel: A Short History from Abraham to the Roman Destruction of the Temple.* Englewood Cliffs, N.J.: Prentice-Hall, 1988.

van der Woude, A. S. *The World of the Bible.* Grand Rapids, Mich.: William B. Eerdmans Publishing Co., 1986.

Histories and Background Studies of Palestine in the Hellenistic and Roman Eras

Cohen, Shaye J. D. *From the Maccabees to the Mishnah.* Philadelphia: Westminster, 1987.

Grabbe, Lester L. *Judaism from Cyrus to Hadrian: Sources, History, Synthesis.* 2 vols. Minneapolis: Fortress, 1991, 1992.

Hayes, John H., and Sara R. Mandell, *The Jewish People in Classical Antiquity: From Alexander to Bar Kochba.* Louisville: Westminster John Knox, 1998.

Hengel, Martin. *Judaism and Hellenism: Studies in Their Encounter in Palestine During the Early Hellenistic Period.* 2 vols. Philadelphia: Fortress, 1974.

Murphy, Frederick J. *The Religious World of Jesus: An Introduction to Second Temple Palestinian Judaism.* Nashville: Abingdon Press, 1991.

Safrai, S., and M. Stern, eds. *The Jewish People in the First Christian Century: Historical Geography, Political History, Social, Cultural and Religious Life and Institutions. Compendium Rerum Iudaicarum ad Novum Testamentum.* 2 vols. Philadelphia: Fortress, 1974, 1976.

Schürer, Emil. *The History of the Jewish People in the Age of Jesus Christ (175 B.C.–A.D. 135).* English version revised and edited by Geza Vermes, Fergus Millar, and Matthew Black. Vols. 1 and 2. Edinburgh: T & T Clark, 1973, 1979.

Tcherikover, Victor. *Hellenistic Civilization and the Jews.* Translated by S. Applebaum. New York: Atheneum, 1979. Reprint, Philadelphia: The Jewish Publication Society of America, 1959.

Histories and Background Studies of Early Christianity

Aune, David E. *The New Testament in Its Literary Environment.* Philadelphia: Westminster, 1987.

Bruce, F. F. *New Testament History.* Garden City, N.Y.: Doubleday & Co., 1972.

Conzelmann, H. *History of Primitive Christianity.* Nashville: Abingdon Press, 1973.

Ferguson, Everett. *Backgrounds of Early Christianity.* 2nd ed. Grand Rapids, Mich.: William B. Eerdmans Publishing Co., 1993.

Leaney, A. R. C. *The Jewish and Christian World 200 B.C. to A.D. 200.* New York: Cambridge University Press, 1984.

Lohse, Eduard. *The New Testament Environment.* Nashville: Abingdon Press, 1976.

Malina, Bruce J. *The Social World of Jesus and the Gospels.* London and New York: Routledge, 1996.

Stambaugh, John E., and David L. Balch. *The New Testament in Its Social Environment.* Philadelphia: Westminster, 1986.

Exegetical Methodology

Coggins, R. J., and J. L. Houlden, eds. *A Dictionary of Biblical Interpretation.* Philadelphia: Trinity Press, 1990.

Collins, Raymond F. *Introduction to the New Testament.* Garden City, N.Y.: Doubleday & Co., 1983.

Fee, Gordon D. *New Testament Exegesis: A Handbook for Students and Pastors.* Philadelphia: Westminster, 1983.

Harrington, Daniel J. *Interpreting the New Testament: A Practical Guide.* Wilmington, Del.: Michael Glazier, 1979.

————. *Interpreting the Old Testament: A Practical Guide.* Wilmington, Del.: Michael Glazier, 1981.

Hayes, John H., and Carl R. Holladay. *Biblical Exegesis: A Beginner's Handbook.* Rev. ed. Atlanta: John Knox, 1987.

Kaiser, O., and W. G. Kümmel. *Exegetical Method: A Student's Handbook.* Rev. ed. New York: Seabury, 1981.

Marshall, I. Howard, ed. *New Testament Interpretation: Essays on Principles and Methods.* Grand Rapids, Mich.: William B. Eerdmans Publishing Co., 1977.

McKenzie, Steven L., and Stephen R. Haynes. *To Each Its Own Meaning: An Introduction to Biblical Criticisms and Their Application.* Rev. and exp. ed. Louisville: Westminster John Knox, 1999.

Archaeology

Aharoni, Yohanan. *The Archaeology of the Land of Israel.* Philadelphia: Westminster, 1982.

Avi-Yonah, Michael, and Ephraim Stern, eds. *Encyclopedia of Archaeological Excavations in the Holy Land.* 4 vols. Englewood Cliffs, N.J.: Prentice-Hall, 1975–78.

Báez-Camargo, Gonzalo. *Archaeological Commentary on the Bible.* Garden City, N.Y.: Doubleday, 1984.

Ben-Tor, Amnon, ed. *The Archaeology of Ancient Israel.* Trans. R. Greenberg. New Haven, Conn.: Yale University Press, 1992.

Dever, William G. *Recent Archaeological Discoveries and Biblical Research.* Seattle: University of Washington Press, 1993.

Finegan, Jack. *The Archaeology of the New Testament: The Life of Jesus and the Beginning of the Early Church.* Princeton, N.J.: Princeton University Press, 1970.

————. *The Archaeology of the New Testament: The Mediterranean World of the Early Christian Apostles.* Boulder, Colo.: Westview, 1981.

Kenyon, Kathleen. *The Bible and Recent Archaeology.* Rev. ed. by P. R. S. Moorey. Atlanta: John Knox, 1987.

Mazar, Amihai. *Archaeology of the Land of the Bible 10,000–586 B.C.E.* New York: Doubleday, 1990.

Meyers, Eric M., ed. *The Oxford Encyclopedia of Archaeology in the Ancient Near East.* 5 vols. New York: Oxford University Press, 1997.

Meyers, Eric M., and James F. Strange. *Archaeology, the Rabbis, and Early*

Christianity: The Social and Historical Setting of Palestinian Judaism and Christianity. Nashville: Abingdon Press, 1981.

Stern, Ephraim, ed. *The New Encyclopedia of Archaeological Excavations in the Holy Land.* 4 vols. New York: Simon & Schuster, 1993.

Yamauchi, E. M. *The Archaeology of New Testament Cities in Western Asia Minor.* Grand Rapids, Mich.: Baker, 1980.

Collections of Noncanonical Texts and Documents

Barrett, C. K., ed. *The New Testament Background: Selected Documents.* Rev. and expanded ed. New York: Harper & Row, 1989.

Boring, M. Eugene, Klaus Berger, and Carsten Colpe, eds. *Hellenistic Commentary to the New Testament.* Nashville: Abingdon Press, 1995.

Cameron, Ron, ed. *The Other Gospels: Non-Canonical Gospel Texts.* Philadelphia: Westminster, 1982.

Cartlidge, David R., and David L. Dungan. *Documents for the Study of the Gospels.* Philadelphia: Fortress, 1980.

Charlesworth, James H., ed. *The Old Testament Pseudepigrapha.* 2 vols. Garden City, N.Y.: Doubleday & Co., 1983, 1985.

Kee, Howard C. *The New Testament in Context: Sources and Documents.* Englewood Cliffs, N.J.: Prentice-Hall, 1984.

Matthews, Victor H., and Don C. Benjamin. *Old Testament Parallels: Laws and Stories from the Ancient Near East.* Rev. and exp. 2nd ed. New York: Paulist, 1997.

Meyer, Marvin, ed. *The Ancient Mysteries: A Sourcebook.* San Francisco: Harper & Row, 1987.

Nickelsburg, George W. E., and Michael E. Stone. *Faith and Piety in Early Judaism: Texts and Documents.* Philadelphia: Fortress, 1983.

Pritchard, J. B., ed. *Ancient Near Eastern Texts Relating to the Old Testament.* 3rd ed. Princeton, N.J.: Princeton University Press, 1969.

Robinson, James M., ed. *The Nag Hammadi Library in English.* Rev. ed. San Francisco: Harper & Row, 1988.

Reddish, Mitchell G. *Apocalyptic Literature: A Reader.* Nashville: Abingdon Press, 1990. Repr., Peabody, Mass.: Hendrickson, 1995.

Schneemelcher, Wilhelm, and Edgar Hennecke, eds. *New Testament Apocrypha.* 2 vols. English translation edited by R. McL. Wilson. Rev. ed. Louisville: Westminster John Knox, 1991, 1992.

Sparks, H. F. D., ed. *The Apocryphal Old Testament.* Oxford: Clarendon Press, 1984.

Thomas, D. Winton, ed. *Documents from Old Testament Times.* New York: Harper & Row, 1961.

Vermes, Geza. *The Complete Dead Scrolls in English.* London: Penguin Books, 1997.

INDEX

Aaron, 117, 119

Abel, 152

Abraham, 50, 77, 98-100, 103, 108, 151, 154, 219, 401, 410-11, 413

Absalom, 145

Acts of the Apostles, 343-44, 348, 359-77, 386-92

Adam, 152, 154

afterlife, 22, 289

agrapha, 301

Ahab, 162, 182

Ahaz, 165, 168-69, 194-95

Ai, 122

Akiba, Rabbi, 258

Akkadians, 103-4

Alexander the Great, 21, 79, 83, 251, 265, 379

allegorical method, 268

Amarna letters, 92

Amaziah, 187

Ammon, 87, 144

Amorites, 104

Amos, 185-89

Anath, 130

ancestral period, 97-109

angels, 290

anointed, 301

antichrist, 422

Antioch, 328, 338, 344, 351, 364, 373, 392, 446

Antiochus IV Epiphanes, 253, 275-76

Antipater, 256

'Apiru. *See* Habiru

apocalyptic literature, 271-72, 449

Apocalypse. *See* Revelation, book of

Apocrypha, 28, 62-64, 267, 277-87

apostle, 360, 364-65, 370, 426

Aramaic, 266

Arameans, 105

archaeology, 51-52, 89-94

Archelaus, 257

Ark of the Covenant, 118-19, 136, 144, 149, 160

Armageddon, 455-56

ascension, 347, 360, 362

Asherah, 130

Assyria, 82, 137, 164-65, 168-71

Athanasius, 67

Azariah, Prayer of (and Song of the Three Jews), 283

Baal, 130-32

Babel, Tower of, 151, 153-54, 363

Babylon, 104, 149, 173-74, 435, 456

baptism, 310, 312, 346, 364, 415, 434

Barnabas, 366, 372-73

Bar Kokhba, 258

Baruch, 199

Baruch, book of, 284

Bashan, 87

Bathsheba, 145, 339

Beatitudes, 339

Behistun Stone, 90

Bel and the Dragon, 281-82

Belshazzar, 273-74

Beloved Disciple, 350-51

Bethel, 161

Bethlehem, 141, 345

Bible, 28, 31-34, 55-73. *See also* English Bible, King James Version, Rheims-Douay

bishop, 429, 436

Black Obelisk of Shalmaneser, 92

Boaz, 228

Book of Signs, 353

Caesarea Philippi, 329

Caiaphas, 317, 365

Cain, 152

Canaan, 80, 121-34

Canaanite, 80, 108, 130-34

canon, 27-28

canonical criticism, 46-47
canonization
    New Testament, 66-68, 420
    Hebrew Bible, 60-62
Catholic Epistles, 66, 421
Central Highlands, 85-86
Christ, 296, 318, 413. *See also* Messiah
Christology, 413
Chronicler, 156, 167, 171, 225
Chronicles, First and Second, 46, 225
circumcision, 108, 373, 400
Claudius, 300, 444
climate, 87-88
Coastal Plain, 83-85
coherence, criterion of, 306-7
Colossians, letter to the, 418, 424-25, 430
Constantine, 22
Corinth, 392, 399, 402, 404, 406
Corinthians, First letter to the, 402-5
    Second letter to the, 402, 406
Cornelius, 372-73
Council of Carthage, 67
Council of Hippo, 67
Council of Trent, 278
covenant, 108-9, 116-17
Covenant Code, 118
Coverdale, Miles, 70
creation, 42-43, 152
criticisms, biblical, 33-51
crucifixion, 317, 334, 355
Cyrus, 93, 208, 213, 214, 221-22
Cyrus Cylinder, 93, 221

"D" source, 43, 58
Damascus, 370, 372, 389-90, 392
Daniel, book of, 91, 272-77, 280-83
David, 141-45, 233-34, 376
Day of Atonement, 259
Day of the Lord (Yahweh), 189, 196, 226

deacon, 429, 436
Dead Sea, 86-87
Dead Sea Scrolls, 86, 94, 263, 267-68, 422
Deborah, 127-28, 177
Decalogue. *See* Ten Commandments
Delilah, 129
demons, 290, 311
Deuterocanon, 28, 278.
    See Apocrypha
Deuteronomic, 43
Deuteronomic Reform, 173
Deuteronomistic History, 121-24, 155, 156-74, 216-17
Deuteronomistic Theology, 199, 244-45
Deutero-Isaiah. *See* Second Isaiah
deutero-Pauline writings, 66, 395, 397, 418-20
Deuteronomy, book of, 113, 118
Diaspora, 265-66, 284, 387
Diatessaron, 326
Didache, 66
disciples, 296, 310, 334, 337, 350, 355, 362-64
dissimilarity, criterion of, 306
divided kingdom, 155-74
divine-human encounter, 102-3, 106-9, 115-19, 129-34, 150, 154, 156-59, 184, 204, 230-32, 238, 249, 288-91, 334-35, 342, 349-50, 357, 375-77, 412-16, 457-58
docetism, 422, 436
Documentary Hypothesis, 42-43, 58
Domitian, 42, 445-46, 450-52

"E" source, 43, 58, 102, 151
Ebla tablets, 91
Ecclesiastes, book of, 247-49
Ecclesiasticus. *See* Sirach
Edom, 87, 112, 139, 144

Egypt, 82-83, 101, 113-15, 136-37
Eighteen Benedictions, 442
El, 108, 130
Elijah, 163, 182
Elisha, 163, 182-83
Elohim, 42-43, 108
Emmanuel, 339, 341. *See also* Immanuel
emperor worship, 381-82, 446, 450-53
English Bible, 70-73
Enoch, First, 272, 423
Enuma Elish, 152
Ephesians, letter to the, 418, 429-31
Ephesus, 351, 392, 407
Epicureanism, 384
Epicurus, 384, 400
eponym, 102
Esau, 100-101
eschatology, 272, 355-56
Esdras, First Book of, 28, 279
    Second Book of, 28, 61, 283-84
Essenes, 263
Esther, Additions to, 284
    book of, 229-30
Eucharist, 405, 416, 448
Eve, 152, 154
exegesis, 35, 54, 268
Exile, Babylonian, 205-8
Exodus, book of, 109-19
Exodus, "new," 214, 312-13, 364
Exodus from Egypt, 109-12, 113-15
Ezekiel, book of, 208-12, 217
Ezra, 222, 224, 228
    book of, 225

Fertile Crescent, 77-78, 103-6
Flood, the, 152-54, 219
form criticism, 43-44
Former Prophets, 58
Four-Source Theory, 324

Galatians, letter to the, 400-401
Galilee, 85, 310, 328-29, 339, 341, 346, 352
Galilee, Sea of, 86, 327
Gamaliel, 389
Garden of Eden, 151-52, 154
Gemara, 270
gematria, 456
Genesis, book of, 98-103, 152-54
Gentile converts, 372-73
geography, 75-89
Gideon, 127, 133, 138
Gilead, 87
Gilgamesh epic, 153
Gnosticism, 383, 405, 422, 429
God, names of, 42-43, 107-8, 110, 116, 219
Gomer, 191
gospel, literary genre of, 303-4, 321-22
gospels, non-canonical, 301, 357-58
Griesbach hypothesis, 324

Habakkuk, book of, 203-4
Habakkuk Commentary, 204
Habiru, 92, 105-6, 142
Haggai, 222
    book of, 226
Hammurabi, Code of, 104
Hanukkah, 254
Haran, 99, 103
Hasidim, 254, 262
Hasmoneans, 255-56
Hazor, 122, 124, 147
Hebrews, book of, 40, 418-19, 431-34, 448
hellenization, 251-52, 266, 379
henotheism, 118
herem, 122-23, 140
Herod Agrippa I, 257, 440-41
Herod Agrippa II, 257
Herod Antipas, 257

Herod the Great, 39, 149, 256, 339
Hezekiah, 93, 169-71, 195
High Priest, 259, 431-32, 436
historical criticism, 38-42
Hittites, 104-5, 107, 116, 136, 145
Holy Land, 80
Holy Spirit, 349, 355-56, 362-64, 366, 368, 402, 410-11, 416
Hosea, 189-92
Hoshea, 165
Huldah, 177, 180
Hurrians, 104, 137

Ignatius, 446
Immanuel, 197. *See also* Emmanuel
Incarnation, 296
independent attestation, criterion of, 306
Isaac, 99-100
Isaiah, 40-41, 192-97. *See also* Second Isaiah and Third Isaiah
Islam, 23
Israel, meaning of name, 80, 101. *See also* Jacob, Northern Kingdom, and United Kingdom

"J" source, 43, 58, 102, 150-54
Jacob, 100-101
James, book of, 419-21
James, brother of Jesus, 420, 441
James, son of Zebedee, 360, 373, 440-41
Jamnia, 61, 258
Jehoiachin, 39, 174, 208, 217
Jehoiakim, 173
Jehoram, 163
Jehu, 163-64, 183-84
Jeremiah, 198-202
    letter of, 283
Jericho, 122
Jeroboam I, 159-62

Jeroboam II, 164, 186
Jerome, 69-70, 278
Jerusalem, 160, 330, 346-47, 362, 364, 367-68, 389, 392, 401, 407, 410, 441, 457
Jesus, 295-318, 328-42, 345-60, 376-77, 422
Jezebel, 162-63, 182
Jezreel, city of, 163, 191
Jezreel, Valley of, 83-85
Joab, 146
Job, book of, 244-47
Joel, book of, 226
John
    Gospel of, 324-26, 350-58, 422
    letters of, 351, 421-22
    of Patmos, 449
    son of Zebedee, 350, 360, 365, 368, 439
    the Baptist, 310, 312-13, 328, 339, 345-46, 363, 376
John Hyrcanus, 255
John Mark, 326-27, 364
Jonah, book of, 228-29
Jordan Rift, 86-87
Jordan River, 86-87
Joseph
    father of Jesus, 309
    of Arimathea, 317, 330
    son of Jacob, 77, 101
Josephus, 61, 263, 268, 298
Joshua, 121-34
Josiah, 171-73, 199, 217
Judah, nation, 82, 85-86. *See* Southern Kingdom
Judaism, 22-23, 286, 341, 364, 441-43
Judas Maccabeus, 317
Jude, letter of, 419, 423
Judges, book of, 121-34
judges (leaders), 127-29

Judith, book of, 280
justification, 414

Kenites, 116
kerygma, 375, 420
King James Version, 72
kingdom of God, 310, 312-15, 329,
	340, 342, 363
Kings, First book of, 155-74
	Second book of, 155-74
King's Highway, 87

Laban, 100
Lachish, 196
lament, 236
Lamentations, book of, 205-7
Latter Prophets, 58
letters
	in the ancient world, 397-98
	of Paul, 64, 66-67, 386-87, 395-
	416
Levites, 259
Leviticus, book of, 113
literary criticism, 48-50
Logos (Word), 352-53
Lord, 116, 296
Lord's Supper. *See* Eucharist
Luke, Gospel of, 322-26, 343-50, 359-
	60
LXX. *See* Septuagint

Maccabees, 253-55
	First book of, 279
	Second book of, 279-80, 286
	Third book of, 28, 285
	Fourth book of, 28, 285
Magnificat, 350
Malachi, book of, 226-27
Manasseh, 171
	Prayer of, 28, 282-83
Marcion, 67, 326

Marduk, 206
Mari tablets, 92, 175
Mark. *See* John Mark
Mark, Gospel of, 321-36
Martyrdom, 392, 444, 452, 457
Mary, mother of Jesus, 309, 338-39
Masada, 256, 258
Matthew, Gospel of, 322-26, 337-42
Megiddo, 129, 147, 456
Mesopotamia, 77, 107-8, 154
Messiah, 277, 290-91, 329, 331, 338,
	340, 342, 355, 363, 389-90, 413,
	442
Messianic secret, 330-31
methods of biblical study. *See*
	criticisms, biblical
Micah, 197-98
Midrashim, 270
Miracles, 311
Miriam, 110, 177
Mishnah, 270
Moab, 87, 112, 139, 144
monotheism, 213
Mordecai, 230
Moses, 77, 110, 115-19, 219, 339,
	413
Mot, 130
mystery religions, 382

Nahum, book of, 203
Naomi, 228
narrative criticism, 48-49
Nathan, 145, 180
navi (prophet), 177
Nebuchadnezzar (Nebuchadrezzar),
	173-74, 202, 221, 273-75
Negeb, 86
Nehemiah, 224-25, 228
	book of, 225
Nero, 300, 392, 444-45
New Testament Apocrypha, 301

Nicodemus, 353
Nineveh, 228
Noah, 219
Northern Kingdom (Israel), 160-66
Numbers, book of, 112, 113
Nuzi tablets, 92, 104

Obadiah, book of, 226
Omri, 162-63
Onesimus, 409
oral law, 262
oral tradition, 44, 55-57, 64, 101-2, 319-20

"P" source, 43, 58, 102, 113, 151
Palestine, 80-89Palm Sunday, 315
parables, 311
parallelism (poetic), 238
Parousia, 320, 356, 398-99, 403, 424-26
parity covenant, 117
passion accounts, 301
Passover, 330, 353
Pastoral Epistles, 418, 428-29
Patmos, 450
patriarchs. *See* ancestral period
Paul, 344, 360, 362, 365, 367, 370-416, 418-20, 424, 428, 440, 444
pax Romana, 317, 379-81
Pentateuch, 42-43
Pentecost, 363-64
persecution, 439-41, 443-58
Persia, 82, 221-23
Peter, 327, 329, 360, 362, 364-68, 372-73, 376, 439, 444
Peter, First letter of, 418, 431, 434-35, 448
Second letter of, 418, 423-24
Pharisees, 262, 339, 365
Philemon, letter to, 409-10

Philippi, 398, 407-8
Philippians, letter to the, 407-9
Philistines, 84, 135-137, 139-43
Philip
    disciple of Jesus, 367-69
    son of Herod, 257
Philo, 22, 263, 268
philosophy (Greek), 352-53, 384-86, 422
Phoenicia, 147
Plagues, 110, 454-56
Plato, 384-85
Platonism, 384-85, 405
Pliny the Younger, 300, 446-48
poetry (biblical), 238
polytheism, 108, 116
Pontius Pilate, 257, 300
priesthood, 119
Priestly Code, 118
Priestly History, 217-19, 229
promised land, 80, 99, 364
prophecy, 175-184, 231-32, 449
    ex eventu, 272
prophets, 28, 58, 60, 175
Proverbs, book of, 240-44
Psalms, book of, 233-38
Pseudepigrapha, 61, 267
pseudonymity, 40, 272, 419-20
Ptolemies, 79, 253
Ptolemy, 251-52

"Q" source, 323-25, 399
Qoheleth. *See* Ecclesiastes
Qumran, 86, 94, 263, 310, 422

rabbi, 270
rabbinic literature, 270
Ramesses II, 109, 114
Ramesses III, 136-37
reader-response criticism, 49-50
realized eschatology, 355-56

Rebekah, 100
Red Sea, 114
redaction criticism, 45-46
Reed Sea, 110, 114
Rehoboam, 159-60, 167
resurrection, 22, 277, 289, 317-18, 330-31, 335, 362, 365, 377, 405, 413-14
Revelation, book of, 41-42, 351, 446, 448-58
Rheims-Douay Version, 72
righteousness, 340-42, 410, 413
Romans, letter to the, 410-12
Rome, 78-79, 83, 328, 344, 410, 412, 435, 443-48, 452, 456
    Roman Empire, 370-86, 412
Rosetta Stone, 90-91
royal theology, 150, 198
Ruth, book of, 228

sabbath, 218-19
sacrifice, 99-100, 118, 404, 415, 432-33, 436
Sadducees, 262-63, 365
Samaria, 85, 162, 362, 367, 369
Samaritans, 223-24, 265, 313, 368
Samson, 127-29
Samuel, 137-39
    First book of, 46, 137-42
    Second book of, 46, 142-43
Sanhedrin, 259, 439
Sarah, 98-100
Sargon II, 165
Satan, 245, 290, 455-56
Saul (king), 137-42. *See also* Paul
Sea Peoples, 104, 136-37
Second Isaiah, 212-16, 312
Semitic Quadrangle, 78-79
seer, 137, 176
Seleucids, 79, 253
Seleucus I, 253

Sennacherib, 93, 170-71, 195
Septuagint (LXX), 62, 68, 268-69
Sermon on the Mount, 314, 339-41, 346
Servant of the Lord (Yahweh), 47, 215
Servant Songs, 215
Shalmaneser III, 92
Shalmaneser V, 165
Shechem, 122, 134, 162
Sheol, 249, 277
Shephelah, 86
Shepherd of Hermas, 66-67
Sicarii, 264
Silas, 398
Siloam Inscription, 93-94
Simon Peter. *See* Peter
sin, 152-54, 402, 410, 413-15
Sinai, Mount, 112, 114-15, 117
    Sinai Covenant, 117
Sirach, 282, 286
slavery, 48, 401, 409, 415
social-scientific criticism, 47-48
Solomon, 137, 146-49, 159-60, 241, 248
Son of God, 332-34, 339, 341-42, 355, 413
Son of Man, 209, 277, 332, 335, 340, 355, 377, 454
Song of Solomon (Song of Songs), 230
Song of the Three Jews. *See* Azariah, Prayer of
sons of the prophets, 176
source criticism, 42-43
Southern Kingdom (Judah), 167-74
Stephen, 366-67, 376, 439
Stoicism, 384
Suetonius, 10, 300, 444, 448
Suffering Servant. *See* Servant of the Lord
Sumerians, 103
Susanna, book of, 280-81

suzerainty treaty, 117
synagogue, 259-61, 384, 392, 399, 402, 442
Synoptic Gospels, 297, 322, 351-53
Synoptic Problem, 322

tabernacle, 119
Tacitus, 300, 444, 448
Talmud, 270, 299
Tanak, 28
Tarsus, 373, 386, 389
Tatian, 326
Teacher of Righteousness, 263
Temple (Jerusalem), 146-49, 212, 259, 317, 328, 364-67, 369, 441
Ten Commandments, 117-18
Tent of Meeting, 119
testament, 28
textual criticism, 36-38
theocracy, 135
theophany, 110
Theophilus, 345, 359, 362
Thessalonians, First letter to the, 398-99, 425-26
    Second letter to the, 418, 425-26
Third Isaiah, 227-28
Thomas, Gospel of, 66, 301-2, 357
Throne Succession Narrative, 146
Tiberias, 300
Tiglath-pileser I, 137
Tiglath-pileser III, 164-65, 195
Timothy, 398, 409, 428
    First letter to, 418, 428-29
    Second letter to, 418, 428-29
Titus, 406-7, 427-28
    letter to, 418, 428-29
Tobit, book of, 280
Torah, 28, 57-58, 60, 340, 342
Trajan, 300, 446-47
Transjordanian Highlands, 87
tribes, 126-27

triumphal entry, 315
Two-Source Theory, 322
Tyndale, William, 70

Ugaritic texts, 91
United Kingdom, 135-54
universalism, 231
Ur, 103, 104
Uriah, 145
Uzziah, 167-68, 193-94

Via Maris, 83-85
virgin birth, 339, 341
Vulgate, 70, 278

Westward Crescent, 79-80
wilderness, 109-19
Wisdom literature, 240-49, 421
Wisdom of Solomon, 282, 286-87
Writings, the, 28, 58-60
Wycliffe, John, 70

Yahweh, 42-43, 116
Yahwistic History, 150-54
YHWH, 116

Zadok, 262
Zealots, 264
Zechariah, 222-23
    book of, 226
Zedekiah, 174
Zeno, 384
Zephaniah, book of, 202-3
Zerubbabel, 222, 227
ziggurat, 153-54
Zion, 150
Zion theology, 150, 161, 198-99
Zipporah, 110
Zoroastrianism, 290